ANOTHER
ALMANAC
OF
WORDS
AT
PLAY

To you, and you too.
Chances are we'll never meet,
but your letters enliven my breakfasts,
and I am grateful to you.

ANOTHER
ALMANAC
OF
WORDS
AT
PLAY

WILLARD R. ESPY

Clarkson N. Potter, Inc./Publishers NEW YORK

DISTRIBUTED BY CROWN PUBLISHERS, INC.

Copyright © 1980 by Willard R. Espy

All rights reserved. No part of this book may be reproduced or utilized in any form or by any means, electronic or mechanical, including photocopying, recording, or by any information storage and retrieval system, without permission in writing from the publisher.

Inquiries should be addressed to Clarkson N. Potter, Inc., One Park Avenue, New York, New York 10016

Printed in the United States of America

Published simultaneously in Canada by General Publishing Company Limited

Library of Congress Cataloging in Publication Data
Main entry under title:

Another almanac of words at play.

First ed. published in 1975 under title: An Almanac of words at play.
Includes index.
1. Literary calendars. 2. Word games. I. Espy, Willard R. II. An Almanac of words at play.
PN6075.A4 1980 793.73 80-16039
ISBN: 0-517-531879 (cloth)
0-517-531887 (paper)

10 9 8 7 6 5 4 3 2 1

First Edition

EPIGRAPH

Doubt, dishonor in the crowd;
  Government by fool or crook;
Acid rain and atom cloud—
  All's absurd, and so's my book.

(This is written for effect:
  Do not take me at my word.
Though the rest may be correct,
  My book's silly, not absurd.)
                                    —W.R.E.

A DEFINITION OF TERMS

ABC LANGUAGE. A substitution of like-sounding letters, digits, or symbols for words or parts of words: AB C D goldfish.

ACRONYM. A word formed from the initial letters of a name, as *Nato* from North Atlantic Treaty Organization; or by combining parts of a series of words: *radar* for *ra*dio *d*etecting *a*nd *r*anging, for instance.

ACROSTIC. A composition, often in verse, in which one or more sets of letters, as the initial or final letters of the lines, taken in order, form a word or words.

ANAGRAM. A word or phrase formed by reordering the letters of another word or phrase: *opts, pots, tops, spot, post.*

ANGUISH LANGUISH. Words so arranged as to evoke overtones of other words: *Ladle Rot Rotten Hut* for *Little Red Riding Hood.*

BOUT RIMÉ. A couplet in which an inappropriate rhyming line is added to a famous first line. Called in English "rhymed endings" or, by Richard Armour, "punctured poems."

BOWDLERIZE. To divest a written work of supposedly offensive material, as Thomas Bowdler edited Shakespeare and Edward Gibbon.

CHAIN VERSE. One in which the last words, word, or sound of each line is the first of the following line: Alas, alas / A lass I knew / Knew an ass / Ask not who.

CHARADE. A kind of riddle, in which each syllable of the word to be guessed, and sometimes the word itself, are enigmatically described.

CLERIHEW. A humorous four-line unscanned verse dealing with some known person. Named after its inventor, Edmund Clerihew Bentley.

ECHOING VERSE. One in which the refrain of each stanza echoes the end of the preceding line.

HOBSON-JOBSON. A folk-etymological alteration of a word or expression, often foreign, as (conjecturally) *Rotten Row* from *Route du Roi.*

LAPSUS COMICUS. A risible slip of the tongue.

LIPOGRAM. A composition lacking a certain letter or letters. The 50,000-word novel *Gadsby,* by E. V. Wright, has no *e.*

MACARONIC. A passage, generally a verse, mingling two or more languages.

MNEMONICS. A system to improve the memory, named for Greek goddess Mnemosyne.

ONOMASTICS. The study of names and their origins.

ONOMATOPOEIA. The formation of words in imitation of natural sounds; words so formed. *Spit, drip, hiss* are examples.

PALINDROME. A word, phrase, verse, or sentence that reads the same forward or backward: *a man, a plan, a canal, Panama.*

REBUS. A riddle composed of words or syllables depicted by symbols or pictures that suggest the sound of the words or syllables they represent.

SPOONERISM. An unintentional transposition of sounds, often the opening sounds, of words: a *bl*ushing *cr*ow, say, for a *cr*ushing *bl*ow.

STINKY PINKY. A noun modified by a rhyming adjective, as *lazy Maisie.*

UNIVOCALIC. A writing containing only one vowel: "Persevere, ye perfect men; ever keep the precepts ten."

INTRODUCTION

The dour deacons of a Scottish kirk censured their minister for skating downriver to church of a frigid February Sunday, the roads being blocked by snow. That the poor fellow had no choice, except to stay home, was irrelevant; he was guilty because he must have taken pleasure in the skating, and pleasure, on a Sabbath, was a sin.

The deacons were right: Pleasure is a sin, and guilt enhances delight. I experience an agreeable frisson at the thought that I have been frittering away time on this book when I should have been out earning a living for my family. Even more gratifying is the knowledge that the book is utterly without redeeming social value. If my readers can treat themselves to the same guilt in the reading as I experienced in the writing, sales will be phenomenal.

Says my dictionary:

> Almanac (ol'm -nak', al-') *n.* 1. An annual publication including calendars with weather forecasts, astronomical information, tide tables, and other related information. 2. An annual publication composed of various lists, charts, and tables of useful information in many unrelated fields.

The word *almanac* is first reported in medieval Latin, possibly deriving from a Greek word meaning "monthly"; but etymologists doubt this. "Of many other conjectures," says the *Oxford English Dictionary*, "none are worthy of notice."

Yet the late Eric Partridge, a peerless etymologist, suggests that *almanac* may originate in Arabic *al + manakh,* "a place where camels kneel"; hence a camp; hence a settlement; hence settled weather; hence weather prognostication.

By this line of thought, *Another Almanac of Words at Play* is a place where camels kneel.

It is only fair to warn you to guard against sleight of hand in certain of the verses, particularly my own, that are scattered through the pages that follow. They are overgrown puns.

This example will show you how the trick works:

> She seized his heart. Till she return it, he
>   (Limp-hung in jaws of cat, like broken bird)
> Pretends the death that his for sure would be
>   If, by so little as a feather stirred,
> She guess him living. He will not go free;
>   She seized his heart till sheer eternity.

Such slight message as that verse holds is mere legerdemain, intended to distract the reader just long enough so that he will feel a pulse of surprise when he glances from the last line back to the first and notices that the two are phonetically identical.

You do not need to remind me that life is not compacted of such whimsies. My book reflects its bitterness and despair as well. Who can read these lines without a gush of tears?

> I met an old man who in deepest dejection
> Reported the loss of his morning erection.

If forced to assert a sober virtue for the pages you are about to read, I would insist that they decently respect the English language. Words in due order intercede between man and God, and I for one need that intercession. To plead my case persuasively, I must make sure He understands what I am saying.

Yet words can be at their most beguiling when they seem most impenetrable. Take this exchange between two lowland Scotsmen, a farmer and a tradesman.* The farmer takes up a fabric, and speaks:

"Oo?"

"Ay, oo."

"Aw oo?"

"Ay, aw oo."

"Aw ae oo?"

"Ay, aw ae oo."

Only another lowland Scotsman could follow that conversation: "Wool?" "Ay, wool." "All wool?" "Ay, all wool." "All white wool?" "Ay, all white wool."

They had simply dropped the consonants. They had boned those words as deftly as a chef bones a trout.

Bless the English language. It is all wool, and a yard wide.

Aw oo?

Ay, aw oo.

—*W.R.E.*
OYSTERVILLE
July, 1980

---

*Richard Grant White, *Every Day English* (Boston: Houghton Mifflin: 1880).

JANUARY

1 JANUARY
♑

For Starters, a Happy New Year

Annette Hickerson says each sign of the zodiac governs a different part of the body. January is the month of the knee; February, of the back; and so on. Here is a checklist:

January. ♑ Great Capricorn shall bring thee to thy Knees;

February. ♒ Aquarius shall throw thee on thy Back;

March. ♓ From Pisces come new Feet, if old thou lack;

April. ♈ Pray Aries, if thy Head be full of fleas—

May. ♉ Or Taurus, if thy Throat prepare a sneeze—

June. ♊ Or Gemini, should well-thewed Arms go slack—

July. ♋ Or Cancer, if thy Stomach's out of whack—

August. ♌ Or Leo, to put flutt'ring Heart at ease.

September. ♍ Call Virgo, be thy Guts in disarray;

October. ♎ Or Libra, should thy Liver lose its savor;

November. ♏ Or Scorpio, for Seat of am'rous play;

December. ♐ Or Sagittarius, thy Legs to favor.

(The Zodiac thy Body thus attends;
But who shall save thy Soul? It has no friends.)
—W.R.E.

1

It is not *my* New Year's resolutions that cause the trouble; it is other people's. Consider the inconsideration of Kay:

> I swore that I would lay off Kay,
>   Not knowing she
> Had sworn, this holy New Year's day,
>   To lay off me.
>   —*W.R.E.*

A different beast presides over each year of the twelve-year Chinese cycle:

LINES ON A CHINESE FAN (OH GEE TRANSLATION)

> On the banks of the Yang-tse I first came awake
> In the year of the Dragon, or Monkey, or Snake,
> Or else, I am told, of the Tiger, or Rat,
> Or the Horse, or the Cow, or if other than that,
> Perhaps of the Ram, or the Dog, or the Duck.
> Whatever the year, it portended bad luck,
> And I died on the Yang-tse, not giving a damn,
> In the year of the Horse, or the Rat, or the Ram,
> Or the Snake, or the Dragon, or Monkey, or Hog,
> Or the Duck, or the Tiger, or maybe the Dog,
> Or maybe the Rabbit, or maybe the Cow.
> Ah well—it is good to be dead, anyhow.
>   —*W.R.E.*

Mike Collins, who teaches elementary grades in Missouri, collects offbeat New Year's resolutions written by his pupils. Among them:

- I resolved to always be fair because it is more important to be fair than rich and famous and happy ... or at least any one of these ... by itself ... in most cases. (Says Mr. Collins: "The idea had melted away like a popsicle.")
- I made a New Year's resolution once. I resolved to always finish everything I start because ... (The recess bell rang at that awkward moment.)
- This year I am going to keep things short and simple. I am stopping now. THE END.

Let this bit of homespun philosophy strengthen you as you lean into the whistling blasts of the coming year:

SONG OF THE SEASONS

> Ter summ(er anyhow a few)
>   Ter win ter win is all
> In spring they spring a spring er two
>   Alas in fall they fall.
>   —*W.R.E.*

2 JANUARY
ъ

A Russian Absurdity

The Russians might take themselves less seriously, and the world might be safer, if only the author of this exercise in illogic, who died in 1942 at the age of thirty-seven, had lived a few years longer.

THE CONNECTION

Philosopher:

1. I am writing to you in answer to your letter which you are about to write to me in answer to my letter which I wrote to you.

2. A violinist bought a magnet and was carrying it home. Along the way, hoodlums jumped on him and knocked his cap off his head. The wind picked up the cap and carried it down the street.

3. The violinist put the magnet down and ran after the cap. The cap fell in a puddle of nitric acid and dissolved.

4. In the meantime, the hoodlums picked up the magnet and hid.

5. The violinist returned home without a coat and without a cap because the cap had dissolved in the nitric acid, and the violinist, upset by losing his hat, had left his coat in the streetcar.

6. The conductor of the streetcar took the coat to a secondhand shop and exchanged it there for sour cream, groats, and tomatoes.

7. The conductor's father-in-law ate too many tomatoes, became sick, and died. The corpse of the conductor's father-in-law was put in the morgue, but it got mixed up, and in place of the conductor's father-in-law, they buried some old woman.

8. On the grave of the old woman, they put a white post with the inscription "Anton Sergeevich Kondratev."

9. Eleven years later the worms had eaten through the post and it fell down. The cemetery watchman sawed the post in four pieces and burned it in his stove. The wife of the cemetery watchman cooked cauliflower soup over that fire.

10. But when the soup was ready, a fly fell from the wall directly into the pot with this soup. They gave the soup to the beggar Timofey.

11. The beggar Timofey ate the soup and told the beggar Nikolay that the cemetery watchman was a good-natured man.

12. The next day the beggar Nikolay went to the cemetery watchman and asked for money. But the cemetery watchman gave nothing to the beggar Nikolay and chased him away.

13. The beggar Nikolay became very angry and set fire to the cemetery watchman's house.

14. The fire spread from the house to the church, and the church burned down.

15. A long investigation was carried on but did not succeed in determining the cause of the fire.

16. In the place where the church had stood a club was built, and on the day the club opened a concert was organized, at which the violinist, who fourteen years earlier had lost his coat, performed.

17. In the audience sat the son of one of those hoodlums who fourteen years before had knocked the cap off that violinist.

18. After the concert was over they rode home in the same streetcar. In the streetcar behind theirs, the driver was the same conductor who once upon a time had sold the violinist's coat in a secondhand shop.

19. And so here they are, riding late at night through the city; in front the violinist and the hoodlum's son; and in the back, the driver, the former conductor.

20. They ride along and don't know what connection there is between them, and they won't know till the day they die.

—Daniil Kharms

3 JANUARY
ҍ

Week Songs

Who marrieth a wife upon a Monday,
If she will not be good upon a Tuesday,
Let him go to the wood upon a Wednesday,
And cut him a cudgel upon the Thursday,
And pay her soundly upon a Friday;
An' she mend not, may the divil take her a' Saturday:
Then he may eat his meat in peace on the Sunday.
—Anonymous

ONE WEEK

The year had gloomily begun
For Willie Weeks, a poor man's SUN.

He was beset with bill and dun
And he had very little MON.
"This cash," said he, "won't pay my dues,
I've nothing here but ones and TUES."
A bright thought struck him, and he said,
"The rich miss Goldrocks I will WED."
But when he paid his court to her,
She lisped, but firmly said, "No THUR!"
"Alas!" said he. "Then I must die!"
His soul went where they say souls FRI.
They found his gloves, and coat, and hat;
The Coroner upon them SAT.
—*Carolyn Wells*

---

7 REASONS TO DIAL
DR. JOYCE BROTHERS THIS WEEK:

Monday Adultery. Part I

Tuesday Adultery. Part II

Wednesday How to have a fair lovers' quarrel.

Thursday First marriage/second marriage: The different problems.

Friday What makes us feel guilt?

Saturday How you can make better decisions.

Sunday The way we talk.

DIAL DR. BROTHERS 936-4444

Which inspires this reflection:

Monday. Adultery. Part one.
Tuesday. Adultery. More fun.
Wednesday. Quarrel courteously.
Thursday. Wedlock. One. Two. Three.
Friday. Guilt. What else is new?
Saturday. Him, her, or who?
Sunday. Talk before you screw.
—*W.R.E.*

4 JANUARY
ち

Sweet Hernia

There is no flaw to be found in words save perhaps that they generally mean something. Walter de la Mare suggested that many essentially beautiful and evocative words have missed their vocation. *Linoleum,* for instance, might be a charming old Mediterranean seaport. Though a transposition of meanings is not as diverting as sheer meaninglessness, it will do for a starter. Familiar words shift identities here:

SWEET HERNIA

Sweet Hernia on the heights of Plasticine
   Sings to the nylon songs of Brassière;
The very aspirins listen, as they lean
   Against the vitreous wind, to her sad air.
I see the bloom of mayonnaise she holds
   Colored like roof of far-away Shampoo
Its asthma sweetens Earth! Oh, it enfolds
   The alum land from Urine to Cachou!
One last wild gusset, then she's lost in night . . .
And dusk the dandruff dims, and anthracite.
                 —Edward Blishen

5 JANUARY
ち

TV Among the Pyramids

This script of a television commercial was recovered from a tomb recently opened under the forepaw of the Sphinx:

IRAS: Why, what's the matter, Charmian? In tears over Uncle Cheops? Come, come, my dear, into the bandages with him, and pop him away.

CHARMIAN: Oh, Iras, how I *dread* embalming day. Standing over the hot oils for hours. Just look at my ugly, red "Sarcophagus Hands!" And look at Uncle Cheops—all those loose ends. I'm sure he'll never "keep." But *your* work always looks as fresh as *you* do. Tell me, what *is* your secret, Iras?

IRAS: It's no secret, you silly little thing. It's LIVE-O, THE WONDER OIL. Just a ten-minute soak, and your work's done. (*Whispers.*) *And* it actually *flatters* the hands. Quickly! Run out and get a bottle now (it's available at all reliable drugstores). I'll give you a hand with the swathing.

Three weeks later.

CHARMIAN: Thank you, Your Majesty. It was a great privilege to preserve Aunt Ptolemy. And remember—she's guaranteed for two thousand years. (*Thinks.*) Thanks to Iras and LIVE-O.

—*D. R. Climie*

6 JANUARY
♄

Playing Toesies

The sprightly Fats Waller musical *Ain't Misbehavin'*, which Louise and I saw this evening, features a song called "Your Feet's Too Big":

> From your ankles up, I'll say you sure are sweet,
> But from there down, baby, you're just too much feet.
> > Your Feet's Too Big,
> > Don't want you 'cause Your Feet's Too Big,
> > Mad at you 'cause Your Feet's Too Big.
> > I really hate you 'cause Your Feet's Too Big.*

The song reminded me of two feet I glimpsed long ago in Lima, Peru. In those days it was customary for Haya de la Torre, leader of the left-wing APRA party, to win the presidential election and be popped into prison for his pains. The authorities would release him in time for the next election, he would win again, and back he would go to confinement.

I passed through Lima on a day when the great man had just experienced a ritual release and was resting at the home of a friend. Being then an aspiring journalist, I set out to interview him. A letter of introduction won me an audience with an APRA lieutenant who arranged an elaborate charade: I was to visit three saloons in succession, drinking a *cerveza* in each. I would be inspected from the shadows; if after the three cervezas I still seemed harmless, I would be conducted, blindfolded, to the house where De la Torre was staying. And that is exactly what happened. When the blindfold was removed, I found myself standing in a hall before a closed door. The man with me opened the door just wide enough so that he could slip through and closed it behind him. A moment later he returned; he was sorry, but the *jefe* was sleeping the sleep of exhaustion and was not to be disturbed.

*"Your Feet's Too Big" by Ada Benson & Fred Fisher.

©1935, 1936 *Edwin H. Morris & Company*, A Division of MPL Communications, Inc., and *Fisher Music Corp.*

©Renewed 1963, 1964 *Morley Music Co.* and *Fisher Music Corp.*

International Copyright Secured. All Rights Reserved. Used by Permission.

My pleas fell on deaf ears and bounced.

Finally, I said, "Can't I at least *look* at him?"

"Well," said the guard, "I'll open the door a crack, and you will see what you will see."

He did, just long enough for me to glimpse, protruding from beneath the quilts of a massive wooden bed, two of the hugest, nakedest, callousedest feet ever to haunt me in my dreams.

I would have interviewed them, but the guard closed the door.

I have given considerable thought to feet and toes since then. Like these, in a couplet supposedly recited to King Edward VII by Frank Harris:

> There is a game played all over town
> Called ten toes up and ten toes down.

I have written about toes myself:

♂ TOES AND ♀ TOES

> I asked you why your toes grew claws,
> While mine grew corns.
>   You said, "Because."
> Why horns upon a woman's toes
> And corns upon a man's?
>   God knows.
>   —*W.R.E.*

A magisterial truth is caught in that verse, but somehow I cannot make it come clear. There is a more domestic tone here, and an intimation of failing health:

IF YOU DO LOVE ME, DO NOT SO

> If you do love me, do not so
> Cry out, "How fast your toenails grow!"
> For toenails, scientists agree,
> Are measures of mortality;
> Each new extension of their length
> Is stolen from our waning strength,
> Till all remaining from our youth
> Is untrimmed nail and gold-capped tooth.
>   —*W.R.E.*

PROGNOSTICATIONS

> Cut your nails Monday, you cut them for news;
> Cut them on Tuesday, a pair of new shoes;
> Cut them on Wednesday, you cut them for health;
> Cut them on Thursday, 'twill add to your wealth;

Cut them on Friday, you cut them for woe;
Cut them on Saturday, a journey you'll go;
Cut them on Sunday, you cut them for evil,
And all the week long you'll be ruled by the devil.
—*Anonymous*

THE SABBATH

Better a man ne'er be born
Than he trim his nails on a Sunday morn.
—*Anonymous*

7 JANUARY

Cooey—C-oo-ey

OYSTERVILLE—For 115 years Espys tended hogs, cattle, chickens, and the like in the bogs of Northern Ireland. Then, in 1725, we came to Pennsylvania and began all over. So I was puzzled when I ran across my surname in an advertisement for coats of arms; the only shield I could imagine for the Espys would feature one or two hogs, drinking swill, with perhaps an ear of corn somewhere about. I eagerly paid $2.25 for the alleged family crest, which turned out to be the work of someone with a sense of humor.

The lower-left and upper-right quarterings pictured not a pig, to be sure, but a bull. The upper-right and lower-left quarterings pictured not an ear of corn, but a sheaf of wheat. The three silver shells in each quarter had no apparent explanation, but after all, Grandpa did co-found Oysterville in 1854.

There was an accompanying explanation: "The surname Espy appears to be occupational in origin, and is believed to be associated with the French, meaning 'one who was a farmer.' Family mottoes are believed to have originated as battle cries in medieval times. A motto was not recorded with the Espy Coat of Arms."

What does the man mean, no battle cry? When I call hogs, they come running for miles.

8 JANUARY
♄

Marblehead and Athol

Detractors of Governor Chubb Peabody of Massachusetts said three cities in the state were named after him—Peabody, Marblehead, and Athol. Scarcely as brilliant a disparagement as this tirade by Henry IV against Sir John Falstaff:

> Why dost thou converse with that trunk of humours, that bolting-hutch of beastliness, that swoln parcel of dropsies, that huge bombard of sack, that stuffed cloakbag of guts, that roasted Manningtree ox with the pudding in his belly, that reverend vice, that gray iniquity, that father ruffian, that vanity in years?

Charles Lamb once joined in hissing a play he had written, to avoid being recognized as the author. Later he wrote to a friend:

> Mercy on us, that God should give his favourite children, men, mouths to speak with, discourse rationally, to promise smoothly, to flatter agreeably, to encourage warmly, to counsel wisely: to sing with, to drink with, and to kiss with: and that they should turn them into mouths of adders, bears, wolves, hyenas, and whistle like tempests, and emit breath through them like distillations of aspic poison, to asperse and vilify the innocent labour of their fellow creatures who are desirous to please them. God be pleased to make the breath stink and the teeth rot out of them all therefor!

Other insults:

THE CURSE

To a sister of an enemy of the author's who disapproved of "The Playboy"

Lord, confound this surly sister,
Blight her brow with blotch and blister,
Cramp her larynx, lung, and liver,
In her guts a galling give her.
Let her live to earn her dinners
In Mountjoy with seedy sinners:
Lord, this judgment quickly bring,
And I'm your servant,

—*J.M. Synge*

ON JACOB TONSON, HIS PUBLISHER

With leering looks, bullfac'd, and freckled fair,
With two left legs, and Judas-colour'd hair,
With frowsy pores, that taint the ambient air.
—*John Dryden*

TO SERGIUS

Thou'lt fight, if any man call Thebe whore:
That she is thine, what can proclaim it more?
—*Sir Charles Sedley*

OF KATE'S BALDNESS

By's beard the Goat, by his bush-tail the Fox,
By's paws the Lion, by his horns the Ox,
By these all these are known; and by her locks
That now are fall'n, Kate's known to have the pox.
—*John Davies*

TO AN ACQUAINTANCE

Thou speakest always ill of me,
I always speak well of thee;
But, spite of all our noise and pother,
The world believes nor one, nor t'other.
—*Anonymous*

9 JANUARY
♄

In Praise of Cocoa

(Lines written on hearing the startling news that cocoa is, in fact, a mild aphrodisiac.)

LEWD SING COCOA

Oh, listen, Mrs. Balhem, I request your full attention,
For cocoa's found to rouse the things you'd rather never mention.
This scientific fact has now been proved beyond a doubt,
So don't let Les have cocoa when he's taking Marlene out.
Go, throw that tin of sin away and do it at the double,
Or cocoa-maddened Les may get his Marlene into trouble.
The neighbors' curtains twitch each time he takes her to the flicks,
So keep him off the cocoa or you'll all be in a fix.
And don't go drinking it yourself before you go to bed.
It doesn't soothe—it causes sex to rear its ugly head.
Unless you want debauchery to lurk within your gates,
Just stick to tea, the cup that cheers—and never titillates.
—*Mrs. J. R. Bainbridge*

10 JANUARY
♄

Carter Didn't Sleep Here

On January 10, 1976, Carter Didn't Sleep Here. It was a close call, though.

During the Massachusetts presidential primary, the *New York Times* published this letter from Louise (I am Louise's husband):

To the Editor:

Jimmy Carter is in danger of losing this bedmaker's vote for President.

According to your man Anthony Lewis, Carter has twice stayed overnight at homes in Cambridge, each time making his own bed the following morning. As any long-suffering bedmaker knows, she is going to have to unmake that bed, strip off the sheets and pillowcase, and make the bed all over again. Thanks, Mr. Carter, but no thanks!

If Mr. Carter ever spends the night at my home (and in these days of peripatetic and penny-pinching politicking anything is possible), common consideration dictates that he (a) hunt up fresh sheets and make the bed, (b) leave the bed the way he gets out of it (recognizing that the bed must be readied for its next occupant), or (c) strip the sheets, put them in the hamper, and remake the sheetless bed, for appearance's sake.

Incidentally, if Mr. Carter should chance to dine at my home prior to sleeping here, I hope he will not fold his napkin after he finishes. I am not going to save it as a souvenir: "Wipe your mouth on the same cloth on which the governor wiped his!" I am going to put it in the washing machine.

Louise M. Espy

Well, who should telephone that afternoon but William vanden Heuvel, who was managing Carter's campaign in New York State. The candidate, he said, had seen the letter, was coming to New York the following Friday, and would appreciate an invitation to spend a night with the Espys. All we had to do was tell our friends he was the best guest we had ever entertained. It was hard to convince Louise that the call was not a practical joke, but the newspapers did report that Carter would be in town, so she went out and bought new sheets.

Friday passed—and Governor Carter never arrived.

On Sunday, though, campaign headquarters called again—to make a definite appointment for Carter to sleep here a week from Monday.

Perfect, said Louise—I would be out in Seattle that night, so Jimmy and she would be alone. Much more cozy that way.

This was before Carter's remark in *Playboy* about lusting after women in his heart. Nonetheless, the caller was not amused; the temperature of her voice dropped swiftly from, say, the mid-seventies to thirty below zero Celsius.

And Carter never slept here.

11 JANUARY

Shaped Verse

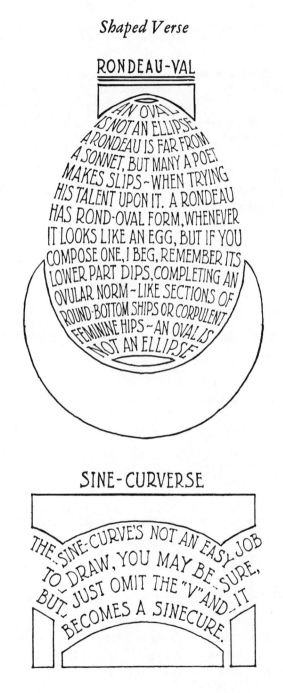

RONDEAU-VAL

AN OVAL IS NOT AN ELLIPSE. A RONDEAU IS FAR FROM A SONNET, BUT MANY A POET MAKES SLIPS ~ WHEN TRYING HIS TALENT UPON IT. A RONDEAU HAS ROND-OVAL FORM, WHENEVER IT LOOKS LIKE AN EGG, BUT IF YOU COMPOSE ONE, I BEG, REMEMBER ITS LOWER PART DIPS, COMPLETING AN OVULAR NORM ~ LIKE SECTIONS OF ROUND-BOTTOM SHIPS OR CORPULENT FEMININE HIPS ~ AN OVAL IS NOT AN ELLIPSE

SINE-CURVERSE

THE SINE-CURVE'S NOT AN EASY JOB TO ~ DRAW, YOU MAY BE ~ SURE, BUT ~ JUST OMIT THE "V" AND ~ IT BECOMES A SINECURE.

—*Gerald L. Kaufman*

12 JANUARY
♄

Meditation and Like That

A number of philosophies that aim at bypassing the world through such devices as transcendental meditation have developed special vocabularies. *Acdac* describes someone who adapts comfortably to any situation. A *blowout center* is any environment to which one can retreat for emotional release.

Joel Homer's definitions of certain metaphysical terms are given here with my comments:

• TADA. A Hindu word that translates as "Let it be." It is used to express acceptance of all things, no matter how dire.

> Tada, tada, there it sits.
>   Everyone has had a
> Blow so stunning it permits
>   Of no response but "Tada."

• ALONE TOGETHER. The title of a song by that inspired lyricist Howard Dietz. The argument runs that we are all finally, irrevocably alone, but that in marriage we may be alone together.

> Alone together is a life
> That unfulfills both man and wife
> And yet still heavier the heart
> That has to live alone apart.

• CHAKRA. A Hindu word meaning "wheel of energy." People operate at top efficiency when their Chakra has been gonged. Or donged.

> Hail him whose Chakra sounds a dong!—
>   Him brave! Him angel-winged!
> Alas!—my Chakra done me wrong:
>   It didn't dong; it dinged.

• NONVERBAL VERBALIZING. A speech system in which words are used, if at all, more as images than as conceptual symbols.

> Nonverbal verbalizing brings to Liz
>   Nonverbalized reward;
> She needs no more than tactile monkey biz
>   To be restored.
>   Liz says words
>   Are for the birds.

- HIQ-up (hick-up). Acronym for High Incompatibility Quotient, justifying divorce between self-aware couples.

> HIQ-up leads to pick-up. Having split,
> We try the singles scene; we cruise a bit.
> We pick up ... HIQ-up ... pick up ... HIQ-up
>   ... pick
> Up ... hiccup ... HIQ-up ... pick up ... hic-...

- EGO FREEGO. A condition in which one's ego has been freed from the crippling effects of insecurity.

> While Ego Freego's ego's free
> From strangling Insecurity,
> This leads to Carelessness, and hence
> To mortifying Accidents.
> I therefore keep my Ego Freego
> Locked in a cellar in Oswego.
>
>   *—W.R.E.*

13 JANUARY

My Chinese Miss

My Chinese miss is dainty as a Chinese fan;
The fare she serves is manna for the inner man.
Her breath is aromatic as her Chinese tea;
My Chinese miss is won ton dumpling soup to me.

Her fingers dip into my heart as chopsticks
    dip in bowls;
Her lashes flutter when I praise her lobster rolls.
Her breasts are silken, tenderer than egg
    foo yong—
No Peking duck could duplicate the savor of
    her tongue.

Ah, blessed feast!—when I arise, so sated
    is my need,
No thought remains of mooshu pork,
    or soup seaweed—
Of bird's nest soup, or sweet and sour,
    or moo gai pen.
(In moments I am hungry for my Chinese miss again.)
                  —W.R.E.

Nor let us slight my Chinese miss's no less dainty Japanese cousin:

JAPANESQUE

Oh, where the white quince blossom swings
    I love to take my Japan ease!
I love the maid Anise who clings
    So lightly on my Japan knees;
I love the little song she sings,
    The little love-song Japanese.
I *almost* love the lute's *ting-tunkle*
    Played by that charming Jap Anise—
For am I not her old Jap uncle?
    And is she not my Japan niece?
                  —*Oliver Herford*

14 JANUARY

First Lines

If you read aloud the first sentence or two of any well-known book, saying "blank" for proper names, chances are that George Axelrod can identify the book. He has hit the jackpot sixteen times in a row. He stumped Edmund Wilson with this one: "First sentence, blank. Second sentence, 'No answer.' Third sentence, blank."

A variation is to identify the title of a book from its first sentence. See how many titles and first sentences you can match here.

1. If you want to find Cherry-tree Lane all you have to do is ask the Policeman at the crossroads.

    A. *The Great Gatsby*, Scott Fitzgerald

2. Nobody could sleep.

    B. *Swann's Way*, Marcel Proust

3. In the late summer of that year we lived in a house in a village that looked across the river and the plain to the mountains.

    C. *Darkness at Noon*, Arthur Koestler

4. Call me Ishmael.

    D. *Catch-22*, Joseph Heller

5. Arms and the man I sing.

    E. *The Good Earth*, Pearl Buck

6. You don't know about me without you have read a book by the name of *The Adventures of Tom Sawyer*, but that ain't no matter.

    F. *The Stranger*, Albert Camus

7. Call me Jonah.

8. The cell door slammed behind Rubashov.

9. My father's family name being Pirip, and my Christian name Philip, my infant tongue could make of both names nothing longer or more explicit than Pip.

10. As Gregor Samska awoke one morning from uneasy dreams he found himself transformed in his bed into a gigantic insect.

11. It was love at first sight.

12. For a long time I used to go to bed early.

13. Mother died today.

14. It was Lung's marriage day.

15. In my younger and more vulnerable days my father gave me some advice that I've been turning over in my mind ever since.

16. It was the best of times; it was the worst of times.

17. I will begin the story of my adventures with a certain morning early in the month of June, the year of grace 1751, when I took the key for the last time out of the door of my father's house.

18. Happy families are all alike; every unhappy family is unhappy in its own way.

19. When the present century was in its teens, and on one sunshiny morning in June, there drove up to the great iron gate of Miss Pinkerton's academy for young ladies, on Chiswick Mall, a large family coach, with two fat horses in blazing harness, driven by a fat coachman in a three-cornered hat and wig, at the rate of four miles an hour.

20. "Take my camel, dear," said my Aunt Dot, as she climbed down from the animal on her return from High Mass.

21. It was a bright cold day in April, and the clocks were striking thirteen.

G. *1984*, George Orwell

H. *The Metamorphosis*, Franz Kafka

I. *Moby Dick*, Herman Melville

J. *The Naked and the Dead*, Norman Mailer

K. *A Tale of Two Cities*, Charles Dickens

L. *Mary Poppins*, P. L. Travers

M. *Farewell to Arms*, Ernest Hemingway

N. *Cat's Cradle*, Kurt Vonnegut

O. *The Aeneid*, Virgil

P. *Huckleberry Finn*, Mark Twain

Q. *Vanity Fair*, William Makepeace Thackeray

R. *Towers of Trebizond*, Rose Macaulay

S. *Great Expectations*, Charles Dickens

T. *Kidnapped*, Robert Louis Stevenson

U. *Anna Karenina*, Count Leo Tolstoy

15 JANUARY
♄

Captain Busby

To me the two paragraphs below don't look like poems, and they don't sound like poems, and they don't feel like poems, but the author insists they are poems.

1.

Captain Busby put his beard in his mouth and sucked it, then took it out and spat on it then put it in and sucked it then walked on down the street thinking hard. Suddenly he put his wedding ring in his trilby hat and put the hat on a passing kitten. Then he carefully calculated the width of the pavement with a pair of adjustable sugar-tongs. This done he knitted his brows. Then he walked on thinking hard.

2.

Captain Busby frowned hard at a passing ceiling and fixed his eye upon a pair of stationary taxis. Suddenly he went up to one of them and addressed himself to the driver. He discharged his socks and continued whistling. The taxi saluted but he put up with it, and puckered a resigned mouth and knitted a pair of thoughtful eyebrows.

—Philip O'Connor

16 JANUARY
♄

Author's Query

This is a further report on a quatrain by the painter Waldo Peirce mentioned in two of my earlier books.

> Busts and bosoms have I known
> Of varied shapes and sizes,
> From poignant disappointments
> To jubilant surprises.

Two readers sent me the entire fifty-two-line verse, a tribute to the lacteal accessories of Mr. Peirce's mother-in-law, Mrs. Isaac Rice. Since the verse is too long and raunchy to quote here in full, I confine myself to these two representative couplets:

> The Redwood or Sequoia's trunk, when levelled to the earth,
> Fell short in full diameter; presented no such girth.
> The greatest Tidal Wave yet known did not provoke the ripple
> That rolled majestically around this charming lady's nipple.

*   *   *

Above these twin Vesuvii great smoke-rings used to curdle,
To mystify topographers, 'twixt nipples and the girdle.
A glacier would have turned aside, lest it should lose its ice
By coming into contact with Mrs. Isaac Rice.

If you would like to have all fifty-two lines, write me.
In the same book I put this inquiry:

> Between my nose and upper lip
> There runs a cleft; a trough; a slip;
> A runnel; furrow; gutter; split;
> I wish I knew the name for it.

The name was philtrum. Nowadays I sing:

> I have a little philtrum
> Wherein my spilltrum flows
> When I am feeling illtrum
> And runny at the nose.

One correspondent reported that *philtrum* is a useful word to have ready at dinner with a pretty girl. Look at her soulfully across the table and murmur, "You have the dearest little philtrum I have ever seen." If she does not stab you with her steak knife, you can look forward to a pleasant evening.

No one has yet reported who wrote this:

> Do you love me, or do you not?
> You told me once, but I forgot.

I have been asked to locate the rest of the following song, which a correspondent heard as a girl at the knee of her grandmother:

> What will be the outcome if the income don't come in?
> From where will come the money for the food and for
>   the gin?

If you know, tell me.

17 JANUARY

Ђ

Interminable Words

When Henry Carey wrote:

> Aldiborontiphoscophornio!
> Where left you Chrononhotonthologos?

he was paying tribute to the perennial, silly fascination of long words. Such words arrive occasionally at my desk, and I have to pay for the extra postage. Louis Phillips sent me *antielectrophotomicrographically,* a thirty-two-letter giant; Eric J. Bowen sent *pneumonoultramicroscopicsilicovolcanoconiosis,* which has forty-five letters. This list is from *Word Ways:*

27   honorificabilitudinitatibus

28   antidisestablishmentarianism

29   trinitrophenylmethylnitramine

30   encephalomyeloraddiculoneuritis

31   dichlorodiphenyltrichloroethane

32   hepatocholangiocystoduodenostomy

33   tetradecamethylcycloheptasiloxane

34   supercalifragilisticexpialidocious

35   azaazoniapentacyclotricosaundecaene

36   dihydroxyphenylethanolisopropylamine

37   praetertranssubstantiationalistically

38   dioxinodioxinobenzopyranobenzopyrylium

39   hepaticocholangiocholecystenterostomies

40   dinitrotetramethyldiaminodiphenylmethane

41   tetradecahydrotetrazoloazacyclohexadecine

42   dibenzenotetrabenzotetraarsacyclohexadecin

43   spironaphthotriazoleoxaazabicyclononatriene

44   dithiatetraazapentacyclotricontatetradecaene

45   pneumonoultramicroscopicsilicovolcanoconiosis

46   bistetramethylenetetrahydrofurodihydropyrazine

47   dispirocyclopentaphenanthrenedioxolanedioxolane

48   lewdningbluebolteredallucktruckalltraumconductor

49   trepignemanpenillorifrizonoufresterfumbledtumbled

50   spirodioxabicyclononaneepoxycyclopentaphenanthrene

51   osseocarnisanguineoviscericartilaginonervomedullary

52   spirofuraniminomethanocyclopentapyrrolotrithiazepine

—Rudolf Ondrejka

Hunter M. Leach is the latest to remind me of the Welsh place name Llanfairpwllgwyngyllgogerychwyrndrobwllllantysiliogogoch, fifty-eight letters. Comedian Red Skelton is credited with discovering the longest word of all—the one that follows "And now a word from our sponsors."

18 JANUARY
ℏ

Malo, Malo, Malo, Malo

It is a marvel that four identical Latin words can be plausibly translated into a complete and complicated English sentence, yet *Malo malo malo malo* means, believe it or not,

> I would rather be
> in an apple tree
> than a bad man
> in adversity.

The first *malo* is "I prefer"; the second is "apple tree"; the third is "bad man"; and the fourth is "hard times." Case endings presumably supply the "in," "than," and "in." But I suspect Lester E. Rothstein is right when he says in *Enigma*: "Even with the addition of prepositions plus the word *quam,* 'than,' the phrase is so ambiguous that it would have been Greek to any classical Roman."

19 JANUARY
ℏ

Uh-oh, Nathan!

The best ethnic jokes are often told in the family.

(Nathan is telling what he calls his Jewish country club joke. I am sorry there is no room to repeat his rich intonations.)

Shapiro, at a banquet, is attempting to propose once more his perennially blackballed friend Max Tannenbaum for membership: "To tell what a great human being Max Tannenbaum is I must use the entire English alphabet! From A to Z I will tell you about this beautiful man!" (Shapiro knows that among the club members is one—now nodding, and dozing—who will try to blackball Tannenbaum. Shapiro trusts that this enemy, Ginsberg, will not wake up.) "A he is Admirable. B he is Beneficial. C he is Charming. D he is Delightful. E he is Educated. F he is Friendly. G he is Good-hearted. H he is a Helluva nice guy. I he is Ina-resting." At this point Ginsberg wakes up. The terrible, the unbudgeable Ginsberg thunders: "J joost a minute! (Majestic pause.) K he's a Kike! L he's a Lummox! M he's a Moron! N he's a Nayfish! O he's an Ox! P he's a Prick! Q he's a Queer! R he's a Red! S he's a Shlemiel! T he's a Tochis! U You can have him! V Ve don't want him! W X Y Z—I blackball the schmuck!"
—*William Styron*

Rabbi Zwi Chaim Yisroel, an Orthodox scholar of the Torah and a man who developed whining to an art unheard of in the West, was unanimously hailed as the wisest man of the Renaissance by his fellow Hebrews, who totalled a sixteenth of one per cent of the population. Once, while he was on his way to synagogue to celebrate the sacred Jewish holiday commemorating God's reneging on every promise, a woman stopped him and asked the following question: "Rabbi, why are we not allowed to eat pork?"

"We're *not*?" the Rev said incredulously. "Uh-oh."

—*Woody Allen*

20 JANUARY
ƀ

Coquin de Sort, Charlie Brown!

Craig Claiborne received a letter from Montreal informing him that "Good Grief, Charlie Brown!" would have different translations in various provinces of France. For instance:

ALSACE:	Ça par example, Charlie Brown!
ANJOU:	Le diable m'emporte, Charlie Brown!
AUVERGNE:	Jarnicoton, Charlie Brown!
BOURGOGNE:	Coquin de sort, Charlie Brown!
BRETAGNE:	Sacre tonnère, Charlie Brown!
CHAMPAGNE:	Par Bacchus, Charlie Brown!
GASCOGNE:	Jarnique, Charlie Brown!
ILE DE FRANCE:	(Région Parisienne, surtout) : Merde alors, Charlie Brown!
LANGUEDOC:	Saperlipopette, Charlie Brown!
LIMOUSIN:	Ma grande, jurée foue, Charlie Brown!
LORRAINE:	Bon sang de bon sang, Charlie Brown!
NORMANDIE:	Nom de Dieppe, Charlie Brown!
ORLEANS:	Pétard de sort, Charlie Brown!
PICARDIE:	Sacre nom d'une pipe, Charlie Brown!
PROVENCE:	Ma fé de Dieou, Charlie Brown!

21 JANUARY
≈

A Wild Raspberry

Deliberate double entendres cannot attain the charm of such innocent blunders as poet Rose Fyleman's "My fairy muff is made of pussy-willow." The authors of the following passages could not have dreamed how low-minded modern readers would construe them:

On barren mountains doth Adonis lie,
A boar's white tusk hath gored his whiter thigh:
His short pants Venus grieve.
—Thomas Stanley's translation of
Bion's "Lament for Adonis"

DAISY

Her beauty smoothed earth's furrowed face
    She gave me tokens three
A look, a word of her winsome mouth
    And a wild raspberry.
—Francis Thompson

WITHIN A CHURCHYARD . . .

Within a churchyard on a recent grave,
    I saw a little cage
That jailed a goldfinch. All was silence save
    Its hops from stage to stage.

There was inquiry in its hopeful eye,
    And once it tried to sing;
Of him or her who placed it there, and why,
    No one knows anything.

True a woman was found the day ensuing,
    And some at times averred
The grave to be her false one's, who when wooing
    Gave her the bird.
—Thomas Hardy

In *Martin Chuzzlewit,* Charles Dickens describes the infatuation of Tom, the church organist, with a member of the choir:

When she spoke, Tom held his breath, so eagerly he listened; when she sang, he sat like one entranced. She touched his organ and from that bright epoch, even it, the old companion of his happiest hours, incapable as he had thought of elevation, began a new and deified existence.

22 JANUARY

≈

Tales Told by Idiots

IDIOT'S LAMENT

Her has come
Her has went
Her has left I all alone
Oh, how can it was
—*Anonymous*

THE BOBOLINK

The bobolink bobbled his brug brimmodaire
  And frabbled his fungo-ozwando;
He spazzled and chuggaed his lyg miffligaire
  While pandigging out his frassmando.

His mushig, however, galog on the siller
  And quinsagged his plag into mink
But the ginzook cowldiggered and piggled the briller
  'Twas the flob sol of our bobolink.

—*Anonymous*

PARDON MY HASTE BUT—

I'm on my way to Wheretown
to dine with Mrs. Who.
If I'm not there by whentime
the guard won't let me through.
There's going to be a why not—
Oh boy I hope I win it—
a pound of homemade whichit
with little whatties in it!
—*Mildred Luton*

LINES BY A HUMANITARIAN

Be lenient with lobsters, and ever kind to crabs,
And be not disrespectful to cuttlefish or dabs;
Chase not the Cochin-China, chaff not the ox obese,
And babble not of feather beds in company with geese.
Be tender with the tadpole, and let the limpet thrive,
Be merciful to mussels, don't skin your eels alive;
When talking to a turtle don't mention calipee—
Be ever kind to animals wherever you may be.
—*Anonymous*

23 JANUARY

≈

What's a Cohort?

Some puns are funny only the first time you hear them; some are never funny; some are funny forever. These always make me smile:

* * *

F.P.A. overheard a woman reciting to her companion at a bar:

> "The Assyrian came down like a wolf on the fold the
>   big bad Assyrian
> And his cohorts were gleaming with purple and gold
>   what's a cohort?"

"Two pints."

* * *

The erudite Lionel Trilling and the erudite Jacques Barzun got into a punning match when a student, discussing Malthus's *Essay on Population,* cited the motto of the Order of the Garter, *Honi soit qui mal y pense*—"Shame on him who imputes ill to it." Barzun remarked, "Honi soit qui Malthus pense." Trilling rejoined, "Honi soit qui mal thus puns."

* * *

The wit, Sydney Smith, heard two women screaming insults at each other from second-story windows on opposite sides of a narrow Edinburgh street.

"Those two will never resolve it," he said. "They are speaking from separate premises."

* * *

In *An Almanac of Words at Play,* I mentioned that Richard Hughes had slipped the following pun into a novel:

> The cat ate cheese and then breathed down a mousehole with baited breath.

Geoffrey Taylor, born the same year as Hughes—1900—used the same pun in a verse; I have always wondered which man thought of it first:

> Sally, having swallowed cheese,
> Directs down holes the scented breeze,
> Enticing thus with baited breath
> Nice mice to an untimely death.

* * *

The Chanler family of New York City had an eccentric Uncle Archie who watched waiters' comings and goings through a pair of binoculars and twirled a silver-headed cane engraved with the words LEAVE ME ALONE. Reports *Sports Illustrated*:

He spent three and a half years involuntarily confined in the Bloomingdale lunatic asylum in White Plains because, among other things, he liked to dress as Napoleon and often went to bed wearing a saber. In a farewell note he left the night he escaped from Bloomingdale in 1900, Uncle Archie wrote to the medical superintendent, "You have always said that I believe I am the reincarnation of Napoleon Bonaparte. As a learned and sincere man, you therefore will not be surprised that I take a French leave."

*   *   *

Here is a fishy story.

There was once a brilliant sturgeon on the staff of the community health fishility. He was, in fact, one of its flounders. Wiser than Salmon, a fin fellow who would never shrimp from his responsibilities, he was successful and happy; he always whistled a happy tuna. One day, one of his patients, a mere whipper snapper, told the sturgeon that his medical theories were full of abalone, and started trouting around telling everybody that the sturgeon's treatments had made him more eel than he had been, and then actually conched him with a malpractice suit!

Well, the sturgeon was in a real pickerel. The board demanded his oyster. But the case smelt to high heaven, so the judge denied the plaintiff's clam. The board tried to hire the sturgeon back, but by then he had hit the bottlenose pretty hard, and the end of our shad tail is that the sturgeon wound up on Squid Roe. Buoy! Isn't that a fine kettle of you-know-what?

—*James Thom*

*   *   *

The late Jimmy Durante crooned these haunting lines at the Parody Club in 1928:

> A boy sat under the Anheuser Busch,
> The rain, 'twas coming down in Schlitz,
> He rose a sad Budweiser boy,
> Pabst yes, Pabst no, Pabst yes.

24 JANUARY

Sol Do Ut Ti Re Do Ut Do Do Do Re Ti Re Do

Guido, eleventh-century father of modern music, named the first six notes of the scale *ut, re, mi, fa, sol,* and *la,* from the first letters of the Latin hymn:

> *Ut* queant laxis   *re*sonare fibris
> *Mi*ra gestorum   *fa*muli tuorum
> *Sol*ve polluti   *la*bii reatum,
>   Sancte Joannes.

Ti was added later, and *ut* was replaced by *do.* If one restores *ut* as the first syllable of the scale, retaining *do* as the last, a considerable number of words can be made by combining musical notes.

It is also possible to make words of the *letters* standing for notes—A, B, C, D, E, F, G. *Baggage* and *defaced* are examples. So is *cabbage-faced,* applied in the comic strip *Mandrake the Magician* to Venusian creatures with lettucelike heads.

I arranged the Guido syllables in the title of today's entry as a message to a friend on his sixty-fifth birthday. Music publisher Eugene Weintraub turned them into two rows of notes, shown below. The first row is in waltz time, and the other in 4/4 time, and the initial *ut* is set in each case an octave higher than the final *do.* If all the notes had been used, this would be a scale exercise, or solfeggio; since *mi* and *fa* are missing, Eugene calls it a

SOLFEGGIETO

My message was not altogether agreeable to my sixty-five-year-old friend. It reads:

SOLD-OUT, TIRED-OUT DODO, DO RETIRE, DO!

25 JANUARY

Declamatory Ode for Dr. Bowdler

Bowdlerize is an eponymous term deriving from Dr. Thomas Bowdler, who in the early nineteenth century mucked out the stews of Shakespearean English, and would have mucked out the stews of the Bible itself if mortality had not stepped mightily in.

There is a lovely if unlikely story that when Bowdler was mucking out *Othello,* he encountered a prurient stage direction: "Desdemona plays the strumpet in bed." Being nothing if not resourceful, the good doctor took but an instant to strike the offending *s.* Henceforth Desdemona was to play the *trumpet* in bed. I suspect that if Othello had caught Desdemona playing the trumpet in bed he would have strangled her much earlier in the play.

Dr. Bowdler is apostrophized, more or less, in the verse *Verecundia* (Latin for modesty):

> O *Verecundia,* modest Muse, arise
> O'er the cold, earthy b*d where *Bowdler* l**s;
> Yet let not sorrow grieve the aching br**st,

That he so soon is taken to his rest;
Let those be p*rg'd the Doctor's praises speak:
Gibbon no more need fl*sh the v*rg*n cheek;
The bard of *Avon*'s cleans'd of moral specks
By cautious *Bowdler,* purest of his s*x.
Virtue his m*str*ss, *Art,* his *nt*m*te,
He tri'd to improve the Bible—but too late.
What he has censor'd none would blush to tell;
Truth's better at the b*tt*m of the well.
                              —*Brian Brindley*

Bowdler would have had his hands full with such American place-names as Maggie's
Nipples and Bastard Peak, Wyoming; or Two Teats, California. A secluded spot
outside of Ontario, Oregon, used to be called Whorehouse Meadows; but a Bureau
of Land Management, haunted by Dr. Bowdler's ghost, changed it to Naughty Girl
Meadows. The bureau also renamed Bullshit Springs Bullshirt Springs.
  This visual wordplay pays tribute to the spirit of the old gentleman:

B WDLER ZE

                              —*Richard Kostelanetz*

26 JANUARY

≋

ODE TO AN ELEVATOR

Capricious, upsy-downsy sweet,
  My patience with thy presence crown!
Pray, when thy rising I entreat,
No more, dear love, rush past my feet
  Down!

Behold thy button burning bright,
  A signal thou wilt be here soon—
If not today, if not tonight,
Some other day, when clappers smite
  Noon.

I hear thee rising! Praise to thee,
  And praise to God, and praise to luck!—
Though well I know that presently,
'Twixt Six and Seven, I shall be
  Stuck.

Thy door slides open. Slightly squiffed,
  I sense too late the empty draft.
A lesser lover would be miffed
To find no life, but only lift
  Shaft.

I pray thee no salt tears to shed;
  I pray thee, drink no hemlock cup.
But I adjure thee, who am dead,
When next I press thy button, head
  Up.

                         —W.R.E.

27 JANUARY
≈

V. B. Nimble, V. B. Quick

*Science, Pure and Applied, by V. B. Wigglesworth, F.R.S.,
Quick Professor of Biology in the University of Cambridge.*
       —A talk listed in the B.B.C. Radio Times

V. B. Wigglesworth wakes at noon,
Washes, shaves, and very soon
Is at the lab; he reads his mail,
Tweaks a tadpole by the tail,
Undoes his coat, removes his hat,
Dips a spider in a vat
Of alkaline, phones the press,
Tells them he is F.R.S.,
Subdivides six protocells,
Kills a rat by ringing bells,
Writes a treatise, edits two
Symposia on "Will Man Do?",
Gives a lecture, audits three,
Has the Sperm Club in for tea,
Pensions off an aging spore,
Cracks a test tube, takes some more
Science and applies it, finds
His hat, adjusts it, pulls the blinds,
Instructs the jellyfish to spawn,
And, by one o'clock, is gone.
                  —John Updike

28 JANUARY

John Hancocks

"When I was a child," recalls autograph collector Charles Hamilton, "there was a story in the local paper saying that some guy had repeatedly written to Rudyard Kipling and never got a reply—until he learned that Kipling got five dollars a word for his manuscripts, and he sent him a check for five dollars. Kipling sent back a one-word unsigned reply: 'Thanks.' Well, this appealed to me immensely. At the time, I was getting ten cents a week from my father for hauling out our furnace ashes, so I sent Kipling a dime, explaining its origin. He sent back a signature. And I was hooked."

Today Hamilton has the most valuable private collection of autographs there is, including these. See how many of the signatures you can identify.

1. Outspoken diplomat

2. The Blue Angel

3. Mideast mastermind

4. The Sundance Kid

5. Nancy's "Special K"

6. Famous plumber

7. The père of a famous trio

8. European statesman

9. Siamese potentate, once

10. Leading leaper

11. Son of Don Brando

12. Famous Minnesotan

13. Thespian famed for his trans-world trip

14. "Notorious" for his dimpled chin.

15. An auld acquaintance

16. Cinderella, Italian style

17. Mime's the word

18. Yankee Doodle Dandy

29 JANUARY
≈

Some Are Right

Some of the word origins below, that is; and some are wrong. Say which are which:

1. *Albatross.* Upon first encountering this white seabird, Portuguese mariners mistook it for a pelican. It was only natural that they would refer to it by its Portuguese name, *alcatraz.* (The island in San Francisco Bay was originally inhabited by pelicans.) *Albatross* is a corruption of *alcatraz,* itself derived from the Arabic *al gadus* ("water bucket"), a reference to the pelican's pouch.

2. *Amazon.* In Greek mythology, a tribe of fierce warrior females. The term evolves through the prefix *a* ("without," as in *atypical*), and *mazos* ("breast"). The Greeks believed that these women cut off their right breasts to eliminate any impediment to archery and assure the true flight of their arrows.

3. *Ambush.* According to legend, a general, suspecting that his enemy lay concealed in a forest, had his men throw stones into the trees. The stones would dislodge birds, *if* the birds hadn't already been flushed by enemy soldiers hidden *in boscis* (Latin for "in the woods"). Gradually modified to *ambush,* the term still denotes a surprise attack by hidden enemies.

4. *Gibberish.* This word is derived from the first name of Jabir ibn Hayyan, an eighth-century scholar and alchemist, who was said to have written more than 2,000 learned treatises. The "scientific" language he used was so abstruse as to sound unintelligible to the uneducated ear.

5. *Corduroy.* At one time, an elegant cloth of woven silk, worn only by the kings of France as part of their hunting attire. It derives from *corde du roi* ("cord of the king"). Both the word corduroy and the cloth it designates are corrupted and decidedly more humble versions of the originals.

6. *Hoax.* A shortening of *hocus pocus* (itself a piece of dog Latin), *hoax* is said to derive from the words of the mass (*Hoc est enim corpus meum; hoc est corpus fili*). Because of its sacred origin, the term *hocus pocus* supposedly possessed occult powers and was frequently intoned as a catalyst to magic or trickery. En route the word *hoax* has come to denote a trick or fraud.

7. *Hysteria.* From the Greek *hustera,* meaning "womb." Ancients believed that the womb was not connected inside the body, and when it moved within the abdomen, the sensation caused women to scream, weep, and act irrationally.

8. *Ketchup.* The term is derived from the onion-and-spice-flavored tomato preserves used in remote mining areas or lumber camps of the American West

where vegetables could not be grown. The sauce was referred to as *cat's blood,* but lumberjacks, drawing upon their arboreal habitat, euphemistically termed it *cat sap.* The word progressed through attrition to *catsup* and, eventually, *ketchup.*

9. *Marmalade.* An elision of *Marie malade,* "sick Mary." The lady referred to was Mary, Queen of Scots, who during an illness could only keep down the sweet conserve of fruit prescribed by her physicians. The "medicine" eventually came to be known by the name and condition of the patient.

10. *Piker.* During pioneer days a group of migrants to California became notorious for their cheapness and small-stake gambling practices. They came from Pike County, Missouri. The region remains under that stigma to this day—home turf of any individual who does things in a small, contemptible, or miserly way.

11. *Praline.* Named for the Marshal du Plessis-Praslin, a French soldier and diplomat, who became minister of state in 1652. As the story goes, the almonds he enjoyed eating gave him indigestion. The suggestion was made that sugar-coating the nuts would eliminate the problem. A variant of this confection came to be known to the Creoles of Louisiana as pralines.

—*Nort Bramesco*

30 JANUARY
≈

This Is Progress?

WASHINGTON—A couple I know checked into one of the new Detroit hotels a few months ago and in due course left a 7 A.M. wake-up call.

Being an early riser, however, the husband was up long before seven and decided he'd go down to breakfast and let his wife sleep late. He dialed the hotel switchboard, explained the situation, and said he'd like to cancel the wake-up call.

"Sorry, sir," the answer came, "but we can't do that. It's in the computer, and there's no way to get it out now."

• A while back, a reporter phoned a congressional committee and asked to speak to the staff director. Unfortunately, he was told, the staff director wouldn't be in that morning; there'd been a power failure at his home. Well, the reporter persisted, that was certainly too bad, but just why did a power failure prevent him from coming to work?

"He can't get his car out of the garage," the secretary explained. "The garage doors are electrically controlled."

• A friend recently went to make a deposit at her local bank in upstate New York.

The deposit couldn't be accepted, she was informed, "because it's raining too hard." Seems that when the rain gets beyond a certain intensity, the wires transmitting the message from the branch banks to the computer at the main bank in Albany send jumbled signals—and so branch bank operations have to be suspended.

• A number of high schools in this area have been built with windows that don't open; when the air conditioning fails on a hot spring or fall day, pupils are given the day off.

• Last fall, when the nation moved back to Standard Time, a young friend was appalled to find she was going to have to turn her time-and-date digital wristwatch ahead thirty days and twenty-three hours.

• Still another acquaintance had his car battery go dead while his power windows were rolled down—and then the rains came and poured in while he was parked alongside the highway waiting for help.

*   *   *

In all likelihood, corrective measures are being developed for many of the problems described above, and helpful correspondents will be writing in to tell me all about it. Yet I am confident that new examples will come along to fill the gap. After all, that's progress.

—Alan L. Otten

31 JANUARY
≈

Wede and F.P.A.

Let me tell you why the following verses are signed "Wede."

At the age of four I fell in love with a twelve-year-old boy named Aquila. We were inseparable. Wherever Aquila went, I followed: through the hayfields, the stands of huckleberry, the alder trees, the gorse; through the marshes; along the ocean surf; out onto the sand flats of the bay.

The locals first called us Aquila-and-Willard, liking the echo; and when they learned that Aquila's nickname was Quede, they said Quede-and-Wede. I don't know why Aquila was nicknamed Quede, though.

When I was one-and-twenty, no use to talk to me, and bound to be a poet, I signed my verses "Wede."

In those days, an aspiring poet's dearest dream was to be published in F.P.A.'s legendary newspaper column, "The Conning Tower." For two years I sent F.P.A. an incessant sighing stream of verses on blighted love and the inevitability of the grave—topics which I continue to treat, albeit more gingerly, to this day. I light a candle to F.P.A. each January 31 because January 31, 1934, was the day he first printed one of my verses. He used five in all, and I clipped and filed them with trembling hands. Here are two of them.

Make a fellow feel old, don't they?

From the *New York Herald Tribune*

The Conning Tower

COQUETTE

Out of gladness first I sung
Into Beauty's ears;
Beauty fled my tinkling tongue,
Weeping silver tears.

Later sang I out of love,
Sang that one was fair,
Conjured Beauty to approve;
Beauty was not there.

Sang I then on bated breath
Music overcast
With a sorrow sweet as death;
Beauty heard, and passed.

When I hushed my bootless tongue,
Finding peace more meet,
Beauty, wench-like, smiled; and flung
Daisies at my feet.

—*WEDE*
17 April, 1934

"I WOULD TO GOD THAT I MIGHT FIND A PHRASE"

I would to God that I might find a phrase
Telling the slow decay of life alone;
How loss of her has damned my flesh and bone
To walk with ghosts, and endlessly reblaze
The dimming landmarks of our dozen days.
Could I have changed the end if I had known,
Leaving a wish unspoke, or path ungone,
That foredecreed the sundrance of our ways?

Some be indeed who profit from each jot
Superimposed today on yesterday,
Setting their course by period and blot
Until the page is filled, or put away;
I can but stand bemused, staring across
The irrevocability of loss.

—*WEDE*
29 October, 1934

FEBRUARY

ı FEBRUARY
～

The Problem of Tragedy

University of Gary
THE BIRCHING ROOM

Dear Mr. Hayford,

Thank you very much for sending me your article on the "Chicago Telephone Directory."

I can't agree with you at all that Placy F. Lagoia is the hero of the "Directory," and that he meets Aristotle's definition of the hero of tragedy. You base your argument upon the fact that Mr. Lagoia appears on page 1030, just half-way through the "Directory"—in short, in a position which you call most significant with respect to Aristotle's definition. But I can find no support in the *Poetics* for your view, but quite the contrary. For Aristotle's description of the hero involves, you may recall, a man of the middling sort, neither entirely good nor entirely wicked, who through some error of judgment or *hamartia* brings about a change from good to bad fortune which involves himself and his friends and relatives. Now I think you have confused this conception of the middling man, a moral conception, with crude notions of position. Mr. Lagoia occupies the middling position in the "Directory," but he is not therefore a middling sort of man in Aristotle's sense. If we assume that the hero of tragedy must suffer a change from good fortune to bad fortune through some sort of peripety, we must also assume·that he is present throughout much of the action, which must have a beginning, a middle, and an end. Now Mr. Lagoia does not appear before the mention of his name on page 1030, nor does he ever again appear in the "Directory," and while he may be said to have a middle, he doesn't have either a beginning or an end. Far from calling him a tragic hero, I think we must put him down simply as one of the many incidental characters with which this work of the Bell Company is somewhat overcrowded.

If we assume that the hero must be present throughout much of the action, the place to seek his first appearance is clearly not halfway through the work, but towards the beginning, as in "Hamlet," or at the beginning, as in Sophocles' "Oedipus Rex."

The first person mentioned in the "Directory" is Nathan Aabel. Nathan Aabel, then, is the hero, to the extent that the work may be said to have a hero. And this qualification is an important one. For what, after all, do we know about Nathan Aabel? That he is an accountant. That his address (whether business or home or both is not made clear) is 902 W. Addison. That his telephone number is Lakeview

5-8819. But beyond these facts we know nothing about him, nor do we ever learn anything more. He appears once, briefly, and is gone; certainly he is far from being a tragic hero in Aristotle's sense; there is no change from good to bad fortune; there is not even a change from bad to good fortune; there is no change at all. What the Bell Company has done is cynically to reduce the character almost to a nullity: notice such elements of style as "acct" for "accountant," "LAKvw" for "Lakeview," and so on. If, then, we can't accept your theory that Placy F. Lagoia is the hero, and if Nathan Aabel manifestly isn't the hero (for while *he* has a *beginning,* he has neither a middle nor an end), who then *is* the hero? I think we must conclude that there is no hero in this tragedy, and lacking a hero no tragedy, and lacking a tragedy no pity and fear, and lacking pity and fear none of the emotions proper to a tragedy.

I suspect that the Bell Company started the work with some intention (which it would not be legitimate to mention) of dealing with the tragedy of Nathan Aabel, but soon let themselves be turned from this original purpose by thoughts of the large mixed public audience at which the "Directory" was directed.

Very cordially yours,
Donald Egret

—*W. B. Scott*

2   FEBRUARY

Damfino, Damfinare

If we aren't willing to learn Latin, why do we insist on using it to decorate English? Instead of misusing Latin plurals (making "media" and "criteria" single nouns, for instance), why not settle for "criterions," "mediums," "curriculums," "hippopotamuses"?

A syndicated columnist, apparently assuming that since *media* and *criteria* are identical in their plural endings they must be identical in the singular, headed his column, "Accuracy: The Only Criterium." You say criterium, I say criterion; I think we two shall have to part.

I have before me a third-grade workbook, issued for classroom use. The masthead glitters with Ph.Ds. The first line reads *"Solus* is the Latin word meaning sun." Any beginner's Latin grammar confirms that *solus* has nothing to do with *sol,* "sun"; it is not even one of the ten forms of that word.

We might give our speech classical flavor by throwing in *umquam* and *numquam*— "never" and "ever." Instead of the enthusiastic affirmative, "Brother, did I ever!", why not, "Brother, did I *umquam!*" A girl asked to compromise her virtue might cry out, *"Numquam!"*

I studied Virgil in a bare-walled classroom. Our professor, deciding that the medicine we needed was a drill in Latin grammar, slammed shut his book and pounced: "J.T., give me the principal parts of a verb in the first conjugation."

J.T. froze. "What's a verb in the first conjugation?" he whispered to his neighbor. "Damn 'f *I* know," came the mumbled reply. J.T. gamely blurted, *"Damfino, damfinare, damfinavi, damfinatus . . ."*

—*Mildred Luton*

3 FEBRUARY

Opposites

What is the opposite of *nuts*?
It's *soup!* Let's have no ifs or buts.
In any suitable repast
The soup comes first, the nuts come last.
Or that is what *sane* folk advise;
You're nuts if you think otherwise.

*   *   *

What is the opposite of *doe*?
The answer's *buck,* as you should know.
A buck *is* doe, you say? Well, well,
Clearly you don't know how to spell.
Moreover, get this through your head:
The current slang for dough is *bread.*

*   *   *

The opposite of *squash*? Offhand,
I'd say that it might be *expand,*
Enlarge, uncrumple, or *inflate.*
However, on a dinner plate
With yellow vegetables and green,
The opposite of squash is *bean.*
—*Richard D. Wilbur*

The foregoing insights appear in a book by Mr. Wilbur called, of course, *Opposites.* The device is addictive, and I cannot help adding my four lines' worth:

What is the opposite of *thought?*
"Many," I allowed.
Two thoughts are a lot—
Three's a crowd.
—*W.R.E.*

4 FEBRUARY

The Other Point of View

Whether or not the grass looks greener from the other side of the fence, says *Word Ways,* at least it looks different:

• From a clock's point of view the hands move counterclockwise.

• From a chicken's point of view every egg is poached.

• The sun never rises on the British Empire.

• The tardy worm avoids the early bird.

• Babe Ruth struck out 1,330 times.

• A hen is only an egg's way of making another egg.

• The way they are making things today, antiques will be things of the past in the future.

• It may be garbage to you, but it's bread and butter to the garbage collector.

• How come there's so much month left at the end of the money?

5 FEBRUARY
≈

Unified Field Theory

In the beginning there was Aristotle
And objects at rest tended to remain at rest,
And objects in motion tended to come to rest,
And soon everything was at rest,
And God saw that it was boring.

Then God created Newton,
And objects at rest tended to remain at rest,
But objects in motion tended to remain in motion,
And energy was conserved and momentum was conserved
    and matter was conserved,
And God saw that it was conservative.

Then God created Einstein,
And everything was relative,
And fast things became short,
And straight things became curved,
And the universe was filled with inertial frames,
And God saw that it was relatively general,
    but some of it was especially relative.

Then God created Bohr,
And there was the principle,
And the principle was quantum,
And all things were quantified,
But some things were still relative,
And God saw that it was confusing.

Then God was going to create Furgeson,
And Furgeson would have unified,
And he would have fielded a theory,
And all would have been one,
But it was the seventh day,
And God rested,
And objects at rest tend to remain at rest.

—*Tim Joseph*

6 FEBRUARY

You Can't Always Be Right

Jean Harlow, meeting Lady Asquith, addressed her by her first name, Margot, pronouncing the word as if it rhymed with *rot*. Lady Asquith reproved her gently: "My dear, the *t* is silent, as in 'Harlow.'"

There is no perfect pronunciation, or rather there are several perfect pronunciations; those listed in dictionaries are the ones most used by educated people at the time dictionaries were assembled. Sounding an *h* before words beginning with vowels (*h'article, h'enemy, h'ecstasy*) while dropping it when it is really there (*'at, 'ungry, 'orse*), now a Cockney aberration, was first affected by the aristocracy. Englishmen started saying *either* as if it were spelled "eyether" in imitation of the first Hanoverian king, who being German pronounced all *ei*'s as $\bar{i}$'s.

Words change in meaning as well as pronunciation, and it is useful to know earlier meanings for accuracy of expression. These evolving words are listed by a man who knows his English better than most:

METICULOUS	Copywriters for men's stores think this is a good word; actually it still carries the pejorative connotation of being "excessively careful about minute details."
PLETHORA	Not just abundance; "harmful excess over abundance."
TERRAIN	A technical military term, meaning "a tract of land viewed for battle possibilities."
INNER MAN	Meant "the soul" until some impious eighteenth-century humorist used it as a synonym for stomach.
TREK	More than mere traveling. Migration.
INTRIGUE	At the end of the last century, this meant only "to plot, conspire," not "to fascinate."
FRANKENSTEIN	He is not the monster; he's the man who *made* the monster.

—*Wesley Price*

7 FEABRUARY

Two Old Crows

Two old crows sat on a fence rail.
Two old crows sat on a fence rail,
Thinking of effect and cause,
Of weeds and flowers,
And nature's laws.
One of them muttered, one of them stuttered,
One of them stuttered, one of them muttered.
Each of them thought far more than he uttered.
One crow asked the other crow a riddle.
One crow asked the other crow a riddle.
The muttering crow
Asked the stuttering crow,
"Why does a bee have a sword to his fiddle?
Why does a bee have a sword to his fiddle?"
"Bee-cause," said the other crow,
"Bee-cause,
B B B B B B B B B B B B B B B B-cause."
Just then a bee flew close to their rail:—
"Buzzzzzzzzzzzzzzzzzzzz zzzzzzzzz zzzzzzzzzzzzzzzz
    ZZZZZZZZ"
And those two black crows
Turned pale,
And away those crows did sail.
Why?
B B B B B B B B B B B B B B B B B-cause.
B B B B B B B B B B B B B B B B B-cause.
"Buzzzzzzzzzzzzzz zzzzzzzzz zzzzzzzzzzzzzzzz
    ZZZZZZZZ."

—Vachel Lindsay

8 FEABRUARY

Mind Your P's and Q's

Radio actor Joe Julien raised his hand during rehearsal and was excused by director Norman Corwin on the ground that all actors should mind their p's and q's.

Unfortunately, this fine double pun throws no light on the mystery of where the expression "to mind one's p's and q's" comes from.

One theory is that since *p* and *q* are similar in appearance, orthography teachers used to stress that the tails of the two letters curve in opposite directions. Another is that in English pubs the bartender kept a blackboard record of his patrons' consumption by p's (pints) and q's (quarts).

Some say that in the days when manners were taught by maxim, elders told their children to mind their "pleases and excuses."

In the levees of pre-revolutionary France, gentlemen about to be admitted to the royal presence were warned not to trip over their long dress swords or lose their wigs during the conventional flourishes and bows: *"Messieurs, regardez vos pieds et vos queues"*—"Gentlemen, mind your feet and wigs."

9 FEBRUARY

Variable Verbs

A boy who swims will soon have swum,
But milk is skimmed and seldom skum,
And nails you trim, they are not trum.

When words you speak those works are spoken,
But a nose is tweaked and can't be twoken,
And what you seek is seldom soken.

If we forget, then we've forgotten,
But things we wet are never wotten,
And houses let cannot be lotten.

The goods one sells are always sold,
But fears dispelled are not dispold,
And what you smell is never smold.

When young a top you oft saw spun,
But did you see a grin e'er grun,
Or a potato neatly skun?

—Anonymous

Use each of the following past tenses, all looking like products of ignorance, correctly in a sentence:

1. Flied	6. Shined
2. Hanged	7. Spitted
3. Leaved	8. Sticked
4. Letted	9. Treaded
5. Ringed	10. Weaved

—Richard Lederer

10 FEBRUARY

Twisted Proverbs

- Perversity makes strange bedfellows.   —*R. Cecil Owen*
- The parrot does not believe all he says.   —*F. G. Messervy*
- The cock crows, but the hen lays the eggs.   —*Olric*
- The fortunate always believe in a just providence.   —*Irene Williams*
- Don't join a queue unless you know what's at the end of it.   —*Gerald Challis*
- The fighter calls the bomber slow.   —*N.B.*
- Second thoughts in the train are better than impulse in the taxi.

—*Miss D. N. Daglish*
- A butterfly lives long enough.   —*Lucifer*
- The crunching of a man's own toast is louder than God's own thunder. —*F.C.C.*
- The fire that melts lead tempers steel.   —*Phiz*
- A patriot is known by his income-tax returns.   —*Pibwob*

Here are some bastardized proverbs:

A rolling pin gathers no moss.

Footsore and fancy free.

Many hands make housework.

A penny saved is a Penny Dreadful.

Faint heart never won fair weather.

Don't look a saw horse in the mouth.

Let sleeping bags lie.

Half a wit is better than none.

Cleanliness is next to impossible.

Fools fall in where angels fear to tread.

You can't teach an old dog card tricks.

Don't kill the goose that laid the deviled egg.

One picture is worth a thousand dollars.

There's no fool like an old maid.

Out of sight, out of order.

A healthy dog has a cold beer.

Politics makes strange bedbugs.

Don't cross your eyes before you come to them.

Don't cross your blessings before they hatch.

People who live in glass houses shouldn't throw parties.

Don't burn your bridges at both ends.

Procrastination is the nick of time.

Penny wise, pound cake.

Into each cellar some rain must fall.

—Mary J. Youngquist

Identify the proverbs below by the single word given:

1. X dog X X X.
2. X X X X eggs X X X.
3. X X X mended.
4. X X X X pudding X X X X.
5. X X X X X X Romans X.
6. X X X feather X X.
7. X X X X kettle X.

11 FEBRUARY

≈

<i>My Weight, Sir, You Must Not Survey</i>

A univocalic—a passage using but one of the five vowels—is difficult to arrange, unless you keep it short:

> Weep, weep.
> Then sleep
> Deep, deep.

Easier is the lipogram, which drops one vowel from each passage. The following lipograms retain the sound of the deleted vowel:

No *A*:

> My weight, sir, you must not survey.
> Sir, weigh me not—no weigh, no weigh.

No *E*:

> Snow falling fast. On snowy quai
> A Spanish miss shows how to ski.
> What sport, slaloming vis-à-vis
> Such fair companion! . . . *Si, ah, si!*
> But lacking ski-facility
> I wind up upsy-daisily.

No *I*:

> Why doth the eyeless fellow cry?
> Why, so would you, had you no eye.

No *O*:

> Il y a une lettre
>   Que je ne puis
> Pas permettre
>   Ici.
> Elle s'entend
> En
> Eau
>   Beau
>   Bateau
>   Chateau
>   Chapeau
>   Plateau
>   Tableau
> Et
> (En anglais)   Sew.

No *U*:

> A Vowel living in my town,
> Heard oftener than written down,
> Gives voice in words like *brew, eschew,*
> *Do, drew, anew,* and *interview.*
> I now declare this Vowel Moot,
> And Ban it from the Alphaboot.
>   —*W.R.E.*

12 FEBRUARY

Spaghettibird Headdress

Anguish languish, popularized by the late Howard L. Chace, is a form of punning in which words overlap to give an impression of other words, as clouds assume forms according to the fancy of the observer. Take, for instance, these:

heresy	warts	firmer
ladle	warts	once
furry	welcher	inner
starry	altar	regional
toiling	girdle	virgin
udder	deferent	

Now read the list aloud, listening for the overtones:

"Here is a little fairy story told in other words, words which are altogether different from the ones in the original version."

You knew it all the time.

The anguish languish that follows is appropriate to this date:

SPAGHETTIBIRD HEADDRESS

bar Labour Ham Winking

Fors oar in shaving ear she goes, awful fodders broad fart hunter dish consonant hay noon action, corn sieved inebriety and addict hated tutor preposition dot omen or crated inkwell.

Non wiring caged integrate cymbal wart, tasting wither damnation, our runny gnashing, socking seed end sod defecated ken logging door. Worm head honor grape batter veal doff fat whore. Wave counter defecator potion audit felled azure vinyl roasting piece fort hose hoe hair gater wives tit tat gnashing mike leaf. Assault her gutter footing in pepper dot weigh shoe duties.

Budding awl archer since, weaken opt defecate, weekend not concentrate, working ought hello disk round. Depravement, livid indeed, hue straggle deer, heft cancer traded hit, pharaoh buff harp burp hours tatter distract. Twirled wheel ladle node orlon ram umber wad wheeze hay year, buttock an if veer fork add catered hairdo done finest walk witch day hoof otter heft dust floor show nobody at fenced. I doze rudder forest tubing hair debtor catered tuba grape tusk rim onion beef harass—dot form tease own whored did, wheat aching greased dim notion tutor cows far wish dig rave do lustful miss shore add dive ocean; dewy her holly dissolve daddies dad shell nut heft tiding feign; end it grubby men, other pimple, brother pimple, father pimple, shell nut pair rich fern dirt.

—*Jim Anderson, Jeffrey Brown, John Spencer*

APE OWE 'EM

When fur stews can this sill leer I'm
   Toot rye tomb ache theme e'en ink Lear,
Youth inked wood butt bee weigh sting thyme
   Use eh, "It's imp lean on scents shear!"
Gnome attar; Anna lies align!
   Nation mice lender verse says knot—
Fork rip tick poet real Ike mine,
How Aaron weal demesnes allot.

—*Leonard Switzer*

13 FEBRUARY
≈

The First Kiss

OYSTERVILLE—I remember walking at the age of eight or so down the two hundred yards of hay-covered lane that separate our house from the bay, and wondering.

I had heard on the radio—it must have been on the radio, though I don't recollect that we had a set then—a song of which two lines ran something like this:

> I'm nervous ... so nervous ... I'm worried ... and blue.
> If that's what her kissing does, what would her hugging do?

There was a mystery here. Kissing, in our family, was a gesture of special tenderness; when my father or mother kissed me, I was knighted. Hugging was as unimportant as scratching behind a dog's ears. What, then, were the special emotions connected with hugging?

I was still wondering when, at the age of fourteen, I experienced for the first time a kiss in the category of what might be called preliminaries. We were on our way back from a school party. My brother Edwin was driving the Dodge, with our teacher (of typing) sitting a bit closer to him than he found comfortable. I was in the dark back seat with the girl I had taken to the party. A kiss was called for. In those days schools did not yet provide diagrams for such encounters, so I made the approach frontally; our noses struck like colliding automobiles. I was blinded with pain; was this, I thought incredulously, the heavenly sensation my more knowledgeable schoolfellows had been exalting? I bled like a slaughtered bull; I am probably the first man to ejaculate through the nose. The girl refused to go out with me again, so I could not correct my mistake. I like to think that she profited from the experience. I can't be sure; she never thanked me.

What *is* so special about hugging anyhow?

14 FEBRUARY
~

Ohne Deine Amor

Macaronics, poems mixing two or more languages, were called *contrasto plurilingue* in medieval times. The form hit its apogee when Rambaut de Vaqueiras, a Provençal poet, assembled a verse with the first stanza in Provençal, the second in Italian, the third in Old French, the fourth in Gascon, the fifth in Spanish and Portuguese, and the sixth in two lines of each language.

This Spanish-German macaronic suits Valentine's Day:

> Me falta immer deine Lieb;
> ¿Porqué kommst nicht aquí?
> Kein Himmel Scheint; kein pájaro
> Fliegt wann du bleibst allí.
>
> Joyas como flores raras,
> Y Königsessen möcht Ich bringen ...
> Lieb und Treu nach tigo siempre ...
> Sin dich ningun puede singen.

Wäre besser wenn la muerte
Me permitiera schlafen.
Vielgeliebte, meine puerta
Immer wartet, abierta.
                    —*Carolyn S. Foote*

An English-language approximation of the author's mood:

The loss of love's perhaps least loss of all—
A raindrop stolen from a brimful sea.
Why stars should cease to shine, and birds to call,
Must puzzle you—I know it puzzles me.

I offered flow'rs like gems; you, gems like flow'rs;
I, manna; you, the milk of paradise.
(Mere idle promises in idle hours:
Their unfulfillment comes as no surprise.)

I wonder . . . is your latch undrawn tonight
As mine is? Is your night lamp by the bed? . . .
We shall sleep better, when we've snuffed the light . . .
When we are dead, are dead, are dead, are dead.
                    —*W.R.E.*

15 FEBRUARY
~

On a Book Cadger

In 1951 I wrote a book which sold in its hard cover version for $2—then a standard price—and in paperback for 25¢. I handed out the paperbacks like calling cards. But now that even paperbacks cost a finger and a thumb, I dole out the handful of books allotted me by the publisher as reluctantly as Midas gave away gold pieces:

Says he, "I hear you've wrote another book."
   Says I, "Just so."
Says he, "No problem if I take a look?"
   Says I, "Gosh, no."
Says he, "Just sign it with a funny line
   To make folks laugh."
Says I, "Pay cash and I'll be glad to sign
   My autograph."
He says, "All right, I'll buy one"; but I know
   That's only crock;

He 'phones me from the store, and says, "Hello?
   They're out of stock.
You'll hold a copy for me? Hey, that's great;
   I know you've got 'em."
(I'm ten floors up, and I'll defenestrate
   Him to the bottom.)
                —W.R.E.

16 FEBRUARY
##

A Chesterton of Hilaireity

A stately old gentleman walked into Brentano's, the New York bookstore, and asked
for a copy of *History of England,* by Hilary Belloc. The clerk said, "You mean
Hil*aire* Bel*l*oc—it's a French name." "I do not," he said. "I mean *Hilary Bel*loc."
The clerk brought the book and wrapped it. "Will this be charge or cash, sir?" she
asked. "Charge," said he. "Very good, sir. To whom shall I charge it?" "*Hi*lary
*Bel*loc," said the old gentleman.

But the clerk had a point; Belloc was born in France, and his given names were
Joseph Hilaire Pierre.

He was a Hilaireious poet:

THE MICROBE

The Microbe is so very small
You cannot make him out at all,
But many sanguine people hope
To see him through a microscope.
His jointed tongue that lies beneath
A hundred curious rows of teeth;
His seven tufted tails with lots
Of lovely pink and purple spots,
On each of which a pattern stands,
Composed of forty separate bands;
His eyebrows of a tender green;
All these have never yet been seen—
But Scientists, who ought to know,
Assure us that they must be so . . .
Oh! let us never, never doubt
What nobody is sure about!
           —Hilaire Belloc

Belloc and G. K. Chesterton were contemporaries (Belloc, 1870–1953; Chesterton,
1874–1936). Both were dexterous wits, as well as firm Roman Catholics; even their
light verse frequently reflected their religious beliefs, as in the first two of these verses:

A BROAD MINDED BISHOP
REBUKES THE VERMINOUS ST. FRANCIS

If Brother Francis pardoned Brother Flea,
There still seems need of such strange charity,
Seeing he is, for all his gay goodwill,
Bitten by funny little creatures still.
—*G. K. Chesterton*

ON READING "GOD"

(Mr. John Middleton Murry explained that his book with this title records his farewell to God.)

Murry, on finding *le Bon Dieu*
Chose difficile à croire
Illogically said *"Adieu"*
But God said *"Au revoir."*
—*G. K. Chesterton*

TRIOLET

I wish I were a jelly fish
That cannot fall downstairs:
Of all the things I wish to wish
I wish I were a jelly fish
That hasn't any cares,
And doesn't even have to wish
"I wish I were a jelly fish
    That cannot fall downstairs."
—*G. K. Chesterton*

FOR BOB KNILLE, EASTERN U.S. SECRETARY, THE CHESTERTON SOCIETY

That Chesterton and Belloc were
    Both Roman Catholics
Is cause sufficient to concur
    In burning heretics.
—*W.R.E.*

17 FEBRUARY
〜

Memory Lane

Israel Shenker recalls in the *New York Times* a woman who remembers people as what they eat.

Her name is Phyllis Brienza, and she is a waitress at a fast-food restaurant. She recognizes people by the orders they give. The customer in the Nehru jacket is "medium with half a bun and French." The man who always keeps his raincoat on is not the man in the raincoat; he is a "well"—i.e., a well-done hamburger.

She greets a customer with "Hi," and adds to the chef, "Rare," mentally reviewing the full identification: "Rare, an apple pie, and coffee."

"When someone new comes in," says Mrs. Brienza, "I think to myself, 'That's a medium,' or 'That's a rare.' Sometimes they have this serious look and I think, 'That must be a well.' Usually I'm right."

"Last Christmas," says Mr. Shenker, "she got a card from a client whom she remembered at once. It was signed simply: 'Medium rare, pressed.' "

* * *

Novelist Eudora Welty draws an affectionate portrait of an elderly black woman who regularly warned visitors, "Don't tell me your name, for I'm resting my mind."

Anyone past fifty will know what she means. A friend of mine asked his eighty-two-year-old father the names of his two constant luncheon companions. "My dear boy," replied his father, "I haven't remembered their names in years."

He was approaching the state of the old woman who was given pills to improve her memory but could not remember to take the pills.

Florenz Ziegfeld of the *Ziegfeld Follies* was a famous man in his day, and his wife, actress Billie Burke, was a famous woman. But no more. Columnist Earl Wilson reports this exchange between a teen-ager and a forty-year-old:

TEEN-AGER: Florence Ziegfeld? I never heard of her.

FORTY-YEAR-OLD: I mean the Florenz Ziegfeld who married Billie Burke.

TEEN-AGER (yawning): Billy Burke? I never heard of him either.

Shortly before the death of the famed columnist Walter Lippmann, a young woman complained to him at a party that a network had turned down her television script because it contained certain racy words, which she lovingly repeated. Lippmann asked blankly, "What do they mean?" The exchange amused Fred Friendly, who was standing by, and he repeated it next morning at breakfast to his teen-age daughter. The racy words were old hat to her; but "Who," she asked, "is Walter Lippmann?"

Writer Julian Street described a Denver suburb for the *Saturday Evening Post*. The city fathers were displeased by Mr. Street's concentration on their red-light district. In retaliation, they changed the name of the thoroughfare most frequented by local prostitutes to Julian Street.

18 FEBRUARY
≈

Some Mothers and Others I've Seen

ORMONYM: A verbal pair of charade sentences, as "some others I've seen" and "some mothers I've seen"—*Verbatim*

Some fathers I've seen
Are inclined to be mean,
And also some mothers,
Some mothers I've seen—

And also some brothers,
Some sisters, some others,
Who, had I my druthers,
Would drown in their spleen—
Some others, some others,
Some others I've seen.
　　　　　　—W.R.E.

DEAR LIZ

Dear Liz:
　　　　Your chamber, dear, 's designed
　For monkey biz;
An aph-ro-dis'-i-ac-al kind
　Of room it is.

And if to enter I've declined
　The reason is
That to *my* chamber I'm confined
　By rheumatis.
　　　　　　—W.R.E.

Paris's theft of Helen from Menelaus was the proximate cause of the Trojan War. When Helen rejoined her husband after the Greeks' victory, the homecoming could hardly have been ecstatic:

WHICH MENELAUS?

Though Menelaus grew by luck old,
　While greater heroes perished,
None held in awe that kingly cuckold
　Who wanton Helen cherished.
The other ladies of the court
Were very much of Helen's sort:
Each night, anticipating sport,
　They asked, "Which Menelaus?"
　　　　　　—W.R.E.

CONCEDE, MY OWN

Insinuate
　I need but briefly bide alone
　While my ontogenies (in bone,
In breath, in blood, in pore, in pate,
In sinew) wait

To crest concurrent with your own
In sin. You ate
Long since this fruit; why hesitate
To taste it now? Concede, my own—
In sin you wait.

—W.R.E.

19 FEBRUARY
X

Chivers to Coogler to Moore

The man who wrote the verse that follows was not joking; indeed, he was mourning the death of his firstborn son; but sorrow is no excuse for bathos.

As an egg, when broken never
Can be mended, but must ever
Be the same crushed egg forever—
So shall this dark heart of mine!
Which, though broken, is still breaking,
And shall never more cease aching
For the sleep which has not waking—
For the sleep which now is thine!

—*Thomas Holley Chivers*

J. Gordon Coogler is as bad a poet, and as irresistible:

ALAS! FOR THE SOUTH!

Alas! for the South, her books have grown fewer—
She never was much given to literature.

—*J. Gordon Coogler*

ALAS! CAROLINA!

Alas! Carolina! Carolina! Fair land of my birth,
Thy fame will be wafted from the mountain to the sea
As being the greatest educational centre on earth,
As the cost of men's blood thro' thy "one X" whiskey.

Two very large elephants* thou hast lately installed,
Where thy sons and thy daughters are invited to come,
And learn to be physically and mentally strong,
By the solemn proceeds of thy "innocent" rum.

—*J. Gordon Coogler*

*Elephant was slang of the day for a university.

Julia Moore, "the sweet singer of Michigan," turned out mountains of claptrap, and I understand had an admiring audience. This excerpt should be enough to spoil your day:

LITTLE LIBBIE

While eating dinner, this dear little child
    Was choked on a piece of beef.
Doctors came, tried their skill awhile,
    But none could give relief.

She was ten years of age, I am told,
    And in school stood very high.
Her little form now the earth enfolds,
    In her embrace it must ever lie.

Her friends and schoolmates will not forget
    Little Libbie that is no more;
She is waiting on the shining step,
    To welcome home friends once more.
                    —Julia Moore

20 FEBRUARY
♓

Clerihews

1. CLERIHEWS ON ENGLISH HISTORY

One of Henry's peeves
Was that Anne of Cleves
Was cold
To hold.
        —J. C. Walker

Good Queen Bess
Said English sanitation was a mess.
Sir John Harrington cried: "I agree!"
And invented the W.C.
        —Allen M. Laing

The venerable Bede
Could read.
It's a pity he couldn't spel
As wel.
        —Lakon

When Charles II
Beckoned
Nell
   Fell.
   —Ruth Silcock

Edward the Confessor
Was not in any way an Aggressor;
Some who were afterwards King
Were much more that sort of thing.
   —Silvia Tatham

2. CLERIHEWS BY THE SCORE

Poor old Wagner
Was not a good bargainer.
He once sold an opera four hours long
For a song.

     —R.L.O.

Mozart
Could never resist a tart.
In the ordinary way
He ate seven or eight a day.
   —Stanley J. Sharpless

21 FEBRUARY
)(

For Planets Forsaken

For planets forsaken;
   For galaxies lorn;
For youth from me taken—
   Forever I mourn.

For sin unforgiven;
   For passion forbörne;
For youth from me riven—
   Forever I mourn.

For life without leaven;
   For duty forsworn;
For forfeiting heaven—
   Forever I mourn.
     —W.R.E.

22 FEBRUARY
♓

Presidential Rectangle

OYSTERVILLE—Here we are at midnight, after a five-hour flight from New York and a four-hour drive from Seattle. Louise says sitting in a Boeing 747 and staring at white clouds is not her idea of the way to celebrate her birthday. I tell her to stop complaining; George Washington spent his forty-fifth birthday at Valley Forge.

He also started the American presidency, surely the most closely linked club in the world:

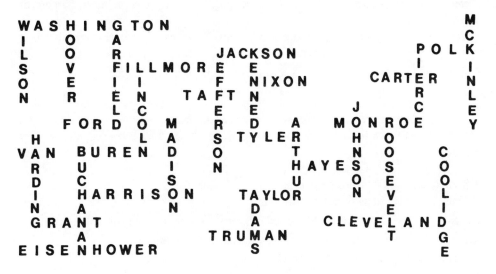

—*Sam Harlan*

23 FEBRUARY
♓

Who Says I Transpire?

By the nature of things, the dictionary lags behind current usage—sometimes, in fact, hundreds of years behind.

Take the word *transpire*. Derived from the Latin for "breathe through," it first meant "to give off through the skin" (the body *transpires* sweat); "to exhale" (the flower *tranpires* fragrance); "to breathe forth" (the dragon *transpires* fire). In a 1647 hymn Crashaw exulted:

> With wider pores . . .
> More freely to transpire
> That impatient fire.

It was natural for a word meaning "to breathe forth" to develop the more abstract sense of "to leak out," "to become known." "Yesterday's quarrel must not transpire" sounds odd today, but it was correct in 1641 and is technically correct now. Thomas Jefferson wrote, "What happened between them did not transpire," a seeming contradiction in terms, but as right as rain. Said a letter of Lord Chesterfield's: "This goes to you in confidence; you will not let one word transpire."

By 1802 the word had added a third meaning: "to occur, take place," as in "He did not know what had transpired during his absence." Noah Webster accepted "take place" as a correct definition of *transpire* in 1828. Yet more than 150 years later, the *Oxford English Dictionary* still calls this third—and most common—meaning a misusage; *Webster's Second* says it is "disapproved by most authorities"; and the *American Heritage Dictionary* lists it as "disputed . . . not acceptable to 62 percent of the Usage Panel."

You are speaking correct, if redundant, English if you say, "It transpired that it transpired that the horse transpired"—"It became evident that the fact was the horse was sweating."

*　*　*

In 1935, when my edition of *Roget's Thesaurus* appeared, many of today's common expressions had not been heard of—among them these, duly recorded in the 1977 edition:

The category	*The word or phrase*
Business	Bottom line; bottom out.
Drugs	Down, downer, turned off, turned on, spaced out, stoned, zonked.
Entertainment	Sitcom, soap, spaghetti western, groupie, dingbat.
Environment	Biodegradable, recycle.
Food	Junk food, fast food, macrobiotics, stir-fry.
General slang	Bananas, bazoom, bonkers, boss, crunch, honcho, the pits, shades.
Politics	Bite the bullet, clout, deep-six, eyeball-to-eyeball, jawbone, stroke.
Space	Go.
Transportation	Jet lag, skyjacking.

24 FEBRUARY
)(

A Smidgin of Pidgin

In the old treaty ports of China, "pidgin" was a corruption of "business," and "pidgin English" was "business English," used by traders. "Look-see pidgin" is hypocrisy; "joss pidgin" is *religion*; "love-pidgin" is *making love*. Fool is *foolo*, devil *debilo*, gold *golo*, wife *waifo*, child *chilo*, all *allo*, always *alloway*, squeeze *squeezey*, think *tinkee*, suppose *supposey*, belong *blongey*. *Maskee* stands for "without, no matter, also, anyhow, but, in spite of." *Galow*, even more common, has no meaning I can grasp. *R's are l's*.

Excerpts from a verse in pidgin:

ONE PIECEE CAT

One time lib China-side one piecee cat,
One day he massa take Joss-pidgin beads
He put bead lound cat neck.
Wat-time he mousey walk outside he hole,
Look-see dat pidgin—see dat cat hab catch
One piecee bead, he mousey too much glad.
(Here the mice celebrate the presumed conversion of the cat to vegetarianism:)
 . . . "One time he *velly* bad—but now he 'pent
An' nevva chow-chow mousey any more,
An' allo mousey lib all plopa now;
He go outside what-tim he wantchee go,
An' nevva blongey flaid—he cat no fear.
An' mousey go to sing-song allo tim,
An' takee waifo, chilos walk outside,
An' allo day for allo mousey now,
He be one Feast ob Lantern, *hai! ch'hoy!*
T'at mousey tink t'at pidgin velly nice,
He catchee too much happy inside,
He makee dancee, galantee, maskee."
(The cat creeps man-man—slowly—toward the unsuspecting mice:)
He cat look-see t'at dance, he walk man-man,
No makee bobely till wat'tim he come
Long-side he dancee—t'en he lun chop-chop
Insidee dance and catch one piecee mouse,
An' makee chow-chow all same olo time.
                                    —*Charles Godfrey Leland*

25 FEBRUARY
✕

Upper Plate, Lower Plate, and Bite

Bennett Cerf called my three eldest daughters Upper Plate, Lower Plate, and Bite because in their preteens they wore braces, reflecting a dental preoccupation that our family has handed down for a hundred years. In 1889 Great-aunt Mat wrote in a Denver newspaper:

Will another century of experience teach dentists how to pull out a whole set of teeth without administering chloroform, yet so painlessly that one would sooner have them out than not? Will the false sets made in the distant future retain the vermilion hue which now characterizes the gums, giving one away the moment he smiles? Or will they be such an improvement on Nature's supply that men and women will rush to the dentist at the first jumping tooth, have out the whole miserable lot, and put "store teeth" in their place?

The idea that teeth might be repaired rather than pulled—perhaps even immunized against caries—never entered her head.

Grandpa's third wife, Aunt Kate, considered herself blessed that at eighty she had one tooth remaining.

"I can scrape an apple with it," she would say proudly.

At ninety-two, Uncle Will suffered his first extraction. Shortly afterward he told a visitor, "Yes, I have been fortunate; I still have every tooth in my head." When the visitor had gone, his daughter Alice reproached him: "But Father, you know perfectly well you had a tooth pulled last year."

"It is right here in my wallet," said Uncle Will, patting his hip complacently.

And it was.

26 FEBRUARY
Ж

To My Greek Mistress

All you need to read off this verse as if it were English is a vague recollection of the Greek alphabet.

> With many a Ψ I ate a Π
>   That you had baked, my dear;
> This torpor N I you—
>   I'm feeling very queer.
> Ο Φ Ο Φ upon your Π!—
>   You Δ cruel blow!
> Your dreadful Π has made me X;
>   My tears fall in a P.
> I would have Λnother lass
>   Who baked that Π, I vow;
> But still I M and M for you,
>   As sick as any cow.

> —W.R.E.

27 FEBRUARY
)(

Who's Me?

Who's Who has a new gimmick, irresistible to egomaniacs: The chosen people are asked to provide summaries of their views on life. I sent this, but it did not appear:

Who's me?	Who's he?
Who's you?	Who's who?
	—W.R.E.

Nor did my suggested postscript to the biographical sketch of a friend, the late language stylist Theodore Bernstein:

Ted Bernstein, damner	Takes up considerable room
Of bad grammar,	In Whom's Whom.
	—W.R.E.

28 FEBRUARY
)(

Crazy Like a Fox

If these comments don't lie, the way men describe animals tells more about the men than about the animals:

Animals seen as sport become to the mind meat, and cease to be individual creatures, so that you may feed fishes, but catch fish, ride elephants, but hunt elephant, fatten turkeys and pigs, but chase turkey and pig, throw bread to ducks, but shoot duck; and some creatures, whom God would seem to have created merely for the chase, such as grouse and snipe, require no plural forms at all.

—Rose Macaulay

IN DEFENSE OF BEASTLINESS

It is an old habit of man's to draw his most contemptuous expressions from animals and their ways. Nothing seems to signify stupidity more fully than such terms as ape, baboon, gorilla, ox, goose, cow, birdbrained, or bullheaded. Do you want to put someone down as craven or contemptible? Then call him chicken or sheeplike, a rat, a snake, a louse, or, most crushing, a worm. Just as great a variety of animals convey cruelty and ruthlessness: hawk, vulture, jackal, hyena, wolf, shark. Among the most worn clichés in the vocabulary of insult are filthy as a pig, vain as a peacock, stubborn as a mule, puffed up as a toad, changeable as a chameleon, blind as a bat, lecherous as a goat, crazy as a loon. An acid-tongued woman is catty and a nasty one is a bitch. Anyone we don't trust is a skunk. To harass someone is to hound or badger him. To be mad is to be batty or cuckoo. Anything we don't believe is fishy.

The idea that man himself has outgrown his primitive and savage animal characteristics got its greatest boost a century ago from the Victorians. They interpreted Darwin's theory of man's evolution from the apes as an ascent. Today we aren't so sure. Most studies of animal behavior in the recent past have revealed more and more estimable characteristics in a great variety of animals: the docility and affection of creatures once thought to be intractable, such as wolves and wolverines; the solicitude of mothers for their young, including not only such familiar examples as birds, kangaroos, and bears, but sea otters and the fish that takes its young into its mouth when danger threatens. Scientists have uncovered astonishing facts about the learning ability and personalities of, among others, dolphins and seals; the marvelous faculties that guide migrating birds and spawning salmon; the wonderfully complex social structure of termites, bees, and ants.

Is it too much to expect that we should acquire a little humility?

—*Milton Rugoff*

29 FEBRUARY
♓

Cut It Short

February, the shortest month, is a good time to discuss brevity. If you are not reading during a leap year, skip this entry.

Keep it short and simple, use the active voice—such adjurations, staples of present-day journalism classes, pervade this two-hundred-year-old poem:

EN DEUX MOTS

Il faut dire en deux mots
  Ce qu'on veut dire;
  Les longs propos
    Sont sots.

Il ne faut pas toujours conter,
  Citer,
  Dater,
Mais écouter.

Il faut éviter l'emploi
  Du moi, du moi,
  Voici pourquoi:

Il est tyrannique,
Trop académique;
  L'ennui, l'ennui
  Marche avec lui.

Je me conduis toujours ainsi
    Ici,
    Aussi,
J'ai réussi.

Il faut dire en deux mots
    Ce qu'on veut dire:
    Les longs propos
    Sont sots.
—*Marie-Françoise Catherine de Beauveau,*
Marquise de Boufflers

En deux mots—"in two words." If two, why not one?

IN A WORD

By a single word
Be heard.
Two, and it
Is shit.

To tell
Heaven from Hell,
First, listen well.

Drop the cry
Of *I*;
Here's why:

When *I* comes on,
Folks yawn;
What's more,
They snore.
I get by
By dropping *I*.

By a single word
Be heard.
Two, and it
Is shit.
            —*W.R.E.*

Dr. John Sampson, librarian at the University of Liverpool, found that he could boil down famous poems by successive excisions, with very little alteration of sense and without metrical difficulty. He first shortened the initial stanza of Thomas Gray's *Elegy in a Country Churchyard* as follows:

The curfew tolls the knell of day,
    The lowing herd winds o'er the lea,
The plowman homeward plods his way
    And leaves the world to dark and me.

He then cut deeper:

The curfew tolls the knell of day,
    The herd winds o'er the lea,
The plowman homeward plods his way
    And leaves the world to me.

And finally:

Dusk tolls,
    Herds flee,
Hinds scoot:
    Not me.

MARCH

1 MARCH

♓

Love, Ever Faithful

—Ed Fisher

2 MARCH

♓

Due Respect and Sunglasses

[Members of teen-age gangs] are respectful of their parents and particularly of their mothers—known as "moo" in their jargon.

—New York Times Magazine

> Come moo, dear moo, let's you and me
> Sit down awhile and talk togee;
> My broo's at school, and faa's away
> A-gaaing rosebuds while he may.
>
> Of whence we come and whii we go
> Most moos nee know nor care to know,
> But you are not like any oo:
> You're always getting in a poo

Or working up a dreadful laa
Over nothing—nothing. Bah!
Relax. You love me. I love you.
And that's the way it shapes up, moo.
                —*John Updike*

SUNGLASSES

On an olive beach, beneath a turquoise sky
And a limeade sun, by a lurid sea,
While the beryl clouds went blithely by,
We ensconced ourselves, my love and me.

O her verdant hair! and her aqua smile!
O my soul, afloat in an emerald bliss
That retained its tint all the watery while—
And her copper skin, all verdigris!
                —*John Updike*

3 MARCH
♓

Sparrows Cheep

Today I met an eighty-four-year-old woman who appeared as fragile and permanent as a dried leaf. She told me about a village on the line between Hungary and Rumania, inhabited—perhaps "infested" is the word—by two families of sparrows. The sparrows on the Rumanian side never cross into Hungary, and the sparrows on the Hungarian side never cross into Rumania. This is the extreme of nationalism; how do you suppose the immigration officers can be sure which sparrows are citizens of Rumania, and which of Hungary?

Some naturalists say the story is apocryphal, since over the centuries the border between the two countries has shifted repeatedly, and sometimes there was no border at all. But I have good reason to believe my informant. John Cassin, several times great-uncle to my children, had a breed of sparrow named after him. Reginald Denham, the play director and birder, assures me that a road in Texas separates Cassin sparrows from a subspecies identical in appearance and that neither breed ever crosses into the territory of the other.

How can Mr. Denham be so certain?

By the cheeps.

*   *   *

The three species of owl that the English call the common scops, long-eared owl, and eagle owl are in French *le petit-duc, moyen-duc,* et *grand-duc.*

4 MARCH
♓

Pig Latin, Columbus and a Polka

Pig Latin, a juvenile version of macaronics, may add Latin suffixes to English words:

PIG LATIN LOVE LYRIC

Lightibus outibus in a parlorum,
Boyibus kissibus sweeti girlorum;
Daddibus hearibus loudi smackorum,
Comibus quickibus with a cluborum.
Boyibus gettibus hardi spankorum,
Landibus nextibus outside a doorum;
Gettibus uppibus with a limporum,
Swearibus kissibus girli nomorum.
                    —Anonymous

This is a true macaronic:

COLUMBUS SAILED THE OCEAN BLUE

Columbus sailed the ocean blue
Nelle mille quattro cento novanta e due
But when he got there he had to stay
Fion al mille quattra cento novante e tre.
                    —Anonymous

A POLKA LYRIC

This macaronic translates itself:

Qui nunc dancere vult modo
Wants to dance in the fashion, oh!
Discere debet—ought to know,
Kickere floor cum heel and toe,
        One, two, three,
        Hop with me,
Whirligig, twirligig, rapide.

Polkam jungere, Virgo, vis,
Will you join the polka, miss?
Liberius—most willingly,
Sic agimus—then let us try:
        Nunc vide,
        Skip with me,
Whirlabout, roundabout, celere.

Tum laevo cito, tum dextra,
First to the left, and then t'other way;
Aspice retro in vultu,

You look at her, and she looks at you.
Das palmam
Change hands, ma'am;
Celere—run away, just in sham.
                    —*Barclay Philips*

5 MARCH
)(

The Social Contract

The Social Contract, postulated by Hobbes and Locke, is an implied agreement between the members of society to refrain from certain antisocial actions—say, kicking dogs—and to carry out certain social obligations—say, kicking cats. I once met at a cocktail party a professor who argued furiously that there is no such thing as a social contract; everyone is entitled to anything he can get away with—a disturbing notion. Later this man brought out a fad book on the subject which burgeoned green on bookshelves for a few months and then crumbled into gray powder.

I have been considering the Social Contract off and on since then. I now deliver my conclusion:

Last evening, Rosalie returned my kiss.
The Social Contract's built of bricks like this.
                    —*W.R.E.*

6 MARCH
)(

Words in Color

OYSTERVILLE—Buddy Basch, proprietor, stockholder, and sole employee of Creative Communications Unlimited, telephoned from New York this morning to ask if I knew the origin of the expression *green with envy*. I did not. Shrugging off toll charges, Mr. Basch went on to list other figures of speech similarly involving color. I have incorporated some of them here.

A DIRGE OF BLACK, A DIRGE OF BLUE

O berry-brown and green as grass
    Was in the days of yore I;
When once I met a rosy lass,
    Rose-colored glasses wore I.

But lily-livered was I too,
   And yellow to the core I.
   (Repeat.)

I had no silver tongue to woo,
   No golden throne to bid-O,
Yet begged, "I'd call it white of you
   If you would kiss me, kiddo."
A blush of scarlet fired her face;
   She answered, "Lord forbid-O!"
   (Repeat.)

I stood there ashen with disgrace,
   Then purpled, and saw red-O;
In black despair I left that place,
   And gray days loomed ahead-O.
No more in pink of health I clown—
   I spent two weeks in bed-O.
   (Repeat.)

In blue funk and in study brown,
In green-eyed jealousy I frown;
My rosy lass has let me down.
(Repeat.)

              —W.R.E.

RED HOT

Deduce from each of the clues below a word or phrase that contains the word *red*. For instance, "Old Glory" would be *Red, White, and Blue*. "Owing money" would be *in the red*.

1. Bureaucratic routines   _____
2. Relief organization   _____
3. False clue   _____
4. "The Galloping Ghost"   _____
5. Delicacy for a wolf?   _____
6. First professional baseball team   _____
7. Biblical waters   _____
8. *Poe* tale   _____
9. Voice of the Brooklyn Dodgers   _____
10. Sherlock Holmes case   _____
11. Tallest conifer   _____
12. Be angry   _____
13. Feminist singer   _____
14. Women's magazine   _____
15. Warning for sailors   _____

16. Ballet movie   ————————————————
17. Russian "tourist trap"   ————————————————
18. Vigorous   ————————————————
19. Porter   ————————————————
20. Christmas song   ————————————————

—Gene Traub

7 MARCH
♓

Inflation

Our forebears too worried about inflation. This commentary was written before 1905:

AVOIRDUPOIS

The length of this line indicates the ton of coal as dug by the miner.
This one indicates the ton shipped to the dealer.
The small dealer gets a ton like this.
This is the one you pay for.
This is what you get.
The residue is:
Cinders and
Ashes.
And this line will give you some conception of the size of the bill.

—Anonymous

*   *   *

A ninety-seven-year-old bulldozer operator in Kilmoganny, Ireland, traced the inflation spiral this way:

The price of admission to the coronation of Henry I was one crocard.
But Henry II's went up to a pollard. At any of King John's frequent coronations, it soared to a suskin, and by Henry III's time it cost a dodkin.

A crocard was a coin of base metal, circulating at two to the penny in England during the thirteenth century.

A pollard was a "clipped coin"; I do not know what that means.

A suskin, or seskin, was a small coin current in the fifteenth century, passing for a penny.

A dodkin, or doit, was a minor Dutch coin, equal to one-eighth of a stiver or about one-half of a farthing; hence, a whit; a bit. A bit is the equivalent of a real, or one-eighth of a Spanish peso, once worth 12½ cents. It is usually referred to in multiples, as two, or four, bits.

A CROQUARD, A DOLLARD, A SUSKIN, A DODKIN

In days of Harry One, long lost,
A croquard would pay for a look at a king.
A glimpse of Harry Two, though, cost
A dollard—a far more extravagant thing.

John One robbed realm of bread and buskin;
A peek at the monarch went up to a suskin.
When Harry Three came on, odds bodkins!—
The croquard and dollard had doubled to dodkins!

I hear from a respected scholar
A President once could be seen for a dollar.

—W.R.E.

8 MARCH
)(

An Explosion of Drummers

Two *San Francisco Chronicle* columns by Ralph J. Gleason list multitudinous nouns—also called venereal nouns and collectives—that might be used in the world of entertainment. (*Venereal,* from "Venus," is commonly limited today to sexual matters but relates also to hunting, the goddess being patroness of both; indeed, there are analogies between them. Young noblemen in the Middle Ages had to memorize such venereal terms as *a pride of lions, a gaggle of geese,* and *a trip of dottrel.*)

To start the game, Mr. Gleason offered *an explosion of drummers, a honk of tenors, a hipness of fans, an ego of soloists, a stride of pianos, a slush of trombones,* and the like. My favorite was *a pox of critics.*

In the next column it was the reader's turn. Charles F. Dery suggested a *clique of castanets.* Other inspirations, not all connected with the business of entertainment, were *a fuzz of policemen, a titter of thrushes, a quest of stags, a palm of hatcheck girls, a trance of jazz fans, a pomade of washroom attendants, a stack of chorus girls,* and *a drag of squares.*

Ethel Lanselt wrote:

"Dear Sir: As one who doesn't like jazz—doesn't understand it—I say don't forget an *exasperation of listeners.*"

Other collectives:

> • A corruption of courts • An indignation of litigants • An arrogance of attorneys • A corpulence of bailiffs • A petulance of judges • A somnolence of jurors.

—Jack Bailey

• A parley of diplomats.

—Ronald F. Kennedy

• A swarm of people is called a crowd. A crowd of clouds is called an over-cast. An overcast of a Broadway play is caused by too many under-studies.
• A convention of surgeons is called a flotilla of cutters.

—Gerald Pocock

• A clutch of straws • A fleet of foot • A litter of picnickers • A peel of strippers • A cast of fishermen • A crew of interest • A brood of tea • A s'warm of summer greetings • A s'cool of winter greetings.

—Alan F. G. Lewis

• A pall of mourners.
• A strike of workers.
• A chowder of clams.
• A conversion of sinners.

—Roy Wilder, Jr.

From *Reader's Digest*:
• A brace of orthodontists.

—Don Tewksbury

• A quibbling of siblings.

—Ann Menconi

• A scoop of reporters.

—Christine Heffner

9 MARCH
♓

What Acts! They Ap-Paul!

Half of the entries in a book I wrote recently on word origins have vanished from my mind. With a memory that bad, how can I be expected to learn from experience? How, on my deathbed, can I repent a life ill-spent?

By the time I have fixed the name of a fellow club member in my mind—say it takes about twenty-five years—he dies. The result is that some of my best friends avoid telling me who they are.

Mnemonics is a system that seeks to counteract such faulty memory through word associations. Thus:

For avoiding hangover:
    Beer on whiskey very risky.
    Whiskey on beer never fear.

For remembering the excretory organs:
SKILL is an anagram of *S*kin, *K*idneys, *I*ntestines, *L*iver, *L*ungs.

For the rule of division of fractions:
The number you are dividing by
Turn upside down and multiply.

(But if I turn 75 upside down it becomes SL . How can I multiply by *that?*)

For the successive fates of the wives of Henry VIII (Catherine of Aragon, Anne Boleyn, Jane Seymour, Anne of Cleves, Catherine Howard, Catherine Parr)
Divorced, beheaded, died;
Divorced, beheaded, survived.

For the Great Lakes, west to east:
*S*ergeant-*M*ajor *h*ates *e*ating *o*nions (Superior, Michigan, Huron, Erie, Ontario)

For the Seven Hills of Rome:
*C*an *Q*ueen *V*ictoria *e*at *c*old *a*pple *p*ie? (Capitoline, Quirinal, Viminal, Esquiline, Caelian, Aventine, Palatine)

For the planets in their order from the sun:
*M*en *v*ery *e*asily *m*ake *j*ugs *s*erve *u*seful *n*octurnal *p*urposes. (Mercury, Venus, Earth, Mars, Jupiter, Saturn, Uranus, Neptune, Pluto)

A mnemonic on the British royal line:

> Willie, Willie, Harry, Stee
> Harry, Dick, Harry Three
> One, Two, Three Neds, Richard Two
> Harry Four, Five, Six. Then who?
> Edward Four, Five, Dick the Bad,
> Harrys twain and Ned the Lad,
> Mary, Bessie, James the Vain,
> Charlie, Charlie, James again,
> William and Mary, Anna Gloria,
> Four Georges, William, and Victoria.
> Edward the Seventh next, and then
> George the Fifth in 1910.
> Edward the Eighth soon abdicated,
> And so a George was reinstated.
>   (I add:)
> Then Bessie Two was coronated.

I started to write a mnemonic passage that would fix in mind the order of the books of the New Testament:

O Matthew—Mark Luke in the John! What Acts; They Ap-Paul!

But the next book was Romans, and since I could not imagine a devout Christian sharing his bathroom with a Roman heathen, I gave up.

10 MARCH
♓

The Irish Pig and Other Reflections on Alcohol

'Twas an evening in November,
And I very well remember
I was walking down the street in drunken pride.
But my knees were all aflutter,
So I landed in the gutter,
And a pig came up and lay down by my side.

Yes, I lay there in the gutter,
Thinking thoughts I could not utter,
When a colleen passing by did softly say,
"Ye can tell a man that boozes
By the company he chooses."—
At that the pig got up and walked away.
                                            —*Anonymous*

I have quoted Henry Aldrich's "If all be true that I do think/ There are five reasons we should drink;/ Good wine—a friend—or being dry—/ Or lest we should be by and by—/ Or any other reason why."

Now comes Henry G. Fischer—curator in Egyptology at New York's Metropolitan Museum of Art—with what appears to be the Latin original of this verse, given him in Brussels by Professor Baudouin van de Walle:

Si bene commemini, sunt causae quinque bibendi:
Vini bonitas, hospitis adventus, sitis praesens
                    atque futura
Et quelibet altera causa.

Some scholars believe Aldrich himself wrote the Latin and then translated it into English. But in *L'ape latina* (Milan, 1936), Giuseppe Fumagelli attributed the Latin verse to P. Sirmond.

This led Mr. Fischer to send Professor van de Walle his own variant, as follows:

If all be true as one divines,
There are five authors for those lines:
Aldrich, Sirmond, you, and I,
And any other, by and by.

The Compleat American Housewife, supposedly written by Julianne Belote in 1776, claims that in that year one Betsy Flanagin, a barmaid at the Halls Corner inn in Elmsford, New York, "had the fanciful notion of adding a brightly colored cock tail feather, as a sort of stirrer, to each drink," thus inventing the cocktail. This story bobs up from time to time but is generally discredited.

Linguist J. L. Dillard theorizes that *cocktail* is from the Krio word *kaketel,* "scorpion . . . a creature with a sting in its tail."

Drunk or sober, nobody knows.

11 MARCH
♓

Cliché Interruptus

Orwell said never to use a metaphor that you recognize from the public prints. A poet here applies a comparable principle to such Inevitable Rhymes as tomorrow and sorrow, planet and granite, tomb and womb:

UNCOUPLETS

All's wrong—I don't want today ending tomorrow;
I want joy following
                               joy.

O uninhabitable planet,
Hard as
                     quicksand,

Stop it—earth-mom—stop "tomb"
From gloat-rhyming with
                                     lips.

But then, you were always a trap-choice: between duty
And
           ugly.

Even on the day love and I went tramping together
Through the Scotch
                                highballs,

I remember, I remember
Love's leaf fell in
                          July.

I desire, I desire
To live forever; in the end I flame like
                                                  ash.

Beaming ogre of our nursery,
Our trust in you has set us
                                     slave.

From graves, green rouge diverts your prey;
We're gift-wrapped in the end for Mother's
                                                        Diet.

Now when your sky-queen eyes of blue
Swear to be
                     false,

At least I'll go down without blah or blink: my dove
Coos
         hate.

                                        —*Peter Viereck*

In the following verse, says Mr. Viereck, he seeks to "violate a sacred schoolma'am rule of grammar in every line, sans losing a certain lyric pathos":

TO HELEN (OF TROY, NEW YORK)

I sit here with the wind is in my hair;
I huddle like the sun is in my eyes;
I am (I wished you'd contact me) alone.

A fat lot you'd wear crape if I was dead.
It figures, who I heard there when I phoned you;
It figures, when I came there, who has went.

Dogs laugh at me, folks bark at me since then;
"She is," they say, "no better than she ought to";
I love you irregardless how they talk.

You should of done it (which it is no crime)
With me you should of done it, what they say.
I sit here with the wind is in my hair.
                                        —*Peter Viereck*

Mr. Viereck's tilt of the lance against clichés reminds me that there are clichés of perception, too. A friend of Phil Silvers, for instance, who perceived the comedian as the Man Who Has Everything and could think of no gift special enough for him, considered the problem solved when Silvers arrived for a weekend visit driving, appropriately, a Rolls-Royce Silver Cloud.

"You won't need that bus this weekend," said the host. "Let me take it in for a check-up." Silvers not objecting, his friend arranged for the surreptitious overnight installation of a built-in bar, a high-fidelity cassette player, a color television set, and a device for preserving programs visually on tape. The Rolls was delivered just before Silvers was to leave Monday morning, and his friend remarked casually, "You'd better check before you start out, Phil, just to be sure everything is in shape."

"Oh, that doesn't matter," said Silvers. "It's a rented car."

12 MARCH
☓

Pumcodoxpursacomlopar

Pumcodoxpursacomlopar stands for pulse-modulated coherent Doppler-effect X-band pulse-repetition synthetic-array pulse compression lobe planar array. It is an acronym—a word built of initials or abbreviations—and it means something or other having to do with physics and airplanes.

President Carter announced a massive energy-saving program called the Moral Equivalent of War. Since little came of it, the program came to be known by its acronym—MEOW. Some people consider it significant that the acronym for the Organization of Oil Producing States is—OOPS.

Fatah, which reverses the initials of the Arabic name of the Movement for the Liberation of Palestine, is a double-edged acronym, and an ominous one. *Fatah* means "victory"; *hataf* means "death."

Equally ominous for those who distrust nuclear power are *rads* (radiation-absorbed doses) and *rems* (roentgen equivalents, man), measurements of radioactive emissions.

If you fear tobacco more than nuclear fallout, you may belong to one of the concerned organizations with such acronymic names as *Ash, Gasp, Puff,* and *Cigar*.

The *Fiat* automobile is manufactured in Torino, Italy. The name is an acronym of *Fabricato Italia Automobilia Torino*.

Dr. David B. Pearce asserts that *stomach* is an acronym and cites as supporting evidence this spoof from *The Lancet*:

> Septimus Thaddeus O'Mach's great treatise on gastrointestinal anatomy led to the general use of the term "the gastric organ of Septimus Thaddeus O'Mach." However, O'Mach's contemporaries got fed up with such a mouthful, and it was digested down to "the organ of S. T. O'Mach," and finally just "Stomach."

*   *   *

Bob Knibbe says the proposed names of these three government agencies were changed for fear of undesirable acronyms:

Department of Urban Development

Federal Information Bank

Forward Error-Control Electronics System

Do you know what a Poossl-Q is?

It is the acronym used in the 1980 census for a *Person Of Opposite Sex, Same Living Quarters*. A Posssl-Q, now out of the closet, is a *Person Of Same Sex, Same Living Quarters*. But the Census Bureau doesn't list that.

13 MARCH
Ж

My Name Is Ozymandias

This takeoff on Shelley's sonnet appeared, without attribution, in my files. I hope the author will speak up, so that I can thank him—or her and find out what the devil the title in heiroglyphics means. The other two lines are translated in answers and solutions.

I met a traveller from an antique land
Who wore upon his brow a cotton band
Which ill concealed the nasty bump that swelled
When by an ancient curse he there was felled;
For, roaming through the desert, blind with heat,
He stumbled on a pair of crumbling feet.
And on the pedestal these words he read
As, wonderingly, he rubbed his battered head:

Nothing beside remains; between the toes
Of that colossal hoax the nettle grows.
And when I'm nettled by the frauds I meet,
I think upon the mystery of those feet.
                              —*Author unknown*

14 MARCH

Bricklayer's Lament

Octave Romaine handed me this letter from a luckless bricklayer in Barbados to his employer:

> ... When I got to the building, I found that the hurricane had knocked some bricks off the top. So I rigged up a beam with a pulley at the top of the building and hoisted up a couple of barrels of bricks. When I fixed the building, there was a lot of bricks left over. I hoisted the barrel back up again and secured the line at the bottom, and then went up and filled the barrel with the extra bricks. Then I went down to the bottom and cast off the line.
>
> Unfortunately, the barrel of bricks was heavier than I was and before I knew what had happened the barrel started down, jerking me off the ground. I decided to hang on and halfway up I met the barrel coming down and received a severe blow on my shoulder. I then continued on to the top, banging my head against the beam and getting my fingers jammed in the pulley. When the barrel hit the ground it bursted its bottom, allowing the bricks to spill out. I was now heavier than the barrel and so I started down again at high speed.

Halfway down I met the barrel coming up and received severe injuries to shins. When I hit the ground I landed on the bricks, getting several cuts from the sharp edges. At this point I must have lost my presence of mind because I let go of the line. The barrel then came down giving me another heavy blow on the head and putting me in the hospital. I respectfully request sick leave.

15 MARCH
♓

The Frog He Would a-Wooing Go

The wood frog pleads for reciprocal affection in a creaky clatter; the peeper, with a jingling of sleighbells; the toad, with a trill or bleat, depending on the species; the green frog, with the sound of a plucked banjo; the bullfrog, with "jug-o'rum."

—Newspaper story

> Now doth the serenading frog
>   The pond and valley vex,
> And also tree, lake, marsh, and bog,
>   Panegyrizing sex!
>
> That creaky clatter on your right
>   Is Wood Frog at his wooing;
> That sound of sleighbells in the night
>   Is Peeper, up and doing.
>
> Toads trill (save Fowler's toads, which bleat).
>   A *ping,* like banjo plucking,
> Denotes a Green Frog is in heat,
>   And signaling for fucking.
>
> The bloated bullfrog calls his mate
>   By booming on his drum;
> But gladly settles, if she's late,
>   For jug o'rum, o'rum.

—W.R.E.

A THREE-TOED TREE TOAD'S ODE

The following verses, according to Stephens G. Croom, appeared in the *Mobile Register* (Alabama), August 12, 1892:

> A tree toad loved a she toad
>   That lived high in a tree.
> She was a two-toed tree toad
>   But a three-toed toad was he.

The three-toed tree toad tried to win
   The she toad's nuptial nod;
For the three-toed tree toad loved the road
   The two-toed tree toad trod.

Hard as the three-toed tree toad tried,
   He could not reach her limb.
From her tree toad bower, with her V-toe power
   The she toad vetoed him.
                  —*Anonymous*

16 MARCH
)(

Presidents in Prime Rhyme

This is the birthday of President James Madison, born March 16, 1751. President
Madison shares with several thousand other people, alive and dead, the distinction
of being my second cousin four times removed. Two other presidents similarly
distinguished are James Monroe and Andrew Jackson. When I was too young to
know better I spent an inordinate amount of time calculating my relationship to
various presidents (anyone whose people came over before the middle of the eigh-
teenth century can find a few in his line), but these three were the closest kin I
could find. Second cousins four times removed, even presidents, count for little on
a credit application at the bank; but at least a man can write verses about them.

JAMES MADISON

James Madison was puny;
   James Madison was small.
He built a Constitution
   Ten Constellations tall.

We wake the better mornings,
   We sleep the better nights,
For Jimmy's Constitution,
   And Jimmy's Bill of Rights.

JAMES MONROE

When the most allowed to lovers
Was to snuggle through the covers,
James Monroe arranged a deal
Called the Era of Good Feel.
Slap and tickle, touch and go!
Hail the Doctrine of Monroe!

ANDREW JACKSON

Andy Jackson started school,
  Ding, dang, and tallyho;
First durned day he fought a duel,
  Ding, dang, and tallyho.

Andy warn't so good at writing,
  Ding, dang, and tallyho;
But he got straight A's at fighting,
  Ding, dang, and tallyho.

Licked the British in his teens,
  Ding, dang, and tallyho;
Won the Battle of New Orleans,
  Ding, dang, and tallyho.

Got his presidential innings,
  Ding, dang, and tallyho;
Said, "The victor takes the winnings,"
  Ding, dang, and tallyho.

Whopped the banks and whopped the Court,
  Ding, dang, and tallyho.
Don't sell Andy Jackson short,
  Ding, dang, and tallyho.
                              —*W.R.E.*

17 MARCH
){

A Bellowing of Irish Bulls

An Irish bull is a saying that contradicts itself in a manner palpably absurd to listeners but unperceived by the speaker. Charles McCabe, writing in the *San Francisco Chronicle,* cites as a master of the genre one Jim McSheehy, who served on a San Francisco civic board. Mr. McSheehy once interrupted a debate on buying a gondola to dress up Stow Lake in Golden Gate Park.

"Why not buy two gondolas," he proposed, "and let nature take its course?"

Irish bulls are kissing kin to malapropisms:

• Now we've got to flush out the skeleton.
• He deals out of both ends of his mouth.
• Let's do it and listen to how the shoe pinches.
• The project is going to pot in a handbasket.
• Don't rock the trough.

- Professor Mahaffy, provost of Dublin University, on the difference between an Irish bull and another bull: "An Irish bull is always pregnant."

- The accused, in a Dublin court: "Your hanner, I was sober enough to know I was dhroonk."

- Beggarwoman: "Help me, kind sir! I'm the mother of five children and a sick husband!" And on receiving a donation: "May you never live to see your wife a widow!"

- He lay at death's door, and the doctor pulled him through.

- We find the man who stole the horse not guilty.

- Half the lies people tell about me aren't true.

- Such is the corruption of the age that little children, too young to walk or talk, are rushing through the streets cursing their Maker.

- There I stood, thinking every moment would be the next.

- On hearing an Anglican priest referred to as "father": "Imagine calling the loikes of him father—a married man with foive children!"

- Talk about thin! Well, you're thin, and I'm thin, but he's thin as the pair of us put together!

- At the poorly attended wake of a prominent figure: "Ah, if this had happened during his lifetime, the place would be packed."

  From Bennett Hammond and Melinda Ogilvy:

- Gentlemen, is not one man as good as another? "Uv course he is," shouted an excited Irish Chartist, "and a great deal betther!"

- Invalid, returning from a trip: "Oh, shur an' it's done me a wurrold of good, goin' away. I've come back another man altogether. In fact, I'm quite meself again."

- Gentlemen, the time has come to grab the bull by the horns and look the matter squarely in the face.

- Gentlemen, this matter deserves careful consideration. The money involved comes within a few pennies of being a vast and astronomical sum.

18 MARCH
♓

Iorz Feixfuli

Robert Ripley, from whom most of my erudition derives, said there are ten ways to spell the sound *r* in English, thirty-three ways to spell *e*, seventeen ways to spell *v*, thirty-six ways to spell *i*, and seventeen ways to spell *s*. Even if he is a bit off on one side or the other, that is a lot of spellings to memorize.

Among many savants to urge spelling reform was George Bernard Shaw, who proposed that one letter of the alphabet be altered or deleted each year, thus giving the populace time to absorb the change. Here, according to one critic, is how his suggestion would work:

In Year 1 that useless letter "c" would be dropped to be replased by either "k" or "s," and likewise "x" would no longer be part of the alphabet. The only kase in which "c" would be retained would be the "ch" formation, which will be dealt with later. Year 2 might well reform "w" spelling, so that "which" and "one" would take the same konsonant, wile Year 3 might well abolish "y" replasing it with "i," and Iear 4 might fiks the "g-j" anomali wonse and for all.

Jenerally, then, the improvement would kontinue iear bai iear, with Iear 5 doing awai with useles double konsants, and Iears 6–12 or so modifaiing vowlz and the rimeining voist and unvoist konsonants. Bai Ier 15 or sou, it wud fainali bi posibl tu meik ius ov the ridandant letez "c," "y," and "x"—bai now jast a memori in the maindz ov ould doderez—tu riplais "ch," "sh," and "th" rispektivli.

Fainali, xen, aafte sam 20 iers ov orxogrefkl riform, wi wud hev a lojikl, kohirnt speling in ius xrewawt xe Ingliy-spiking werld. Haweve, sins xe Wely, xe Airiy, and xe Skots du not spik Ingliy, xei wud hev to hev a speling siutd tu xer oun lengwij. Xei kud, haweve, orlweiz lern Ingliy as a sekond lengwij et skuul.

> Iorz feixfuli,
> M. J. Yilz.
> —*M. J. Shields*

If you cannot spell, take comfort; neither could Shakespeare.

AMPLIFIED SPELLING

A little buoy said "Mother deer,
　　May eye go out two play?
The son is bright, the heir is clear;
　　Owe mother, don't say neigh."

"Go forth, my sun," the mother said;
　　His ant said, "Take ewer slay,
Ewer gneiss knew sled awl painted read,
　　But do not lose ewer weigh."

"Owe, know!" he cried, and sawt the street
　　With hart sew full of glee.
The weather changed, and snow and sleet
　　And reign fell fierce and free.

Threw snowdrifts grate, threw water pool,
　　He flue with mite and mane.
Said he, "Tho eye wood walk by rule,
　　Eye may not ride, 'tis plane.

"I'de like two meat some kindly sole,
    For hear gnu dangers weight,
And yonder stairs a treacherous whole;
    Two sloe has bin my gate.

"A peace of bred, a bneiss hot stake,
    Eye'd chew if eye were home;
This crewl fair my hart will brake;
    I love knot thus two Rome.

"I'm week and pail; I've mist my rode,"
    But here a carte came passed.
Buoy and his slay were safely toad
    Back to his home at last.
                —*Anonymous*

19 MARCH
♓

Slicing Cooper in Twain

OYSTERVILLE—It has been raining for a week. In the words of Edward Lear:

O pumpkins! O periwinkles!
O pobblesquattles! how him rain!

Since it is too wet to stick my nose outdoors, and since I have no interest in exercising my mind, I am drifting through Mark Twain's comments on J. Fenimore Cooper's early-nineteenth-century "Leatherstocking Tales." How lucky I feel that Mark Twain is not around to review any book of mine!

''THE BROKEN TWIG SERIES''

In his little box of stage properties Cooper kept six or eight cunning devices, tricks, artifices for his savages and woodsmen to deceive and circumvent each other with, and he was never so happy as when he was working these innocent things and seeing them go. A favorite one was to make a moccasined person tread in the tracks of the moccasined enemy, and thus hide his own trail. Cooper wore out barrels and barrels of moccasins in working that trick. Another stage property that he pulled out of his box pretty frequently was his broken twig. He prized his broken twig above all the rest of his effects, and worked it the hardest. It is a restful chapter in any book of his when somebody doesn't step on a dry twig and alarm all the reds and whites for two hundred yards around. Every time a Cooper person is in peril, and absolute silence is worth four dollars a minute, he is sure to step on a dry twig. There may be a hundred handier things to step on, but that wouldn't satisfy Cooper. Cooper requires him to turn out and find a dry twig; and if he can't do it, go and borrow one. In fact, the Leatherstocking Series ought to have been called the Broken Twig Series.

—Mark Twain

20 MARCH
♓

Wouldn't That Be Silly?

Put "Do not" before each of the lines in this verse. You will change the meaning of the verse, but not its note of doubt:

> Tell me I am fair;
>   Tell me I am wise.
> Tell me you will care:
>   Tell me lies.
>   *—W.R.E.*

Here, put "Wouldn't that be silly?" after each line:

> If I were a hive of bees,
>   Or a pig with a silver collar,
> Or a blanket full of fleas,
>   Or a Susan B. Anthony dollar—
> If I were any of these,
> I'd charge a penny a squeeze.
>   *—W.R.E.*

21 MARCH
♈

The Price of Redundancy

In England, laid-off workers are *redundant*. The italicized words in the expressions below are redundant and should be laid off:

- She was modest *about herself*
- He was optimistic *about the future*
- She promised to reform *from now on*
- He nodded *his head*

- *Past* experience
- Skirted *around*
- *Wall* murals
- *Personal* friend

- She had no plans *for the future*
- *New* recruit
- The *general* public
- *False* mirage
- *Mutual* cooperation
- *Contributing* factor
- *End* result
- *Connecting* links
- *New* developments

- *Prior* notice
- He removed *both* his shoes and socks
- *Previous* history
- He thought *to himself*
- Sahara *desert*
- Strangled *to death*
- Set a *new* record
- The *true* facts
- Face *up to* the problem

—*Wesley Price*

22 MARCH
♈

If You Lithp, Thay "He Grunth"

In John Barth's *The Sotweed Factor,* a pupil of Poet Laureate Ebenezer Cooke rhymes several difficult words for his master by, well, cheating—pronouncing *imPORTunacy,* for instance, importunACy and *procrUStean* procrusteAN. Even by cheating, though, he cannot rhyme *month.* Ebenezer comforts him; there is no such thing as a rhyme for month, he says; it "hath not its like."

But Christina Rossetti wrote:

> How many weeks in a month?
> Four, as the swift moon run'th

—surely a correct, if tortured rhyme. Then again, why should a man willing to mispronounce *importunate* for the sake of a rhyme object to breaking a word in two for the same reason?

> It is unth-
> inkable to find
> A rhyme for month,
> Except this special kind.
> —*W.R.E.*

See how easy it is?

*   *   *

Etymologically, the very word *rhyme* is an accident. It was introduced around 1550 through a mistaken correspondence with *rhythm. Rime,* the older and correct spelling, is from the Anglo-Saxon *rim*—"number, computation."

Rhyme is only one aspect of the science of versification. The two subdivisions defined below are as essential, if less familiar:

ARSIS AND THESIS

Two antonyms to you I put:
The *arsis* tiptoes through the foot;
The *thesis,* on the other hand,
Calls out in clamorous command
(Unless, of course, they're turned around,
And each assumes the other's sound.
Then loud is arsis, thesis low,
As all you arses ought to know.)
— *W.R.E.*

23 MARCH
♈

Ypres into Wipers

I repeat that a *hobson-jobson* transforms a difficult phrase, generally of foreign origin, into something familiar and easy, "hobson-jobson" itself being an adaptation by the English of the Shiite mourning cry "O Hasan! O Husain!" By the magic of hobson-jobson, French *chemin couvert,* "covered road," became *smackover; Purgatoire,* "purgatory," *Picketwire; Le Mont Vert,* "the green mountain," *Lemonfair.*

Rotten Row in London was long considered a corruption of *Route du Roi,* "The King's Road," but probably reflects also the fact that the way was much traveled by incontinent horses. *Chère Reine,* "dear queen," became *Charing Cross.* The Tommy Atkinses of World War I called the foreign towns *Premysl* and *Ypres Penny-Whistle* and *Wipers. Ste. Anne de Beaupré* became *Burpy; Aix-les-Bains, Aches and Pains; Place Pigalle, Pig Alley. Cape Despair* hobson-jobsons its opposite in meaning, *Cap d'Espoir,* "Cape of Hope."

French foods, too, took on new associations in English. Kickshaw, describing any fancy food, corrupts *quelque chose,* "something." *Crévis* became *crayfish,* and *mousseron, mushroom.*

Invading Spaniards, unable to pronounce the name of the Mexican town *Quahna-huac,* called it *Cuernavaca,* "the horn of a cow." Americans say *Tom and Charley* for *Tamaunchale.*

E. C. Sharon reminds me that there is no connection between the gallons in a ten-gallon hat and the English measure. The former derive from Spanish *galon,* "ribbon, braid." The hat has a brim broad enough to hold ten *galones.*

A ball-buster, from Yiddish *baleboosta,* is not (as sometimes fancied) a woman who deliberately destroys the ego of a man, but a "head of the household, manager"; thus anyone of either sex who is particularly competent.

French *à toute à l'heure* became *toodleoo* in English. Spanish *Cayo hueso,* "peninsula of the bones," rearranged itself to *Key West.* Irish *shebeen,* "roadhouse," is now *shebang*. *Pinky* for the little finger corrupts Dutch *pinkje*, small. *Bulldog* has nothing to do with our bull; the first syllable alters French *boule*, "ball," referring to the dog's round, thick, brainless head. *Dismal* derives from Latin *decima*, "a tenth," and commemorates the cruel extortions practiced by feudal lords in exacting tenths, or tithes, from their vassals.

German soldiers occupying Paris in the war of 1870, seeing a transom for the first time, asked *"Was ist das?"*; the French still call a transom a *vasistas*. Malta's one-and-only railway system, which operated on an eight-and-a-half-mile track for nearly fifty years, from 1883 to 1931, was named *Xmundifer*—as close as the Maltese could come to pronouncing French *chemin de fer*.

Under early English common law, any neighbor who heard a "human cry" was obliged to investigate, and if it came from the victim of a crime, to pursue and, if possible, to subdue the criminal. *Human cry* evolved into *hue and cry*.

Spirit and image similarly advanced to *spi't 'n' image,* and thence to our present *spitting image.*

24 MARCH
♈

Up and Down Counting Song

1. Dear ewe, dear lamb, I've **1** thee: we
2. Will **2**tle through the fields together;
3. With **3**d and pipe we'll jubilee;
4. We'll gambol back and **4**th in glee;
5. If **5** your heart, who gives a D.
6. How raw and **6** the weather?
7. In **7**th heaven me and thee
8. Will **8** and soon find ecstasy—
9. My ewe be**9** is tied to me,
10. And **10**der is the tether!

10. Yet there may be a **10**dency
9. (Someday when **9** no more know whether
8. You **8** for me still longingly
7. Or find our love less **7**ly)
6. For you in class**6** sulk to flee—
5. Off **5** no doubt to new bellwether
4. And fresher **4**age.... It may be
3. We'll both **3**quire a style more free,
2. And find the Bird of Love **2** be
1. Reduced to **1** Pinfeather.

—W.R.E.

ILL DONE

Of all the ill deeds you have done,
Which would you undo now? Name one.

Of all ill deeds you hoped to do,
Which still remain undone? Name two.

Of ill deeds in your memory,
Which would you do again? Name three.

Of ill deeds you should most abhor,
Which do you treasure most? Name four.
—*W.R.E.*

25 MARCH
♈

Jovanovich

Sandy Choron says this takeoff on Lewis Carroll's "Jabberwocky" has been circulating for a quarter of a century or more in New York publishing offices, with changes from time to time in the names of publishers listed.

'Twas potter, and the little brown
Did simon and schuster in the shaw;
All mosby were the ballantines,
And the womraths mcgraw.

Beware Jovanovich, my son!
The knopfs that crown, the platts that munk!
Beware the doubleday, and shun
The grolier wagnallfunk!

He took his putnam sword in hand,
Long time the harcourt brace he sought;
So rested he by the crowell tree
And stood awhile in thought.

And as in harper thought he stood,
Jovanovich, with eyes of flame,
Came houghton mifflin through the wood
And bowkered as it came!

Dodd mead! dodd mead! and from his steed
His dutton sword went kennicatt!
He left it dead, and with its head
He went quadrangling back.

"And hast thou slain Jovanovich?
Come to my arms, my bantam boy!
Oh, stein and day! Giroux! McKay!"
He scribnered in his joy.

'Twas potter, and the little brown
Did simon and schuster in the shaw;
All mosby were the ballantines,
And the womraths mcgraw.
—*Author unknown*

26 MARCH
♈

Stroke, Strike, and Other Epigrams

To stroke, meaning "to butter up," was used hundreds of years before Watergate:

TO FOOL, OR KNAVE

Thy praise, or dispraise is to me alike,
One does not stroke me, or the other strike.
—*Anonymous*

Other epigrams:

A SENSIBLE GIRL'S REPLY TO MOORE'S

"Our couch shall be roses all spangled with dew."
It would give me rheumatics, and so it would you.
—*Walter Savage Landor*

THE GEORGES

George the First was always reckoned
Vile, but viler George the Second;
And what mortal ever heard
Any good of George the Third?
When from earth the Fourth descended
(God be praised!) the Georges ended.
—*Walter Savage Landor*

In fairness, I add this couplet:

Nay! The Fifth was much improved;
George the Sixth was even loved.
—*W.R.E.*

ON QUEEN CAROLINE

Most Gracious Queen, we thee implore
To go away and sin no more,
But if that effort be too great,
To go away at any rate.
—Anonymous

LE JEUNE HOMME DE DIJON

Il y avait un jeune homme de Dijon,
Qui n'avait que peu de religion.
Il dit: "Quand à moi,
Je déteste tous les trois,
Le Père, et le Fils, et le Pigeon."
—Norman Douglas

LINES FOR AN EMINENT POET AND CRITIC

He has come to such a pitch
Of self-consciousness that he
Dares not scratch, if he has the itch,
For fear he is the flea.
—Patric Dickinson

A man said to the universe:
"Sir, I exist!"
"However," replied the universe,
"The fact has not created in me
A sense of obligation."
—Stephen Crane

27 MARCH
♈

Schizophrenic Words

In Hebrew, says Harvey Minkoff in *Verbatim*, the root consonants *ZBL* led to both *ZrBuL,* meaning "exalted," and *ZeBeL,* meaning "manure"; *KDS* diverged to *KoDeS,* "holy," and *KeDeSah,* "prostitute." In Chinese, *kungfu* translates, on the one hand, as "task, accomplishment," and, on the other, as "leisure."

Each word in the following list has at least one definition which runs contrary to normal usage or two or more definitions which seem to contradict each other. The authority is *Webster's Second.*

- *Acidity* means "alkalinity." *Affection* means "animosity."
- *Bent* means "leveled." *Bleach* means "blacking." *Bless* means "curse." *Bluefish* means "greenfish." *Bosom* means "depression." *Bride* means "a spouse of either sex."
- *Emancipate* means "to enslave."
- *Fill* means "to pour out."
- *General* means "Admiral."
- *Harlot* means "male menial." *Help* means "hinder." *Host* means "guest."

—Tom Pulliam

Additional examples appear in Answers and Solutions.

28 MARCH
♈

Hello, Honey, Everything Is Mighty Nice Up Here

A woman willed her estate to her husband but cautioned him in a videotaped message:

> Don't go to Vegas, or play with stock,
> Or drink much after six o'clock,
> Or party far into the night,
> You'll join me if you don't live right.
> And sports cars and funny hats,
> You're really much too old for that.
> And please, when all my songs are sung,
> Don't fall for someone sweet and young.

Here is mortality abbreviated:

ALPHA AND OMEGA

> From ABC to Ph.D.
> Takes 30 years or so,
> Then FHA and PTA
> May be the route to go.
> So PDQ the years go by,
> From IOUs we're free,
> And in the end we can expect
> A well-earned R.I.P.!
> —*Jean B. Boyce*

CHRISTMAS 1924

"Peace upon Earth!" was said. We sing it,
And pay a million priests to bring it.
After two thousand years of mass
We've got as far as poison gas.
—*Thomas Hardy*

CHRISTMAS 1980

Praise God for still small voice of calm,
And also for the atom bomb.
—*W.R.E.*

As Dog to me, to God am I,
    And thus the matter prove:
When kicked, I wag my tail, and cry,
    "How kind, dear God of Love!"
—*W.R.E.*

29 MARCH
♈

Palimpsest and Hermit Crab

A palimpsest is a piece of parchment designed for easy and frequent erasures.

PALIMPSEST

My name's writ large upon her palimpsest;
    I kissed the fingers that inscribed it there.
Ten thousand years from now, sir, you will swear
    That I above all mortals have been blessed.
Yet if with probing chemical you quest—
    If precedent erasures you restore—
You'll find she blessed Joe, Johnny, and the rest,
    Between this evening and the one before.
—*W.R.E.*

ON THE HERMIT CRAB

The hermit crab lives safely curled
Inside the shell that is his world.
If you expose him to the sky,
He moans, "I faint!"; he groans, "I die!"

Next day you'll find him doing well
Inside another hermit shell.
(Come back, dear!—I'm inferior ab-
solutely to the hermit crab.)

—*W.R.E.*

30 MARCH
♈

The Most Unkindest Cut of All

I mentioned Mark Antony's "the most unkindest cut of all" in a manuscript. The copy editor penciled in the margin, "Poor grammar. Cut 'most' or 'est.'" In fact, the double comparative and double superlative have long and honorable histories in English. These examples are cited by the *Oxford English Dictionary*:

> I should be glad . . . to see a more equaller Balance among Sea-men, and their Imployers (1669).
> I have heard, good Sir, that every Body has a more betterer and a more worserer Side of the Face than the other (1752).
> But Paris was to me / More lovelier than all the world beside (Tennyson, 1832).
> I was always first in the most gallantest scrapes in my younger days (Hardy, 1878).
> My most extremest time of misery (1881).

Improper usages today, certainly; yet they come trippingly, and add emphasis. Why not revive them?

31 MARCH
♈

Witty Word Square

Word squares generally bore me; I am reminded of Samuel Johnson's comparison of a woman preacher with a dog that has learned to stand on its hind legs: "It is not done well; yet you are surprised to find it done at all." Any word square created by Mary Youngquist, however, tickles brain cells and risibilities alike. This one contains twelve lines, most consisting of doubled words. The lines are sometimes repeated, and the whole reads the same from left to right or top to bottom.

```
G O R G E S G O R G E S
O M O O V E O M O O V E
R O B B E R R O B B E R
G O B B L E G O B B L E
E V E L Y N E V E L Y N
S E R E N E S E R E N E
G O R G E S G O R G E S
O M O O V E O M O O V E
R O B B E R R O B B E R
G O B B L E G O B B L E
E V E L Y N E V E L Y N
S E R E N E S E R E N E
```

Miss Youngquist (now Mrs. Hazard) explains her creative process as follows:

- GORGES! GORGES! was the enthusiastic cry of the first explorers to view the expanse of the Grand Canyon; it is recorded in the *Journal of Unusual Nature Kingdom* (*JUNK*), February 30, 1818.

- O M-O-OVE! O M-O-OVE! is the anguished utterance of a camel driver whose beast is clumsily standing on his master's foot (see *Handbook of Camel Drivers,* page xiv).

- ROBBER, ROBBER! (heard often in New York City) is an expression common to persons discovering a thief on the premises (so common, indeed, that no source need be given).

- GOBBLE, GOBBLE is from "Old MacDonald Had a Farm," a standard study of husbandry. The section on turkeys (*Meleagris gallopavo*) is frequently cited: "Here a gobble, there a gobble, everywhere a gobble, gobble."

- EVELYN, EVELYN! The impassioned outburst to his leading lady of the star of the classic silent movie *The Ecstasies of Evelyn* (see the Late, Late, Late Show).

- SERENE, SERENE. The reply of a one-hundred-year-old guru when asked the state of his mind (quoted in *Gurus I Have Known and Loved*).

APRIL

1 APRIL
♈

April Fool

There are days when life seems like an elaborate April Fool's joke:

I THOUGHT AND I THOUGHT

I thought and I thought, till I thought
The thought that the ages had sought.
Unfortunately
It turned out to be
Not the thought that I ought to have thought.
—*W.R.E.*

WORMS

Worms aren't witty;
Worms aren't pretty;
Worms just
        squirm.
This, I think,
Serves to link
Man and
      worm.
—*W.R.E.*

2 APRIL
♈

Name-Dropping

Norman St. John-Stevas, the British arts minister, broke off during a speech to apologize for referring so often and familiarly to celebrities.

"One must not be a name-dropper," he said, "as Her Majesty remarked to me at luncheon yesterday."

Which reminds me—my third wife's elder sister's first daughter's first husband was the second husband of the third wife of the late Justice William Douglas.

Philip M. Cohen used to go around gathering unusual names from telephone books, and then dropping them into conversations. Some of the names he assembled:

- Atlanta: Joseph Bpuscia, E. M. Fmeets
- Baltimore: Thomas Fpitnale
- Chicago: Mary Fb, E. Fbeswalter, C. Wxmhersji
- Columbus: Jeanette and Joe Fmura
- Dallas: Anna Bella Bparnell
- Houston: Robert D. Pplanck, Arun Pvongnak
- London: Mr. HcYiani
- Manhattan: Edith Wfoulkes

But Mr. Cohen has a fatal weakness: He likes to check his facts. He called the numbers listed and found that all but three of his marvelous names were typographical errors.

The moral is: Let well enough alone.

Letters remain on most telephone dials, and sometimes they can be worked into words. NERVOUS, for instance, got you the correct time in New York, until the telephone company changed the number out of sheer nastiness. Telephone numbers may turn to SEXPLOT, DOGYBAG, and FATHEAD. A while back the number for a First Methodist Church in Hollywood could be dialed as GODDAMN, but the church, or God, disconnected the number.

Mathematicians are hard put to name-drop, because their names are hard to pronounce and spell:

HENRI LEBESGUE HAS GOT NO Q

Weep for the mathematicians
   Posterity acclaims:
Although we know their theorems
   We cannot spell their names.

Forget the things you thought you knew—
Henri Lebesgue has got no Q.

Hermann Grassmann—reader, do
Spell his names with two Ns, too.

Fejér, Turán, Cesàro, Fréchet—
Let's make the accents go that way.

And as for (Radon-) Nikodým,
Let's give his accent back to him.

Put letters in or leave them out,
Dress them with accents round about,
Finish the name with -eff or -off,
There is no way to spell $\gamma\varepsilon\delta\Delta\iota\omega\varepsilon\beta$.

                 —R. P. Boas

3 APRIL
♈

Can You Top This?

Games borrowed a few classic one-line jokes from comedian Henny Youngman, and set them up in puzzle format. You are supposed to develop your own snappers for the stories below. The Master's are in Answers and Solutions.

1. The six fraternity men came weaving out of the off-campus gin mill. The president said to one of the fellows, "Herbie, you drive . . .

2. An empty-headed lovely young girl stood at the bank teller's window. He looked at her and at the check she wished to cash, then asked her if she could identify herself. She . . .

3. A fellow bought a mousetrap for his cellar. When he went to set it, he found that he had forgotten to buy cheese, so he cut a piece of cheese from a picture in a magazine and placed this in the trap. Surprisingly enough it worked. When he went down the next morning, he found in the trap . . .

4. I didn't know what to get my wife anymore. First she wanted a mink, I got her a mink. Then she wanted a silver fox, I got her a silver fox . . .

5. A cross-eyed judge was trying three cross-eyed prisoners. He turned to the first cross-eyed prisoner and said, "What's your name?" The second cross-eyed prisoner said, "John Brown." The cross-eyed judge said, "I wasn't talking to you," and . . .

6. Woman to dentist: "I don't know what's worse, having a baby or getting a tooth pulled." Dentist: ". . .

7. A man brags about his new hearing aid. "It's the most expensive I've ever had—twenty-four hundred dollars." His friend asks, "What kind is it?" He says, ". . .

8. My wife went to the beauty shop and got a mud pack. For two days she looked nice. Then . . .

9. Somebody once asked me, "Henny, do you like bathing beauties?" I said, ".

10. Two kangaroos were talking to each other, and one said, "Gee, I hope it doesn't rain today . . ."

11. One time I came home and my wife was crying because the dog had eaten a pie she had made for me. "Don't cry," I told her, ". . .

12. Did you hear about the rich kid from Dallas who walked up to Santa Claus and said, ". . .

13. My wife will buy anything marked down. She brought home two dresses and an . . .

14. I solved the parking problem. I bought a . . .

15. I'll never forget when I lost my baby teeth . . .

16. Psychiatrist to patient: "What do you do for a living?" Patient: "I'm an auto mechanic." Psychiatrist: ". . .

17. What do you do for a man who has everything? . . .

18. Two fellows were applying for jobs as truck drivers. One said, "This is my partner Sam. My name is Orville." "Okay, Orville, I want to give you a mental test. Suppose you are driving along a road at three o'clock in the morning, you are on a little bridge, and another truck is coming toward you at a hundred miles an

hour. What is the first thing you'd do?"

"I'd wake up my partner Sam, and say . . .

19. Calling all cops, calling all cops, be on the lookout—they are passing a lot of counterfeit tens and twenties . . .

4 APRIL
♈

Macaronic Mother Goose

In November Mother Goose will be talking fractured French. Let us see how she does in April with macaronics:

JACK AND JILL

Jack cum amica Jill,
    Ascendit super montem;
Johannes cecedit down the hill,
    Ex forte fregit frontem.

LITTLE BO-PEEP

Parvula Bo-Peep
    Amisit her sheep,
Et nescit where to find 'em;
    Desere alone,
    Et venient home,
Cum omnibus caudis behind 'em.

LITTLE JACK HORNER

Parvus Jacobus Horner
Sedebat in corner,
Edens a Christmas pie;
Inferit thumb,
Extreherit plum—
Clamans, "Quid sharp puer am I!"
    —Anonymous

SHE LOST HER SHEEP

Arcuconspicilla looks for *perditas*,
"They'll come home, *trahantes caudas!*" What
    absurditas!
    —Anonymous

FOUR AND TWENTY MERULAE

Nummum et saeculis saeculorum cantate!
Four and twenty *merulae* in a pie *paratae;*
Pieum when *apertum est, cecinere crapulae*
Regi quae monstrendae, ecce pretty *epulae!*
—*J. Moyr Smith*

5 APRIL
♈

The Fairer Sex, Etsexera

Aphorisms on men, women, and marriage:

• It doesn't much signify whom one marries, for one is sure to find out next morning it was someone else.   —*Rogers*

• If you are afraid of loneliness, don't marry.   —*Chekhov*

• The most happy marriage I can picture would be the union of a deaf man to a blind woman.   —*Coleridge*

• To marry a second time represents the triumph of hope over experience.   —*Dr. Johnson*

• Home life as we understand it is no more natural to us than a cage is natural to a cockatoo.   —*Shaw*

• Coition is a slight attack of apoplexy.   —*Democritus of Abdera*

• Were it not for imagination, sir, a man would be as happy in the arms of a chambermaid as a duchess.   —*Dr. Johnson*

• A wise woman never yields by appointment.   —*Stendhal*

• There is no fury like a woman searching for a new lover.   —*Connolly*

• A man does not look behind the door unless he has stood there himself.   —*Du Bois*

• There is no sanctuary in one bed from the memory of another.   —*Connolly*

• A lover tries to stand in well with the pet dog of the house.   —*Molière*

• Lovemaking is radical, while marriage is conservative.   —*Author unknown*

• Love is an ideal thing, marriage a real thing; a confusion of the real with the ideal never goes unpunished.   —*Goethe*

• In matrimony, to hesitate is sometimes to be saved.   —*Butler*

• If a man hears much that a woman says, she is not beautiful.   —*Haskins*

• A woman may very well form a friendship with a man, but for this to endure, it must be assisted by a little physical antipathy.   —*Nietzsche*

• Men who cherish for women the highest respect are seldom popular with them.
—Author unknown

• Woman inspires us to great things, and prevents us from achieving them. —Dumas

• You don't know a woman until you have had a letter from her.   —Ada Leverson

• Nature has given women so much power that the law has very wisely given them little.
—Dr. Johnson

• When women kiss it always reminds one of prizefighters shaking hands.
—Author unknown

6 APRIL
♈

Therefore Rejoice

Be active, they say. Say, "He hit me," we are told, not "I was hit by him." Say, "He saw me," not "I was seen by him." Yet if you feel passive, why not talk that way?

1. THE ACTIVE VOICE

One acts, one's acted on. (I ment-
   ion this re subjects of a sent-
ence.) Subjects that commit an act
   Are Male, which may not mean attract-
ive (no!), but *prominent,*
   With bulging Biceps; it's a fact
That virile symbols make a dent
   In ladies who enjoy a gent.
      Wherefore rejoice,
      O subjects of the Active Voice!

2. THE PASSIVE VOICE

Not so the subject of the Pass-
   ive voice; she is not corded round with massive muscles, being of the lact-
   ic or mammalian sort, well stacked—
And virginal (like any lass,
   Till acted on to her content.)
      Wherefore rejoice,
      O subjects of the Passive Voice!
—W.R.E.

7 APRIL
♈

Hymn to the Spring and Villon Too

The initial letters of the following verse, written for Queen Elizabeth I, spell "Elisabetha Regina":

HYMN TO THE SPRING

E arth now is green, and heauen is blew,
L iuely Spring which makes all new,
I olly Spring doth enter.
S weet young sun-beams doe subdue
   A ngry, aged Winter.

B lasts are mild, and seas are calme,
E uery medow flowes with balme,
   T he earth weares all her riches,
H armonious birds sing such a psalm
   A s eare and heart bewitches.

R eserve (sweet Spring) this nymph of ours,
E ternall garlands of thy flowers,
   G reene garlands never wasting;
I n her shall last our state's faire spring,
N ow and for euer flourishing,
A s long as heauen is lasting.
                    —*Sir John Davies*

François Villon's "Ballade des Contrevérités" has this acrostic conclusion:

V oulez vous que verte vous die?
I l n'est jouer qu'en maladie,
L ettre vraie qu'en tragédie,
   L ache homme que chevalereux,
O rrible son que melodie,
   N e bien conseille qu'amoureux.

An English approximation of the sentiment:

V illon! never (else I lie),
I s there joy, except to die;
   L ife is sung in tragic runes
L ofty knights are louts disguised
   O dious sounds dress up as tunes
N aught but love is well advised.
                    —*W.R.E.*

8 APRIL
♈

A Fragrance of Flowers

The morning glory opens at five or six in the morning; the African daisy at eight or nine; the tulip at ten or eleven; the goatsbeard, noonish. The four o'clock retires at around four, and the day lily at around eight.

These horological data came to mind as I considered the verse that follows, listing flowers advertised in a Boston newspaper of March 3, 1760. Exaggerate the beat if you read the verse aloud:

> LAV-en-der; HON-ey-wort (loved by BEES);
> TREE Mal-low; PAINT-ed Dame Top-knot PEAS;
> HON-es-ty (SOLD in bites, so that EACH
> HAS a bit); CATCH-fly; Flower-ing PEACH;
> SNAP-drag-on; COL-chi-cum; Lark-spur SHOOTS;
> FIF-ty-five IN-ter-mixed Tu-lip ROOTS;
> HORN Pop-py; MAR-i-gold; Hol-ly-HOCK;
> EV-er-more; SNUFF Flower; Pur-ple STOCK;
> HYS-sop; Red LAV-a-ter; Wall-eyed PINK;
> ICE-plant; Sweet MAR-jor-am; Bil-ly STINK;*
> SWEET Rock-et; WHITE Lu-pin; Col-ored BOWER;
> YEL-low Chrys-AN-the-mum; Red Wall-FLOWER;
> STRAW-ber-ry SPIN-age; Dear Love Lies BLEED-ing;
> CAR-na-tion POP-py (read-y for SEED-ing).
>   —W.R.E.

9 APRIL
♈

Words of Wood

Pangrams are brief, more or less intelligible passages using every letter of the alphabet: "The quick brown fox jumps over the lazy dog." The goal is to use each of the twenty-six letters as infrequently as possible.

From Spetsai, an island off southern Greece, Clement Wood has sent me three pangrams of his own creation.

Clement Wood is a poet, born in 1888. He wrote *The Complete Rhyming Diction-ary,* first published in 1936 and still a standard reference work.

Since I have in mind to write a rhyming dictionary myself, I am replying instantly to Mr. Wood, thanking him for his pangrams and inviting myself to visit him. Who knows—he may write a splendid introduction to my dictionary!

*The Scottish name. The English say Sweet William.

"I have been reading your *Game of Words*," he wrote, "and lingered over the section 'All Twenty-six Letters of the Alphabet.' Now, several sleepless nights and feverish days later, I'm happy to report to you that

MR. JOCK, TV QUIZ PH.D., BAGS FEW LYNX."

That, reader, is the ideal pangram—each of the twenty-six letters used just once. Moreover, it is intelligible without reference to a dictionary. Purists may complain that Mr. Wood has cheated by using initials; I approve of initials if they further the message.

He appended a commentary:

"Serves Jock right. An academic who sells out to the mass media can expect his marksmanship to suffer."

He also sent the two following pangrams with accompanying reflections:

FEW MOCK QUARTZ GLYPH'S BVD JINX.

("I daresay the handful of union-suit buffs who choose to jeer at the caveat hewn in rocks by the ancients will have cause for regret.")

TV QUIZ DRAG-NYMPHS BLEW COX, JFK.

("Scandalous—and to think I voted for JFK!")

MORE TO COME ON 10 MAY.

10 APRIL
♈

What Is the Word for #?

Occasionally I am asked whether there is one inclusive word for the symbol #. There is not. It has different meanings under different circumstances:

> Many offices encumber
>   My diurnal rounds;
> 1. Before a digit, I'm a #;
> 2.   After digits, #;
> 3. In a printer's proof, a #;
>   While, if at the harp
>   You should pluck me from my place,
> 4.   I would be a #.
> 5. In one game, I'm #;
> 6.   An # on 'phones;
> 7. In business, I'm #, although
> 8.   A # when in bones.

—W.R.E.

11 APRIL
♈

Kicking the Bucket

See if you can determine, without peeking in back, the origins of the hobson-jobsons defined below.

1. Apple-pie order. Perfect order or arrangement.
2. Egg on. Incite, encourage, provoke.
3. Not give a hoot. Not care at all.
4. Kick the bucket. Die.
5. Mealymouthed. Unwilling to tell the truth in plain language.
6. Round robin. A petition with signatures in a circle, concealing who signed first.

12 APRIL
♈

A Man Caught a Magical Fish

I recently submitted a manuscript for a future *Children's Almanac* which contained this limerick:

> A man caught a magical fish
> Which offered to grant him one wish.
> Said the man, "You are kind;
> I hope you won't mind
> Being trout *amandée* on a dish."

The editor approved conditionally: "with changes," she wrote in the margin. Do you suppose she prefers trout *meunière?*

She made no comments on these nonsense limericks:

> The train between Nitwit and Muntz
> Proceeds both directions at once:
> So I frequently flit
> Between Muntz and Nitwit
> Not stirring from Nitwit or Muntz.

> Said a logical pupil named Gunn,
> "Arithmetic's foolishly run.
> $2 \times 2 = 4$;
> So $\times$ = More;
> Yet 1×1 just $= 1$."

He: "Fiddle dee carra wee loop?"
She: "Cramer om ib corser soop."
  He: "Coggle con see?"
  She: "Ara lig dee."
He: "Hoggle O soggle poop poop!"

There's an out-of-reach girl in the skies
Of an astronomical size.
  Each night through my 'scope
  I gaze in the hope
Of seeing the stars in her eyes.

The moon told a newsman in Axing,
"My job is becoming too taxing.
  It isn't the heights,
  Or the working at nights,
But I'm sick of the waning and waxing."

A Cold told a Sneeze, "I won't hurchoo;
I'll loyally honor your virchoo.
  Sweet, what do you say?
  Let us marry today!"
The Sneeze replied, "KER-choo-ah-KER-choo."
                        —*W.R.E.*

13 APRIL
♈

A Wickedness of Willies

Verses in the devilish "Little Willy" tradition of Harry Graham:

Tommy shot Mamma for fun.
Father, as he cleaned the gun,
Said, "That's very wrong, my pet;
Cartridges are hard to get."
                        —*L. V. Upward*

James, reposing on a bank,
Was rudely wakened by a tank;
The ground was soft, the tank was large,
So James was buried free of charge.
                        —*E. W. Fordham*

Herbert, following a tiff,
Pushed his sweetheart o'er a cliff.
Now his action he regrets;
She had got their cigarettes.
                        —*Nancy Gunter*

When Gypsies kidnapped sister Lil,
The folks were all upset but Will.
Said little Willie, "Dry your tears,
She'll love it when they pierce her ears."
                    —*William E. Engel*

"It's three No Trumps," the soldier said;
A sniper's bullet struck him dead.
His cards bedecked the trench's bottom.
A comrade peered—"Yes, he'd 'a' got 'em."
                    —*Guy Inness*

What are we to do with Jim?
    He pushed Grandma down the quarry,
And he knows we're cross with him,
    Yet he *will* not say he's sorry.
                    —*R. E. Kitching*

POLITENESS

My cousin John was most polite.
    He led shortsighted Mrs. Bond,
By accident, one winter's night,
    Into the village pond.
Her life perhaps he might have saved,
    But how genteelly he behaved!
Each time she rose and waved to him,
    He smiled and bowed and doffed his hat.
Thought he, "Although I cannot swim,
    At least I can do *that*."
And when for the third time she sank,
He stood bareheaded on the bank!
                    —*Harry Graham*

14 APRIL
♈

Lo the Poor Indian

INDIAN TRIBES

The Sioux and the Algonquins, where are these?
Where, too, are now the Hurons and Pawnees?
The Chickasaws, Oneidas, and Shawnees,
The Winnebagos and the Muscogees,

The Sauks, the Comanches, and Uchees,
The Kansas, Seminoles, and Weetumkees,
The Mohegans, Nihantics, and Natchees,
The Pequots, Miamis, and Yanasees,
The Tuscaroras and the Waterees,
The Narragansetts, and Menomonees,
The Choctaws, Delawares, and Cherokees,
The Eries, Yamacraws, and Mosokees,
The Mohawks, and the Chicahominies,
The Kickapoos, and tall Walhominies,
The Androscoggins, and the Omahas,
The Alabamas, and Mitchigamuas,
The Tangeboas, and the Pammahas,
The Appalachias, and the Ostonoos,
The Sacs and Foxes and the Onodoos,
The Pottawattomies and Ioways,
The Creeks, Catawbas, and Ojibbeways,
The Senecas, Peorias, and Crows,
Who sank beneath the burden of their woes?
How few remain of all those valiant hosts
That peopled once the prairies and the coasts!

—Anonymous

A WANDERING TRIBE CALLED THE SIOUXS

A wandering tribe, called the Siouxs,
Wear moccasins, having no shiouxs,
   They are made of buckskin,
   With the fleshy side in,
Embroidered with beads of bright hyiouxs.

When out on the warpath, the Siouxs
March single file—never by tiouxs
   And by blazing the trees
   Can return at their ease,
And their way through the forest ne'er liouxs.

All new-fashioned boats they eschiouxs,
Preferring their birch-bark caniouxs;
   These are handy and light,
   And, inverted at night,
Give shelter from storms and from dyiouxs.

The principal food of the Siouxs
Is Indian maize, which they briouxs
   And hominy make,
   Or mix in a cake,
And eat it with fork, as they chiouxs.

—Anonymous

15 APRIL
♈

Snallygaster I

As if it wasn't bad enough to have to pay my income tax today, I also received this letter:

United States Senate
WASHINGTON, D.C. 20510

April 15

Mr. Willard R. Espy
Contributing Editor
Harvard Magazine

Dear Mr. Espy:

I noted with interest on page 64 of the current issue of Harvard Magazine that you quote President Truman as having used the word "snollygoster." I am further dismayed to see that you are under the misapprehension that the word passed out of the language in the mid-Nineteenth Century, and that President Truman thought it meant "a man born out of wedlock." All of this is *wrong!*

The correct way to spell it is "snallygaster." The word probably derives from the German "schnelle Geischter" or "flying ghost." They frequently were reported in rural Maryland, about the time of an election. Voters planning to vote the wrong way would probably find it prudent to stay at home when the snallygaster was on the prowl. Far from having disappeared in the Nineteenth Century, it has been a subject of much newspaper attention in Maryland in the Twentieth Century. One of the papers to most accurately report the appearance of the snallygaster was the Valley Register, published at 123 West Main Street, Middletown, Maryland 21769.

The question of the snallygaster has also been a matter of vital interest to William Safire, distinguished columnist of the New York Times, who unfortunately fell into the same error in misspelling the word.

Knowing your high regard for accuracy, I take the liberty of calling these matters to your attention. Perhaps together we can put this straight and keep coming generations from the ignorance that might have them prey to a snallygaster's claws.

Sincerely,
Charles McC. Mathias, Jr.
United States Senator

cc: Mr. William Safire
The New York Times
Mr. George C. Rhoderick, Jr.
The Valley Register

I suspect that the letter is a fraud and that there is no such person as a Senator Mathias. Should further information transpire, I'll let you know.

MORE TO COME ON 22 APRIL.

16 APRIL
♈

Aesop Revisited: Sun, Moon, and Cloud

Bright as the Morning Star shines Clare
    In hymeneal guise.
"Alack!" I cry; "what groom would dare
    Undo those hooks and eyes?"

"Like pit from cherry she'll pop out,"
    Boasts Sun, "at my first kiss"—
Then flings inflammably about,
    Until the sidewalks hiss.

Like candles drip the wedding guests,
    The maids of honor droop—
Yet not one bangle Clare divests,
    One pantyhose or hoop.

"My music magics maids," says Moon,
    And sings of Lohengrin;
But still her gown stays chastely on,
    And she as chastely in.

But then a cloud spreads modest cover,
    And in that change of weather
The deed is done, the problem's over:
    Clare's in the altogether.
                   —W.R.E.

17 APRIL
♈

Up Here in the (9)

For each number below, substitute a word with that number of letters. By adding the clue letters provided, supply new words until you end with a nine-letter monster.

A. Once upon (1) time a little boy's (2) gave him an unusual pet—a trained baby (3), whose favorite food was not bananas but green (4), cooked in tomato juice to give them a reddish brown, or (5) color. Although the pet, as he grew older, got nothing but (6) for his many accomplishments, nevertheless at times he was saddened almost to the point of (7) by the thought that his present, comfortable little (8) might someday (9).

Clues: 2, p. 3, e. 4, s. 5, i. 6, r. 7, d. 8, a. 9, p.

B. (1) How nice it would be to lie (2) the sand on any (3) of the many Florida beaches, protecting my (4) from the hot sun, far away from this cold city built of (5)! Happy not to have done an (6) day's work, ready to settle into one of those luxurious chairs that look like (7), I would surely feel like a king and would not wish to change my kingdom for (8). (Warning! There's an apostrophe in word (8).) What a delightful way to forget all about the snow and ice up here in the (9).

Clues: 2, n. 3, e. 4, s. 5, t. 6, h. 7, r. 8, a. 9, t.

—*Maxwell Nurnberg*

18 APRIL
♈

Madam, I'm Adam

The briefer the palindrome, the clearer the message: "Madam, I'm Adam"; "A man, a plan, a canal—Panama"; "Able was I ere I saw Elba." Palindromes of as many as sixty letters may retain a certain cogency:

• Straw? No, too stupid a fad. I put soot on warts.
• Eros? Sidney, my end is sore!
• Are we not drawn onward, we few, drawn onward to new era?
• Now, Ned, I am a maiden nun; Ned, I am a maiden won.

As palindromes grow longer—the French wordgame book *Oulippo* has a palindromic passage that I count at around 5,000 letters—the sense diminishes and finally vanishes quite away. If, however, the components of the palindromes are entire words instead of letters, a palindromic poem may be extended indefinitely and quite sensibly. David L. Stephens sent me the following examples. The first, inspired by a German folk song, has been recorded in different translations by Burl Ives and Richard Dyer-Bennett:

Returning exquisite desire,
Burning, then ashes and smoke.
Glowing ember or flaming oak—
Unknowing, unknown secret fire!

Fire, secret, unknown, unknowing,
Oak flaming or ember glowing.
Smoke and ashes; then burning
Desire, exquisite, returning.
            —*Author unknown*

HANNIBAL, MISSOURI

Glimmering, gone—springtime stream
Lapping . . . road winding down
The shimmering hill. Hometown

Napping . . . sweet, solemn dream!
Dreams solemn, sweet . . . napping
Hometown . . . hill shimmering . . . the
Down-winding road . . . lapping
Stream . . . springtime . . . gone, glimmering.
—Author unknown

As far as Anders R. Sterner knows, the oldest surviving graffito is this palindrome found on the wall of a lately excavated tavern of ancient Rome: "ROMA SUMMUS AMOR." Decide for yourself whether the theme is patriotism or a less lofty form of love. Another foreign-language palindrome contributed by Mr. Sterner is the Finnish word for soap salesman: "SAIPPURAKARUPPIAS."

FOUR PALINDROMES

Draw pupil's lip upward.
Swen nixes sex in news.
Do nine men interpret? Nine men, I nod.
Rise to vote, sir.
—Author unknown

Toward the end of 1959, Alastair Reid, uttering the huge hoots that pass for laughter among the Scots, composed a palindrome. He then forced his friends to listen to it willy-nilly. The line became an instant classic. W. H. Auden enjoyed it so, and repeated it so often, that he has sometimes been credited as the author. He is not; the writer of that palindrome is the man to whom it is attributed here:

T. Eliot, top bard, notes putrid tang emanating, is sad. I'd assign it a name: gnat dirt upset on drab pot-toilet.

—Alastair Reid

19 APRIL
♈

Private? No!

Punctuation can make a difference.

Private
No swimming
Allowed

does not mean the same as

Private?
No. Swimming
Allowed.

Other examples:

> The escaping convict dropped a bullet in his leg.
> The escaping convict dropped, a bullet in his leg.

> The butler stood by the door and called the guests' names as they arrived.
> The butler stood by the door and called the guests names as they arrived.

> Go slow, children.
> Go slow—children.

> I'm sorry you can't come with us.
> I'm sorry. You can't come with us.

A punctuation mark omitted or misplaced has upset the intent of many a legal document. Punctuate these sentences for clarity:

1. Said I I said you said I said said said he who said I said you said said I said said is said said said is not said said like said.
2. That that is is that that is not is not is not that it it is.
3. The murderer protested his innocence an hour after he was put to death.
4. He said that that that that that man said was correct.

See what mispunctuation can do:

> A clever dog knows its master.
> A clever dog knows it's master.

> Do not break your bread, or roll in your soup.
> Do not break your bread or roll in your soup.

For more of this kind of thing, read *Fun with Words,* by Maxwell Nurnberg.

A PAEAN OF PUNCTUATION

> Thine eyes, dear one, dot dot, are like, dash, what?
> They, pure as sacred oils, bless and anoint
> My sin-swamped soul which at thy feet sobs out,
> O exclamation point, O point, O point!
>
> Ah, had I words, blank blank, which, dot, I've not,
> I'd swoon in songs which should'st illume the dark
> With light of thee. Ah, God (it's *strong* to swear)
> Why, why, interrogation mark, why, mark?
>
> Dot dot dot dot. And so, dash, yet, but nay!
> My tongue takes pause; some words must not be said,
> For fear the world, cold, hyphen-eyed, austere,
> Should'st shake thee by the throat till reason fled.
>
> One hour of love we've had. Dost thou recall
> Dot dot dash blank interrogation mark?
> The night was ours, blue heaven over all
> Dash, God! Dot stars, keep thou our secret dark!
> —*Marion Hill*

20 APRIL
♈

Metaphysics

Why and Wherefore set out one day
   To hunt for a wild Negation.
They agreed to meet at a cool retreat
   On the Point of Interrogation.

But the night was dark and they missed their mark,
   And driven well-nigh to distraction,
They lost their ways in a murky maze
   Of utter abstruse abstraction.

So they took a boat and were soon afloat
   On a sea of Speculation,
But the sea grew rough, and their boat, though tough,
   Was split into an Equation.

As they floundered about in the waves of doubt
   Rose a fearful Hypothesis,
Who gibbered with glee as they sank in the sea,
   And the last they saw was this:

On a rock-bound reef of Unbelief
   There sat a wild Negation;
Then they sank once more and were washed ashore
   At the Point of Interpretation.
               —*Gelett Burgess*

21 APRIL
♉

Slang That Stays Slang

Some slang has its day in the sun and night in the moon and then fades away. Some slang becomes acceptable speech. Some slang survives but never crashes society. These examples are of the last sort:

Nearly 500 years ago Chaucer described willing wenches as "hot." *Lam* for "to run away" was in use as early as 1555; *powder* in the same sense arrived in the next century. Other slang words in use for more than 300 years are *ad-lib, bull* (for an error), *lousy, crack, uncle, in the bag, potted, rap* (for a bull session), *shake a hoof, nuts, beef* (rhyming slang for "stop thief"), *bracelets* (for handcuffs), *guts, angle, dub, stall, shoestring, vamp, scram, racket, binge, blue, booze,* and *confab.* A *gam* was a leg on a coat of arms.

At least 200 years old are *big gun, big shot, deadhead, free-lance, fuzzy, lay an egg, big house* (for the poorhouse), and *take a fall.*

22 APRIL
♉

Snallygaster II

A letter (see 15 April) to George C. Rhoderick, Jr., with copies to William Safire and the putative Senator Mathias:

22 April

Dear Mr. Rhoderick:

My recent mail contained a letter, of which a copy apparently went to you, by someone who signs himself Charles McC. Mathias, Jr. This writer tried to persuade me that there really is a Charles McC. Mathias, Jr.; that the writer is he; that he is a United States senator; and, by implication, that there is a United States Senate. He also expects me to believe that there exists a place called "rural Maryland."

These are dubious propositions. Fortunately I am able to test them by sending you this letter. If it is returned to me with "No Such Person" stamped on the envelope, I can dismiss the matter. If it is not returned, I can assume that you are real and that Senator Charles McC. Mathias, Jr., probably is, too.

I had mentioned in an article the word *snollygoster*, defined by President Truman as a man born out of wedlock. The self-styled senator declares that the word is correctly *snallygaster*, probably deriving from German *schnelle Geischter*, "flying ghost." The snallygaster, he goes on, prowls around election time to intimidate possibly dissident voters.

After listing my statements about the snollygoster, he declares, "All of this is *wrong!*"

To *underline* the word *wrong* adds insult to injury.

It appears to me that the descriptions of the snollygoster given by the President and the soi-disant senator are much of a piece. The President used the word to describe a cheap and venal politician—nine times out of ten a shyster lawyer. A shyster lawyer is a bastard, and no doubt your monster is, too. QED.

Still, I should like to know more about snollygosters (snallygasters?), and you appear to be the authority in the field. What do they feed on? Are they social or solitary? Do they lie with humans? Is the bite, or sting, poisonous?

And *is* there a Charles McC. Mathias? Is he a United States senator? For that matter, is there actually a United States Senate? I am willing to concede that there really is a Commonwealth of Maryland.

If you are not out chasing snollygosters, do tell me what you can. I shall be grateful.

Sincerely,

Willard R. Espy

MORE TO COME ON 5 MAY.

23 APRIL
ỵ

How Mortal These Fools Be

LET US WONDER, WHILE WE LOITER

Let us wonder, while we loiter,
Which of us will die of goiter;
Which of stone or dysentery;
Which of rheum or beriberi;
Which of grippe or diarrhea,
Nettlerash, or pyorrhea;
Which of us turn turvy topsy,
Victim of paretic dropsy.
Be it pox or whooping cough,
Something's bound to bear us off.
All we know is, we're in trouble:
Barman, make my next one double.
                    —*W.R.E.*

NO INTRAVENOUS FOR ME

When faced with terminal disease,
No intravenous feeding, please.
No pumps imparting partial life;
No last-ditch doings with the knife.
When coma comes, please let me slide
Unhindered to the other side:
I want no plastic tubes to mar
My meeting with The Registrar.
                    —*W. H. Von Dreele*

ACTUARIAL REFLECTION

Very, very, very few
People die at ninety-two.
I suppose that I shall be
Safer still at ninety-three.
                    —*W.R.E.*

EARTH DOTH TWIRL

Earth doth twirl—
Furl, unfurl
   The sun . . .
And so will too
After you
   Are done.
                    —*W.R.E.*

A change of subject, but not of mood:

DON'T RUB IT IN

Misericordia,
Lordia!
Take it easy,
Jeesy!
We're born in sin—
Don't rub it in!
—*W.R.E.*

24 APRIL

The Price of a Candle

The Chinese have an epigram, "The couple who go to bed early to save candles wind up with twins":

"My dear, we saved a candle!" ...
"Sillykins!
In nine months we'll dandle
Twins!"
—*W.R.E.*

An olio of epigrams (defined by William Camden as "shorte and sweete poems, framed to praise or dispraise"):

MODERATION

In things a moderation keep,
Kings ought to shear, not skin, their sheep.
—*Robert Herrick*

WHAT'S LIGHTER THAN A FEATHER?

My soul, what's lighter than a feather? Wind.
Than wind? The fire. And what than fire? The mind.
What's lighter than a mind? A thought. Than thought?
This bubble world. What than this bubble? Nought.
—*Francis Quarles*

MANKIND

Clay, sand, and rock seem of a diff'rent birth:
So men; some stiff, some loose, some firm: all earth.
—*Barten Holyday*

BAD COMPANY

Bad company is a disease;
Who lies with dogs, shall rise with fleas.
—*Rowland Watkins*

A SUMMARY OF LORD LYTTLETON'S ADVICE

Be plain in dress and sober in your diet;
In short, my deary, kiss me and be quiet.
—*Lady Mary Wortley Montagu*

TO AN OFFICER IN THE ARMY, INTENDED TO ALLAY THE VIOLENCE OF PARTY SPIRIT

God bless the king—I mean the faith's defender;
God bless—(no harm in blessing)—the pretender;
But who pretender is, or who is king,
God bless us all—that's quite another thing.
—*John Byrom*

25 APRIL

Bad Bab

Imagine (I wrote to my friend Dick Hyman, the jazz pianist and composer) an agitated young man shouting into the ear of a dozing ancient, while pointing at a taxicab fleeing around a corner on two wheels. The driver is a young woman, and a great cabbage is about to roll off the roof.

Now place beneath your mental picture a musical score consisting of the following notes:

G A D D A D D E A F A G E D D A D A B A D A D A G

E B A D E B A B A B A B E F A C E D B A G G A G E

C A D G E A C A B B A G E A B A D A D A G E B A D

E B A B C A D G E A C A B G A D D A D B A B A C C

E D E D B A D G A F F E D A D B A D D E E D B A B

B A D B A B B A D

A moment's examination reveals a tense drama of temptation and fall:

Gad, dad
(Deaf, agèd dad)!—
A bad adage
Bade Bab

(a babe-faced baggage)
Cadge a cabbage!

A bad adage
Bade Bab
Cadge a cab!

Gad, dad,
Bab acceded!
Bad gaffe, dad!—
Bad deed, Bab!—
Bad, Bab, bad!
—*W.R.E.*

The score below arrived from Dick this morning. "It makes a pleasantly quirky tune," he writes, "which I have also elaborated into a little piano piece."

If you would like the elaborated piano tune, just ask me.

* * *

DISHARMONY

She would keep
Harping on about tidiness
Blowing her own trumpet
And drumming it into me

That I mustn't fiddle
With my hair.
I think she was instrumental
In our divorce.
—*Alan E. G. Lewis*

26 APRIL

♉

Everybody Have a Right to Their Oan Language

Let him who is immune to grammatical slips cast the first stone. *The New Yorker* is more fussy about language than most of us, but I have just read there, "The two geniuses—Maynard Keynes and the Woolfs—had distinctive public influence." 1 genius + 2 geniuses = 2 geniuses. Yes, *The New Yorker*.

The chairman of the English Department of the Scarsdale high school, complaining about an article in the *New York Times,* writes the editor, "My first dismay resulted from the careless writing." He then proceeds to demonstrate what careless writing means: "The complexity of the characters in Shakespeare have been ignored," he says; and again: "If Caesar had been guilty, Brutus would be justified." Yes, the chairman of the English Department.

An editorial in the *Portland Oregonian* praises the "laudatory conduct" of a trial judge; another criticizes voters for their "disinterest" in the school budget. A picture caption describes two children in a patch of flowers as "inspecting fauna." Yes, the *Oregonian*.

The New Yorker knew that two and one do not make two; the chairman of the English Department knew that *complexity,* a singular noun, takes a singular verb, and he meant to say that Brutus "would have been" justified; the *Oregonian* knew that *laudatory* is not *laudable, disinterest,* not *lack of interest,* and *fauna* not *flora.* But they all were in a hurry.

So what can I say, except don't be in such a hurry?

I may deplore the slips, but I make slips, too; we are all human. There is a school of thought, however, which actually blesses bad grammar and confused syntax. I do not deplore members of that school; I curse them.

I anathematize, for instance, the Council on College Composition and Communicaton. Insistence on accuracy in spelling, grammar, punctuation, and vocabulary, says the council, inhibits a student's "creativity and individuality." Students have a right to their own language.

Examples of the effects of this criminal approach were assembled by J. Miller Morse, professor of English at Temple University. The passages that follow, says Professor Morse, are all from compositions of college students majoring in English:

• George Orwell makes me feel like I was desserted on some destitute island in Politics and the English languages. He points out the destruction of the language, is caused by people, attempting to decieve the writing and using bad speech practices.

- The victims screems for helping herself was effident thru all the allies around 100 Murch Avenue as if the thick smoke billowing from a factorys exhaust pipe.

- The blind and the death suffer unjustly because of there handicapped which are considered as being dim witness and are felt to be in a class for the retarded even when there not.

- In are times the responcable writer must read the hand writeing on the wall so he can asses the human conditions.

- Joyce was liveing symotanious to Kafka all though the did not aide each other in utilizing the same standart of excellent like stream of conscience.

- The modren day literature has it's good merit's as well as it's bad ones but I don't think so.

The Seattle student who wrote this description of the human innards must be in college by now:

> The human body is composed of three parts: the Brainium, the Borax, and the Abominable Cavity. The Brainium contains the brain. The Borax contains the lungs, the liver, and the living things. The Abominable Cavity contains the bowels, of which there are five: A, E, I, O, and U.

27 APRIL

☿

Metamorphosis

—*Louis Phillips*

28 APRIL
☿

Don't Quote Me

Frequently one's memory of a familiar quotation is off the mark by as little as a single trifling letter or punctuation mark. In the 1930s, columnist-wit F.P.A. devised the following quiz to put people like you and me in the dunce's corner. If you don't miss at least one of these questions, I have no wish to meet you; you are insufferable.

1. Complete the first line of "Rock Me to Sleep" beginning "Backward, turn backward . . ."
2. What is the first line of "The Old Oaken Bucket"?
3. From "The Rime of the Ancient Mariner," complete the line "Water, water everywhere . . ."
4. What words follow "Alas, poor Yorick"?
5. What grow "from little acorns"?
6. Finish the line "Breathes there . . ."
7. Finish the line " 'Twas the night before Christmas . . ."

29 APRIL
☿

Funnels and Salmon

Christian Morgenstern, surrealist German poet of the early twentieth century, was as ingenious as Ogden Nash in his puns and alliterations:

A PAIR OF FUNNELS

A pair of funnels stroll by night. They both
collect inside themselves the white moonlight, so clear, so calm, so bright,
which then runs down the runnels
of these funnels, making
their woodland way
much brighter,
und so
weit-
er.
—*Christian Morgenstern*
(translated by
Geoffrey Grigson)

THE SALMON

To Switzerland, right up the Rhine,
A salmon swam.

He managed one by one each
Salmon-dam.

Up, up he went, to God knows where,
And there,

Twelve feet or more above him, rose
A weir.

Ten feet he jumped, so well, and fell,
Dismayed.

Below that Alp three
Weeks he stayed.

And then turned round at last
And swam,

In silence, back to Amst-
erdam.

—Christian Morgenstern
(translated by
Geoffrey Grigson)

 **30 APRIL**

Assault and Battery

—Bruce McMillan

MAY

1 MAY
♉

Sing a Song of Tupping

The English leap from bed each May Day morning, crying out:

> Hurray, hurray! the first of May!
> Hedgerow tupping begins today!

Wherefore:

> Welcome to the month wherein
> Hedgerow tupping doth begin.
> (Just in England, though, my dear;
> We are much too moral here.)

Tupping is a euphemism, but it will serve. This is a day for praising the Lord who created us male and female. Here, tupping was clearly on the mind of the Prince of Wales, later Edward VII. He was ogling Lillie Langtry, an actress and professional beauty whose birthplace was the Isle of Jersey. The sweater known as the jersey is named in her honor.

> The Prince of Wales saw Lillie in her sweater,
> And approved.
> He liked the look of Lillie even better
> When the sweater
> Was removed.
>   —*W.R.E.*

Gerontologic tupping:

> He would tup and she would tup
> Fanning faded fire
> Tickle up and tickle up
> Ashes of desire.
>   —*W.R.E.*

This is a day for a second honeymoon:

TWO WHO SINGLE

> Two who, single,
> Learned that tingle
> Turns to trouble,

121

> Now, yoked double,
> Guiltless mingle.
> No more trouble;
> No more tingle.
> —*W.R.E.*

It is also a day for ending such frustrations as this:

INFLATION IS A BAD THING

> Inflation is a bad thing,
>   But unemployment, worse;
> All men derived from Adam
>   Have felt this double curse:
>
> Have tossed at night, recalling
>   Past rapturous enjoyment—
> Bemoaning the inflation
>   That stems from unemployment.
> —*W.R.E.*

> 'Twixt sleep and wake the prick she plied
>   Until it took a stand;
> And still it stands, unsatisfied,
>   Awake in sleeping hand.
> —*W.R.E.*

REPLYING TO THE CONTENTION OF JOSEPH BRODSKY IN THE NEW YORK REVIEW OF BOOKS THAT NINETY PERCENT OF THE BEST LYRIC POETRY IS WRITTEN AFTER SEXUAL INTERCOURSE

> A poetry critic named Brodsky
> Came up with this theory oddsky:
>   "Most love songs to sweetum
>   Are writ postcoitum."
> Not mine, Joe; more often I nodsky.
> —*W.R.E.*

2 MAY

Last Words of Animals

1. The Mouse: Precious dark and smells of cheese.
2. The Turtle: They are mocking me.

3. The Hare: Over to you, tortoise.
4. The Flea: And now for Abraham's bosom.
5. The Dog: I have passed the last lamppost.
6. The Tarantula Spider: Darling, this is the greatest moment of my life.
7. The Worm: I turn—to dust.
8. The Phoenix: May I trouble you for a match?
9. The Steer: What bloody man is this?
10. The Skunk: Strew over me roses, roses.
11. The Pig: I hope to save my bacon.
12. The Bee: No flowers, if you please.
13. The Dragon: Where's George?
14. The Snail: This house to let.
15. The Wasp: Stung.
16. The Ant: So much to do, so little done.
17. The Locust: I have no more territorial claims.
18. The Ostrich: Where's that sand?
19. The Lark: I shall not be getting up early tomorrow.
20. The Slug: How I regret my salad days.
21. The Rooster: What will happen to the sun?
22. The Cat: I'm going to look at a king.
23. The Camel: I feel the penultimate straw.
24. The Walrus: The time has come.
25. The Lobster: Why are you all blushing?
26. The Crocodile: Tears, idle tears.
27. The Swan: I think I am going to sing.
28. The Chameleon: I wonder, shall I wear my flame or my white?
29. The Weasel: Pop.
30. The Peacock: Pray put out my tails.

—New Statesman

3 MAY

"*The Black Stinking Fume Thereof*"

"Warning," says the legend on your package of cigarettes: "The Surgeon General Has Determined That Cigarette Smoking Is Dangerous to Your Health." This excoriation by King James I is considerably more eloquent than that of the Surgeon General:

> Should men not bee ashamed, to sit tossing off tobacco pipes, and puffing of the smoke of Tobacco one to another, making the filthy smoke and stinke thereof, to exhale athwart the dishes, and infect the aire, when very

often men that abhorre it are at their repast? . . . it makes a kitchin also oftentimes in the inward parts of men, soiling and infecting them, with an unctuous and oily kind of Soote, as hath bene found in some great Tobacco takers, that after their death were opened.

. . . Have you not reason then to bee ashamed, and to forbear this filthie noveltie . . . a custome loathsome to the eye, hateful to the nose, harmefull to the braine, dangerous to the Lungs, and in the black stinking fume thereof, nearest resembling the horrible Stigian smoke of the pit that is bottomless.

4 MAY
♉

Odd Ends

- *Sanka* brings five cups of coffee in French Canada. *Dry martini* brings three servings in Germany. (*Word Ways* does not mention that the natural response to "sanka" in the United States is "You're welcome.")
- Logophiles call a word that remains a word after dropping any one letter a *charitable* word. The charitable word *seat* can shrink to *sea, set, sat,* or *eat.*
- A word that becomes a different word through the addition of an appropriate letter is a *hospitable* word. The hospitable word *rap* welcomes *trap, reap, rasp,* and *rapt.*
- The longest common word having only two vowels is *latchstrings.*
- *Strengthlessness* is not only a common three-syllable word of staggering length, but also a univocalic; it employs only the vowel *e.*
- A laxative manufacturer coined the name *Serutan* for its product, and reminded customers that Serutan is "nature's" spelled backward. Such a reversal would be less winsome in the case of the acid neutralizer Tums or the liqueur Bols. And would Embargo be an acceptable name for a brassiere?
- James Rambo devised a sentence that uses the vowels in order, one to a word: "Schmaltz's strength thrills throngs, sculpts rhymes." Somehow, though, an extra *e* slipped into that last word. How about "Ann's bed is old but dry"?
- Fill in the seven missing initials of the words below to spell out a proper noun. Then try again; you may find another:

-umble

-mpire

-atter

-onics

-rinal

-aster

-arely

—Word Ways

5 MAY
☿

Snallygaster III

CHARLES McC. MATHIAS, JR.
MARYLAND

REPLY TO:
358 Russell Senate Office Building
Washington, D.C. 20510

United States Senate
WASHINGTON, D.C. 20510

May 2, 1978

Mr. Willard R. Espy
30 Beekman Place
New York, New York 10022

Dear Mr. Espy:

Your letter to Mr. Rhoderick contains only one
positive statement, and that, alas, is also wrong! You
said, "I am willing to concede that there really is a
Commonwealth of Maryland." There may be a Commonwealth
of Massachusetts and a Commonwealth of Virginia, but
there is no "Commonwealth of Maryland."

Maryland is, in fact, the Free State of Maryland.
It is so called because of highly vocal opposition to the
Volstead Act. Some of us might prefer that we had earned
the title "Free State" by our early practice of religious
tolerance or by the early assertion of the right of women's
suffrage.

The ancient liberties of Maryland are so firmly rooted
that it was not until the Federal Government turned off the
tap on Congressman John Boynton Philip Clayton Hill that
our yelps for freedom established for all the time our right
to the title, the "Free State."

Be that as it may, we are the Free State of Maryland, the
only one in the Union, and proud of it.

As for further word on the snallygaster-snollygoster
controversy, I enclose Mr. William Safire's latest comment.

Sincerely,

Charles McC. Mathias, Jr.

CM:lrs

cc: Mr. Safire
     Mr. Rhoderick

The New York Times
WASHINGTON BUREAU
1920 L STREET, N.W.
WASHINGTON, D.C. 20036
(202) 293-3100

WILLIAM SAFIRE

Dear Mac —

A snally gate flies
with its left wing,
while a snally gate
flies with its right
wing. that's the
difference.

Best

Bill

The Senator may be real, after all.

MORE ON 9 MAY.

6 MAY

Nixno, Nixon, and Carter

Shortly after his triumphant reelection in 1972, President Richard M. Nixon ordered a radical change in the spelling of his name—from N I X O N to N I X N O—in order, as he explained in a hastily arranged television appearance viewed by

3,281,000,028 people around the world, "to make everything perfectly clear." His standing in the polls plummeted, and soon afterward he was driven from office.

He can't blame me. During the campaign I had sent him this warning, for which no acknowledgment is to be found in my files:

> You'll make it, Mr. Nixon,
>   Unless you change your name;
> As Onnix, Xinno, Noxin,
>   You'll never be the same.
>
> A candidate named Innox
>   Will find his chances few,
> And if your name is Xonni
>   I will not vote for you.
>   —*W.R.E.*

*   *   *

The Greek palindrome below, inscribed upon a baptismal font in Hagia Sophia, in Istanbul, may go back to the sixth century, fourteen centuries before Nixon and Watergate. I hope some traveler will inform me whether it is still there.

N I 4 O N   A N O M E M A T A   M H   M O N A N   O 4 I N

νίψον	ἀνομήχτλ	μψ̀	μοναν	ὄψιν
wash	sins	not	only	face

In the 1980 elections, President Carter was charged with reversing himself on major issues to save votes. Professor Edward Scher of New York University summed up the accusation in an immortal palindrome:

TO LAST, CARTER RETRACTS A LOT.

At about the same time, the French press coined *carterisme,* to signify confusion.

7 MAY
♉

The Musical Ass

> The fable which I now present
> Occurred to me by accident;
> And whether bad or excellent,
> Is merely so by accident.
>
> A stupid ass this morning went
> Into a field by accident;

And cropped his food, and was content,
Until he spied by accident
A flute, which some oblivious gent
Had left behind by accident;

When, sniffing it with eager scent,
He breathed on it by accident,
And made the hollow instrument
Emit a sound by accident.
"Hurrah, hurrah!" exclaimed the brute,
"How cleverly I play the flute!"

Moral.

A fool, in spite of nature's bent,
May shine for once—by accident.
                    —*Tomaso de Yriarte*

8 MAY

Ce Même Vieux Coon

Ce même vieux coon n'est pas quite mort,
    Il n'est pas seulement napping.
Je pense, myself, unless j'ai tort,
    Cette chose est yet to happen.

En dix-huit forty-four, je say,
    Vous'll hear des curious noises;
He'll whet ses dents against some Clay,
    Et scare des Loco—Bois-es!

You know qui quand il est awake,
    Et quand il scratch ses clawses,
Les Locos dans leurs souliers shake,
    Et, sheepish, hang leur jaws-es.

Ce même vieux coon je ne sais pas why,
    Le mischief's coming across him,
Il fait believe he's going to die,
    Quand seulement playing 'possum.

Mais wait till nous le want encore,
    Nous'll stir him with une pole;
He'll bite as mauvais as before
    Nous pulled him de son hole!
                    —*Anonymous*

AESTIVATION

In candent ire the solar splendour flames;
The foles, languescent, pend from arid rames;
His humid front the cive, anheling, wipes,
And dreams of erring on ventiferous ripes.

How dulce to vive occult to mortal eyes,
Dorm on the herb with none to supervise,
Carp the suave berries from the crescent vine,
And bive the flow from longicaudate kine!

To me, alas! no verdurous visions come,
Save yon exiguous pool's conferva-scum—
No concave vast repeats the tender hue
That laves my milk-jug with celestial blue.

Me wretched! let me curr to quercine shades!
Effund your albid hausts, lactiferous maids!
Oh, might I vole to some umbrageous clump,—
Depart,—be off,—excede,—evade,—erump!
                    —*Oliver Wendell Holmes*

Paul Hollister recalls this semi-macaronic from his high school days:

Amo, amas
I loved a lass
Ah me, but she was tender!
Amas, amat
She left me flat
I hate the feminine gender.
                    —*Anonymous*

9 MAY
♉

Snallygaster IV

O me of little faith! There truly is a George Rhoderick, and therefore a Senator Mathias, and therefore a United States Senate, and, therefore, perhaps, even a United States of America. How good it is to know these things!

Here are extracts from a letter which arrived today:

Dear Mr. Espy:
   I assure you that I am very much alive, and have been since the year 1895, and thus can offer some first-hand information concerning the animal (or bird, or beast) which has generated the present exchange of letters.

First, let me assure you that Senator Charles McC. Mathias is indeed the legislative solon he claims to be. He is a native of our own Frederick County, which is delightfully referred to by its many residents as "rural Maryland."

President Harry S. Truman's "Snollygoster" must not have been an ancestor of Maryland's famed "Snallygaster," for according to your own research this nineteenth-century phenomenon was a member of the human race—albeit a "bastard." This "Snollygoster," which was called into being in the 1860s, according to your own report, and which is affirmed by William Safire, of the *New York Times,* in his *The Language of Politics,* apparently did "fall asleep" after the "pressing need for it no longer existed," and was only revived by President Truman as one of his many familiar and cogent expletives with which he blasted his political antagonists.

But it was in the year 1909 that the monstrous and reason-defying "Snallygaster" appeared over the reaches of the beautiful and historic Middletown Valley of western Maryland.

Its introduction to the people of the Middletown Valley was made by my father, the late George Carlton Rhoderick, who was in the year 1909 the editor and proprietor of the *Valley Register.* I am sending you a copy of the article which introduced the creature to the paper's readers. Later I will send you copies of the following two articles.

Sincerely yours,
Geo. C. Rhoderick, Jr.
President, *The Valley Register, Inc.*

Perhaps Senator Mathias and I have been talking at cross-purposes. There is a snollygoster, and there is a snallygaster, two distinct breeds, both still extant.

MORE ON 16 MAY.

10 MAY

Ȣ

More Words of Wood

Arthur Miller, sitting alone in a bar, was approached by a well-tailored, slightly tiddly fellow who addressed him thus:

"Aren't you Arthur Miller?"

"Why, yes, I am."

"Don't you remember me?"

"Well . . . your face seems familiar."

"Why, Art, I'm your old buddy Sam! We went to high school together! We went out on double dates!"

"I'm afraid I—"

"I guess you can see I've done all right. Department stores. What do *you* do, Art?"

"Well, I . . . write."

"Whaddya write?"

"Plays, mostly."

"Ever get any produced?"

"Yes, some."

"Would I know any?"

"Well . . . perhaps you've heard of *Death of a Salesman*?"

Sam's jaw dropped; his face went white. For a moment he was speechless. Then he cried out, "Why, you're ARTHUR MILLER!"

I was reminded of this story when I heard this morning from Clement Wood, whose earlier letter is recorded on 9 April.

Alas, my Wood is after all not, it appears, the man who wrote *The Complete Rhyming Dictionary* nearly fifty years ago. My Wood writes: "I revere that master of rhymes. I consult him. I admire his impromptu verses. But I believe he is indeed dead. God rest his soul."

I still plan to call on my Mr. Wood in Greece. I would travel a long way to meet the man whose latest letter encloses this beguiling tribute to the game of Scrabble®:

DEATH OF A SCRABBLE MASTER

This was the greatest of the game's great players:
If you played BRAS, he'd make it HUDIBRASTIC.
He ruled a world 15 by 15 squares,
Peopled by 100 letters, wood or plastic.

He unearthed XEBEC, HAJI, useful QAID,
Found QUOS (see pl. of QUID PRO QUO) and QUOTHA,
Discovered AU, DE, DA all unitalicized
(AU JUS, DA CAPO, ALMANACH DE GOTHA).

Two-letter words went marching through his brain,
Spondaic-footed, singing their slow litany:
AL (Indian mulberry), AI (a sloth), EM, EN,
BY, MY, AX, EX, OX, LO, IT, AN, HE . . .

PE (Hebrew letter), LI (a Chinese mile), KA, RE,
SH (like NTH, spectacularly vowelless),
AY, OY (a cry of grief, pain or dismay);
HAI, HI, HO—leaving opponents powerless.

He, if the tiles before him said DOC TIME,
Would promptly play the elegant DEMOTIC,
And none but he fulfilled the scrabbler's dream,
When, through two triple words, he hung QUIXOTIC.

The day his adversary put down GNASHED,
He laid—a virtuoso feat—beneath it GOUTIER,
So placed that six more tiny words were hatched:
GO NU, AT, SI, then (as you've seen, no doubt) HE, ER.

Plagued by a glut of U's, he racked up TUMULUS,
Produced ILLICIT when he had a boom in I's.
When once he couldn't hang his pretty AZIMUTH,
He found a dangling E, created HUMANIZE!*

Receive him, EARTH (HEART's anagram is there);
His memory all players BLEES (var., BLESS, Scot.).
Inscribe his CENOTAPH (CAT PHONE) "I ACTS QUEER,"
for which he would of course read "REQUIESCAT."

—*Clement Biddle Wood*

11 MAY

♉

Why Are You So Tired?

The bathtub, says a legend on a paper napkin, was invented in 1850, and the telephone in 1875. This means that if you had been living in 1850, you could have rested in the bathtub twenty-five years without the phone ringing.

Modern conveniences notwithstanding, we seem to be tired most of the time these days. Here is a possible explanation:

> The next time people ask you why you are tired, tell them. Your exhaustion is fully justified and you can prove it by a few simple statistics: The U.S. has a population of over 200 million. Of these, 72 million are over 65, leaving 128 million to do the work. When you subtract from this the 75 million people under 21, you get 53 million. There are also 27,471,002 employed by the federal government in one capacity or another which leaves 25,528,998 to do the work. The 8 million in the armed forces leaves only 17,528,998 to do the work, and when you subtract from this the 15 million on state and city government payrolls, and the 1,520,000 in hospitals, mental institutions, and similar places, the work force is reduced to 1,008,998.
>
> Fine, but there are an estimated 800,500 bums, vagrants, and others with a pathological fear of work. That leaves 208,498 people to carry the national workload, 208,496 of whom are presently behind bars. Which, brother, leaves you and me. And I don't know about you, but I'm getting tired.
>
> —*Author unknown*

There are reports that we have grown too tired to keep the economy, not to mention society itself, under control:

---

*An examination of tournament records confirms that the T in AZIMUTH was a blank.—*CBW*

SOLOMON GRUNDY

Solomon Grundy
Bought gas on Monday,
Filled up on Tuesday,
Once more on Wednesday,
Two tanks on Thursday,
Also on Friday,
Ditto on Sunday.
Anybody want to trade a Datsun even-up
For the powder-blue, all-optionals-included,
Comfort-Control, 1981 Cadillac of Solomon Grundy?
—*Frank Jacobs*

12 MAY
♉

Philander Is a Wallaby?

Which of the following definitions (per *Webster's New International Dictionary,* second edition) is correct?

1. bole—*a.* a crumbly clay; *b.* a dose; *c.* the momentum of one gram moving with a velocity of one centimeter per second; *d.* a recess or cupboard in a wall.

2. breve—*a.* a letter of authorization; *b.* a double whole note; *c.* to post accounts; *d.* one of a family of Asian and Australian birds.

3. brock—*a.* a male red deer two years old; *b.* a horse; *c.* the European badger; *d.* a cow.

4. cade—*a.* a European juniper; *b.* a barrel, cask, or keg; *c.* a measure of herrings, orig. 720; *d.* a spoiled child.

5. cope—*a.* to muzzle a ferret by sewing up its mouth; *b.* the tongue or pole of an oxcart; *c.* the duty paid to the lord of a manor on the ore raised; *d.* the top part of a set of flasks.

6. crap—*a.* buckwheat; *b.* residue from rendered fat; *c.* money; *d.* the gallows.

7. drag—*a.* a planker; *b.* a fox's trail; *c.* a drogue; *d.* a kind of coach.

8. dun—*a.* to cure codfish; *b.* a fortified residence surrounded by a moat; *c.* a May fly; *d.* to resound.

9. flag—*a.* a slice cut in plowing; *b.* a partitition between grate rooms; *c.* a groat, fourpence; *d.* a woman.

10. frith—*a.* a narrow arm of the sea; *b.* a hedge, esp. a wattled hedge; *c.* to preserve in peace; *d.* unused pasture land.

11. gib—*a.* to act like a cat; *b.* a removable plate to hold other parts in place; *c.* a male salmon; *d.* a prison.

12. hob—*a.* the male ferret; *b.* a quoits pin; *c.* to clear of tufts; *d.* a cutting tool consisting of a fluted steel worm.

13. kip—*a.* a piece of wood used in playing two-up; *b.* 1,000 pounds; *c.* 40.68 pounds; *d.* the common tern.

14. moil—*a.* a steel bar sharpened to a point; *b.* a hornless ox; *c.* to moisten or wet; *d.* to burrow.

—*Girard Orway*

13 MAY

♉

Morituri Te Salutamus

A verse to impress on my readers the correct spelling of *minuscule*:

MORITURI TE SALUTAMUS

(When publishers war, says a book column, marginal writers perish.)

About to die, we hail you as we goosestep to the field;
We'll be back a little later, either with or on our shield.
We're a thin red line o' 'eroes, yet you look at us askance
If we but hint you might increase our minuscule advance—
Minu, minu, minuscule Advance, VANCE, V A N C E.

For you, O Caesar, we expend our cannonades of prose;
We slash, we stab, we lop a limb, we bloody up a nose.
Like bayonets our vowels rage, like swords our conson*ants*;
O, can't you add a tittle to our minuscule advance—
Minu, minu, minuscule Advance, VANCE, V A N C E?

While you stick pins in battle maps, we to the death contend
With someone not our enemy, who might have been our friend.
For you we draw and quarter him with verbal ele*gance,*
And you come up, dear Caesar, with a minuscule advance—
Minu, minu, minuscule Advance, VANCE, V A N C E.

Though *Roots* he raise against us—yea, though *Jaws* against us raise he—
We'll sweep the field with *Scruples,* and repeat with *Princess Daisy.*
About to die, we hail you. But, O Caesar, do enhance . . .
Enlarge . . . augment . . . aye, multiply our minuscule advance—
Minu, minu, minuscule Advance, VANCE, V A N C E.

(A muttering as of distant thunder, with heat lightning on
the horizon:)

You haven't got a minu-, minu-, minusculish chance.
—*W.R.E.*

14 MAY
☿

Must I Undress, Tovarich?

Time says Russian tourists generally carry the official Russian-English phrase book. If asked how he enjoyed his flight to the United States, a tourist may consult his phrase book and reply, "Flying in the TU-114, I felt myself excellently." Confused by a question, he may read out, syllable by syllable: "I don't know En-glish. I know no other lang-uage except my native tongue. The study of foreign lang-uag-es is greatly de-veloped in our coun-try." Dining in a restaurant, he may call the waiter and recite: "Please give me curds, sower cream, fried chicks, pulled bread and one jel-ly fish."

Time reports that if the tourist falls sick, he is likely to complain to the doctor of "a poisoning, a noseache, an eye-pain or quinsy," followed by a plaintive "Must I undress?"

If shopping for his wife, he may request "a ladies' worsted-nylon swimming pants."

A Russian woman at a beauty salon is likely to say, "Make me a hairdress," "sprinkle my head," or (God forbid, says *Time*), "I want my hair frizzled."

Nor does the Russian tourist neglect subjects of more significance. "Show us your devices for outer space research work," he may read from his handbook; "how powerful is this reactor? Show me a working diagram of this reactor." Or, "Whose invention is this? When was this invention patented? This is a Soviet invention."

Frederick F. Snyder, who teaches Russian at Harvard, admires the language for its down-to-earth character. "A dredge," he says, "is called, literally, an earth sucker, and a vacuum cleaner, by analogy, a dust sucker. Since the root is the verb *to suck,* you can imagine how a student's mind expands on the basic pattern."

Professor Snyder wrote me of a perhaps apocryphal dialect called Blue Russian, "spoken by about sixteen persons scattered widely over the Valdai Hills." Blue Russian is so called "because of the characteristic tint of the faces of speakers as they hold their breaths while pronouncing imperfective—frequentative and durative—word forms."

In Blue Russian, *bit'* means "to beat"; *pobit'* means "to do a little beating." The secondary imperfective form is *pobivyvat'*. *Zapobit'* means "to start to do a little beating," and its imperfective is *zapobivyvat'*. *Perezapobivyvat'* means "to begin all over again to do a little beating"; its imperfective is *perezapobivyvat',* which may be rendered "to make a practice of making fresh starts on projects involving a limited amount of beating." Hence, says Professor Snyder, the handy expression: *shkol'-nodvorovyj perezapobivyvujushchij,* "schoolyard bully."

A computer was asked to translate the English phrase "Out of sight, out of mind," into Russian and then translate it back into English. Consider the modern miracle of what came back: "Invisible insanity"!

15 MAY
Ȣ

A Windiness of Words

Windy phrases that drive editors up the wall:

- Did not have   for   lacked
- Did not succeed   for   failed
- Are able to   for   can
- Would be able to   for   could
- Will have to   for   must
- Most of the time   for   usually
- The great majority   for   most
- Almost never   for   seldom
- With regard to   for   about
- More than a few   for   several
- In spite of the fact
  that   for   although
- In the near future   for   soon
- Is well aware   for   knows
- Making a particular
  point of   for   emphasizing
- Made up his mind   for   decided

—Wesley Price

Mr. Price also lists "sentence openers we can do without," to wit:
Paradoxically . . . typically . . . ironically . . . curiously . . . surprisingly . . . furthermore . . . consequently . . . significantly . . . essentially . . . amazingly . . . and hopefully.

I am guilty of most of these lapses. Not, hopefully, of hopefully.

LOVE SONG OF A GRAMMARIAN

You hint—you "take it"—you *pretend*
    That I implied what you infer—
Count written what I haven't penned;
    Count promised what I won't aver.

Inferring what I'm not implying,
    You throw into a parlous state
Our pretty game; you lie unlying;
    You intimately intimate.

'Twixt inference and implication
It takes a Solomon to span
The gulf of misinterpretation
Between a woman and a man.
—*W.R.E.*

16 MAY
☿

Snallygaster V

From the *Valley Register,* Middletown, Maryland, February 12, 1909:

MONSTER GO-DEVIL, OR WINGED BOVALUPUS, IN THIS SECTION OF MARYLAND

It Killed Bill Gifferson in New Jersey—Nearly Caught a Woman at Williamsport—Shot at Near Hagerstown—Seen at Shepherdstown—Laid Egg Near Burkittsville—Government to Send Troops After It.

The terrible beast that has been causing so much alarm in New Jersey is undoubtedly headed this way. The creature was first heard from in New Jersey about a month ago, when its tracks in the snow were observed. They could be seen in a field, and then they would entirely disappear. This was the source of much mystery until it was discovered that the fearful beast could fly as well as it could walk. James Harding was the first man to see it, and he described it as a sort of cross between a vampire, a tiger, and a bovalupus. It has enormous wings, a long pointed bill, four legs armed with claws like steel hooks, one eye in the center of its forehead, and it screeches like a locomotive whistle. . . . Bill Gifferson was the first victim of the Go-Devil, or whatever it may be called. He was walking along a country road when it swooped down upon him, carried him to the top of a high hill and, perching there, pierced his jugular vein with its needle-like bill and slowly sucked his blood while it gently fanned him with its wings.

The beast was seen near Hagerstown last week. George Jacobs was out hunting when he saw a strange-looking thing flying over his head. He thoughtlessly fired at it, but the shot rattled from its tough hide as if he had shot against an iron plate. The enraged Go-Devil took after him and he barely escaped by dodging into a stable and slamming the door. Its yawps were fearful.

The *Shepherdstown Register* reports that the great beast was seen along the cliffs about a half-mile above that town last week and that the government was notified of its presence there.

MORE TO COME ON 10 JUNE.

17 MAY

♉

Bowwow, Dingdong, and Pooh-pooh

bowwow theory n : a theory that language originated in imitations of natural sounds (as those of birds, dogs, or thunder).

dingdong theory n : a theory that language originated out of a natural correspondence between objects of sense perception and the vocal noises which were a part of early man's reaction to them.

pooh-pooh theory n : a theory that language originated in interjections that gradually acquired meaning.

—*Webster's Third New International Dictionary*

Apple-biting Adam spied
  Lovely Eve anew.
Did he imitate a dove?
  Did he bill and coo?
Or did sense perceptions speed
  To his brain and through,
Causing him to voice a noise
  Meaning "I love you"?

Which are right and which are wrong,
Bowwow theorists or dingdong?

Other scholars base their claim
  On another clue:
They say Adam blurted, "Ah!
  "Wow!" "Oho!" or "Ooh!"—
Interjections which would all
  More than likely do,
So that their conjecture seems
  Sound as the other two.

Which one's got it, anyhow—
Pooh-pooh, dingdong, or bowwow?

Happy breed whose chase has such
  Cheerful beasts in view!

We, the others, wonder, as
    Thunderclouds accrue,
What new sound will signify
    Human speech is through—
Whimper? Bang? Old Gabriel's
    Final view halloo?

Cataclysm, which are you:
Bowwow, dingdong, or pooh-pooh?
          —Ormonde de Kay

18 MAY

♉

Quis Praecipiet Praeceptorem?

Asked what courses he taught, a distinguished professor of medieval literature said
blankly, "Teach? I do not teach; I *publish*."

"Then you never meet your students?" I inquired.

"Oh, yes—I need them to help with my research."

That night I was troubled by anxiety dreams. In the morning I deciphered the
following scrawl in my bedside notebook:

ELEGIAC STRAINS / FOR ATHELFORD BAINES

Let us mourn the demise of poor Athelford Baines,
    Who died from prostration of overworked brains.
At the age of thirteen he received his B.A.
    And added a Master's the following day;

Then requested of Harvard, and Princeton, and Yale,
    By postcard, a doctor's degree through the mail.
His simple suggestion fortuitously
    Seemed an answer to prayer to Profs. *A, B,* and *C.*

(I conceal their cognomens, lest readers should quail
    Whose *alma ma*'s Harvard, or Princeton, or Yale)—
Titanical scholars, so far above reach
    No provost has ever dared ask them to teach

(Though undergrads trailing them over the quad
    Report they give seminars often to God).
And the wage paid these three turns the comptrollers pale
    At Harvard and Princeton, as well as at Yale.

Their students are rumors, no more, to these three
    (Here cleverly hidden as *C, A,* and *B*),
Except when employed in unnatural acts
    Described by us laymen as Getting the Facts,

To flesh out the tomes even doctors must brew
    To win the applause of *Scholastic Review.*
The text may seem gibberish to the canaille,
    But resplends one's resplendence at Harve, Prince, or Yale.

It happened, when Athelford's postcards came in,
    A was mired in research on the Merits of Sin,
While *B* was proposing to wipe out the cl**
    By keeping us standing, thus leaving no lap.

C was looking for proof that a nursemaid's sly tickle
    Had caused the neurosis of *Peregrine Pickle.*
The three saw at once they were certain to scale
    New glories at Princeton, or Harvard, or Yale,

With a helper so smart he could boil down his brains
    To fit in a postcard signed "Athelford Baines."
So Athelford Baines won his candidacy
    Not for just *one* Ph.D., but for *three.*

From midnight till seven, he putrefied in
    That odious wallow, *The Merits of Sin;*
Then tested till noon this astounding idea:
    To stand at attention will halt gonorrhea.

Till dinner he tickled the various spots
    He thought might have given young Smollett the hots—
Until a synapse went "Synapse!" in his head,
    And, to his annoyance, he found himself dead.

"Alas," his last thought was, "my headstone must read,
    '*Hic jacet* young Baines, who died un-Ph.D'd.' "
Yet what a performance!: *A* had a big win
    In his seminal treatise, *The Merits of Sin;*

While *B*'s war on laps (lacking chastity belts)
    Put a *finis* to cl** and to quite a bit else.
C's tome tickled backs, tickled sides, tickled fronts,
    And part of the time tickled all parts at once.

Each evening as A, B, and C count their kale
    At Harvard, and Princeton, and also at Yale,
Please God they remember, while adding their gains,
    To pray for the soul of poor Athelford Baines.

                                  —*W.R.E.*

19 MAY
☿

Passing the Buck to Magoo

Dr. Magoo, of the animated cartoons, is an acronym for Mark Goodson, the television producer, and looks like him. "Buck," American slang for a dollar, came into use as the post-Revolutionary pioneers in the Appalachian hills traded their hides for goods. A good buckskin was worth a dollar in trade—a "buck." A doe's skin was worth less, since it was smaller; hence "doe" for money in general, not for a specific amount.

—*Larry K. Fosgate*

I know nothing of Dr. Magoo, but there are other possible origins for *buck* and *dough.*

A counter used in a poker pot—sometimes a jackknife—was also known as a buck. The counter went to the winner of the pot, whence "pass the buck" and "the buck stops here." When the silver dollar came on the scene, it commonly served as a buck and took the name. (I have no idea why that counter was called a buck in the first place.) The hide and the counter seem to have joined forces to imprint the slang term in the language.

Doe as the source of *dough,* money in general, is unlikely, though it may have helped. (For Richard Wilbur's opinion, see 13 March.) A more probable connotation is the relationship of money to bread, the staff of life: "Man does not live by bread alone." From "bread" to "dough" was an easy transition, and indeed the round trip is now complete: *Bread* is as synonymous for money as *dough.*

The name *Buffalo,* New York, is an Indian corruption of *belle fleuve,* French for "beautiful river." This was the exclamation of Father Hennepin, the Belgian priest and explorer, when he first saw the Hudson. But *buffalo,* the animal, is from Greek *bubalos*—in turn from *bus,* "ox."

Sabotage is from the French *sabot,* "a wooden shoe." In the recurrent strife between lords and peasants, long antedating the French Revolution, the peasants stomped in their wooden shoes on newly planted fields to prevent growth. They also threw the shoes into the machinery of textile mills, wrecking the apparatus. Presto: *sabotage.*

20 MAY
☿

The Food of Love

R. M. Walsh built a verse in the *Saturday Evening Post* around metaphors of food— "She takes the cake," "some tomato," "full of baloney," and so on. I thank him for these conceits, some of which I have borrowed here:

Johnny boy was top banana,
  Johnny boy was full of beans;
Johnny boy brought home the bacon—
  Plenty lettuce in his jeans.

Johnny boy fell hard for Anna,
  Thought her sweet as apple pie,
Yet could not her love awaken—
  She had other fish to fry.

Johnny boy grows soft as custard,
  In a pretty pickle he;
Milk of human kindness stumbles—
  He's not Anna's cup of tea.

Johnny boy can't cut the mustard,
  Anna keeps him in a stew.
That's the way the cookie crumbles;
  I say fudge, and so should you.
                              —W.R.E.

21 MAY

I Do Not Love Thee

Certain epigrammatic verses recur, written in different languages and attributed to different authors. The first-century Latin poet Martial wrote: "*Non amo te, Sabidi, nec possum dicere quare; / Hoc tanto possum dicere, non amo te.*" ("I do not love thee, Sabidus, nor can I say why; but this much I can say, I do not love thee.") In the seventeenth century an Oxford student named Tom Brown, told to translate this passage, produced the famous quatrain:

I do not love thee, Dr. Fell;
The reason why I cannot tell;

But this alone I know full well:
I do not love thee, Dr. Fell.

An even earlier rendition:

ANTIPATHY

I love him not; but shew no reason can
Wherefore, but this: *I do not love the man.*
                              —*Author unknown*

This French version was contemporaneous with Tom Brown's:

Je ne vous aime pas, Hylas;
Je n'en saurois dire la cause,

Je sais seulement une chose:
C'est que je ne vous aime pas.
                    —*Comte de Bussy-Rabutin*

22 MAY

Maudit Soit Ton Père

Francis H. Wilson believes, and I have no reason to dispute him, that the longest curse word is German: *Himmelherrgottkreuzmillionendonnerwetter!* We cannot touch it. We are backward in anathema; our vocabulary of invective centers on tired obscenities. A magazine named *Maledicta* is trying to reform us, but it has a downhill road to travel.

The Spaniards, ceremonious in polite conversation, convey the ultimate insult with a gesture of the head and a curt, contemptuous phrase: *tu madre,* "your mother." "Not saying the operative word," asserts Robert M. Adams, "seems a particularly devious and deadly form of obscenity, since it forces the victim to contaminate his own mind, to call up the expression that the speaker does not even deign to voice."

The French are more given to Rabelaisian profusion in their obscenity. Herewith some French cursing:

LA COLOMBE DE L'ARCHE

Maudit
soit le père de l'épouse
du forgeron qui forgea le fer de la cognée
avec laquelle le bûcheron abattit le chêne
dans lequel on sculpta le lit
où fut engendré l'arrière-grand-père
de l'homme qui conduisit la voiture
dans laquelle ta mère
rencontra ton père!

—*Robert Desnos*

A rough translation:

FROM THE ARK, A DOVE

Cursèd
be the father of the wife
of the blacksmith who beat out the iron for the ax
with which the woodsman cut down the oak
from whose wood was framed the bed
in which was conceived the great-grandfather
of the man who drove the carriage
in which your mother
met your father!

—*W.R.E.*

I have never heard an American beslime the body's innocent members as foully as do Isabelle and Marie here:

ISABELLE ET MARIE

Isabelle rencontra Marie au bas de l'escalier:
"Tu n'es qu'une chevelure! lui dit-elle.
—et toi une main.
—main toi-même, omoplate!
—omoplate? c'est trop fort, espèce de sein!
—langue! dent! pubis!

—oeil!
—cils! aisselle! rein!
—gorge! oreille!
—oreille? moi? regarde-toi, narine!
—non mais, vieille gencive!
—doigt!
—con!"

—*Robert Desnos*

Or as we might put it:

ISABELLE AND MARIE

Isabelle met Marie at the foot of the stairs:
"You are nothing but an empty wig! she told her.
—and you a hand.
—hand yourself, shoulder blade!
—shoulder blade? That's too much, you mammary gland!
—you tongue! you tooth; you pubic bone!
—throat! ear!
—ear? me? Look at yourself, you nostril!
—you decaying gum!
—finger!
—XXXX!"

—*W.R.E.*

For a translation of *con,* I refer you to Shakespeare's *Henry V,* Act IV, Scene 3.

23 MAY
II

Why Should a Lumberjack Want Last Year's Overcoat?

The father of Nathan, a sickly child, tried to teach him arithmetic:

"Marking Down," he would say, not unlike a recitation student announcing the title of a poem. "A clothing dealer, trying to dispose of an overcoat cut in last year's style, marked it down from the original price of thirty dollars to twenty-four. Failing to make a sale, he reduced the price to nineteen dollars and twenty cents. Again he found no takers, so he tried another price reduction and this time sold it . . . All right, Nathan, what was the selling price if the last markdown was consistent with the others?" Or, "Making a Chain." "A lumberjack has six sections of chain, each consisting of four links. If the cost of cutting open a link . . ." And so on.

The next day, while my mother whistled Gershwin and laundered my father's shirts, I would daydream in my bed about the clothing dealer and the lumberjack. To whom had the haberdasher finally sold the overcoat? Did the man who bought it realize it was cut in last year's style? If he wore it to a restaurant, would people laugh? And what did "last year's style" look like anyway? "Again he found no takers," I would say aloud, finding much to feel melancholy about in that idea. I still remember how charged for me was that word "takers"! Could it have been the lumberjack with his six sections of chain who, in his rustic innocence, had bought the overcoat in last year's style? And why suddenly did he need an overcoat? Invited to a fancy ball? By whom? ...

My father was disheartened to find me intrigued by fantasies and irrelevant details of geography and personality and intention, instead of the simple beauty of the arithmetic solution. He did not think that was intelligent of me and he was right.

—Philip Roth

24 MAY
II

Recovered Charades

Will Shortz sent these charades:

A thing whereon all Princes lie,
And as we all express a sigh,
What man into the world brings in,
An Indian weed whose leaf is thin,
A wood by kings esteemed much,
The part of speech when naming such:
These Initials join'd declare
A town where friendly people are.
   —*Country Magazine, May 1784*

An insect of the smallest kind
If you transpose, you soon will find
That from all mortals I do quickly fly;
When gone, my loss in vain they'll mourn,
In vain will wish for my return,
Tho' now to kill me, ev'ry art they try.
   —Matilda

Weekly Museum, July 16, 1796

25 MAY
II

Solomon's Song, 4: 1–5

1. Behold, thou *art* fair, my love; behold, thou *art* fair; thou hast doves' eyes within thy locks; thy hair *is* as a flock of goats, that appear from Mount Gilead.

2. Thy teeth *are* like a flock *of sheep that are even* shorn, which came up from the washing; whereof every one bear twins, and none *is* barren among them.

3. Thy lips *are* like a thread of scarlet, and thy speech *is* comely; thy temples *are* like a piece of pomegranate within thy locks.

4. Thy neck *is* like the tower of David builded for an armoury, whereon there hang a thousand bucklers, all shields of mighty men.

That is to say:

> My love, your teeth *are* new-shorn sheep,
>   And ev'ry sheep *is* big with twins.
> Your breasts *are* as two roes asleep;
>   Kid, this *is* how our love begins.
>
> An armoury meseems your throat,
>   With shields and bucklers hung about;
> Your tresses smell of mountain goat;
>   Your locks have doves' eyes. Rinse them out.
>   —*W.R.E.*

26 MAY
II

Do Not Mispell or . . .

Two reflections on grammar:

ONCE UPON A TIME I USED

> Once upon a time I used
> To mispell
> To sometimes split infinitives
> To get words of out order
> To punctuate, -badly
> To confused my tenses
> to ignore capitals
> To employ common or garden clichés
> To indulge in tautological repetitive statements
> To exaggerate hundreds of times a day
> And to repeat puns quite by chants.
> But worst of all I used
> To forget to finish what I
>   —*Alan F. G. Lewis*

SPELLING REFORM

With tragic air the love-lorn heir
  Once chased the chaste Louise;
She quickly guessed her guest was there
  To please her with his pleas.

Now at her side he kneeling sighed,
  His sighs of woeful size:
"Oh, hear me here, for lo, most low
  I rise before your eyes.

"This soul is sole thine own, Louise—
  'Twill never wean, I ween,

The love that I for aye shall feel,
  Though mean may be its mien!"

"You know I cannot tell you no,"
  The maid made answer true;
"I love you aught, as sure I ought—
  To you 'tis due I do!"

"Since you are won, O fairest one,
  The marriage rite is right—
The chapel aisle I'll lead you up
  This night!" exclaimed the knight.
  —*Anonymous*

27 **MAY**
II

Tickle, Ben Jon.; Tickle, Anon.!

THE SATYRS' CATCH

Buzz, quoth the blue fly,
  Hum, quoth the bee:
Buzz and hum, they cry,
  And so do we.

In his ear, in his nose,
  Thus, do you see?
He ate the dormouse,
  Else it was he.
  —*Ben Jonson*

THE DEAD PIG

T' owd pig's got mezzles an' she's deead, poor thing.
An' what will you mak o' her poor awd heead?
'T will mak as good a yune as iver baked breead.
An' what will you mak o' her poor awd legs?
As good a set o' bed-props as iver propped beds.
An' what will you mak o' her poor awd skin?
'Twill mak as good a blanket as iver man lay in.
An' what will you mak o' her poor awd tail?
'Twill mak as good a hammer-shaft as iver drove a nail.
An' what will you mak of her poor awd lugs?
As good a pair o' bed flops as iver flopped bugs.
  —*Anonymous*

(In the Yorkshire dialect, *yune* is "oven," *lugs* are "ears," and *bed-flops* are "leather swatters for killing vermin.")

28 MAY
II

Quis Custodiet . . . ?

The next time a newspaper editor tells me that the fourth estate is the only reliable watchdog of the nation's morals, I am going to ask him to explain this wire service dispatch:

```
A204
   D 1
      CUTLERY 5-30
      PARIS(UFI)--FRENCH PRESIDENT VALERY GISCARD D'ESTANG MAY
INVITE FEWER NEWSMEN AND HIRE MORE WAITERS FOR THE NEXT ELYSEE
PALACE LUNCHEON, PRESIDENTIAL PALACE OFFICIALS SAID FRIDAY.
      THEY SAID THAT ALTHOUGH THREE TO FOUR WAITERS PLUS ONE
HEADWAITER WERE ASSIGNED TO EACH TABLE AT THE RECENT 240-
PERSON PRESS LUNCHEON, 13 PIECES OF HEAVY GOLD CUTLERY HAVE
NOT BEEN ACCOUNTED FOR SINCE THE PRESS LEFT THE DINING ROOM.
      UFI 05-30 12:28 FED
```

29 MAY
II

Krazy, Kurt!

Tim Pitkin, of Rensselaer Falls, New York, claims to have created "the world's first sensible pangram," to wit:

JUM FOGHN DSPIT VERY QWCK X-BLAZ.

I doubt whether the record books will agree; the pangram seems to be built around shorthand rather than the dictionary. Here is how Mr. Pitkin interprets it: "Jum, a Norwegian, made a phone call despite the fact that he was in a very fast fire that was coming from two directions."

Kurt Vonnegut jotted down Clement Wood's fine "MR. JOCK, TV QUIZ PH. D., BAGS FEW LYNX" (9 April) and spent, he says, a sleepless night trying to improve on it. Today he reports that he has worked out a variant, as the headline of a likely news story of the future. The headline and dispatch read as follows:

JR. TV QUIZ PHD'S
MOCK FAG WEB LYNX

BURBANK, CAL., May 31—Three young stars of "Preco City," an ABC television quiz show featuring panelists under sixteen who have earned doctors' degrees, heaped scorn in a press conference here today on the title character of their chief competitor in the Wednesday night prime ratings war, NBC's "Gay Wildcat."

UCLA political scientist Dr. Joel Sissman, 15, spokesman for the three, said that they did not object to the human roles in "Gay Wildcat," a situation comedy involving two male homosexuals in a snowbound Montana log cabin with a talking male lynx. "We see nothing wrong in homosexuals having TV shows all their own on a network all their own," he said. NBC has, in a last-ditch effort to retain even a minor fraction of the viewing audience, devoted its programming for the past two years almost exclusively to the tastes and concerns of the gay community.

"We are here," declared Sissman, "to protest the insult to all great cats, most of them now extinct, implicit in the characterization of 'Fire Island,' the NBC lynx. Yet another sin has been invented by mankind," he went on, "which we are prepared with all possible sadness to identify. It consists of exterminating creatures of nearly indescribable beauty and dignity, and then describing them for posterity as, like 'Fire Island,' having been lisping, homophilic Iagos with a mania for Tallulah Bankhead films and chocolate mousse."

—Kurt Vonnegut

30 MAY
II

Well, There Is Another One Out of the Way

This is Memorial Day, Old Style. Hence these verses:

ELEGY FOR MY LATE FRIEND AND TAILOR, CANIO SALUZZI

As spread my waistful span (io),
You never failed, dear Canio,
To prove clothes make the man (io),
    However dropsical his lower part.
Your camouflaging suits (zi)
My ev'ry bulge confute (zi);
Saluto te, Saluzzi,
    Past master of the thread-and-needle art!
You're called aloft, to furbelow
    Our Lord Emmanuel;
Unhid henceforth shall be my slow
    Sure embonpointal swell;
Yet I am comforted to know
    That God is tailored well.

—W.R.E.

REQUIESCAT IN PACE

When reading the obits, I frequently say,
"Well, there is another one out of the way"—
By which I mean one of those clods who refuse
To second my sociological views,
Or one of those humorless, dim-witted blokes
Who yawn in the midst of my favorite jokes,
Or who go through the door first, when I am
        ahead;
The world is improved when such people are dead.
(I know, when *I'm* obited, people will say,
"Well, there is another one out of the way!")
                                        —*W.R.E.*

'ER AS WAS

'Er as was 'as gone from we.
Us as is 'll go ter she.
                    —*Anonymous*

3 1 **MAY**
    II

Did You Ever, Ever, Ever Sipsop?

DID YOU EVER, EVER, EVER

Did you ever, ever, ever,   No, I never, never, never,
In your leaf, life, loaf,   In my leaf, life, loaf,
See the deevel, divil, dovol,   Saw the deevel, divil, dovol,
Kiss his weef, wife, woaf?   Kiss his weef, wife, woaf.
                                        —*Anonymous*

SIPSOP'S SONG

Hang your serious songs, said Sipsop & he sung as follows

            Fa ra so bo ro
                Fa ra bo ra
            Sa ba ra ra rare roro
            Sa ra ra ra bo ro ro ro
            Radara
            Sarapodo no flo ro
                —*William Blake*

JUNE

JUNE
II

To a Cow in June

June is, among other things: Fight the Filthy Fly Month, National Ventilation Month, and June Dairy Month. You can honor all three, according to the Providence *Journal,* by swishing a cow's tail:

> Swish, Month of Ventilation Nash-
> onal! Swish, Month of Dairy, too!
> Swish, Month to Fight the Filthy Fly!
> Thy caudate member swish, dear Moo!
> —*W.R.E.*

June is also a month for idle reflections:

ALL HAIL!

> Hail to thee, blithe spirit!—
> Answer me, I beg!
> Bird thou never wert, but
> Wert thou ever egg?
> —*W.R.E.*

MY DENTAL FLOSS

> My Dental Floss,
> Come Smiles, come Tears,
> Has served my Teeth
> For Years and Years;
> And that is Very
> Nice, my Dears.
>
> And yet I know
> Without a Doubt,
> Some day that Floss
> Will Quite Run Out.
> This gives me Much
> To Think About.
> —*W.R.E.*

CHARLES DICKENS AND THE DEVIL

Charles Dickens found the Devil
  Stealing Charles Dickens's chickens.
"What the Dickens!" said the Devil.
  "What the Devil!" said Charles Dickens.
                    —W.R.E.

2 JUNE
II

S *ay* I *t* L *oud*—L *augh*, Y *ell*

"A re you deaf, Father William?" the young man said,
"D id you hear what I told you just now?
  E xcuse me for shouting! Don't waggle your head
  L ike a blundering, sleepy old cow!
  A little maid dwelling in Wallington Town
  I s my friend, so I beg to remark;
  D o you think she'd be pleased if a book were sent down
  E ntitled 'The Hunt of the Snark'?"

"P ack it up in brown paper!" the old man cried,
"A nd seal it with olive-and-dove.
  I command you to do it!" he added with pride,
"N or forget, my good fellow, to send her beside
  E aster Greetings, and give her my love."
                    —Lewis Carroll

HE SQUANDERS RECKLESSLY HIS CASH

The acrostic below appeared in *Golden Days* on October 10, 1885. Two twelve-letter words, formed one from the fourth and the other from the final letters of the lines—remarkable!

He s*q*uanders recklessly his cas*h*
In c*u*ltivating a mustach*e*;
A sh*a*meless fop is Mr. Dud*e*,
Vai*n*, shallow, fond of being viewe*d*.
'Tis *t*rue that he is quite a swel*l*—
A sm*i*le he has for every bell*e*;
Wha*t* time he has to spare from dres*s*
Is t*a*ken up with foolishnes*s*—
A wi*t*less youth, whose feeble brai*n*
Inc*i*tes him oft to chew his can*e*.
Lea*v*e dudes alone, nor ape their way*s*,
Mal*e* readers of these Golden Day*s*.
                    —Mrs. Harris

The next acrostic may be read three ways—from left to right; vertically; or from right to left and from left to right in alternate lines, a form the ancient Greeks called *boustrophedon,* "as the ox turns in plowing." It uses words instead of letters.

YOUR FACE YOUR TONGUE YOUR WIT

Your face	Your tongue	Your wit
so faire	so smooth	so sharp
first drew	then mov'd	then knit
Mine eye	Mine eare	My heart
thus drawn	thus mov'd	thus knit
affects	hangs on	yeelds to
Your face	Your tongue	your wit

—*Anonymous*

A despairing, not to say sacrilegious, acrostic:

IN GOD WE TRUST

I nsane titterings heard on the stair,
N ightmarish shadows thrown on the wall,
G rim windless blasts felt in the old hall,
O dd ghosts invade my sick mind and soul.
D aily I ail with a strange malaise;
W ild with terror, my lovely Gervaise
E ntreats we leave while my mind is whole . . .
T aut with fear I search this haunted pile,
R oaring her name, but Gervaise has fled.
U nless . . . Why is my hand stained this red?
S adly I recall her tortured smile
T hat now fills my heart with dark despair.

—*Walter Shedlofsky*

3 JUNE
II

Love Song in Brooklyn

There may be a few enclaves of Brooklyn where the traditional accents persist; I have not found them. Once Brooklynites spoke this way:

> Dear Oima, spoin
> Me not; I yoin
> To feel you toin,
> That we may jern
> From lern to lern,
> From grern to grern,

> In sweet sojoin.—
> From stem to stoin
> We'll berl and boin.
> Toin, Oima, toin!
> —*W.R.E.*

Then Brooklyn was naturalized, and the dialect was mongrelized into everyday English:

> Dear Irma, spurn
> Me not; I yearn
> To feel you turn,
>   That we may join
>   From loin to loin,
>   From groin to groin,
> In sweet sojourn.—
> From stem to stern
> We'll boil and burn.
> Turn, Irma, turn!
> —*W.R.E.*

4 JUNE
II

Where the Caribou Play and the Furbish Louseworts Perish

As a staunch friend of the caribou I was pleased to note the following item in today's *Wall Street Journal*:

A friend of ours has just returned from a first-hand look at the Alaskan pipeline, which helps transport North Slope oil to the U.S. at some considerable cost to consumers. One reason the pipeline was so expensive was the added engineering necessary to create special "gates" at the migratory paths of caribou. At these points, the pipeline, which is mostly above ground, was buried and special measures were taken to prevent its heat from melting the permafrost and turning it into mud. But our friend noticed that the caribou don't seem to appreciate what was done for them. They actually like the pipeline—above ground. They sleep under it, play under it, leap over it, enjoy its friendly warmth. What can you do with animals like that?

LITTLE DARTER, LITTLE PEA, DON'T YOU WISH THAT YOU WERE ME?

> Now shed your tears from morn till even
> For six hundred thirty-seven

Styles of *beasts, snakes, bugs,* and *fishes*
Threatened by us avaricious
Homo saps., who all agree
(Whether Afric or Chinee,
Eskimo or Wasp or Bedouin)
The sole good *Injun* is a dead one,
A principle that too applies
To *tigers, elephants,* and *flies.*
E'en the flashing *darter snail*
Must turn up its tiny tail,
Doomed to total terminus
By the cussed likes of us.

When the *Fauna* are no more, a
Chap can still destroy the *Flora:*
Furbish Lousewort, two feet high,
Pax Vobiscum as you die!
Milkvetch Perydberg, dear Pea,
Who on acres two or three
Struggle for your final breath,
Woe for your untimely death!
Texas Wildrice Watergrass,
Grant forgiveness as you pass!
Poor *Persistent Trillium,*
I deplore your martyrdom.
Virginia Roundleap Birch, relax—
Thirty still have missed the ax!
Northern Monkshead Wild, Lord love you,
There are still two thousand of you!
Smile, friends, dying: I remind you
Mankind isn't far behind you.

—*W.R.E.*

(But the darter snail has been transplanted, and, by some reports, is thriving.)

FOUR LITTLE TIGERS

Four little tigers
  Sitting in a tree;
One became a lady's coat—
  Now there's only three.

Three little tigers
  'Neath a sky of blue:
One became a rich man's rug—
  Now there's only two.

Two little tigers
  Sleeping in the sun:
One a hunter's trophy made—
  Now there's only one.

> One little tiger
> Waiting to be had:
> Oops! He got the hunter first—
> Aren't you kind of glad?
> —*Frank Jacobs*

SING A SONG OF SPILLAGE

> Sing a song of spillage—
> A tanker's fouled the shore:
> Four and twenty blackbirds—
> They were white before.
> —*Frank Jacobs*

5 JUNE
II

Alternative Weddings

What is an "Alternative Wedding"?

That's a good question. I'd say, "It depends pretty much on the individual," so let's look at some individual cases.

Sam and *Judy,* for example. They chose to emphasize their mutual commitment to air and water quality, exchanging vows while chained to each other and to the plant gate of a major industrial polluter.

Lyle and *Marcia,* recognizing their dependence on each other, were joined in matrimony in a crowd of total strangers and had but $3.85 and a couple of tokens between them.

Al and *Tammy,* on the other hand, sharing a commitment to challenge and excitement, were married in 6.12 seconds in *Al*'s Supercharged Funny Car, with a minister on her lap and four bridesmaids on the floor (a new track record).

Bud and *Karen* chose a simple ceremony in their own apartment, with *Karen* fixing pizza in the kitchen, *Bud* asleep on the sofa, and their *two children* throwing toys at the guests.

Charles and *Frank,* however, selected the Early Traditional style, complete with morning coats, Wagner and Mendelssohn, and crustless sandwiches.

Others have been married in canoes or small powerboats, under bridges, in tunnels, beside creeks, on towers, over the telephone (with the groom calling from a distant tavern), and on ski tows, islands, mountain peaks, peninsulas, rooftops, and rocks. A New, or Alternative, Wedding means freedom to be married in exactly the way you always wanted to be.

—*Garrison Keillor*

6 JUNE
II

Ananias Was a Layer

—*Saturday Evening Post*

7 JUNE
II

Out of Sight, Out of Mind

The oft'ner seen, the more I lust,
   The more I lust, the more I smart,
The more I smart, the more I trust,
   The more I trust, the heavier heart.

The heavy heart breeds my unrest,
  Thy absence therefore I like best.

The rarer seen, the less in mind,
  The less in mind, the lesser pain,
The lesser pain, less grief I find,
  The lesser grief, the greater gain,
The greater gain, the merrier I,
Therefore I wish thy sight to fly.

The further off, the more I joy,
  The more I joy, the happier life,
The happier life, less hurts annoy,
  The lesser hurts, pleasure more rife.
Such pleasures rife shall I obtain
When distance doth depart us twain.
                    —*Barnaby Googe*

8 JUNE
II

The Frolicsome Flea

When Tom Buckley was writing a *New York Times* column called "About New York," he occasionally asked me to turn a macaronic verse into clear English for his readers. This one came from B. F. Skinner, the behavioral psychologist, who does not know its origin. Each stanza uses successively English, French, German, Latin, and Italian:

There once was a frolicsome flea
Son chien lui dépluit comme abri
  Er wollt' einen Kater
  Sed observat mater
Non lasci i parenti cosi.

But he listened not to their prayer
Il quitta son père et sa mère,
  Er spring t' auf 'ne Katze
  Sed haec rasitat se
Lo mangi, orribile a veder.

Around and about the gore flew
Aie pitié du petit fou
  Mit lautem Geschrei
  Vae mihi, o vae,
Il povero acese in giu.

The moral of this little tale:
Ne tentez la force de vos ailes;
  Bleib', ruhig zu Haus
  Sit domui laus
Alla casa dimora fedel.
                    —*Anonymous*

My approximation of "The Frolicsome Flea":

A Flea, bored with Dog as a diet,
Heard of Cat, and decided to try it.
He cried, "I must go!"
But his parents said, "No!
Stay at home on our Dog and keep quiet."

The Flea didn't heed them a mite;
He jumped on a Cat for a bite.
This maddened the Puss,
Who scratched the Flea loose
And ate him—a horrible sight!

The dying Flea popped with a splat—
Oh, pity the poor little brat,
Crying, "Ma, take me back!"
As, alas and alack,
He slid down the throat of the Cat.

My Moral, dear friends, is a hot one;
What seems like a snack may be not one;
If you live on a pup,
Stay at home and shut up;
Be glad of a home if you've got one.
                    —*W.R.E.*

9 JUNE
II

Fame

Except for Zoltan Zander, everyone listed in this tour de force was or is a living person.

Alfred Adler, analyzing,
  Probed the psyche, saw obsessions;
Béla Bartók, improvising,
  Blended chords in odd progressions;
Calvin Coolidge, silent, solemn,
  Thought of running, didn't choose to;

Dorothy Dix inscribed a column,
  Lulled the lovelorn, made them news, too;
Edward Elgar, mad for marches,
  Wrote five *Pomp and Circumstances*;
Fannie Farmer knew her starches,
  Turned out cookbooks, saved romances;
Greta Garbo, hibernating,
  Fled from films with little laughter;
Henry Hudson, navigating,
  Edged the Arctic, died soon after;
Ilya Ilf, pooh-poohing purges,
  Razzed Red Russians with wry stories;
Jesse James, obeying urges,
  Stole from banks, gained outlaw glories;
Kublai Khan found home-life dreary,
  Conquered Asia, met the Polos;
Lotte Lehmann sang *Valkyrie,*
  Filled up halls for *Lieder* solos;
Margaret Mitchell, done with Scarlett,
  Wrote no more, abandoned Tara;
Nita Naldi, sultry starlet,
  Played the siren, echoed Bara;
Oliver Optic fed the hopper,
  Dashed off books for fledgling readers;
Pontius Pilate came a cropper,
  Proved the least of lesser leaders;
Quisling, quisling, tried for treason,
  Lost his life with few men grieving;
Robert Ripley, straining reason,
  Dug up facts beyond believing;
Sarah Siddons lit up stages,
  Woke the critics from their slumbers;
Thomas Telford earned his wages,
  Threw up bridges in great numbers;
Ugolino, unaesthetic,
  Sold out Pisa, drew damnation;
Vladimir Vasek waxed poetic,
  Mourned in meter Czech privation;
William Wallace sought no respite,
  Rallied clans, was hanged in London;
Xerxes, xenophobic despot,
  Lost a navy, wound up undone;
Yen Yang-chu attained his wishes,
  Streamlined Chinese ways of learning;
Zoltan Zandar, quite fictitious,
  Ends this piece, his fame thus earning.

—Frank Jacobs

10 JUNE ♊

Snallygaster VI

The *Hagerstown Mail* says that the monster was seen on the railroad bridge at Shepherdstown last Monday night by the engineer of No. 83, who described it as having an elastic neck and a very long, sharp beak. From descriptions sent to the Smithsonian Institution at Washington, they write back that it is either a winged bovalupus or a Snallygaster, as it has some of the characteristics of both. These animals are exceedingly rare and the hide of a Snallygaster is said to be worth a hundred thousand dollars a square foot, as it is the only thing known that will properly polish punkle shells used by the people of Umbopeland, in Africa, as ornaments. Telegrams and letters are pouring in from scientists and naturalists, and a strict watch is being kept to try to locate its den or roost.

A gentleman from the southern part of the Valley says that the Go-Devil was seen in the mountains between Gapland and Burkittsville last Tuesday night, where it laid an egg—an egg almost as large as a barrel, covered with a tough, parchmentlike shell of a yellowish color.

What alarms us now is that this terrible beast has been seen in the southern part of the Middletown Valley. This vampire-devil is seldom seen during the day, feeding at night only, and the strange part is that it seems to prefer men to women, though it attacks the latter at times. It never gets after children, unless very hungry, as they do not have sufficient blood to satisfy it.

It is said that President Roosevelt is so anxious to see the monster that he may postpone his African safari until it can be captured.

MORE ON 16 JULY.

11 JUNE ♊

Abby up a Tree

Dear Abby:

Now it has been disclosed that a certain brand of bread whose advertising claims "400 percent more fiber" uses wood in part for that fiber.

The following questions come to mind:

- How much of the bread must I eat in order to bark?
- Will it help in searching for my roots?
- Will it make me a budding genius?

• Will it be easier to get leaves of absence?
• Will it sap my strength?
• Will my son be a chip off the old block?

I'm ready to climb the walls. (Paneled, of course.) I pine for some answers.

—Margaret

Dear Margaret: I wooden know.

DEAR FRUSTRATED

Dear Abby:

My husband and I were married for four years and had one child. Then we separated and I met "Mr. X." Abby, I never knew lovemaking could be so beautiful and fulfilling.

Because of the child we decided to give our marriage another chance, but I can't forget "Mr. X." (Now I have another lover very much like him.) I know that my own mother was never satisfied with one man. She had six children, and we all have different fathers.

My husband's desires are much greater now than before, but he still leaves me unfulfilled and with a sick headache. How can I get this across to him?

—Frustrated

I did not wait to read Abby's response to this letter. I wrote my own:

Dear Frustrated: Don't try. Take aspirin.

12 JUNE
II

Unmailed Letter

Editor
Author's Queries
New York Times Book Review

Sir or Madam:

For an autobiography, I should be grateful for recollections from anyone who can remember me.

Yours faithfully,
Willard R. Espy

(I did not have the brass to send this letter. As you will see from the Answers and Solutions, though, another writer later forwarded a similar request—and, I gather, got good results, too.)

13 JUNE
♊

Jack Be Nimble

"There probably is no commoner name in nursery rhymes and tales than Jack," says *Games*. "We have Jack and Jill, Jack Sprat, Little Jack Horner, Jack in the Beanstalk, Jack the Giantkiller, and, of course, our favorite candlestick hurdler. The name is common in words and phrases as well."

Each clue below leads to an answer containing the name Jack. For example, "Halloween fixture" would be *Jack-o'-lantern*.

1. Handyman _____
2. Hard cider _____
3. Classic dive _____
4. Win big _____
5. "21" _____
6. Toy _____
7. Paul Bunyan, e.g. _____
8. British emblem _____
9. Exceptionally adept _____
10. Singing family _____
11. Game of dexterity _____
12. Autumn "visitor" _____
13. Fast-starting hare _____
14. Tight garment _____
15. Hand-held rock drill _____
16. Warm-up exercise _____
17. Religious plant _____
18. Pancake _____

—Gene Traub

14 JUNE
♊

Sphinx, Sphincter, Sphinctest

The cognomen of *sphincter ani,* essential to civilization and romantic love, is the *Sphinx*, possessor of dark secrets. The Sphinx devoured all passersby who failed to answer her riddle: "What walks on four legs in the morning, two at noon, and three in the evening?" When Oedipus gave the correct answer, "Man" (an infant crawls on all fours, a man walks on two legs, and an ancient uses a cane), the Sphinx slew herself in frustration. The cognominous sphincter still flourishes. It is eulogized here:

> They say man has succeeded where the animals fail because of the clever use of his hands, yet when compared to the hands, the sphincter ani is far superior. If you place into your cupped hands a mixture of fluid, solid, and gas, and then through an opening in the bottom try to let only the gas escape, you will fail. Yet the sphincter can do it. [The gas may precede the solids, uttering hoots and hisses, as the sound of whistles, bells, and hissing brakes precedes a train into the station.—*W.R.E.*] The sphincter apparently can differentiate between solid, fluid, and gas. It apparently can tell whether its owner is alone or with someone, whether standing up or sitting down, whether its owner has his pants on or off. No other muscle is such a protector of the dignity of man, yet so ready to come to his relief ...
>
> —*W. C. Bornemeier*

*   *   *

The sphincter-related graffito that follows was found by Henry G. Fischer on the wall of a men's room in the Fondation Egyptologique Reine Elisabeth, Brussels. I will leave the translation to you:

> *Vous qui venez ici dans une humble posture*
> *Débarasser vos flancs d'un importun fardeau,*
> *Veuillez, quand vous aurez satisfait la nature*
> *Et déposé dan l'urne un modeste cadeau,*
> *Epancher de l'amphore un courant d'onde pure*
> *Et sur l'autel fumant placer pour chapiteau*
> *Le couvercle arrondi dont l'auguste jointure*
> *Aux parfums indiscrèts doit servir de tombeau.*
> —*George Sand*

W. H. Auden remarked that a fart is the desperate cry of a turd trying to get out.

Gary R. Shroat has coined the word *diascetesis,* from the Greek for "motion through a dung heap," to describe what he describes as "that veritable Gresham's Law of Linguistics which states that a sexual or scatological connotation of a word tends to drive all other connotations out of existence":

> For instance, it is a truism that no heterosexual would be happy to be called gay. And how many kinds of "intercourse" is the average person, gay or not, aware of practicing? The typical coffee drinker would switch to saccharine, cancer scare or not, if he knew that "defecation" is a part of the process of sugar refining. And did you realize that "prophylactic," which refers to any device or substance intended to prevent disease, may be used just as properly to describe the kind of rubbers your mother used to tell you to wear on your feet when it rained as to characterize the little items they issue men in the service?

An intriguing conceit, Mr. Shroat:

> Though defecation's rather sweet,
> And intercourse can be a ball
> The gayest enterprise of all
> Is to go splashing down the mall
> With prophylactics on your feet.
> —*W.R.E.*

15 JUNE
‖

School's Out

"Correct English is designed only for school children."
—*Letter to the New York Times*

> No more classes, no more books,
> No more teachers' dirty looks.
> School is out, and left behind
> Childish nonsense—merit, mind.
>
> Answers henceforth go unchecked:
> Two plus two is nine, correct?
> Down with rulings pedagogic—
> Down with philologic logic!
>
> Down with books that clog the shelf!
> Down with thinking for yourself!
> Down with cautionary brain!—
> Why not wet your bed again?
>
> Why not cease to be a man—
> Be instead a 'rangutan?
> Itchy? Scratch it. Hungry? Hunt.
> Care to leave a message?—Grunt.
> —*W.R.E.*

The *Pittsburgh Press* ran a poetry contest to encourage good English. The third line of the quatrain that follows is from one of the prizewinning verses:

GRAMMAR IN EXTREMIS

> The vows that I exchanged with she
> Were broken soon by both of we.
> (The sacred love of you and I
> May also wither by-and-by.)
> —*W.R.E.*

NOUN INTO VERB

"Yesterday," said the college boy home on vacation, "we autoed to the country club, golfed till dark, bridged a while, and autoed home."

"Yesterday," said the father, "I muled to the cornfield and geehawed till sundown, then I suppered till dark, piped till nine, bedsteaded till five, breakfasted, and went muling again."

—Carl Sandburg

16 JUNE
II

What's in a Name?

A nineteenth-century immigrant was so rattled on his arrival at Ellis Island that when asked his name he replied, *"Ich habe vergessen,"* meaning, "I have forgotten." He was written down as Ferguson.

Judy Bosworth asked the Department of Motor Vehicles for license plates bearing her first name. Several Judys were ahead of her, so the plates arrived bearing the legend JUDY 13. She changed her last name from Bosworth to Thirteen.

In college I knew a Fair Virgin, and fair she was. Curious surnames are legion: Tennis, Roof, Opacity, Maiden, Into, Oyster, Cutie, Hidden, Shoals, Miscall.

John Train wrote a book called *Remarkable Names*. Here are some remarkable names he chose:

- Ave Maria Klinkenberg
- Private Baby Cherry
- Mrs. Belcher Wack Wack
- Buncha Love
- Carlos Restrepo Restrepo Restrepo de Restrepo
- Reverend Christian Church
- George Baretits
- Hugh Pugh
- John Senior, Junior
- Joy Bang
- Katz Meow
- Lettice Goedebed
- Memory Lane
- Ophelia Legg
- Miss Pinkey Dickey Dukes
- Shine Soon Sun
- T. Hee
- Mrs. V. D. Whynot

17 JUNE
II

Collegiate Quiz

It is commencement time; across the country, speakers on campus daises explain to students what has gone wrong. Here are the meanings of the names of some well-known colleges and universities. How many can you identify?

1. By God. 2. A dove. 3. Famous spearman. 4. Big hill. 5. New town. 6. Bold friend. 7. Army guard. 8. Sacred oak on a hill. 9. A leader. 10. Fertile upland. 11. A servant. 12. Elm wood. 13. Upper linden tree. 14. Chief guardian. 15. A place to sit. 16. Brave as a bear. 17. Birch meadow. 18. Dark wasteland. 19. From the mound. 20. Springs in the meadow.

—*Thomas L. Bernard*

18 JUNE
II

Bugs of State

OYSTERVILLE—Considering the tent caterpillars in my rhododendrons, I don't understand how some people can admire insects so much as to make them official symbols of a state. Yet North Carolina and Kansas have chosen the honeybee as official insect; California, the dog-butterfly. Bugs have constituencies elsewhere— the honeybee in West Virginia, Kansas, and Michigan; the praying mantis in Florida; both the ladybug and the earthworm, which I had never considered an insect, in Indiana. Someday I may have an opportunity to vote for a bug for President. Perhaps, indeed, I have already done so.

See the Legislature   Vie
Heed the Call of Nature   The Butterfly
Solons all a-dote   The Mantidae
On the Insect vote   The prolific
Enfranchise   Apis Mellific
    Flies   All hail
See each Candidate   Snail!*
For Bug of State   —*W.R.E.*

19 JUNE
II

Love in Shadow

A bow to bathos:

ONCE MORE THE FIR ACCRETES ITS ANNUAL RING

Once more the fir accretes its annual ring
Around the sapless core;
I do not think it recollects a thing
Of rings it drew before.

*The snail is a mollusk, really.

I shall not find your eyes less violet
If you should scarce recall
The look of me next spring, and quite forget
That we two loved at all.

—*W.R.E.*

OUR LOVE WILL NEVER DWINDLE, BEING NEVER

Our love will never dwindle, being never;
It could not be so dear if it could be.
The babe we never bore is ours forever;
There is no need to set the wild deer free.

I know a land that has no dawn nor setting:
No summer there, or winter; spring, or fall;
No memories are there, and no forgetting;
The lovers there breathe barely, if at all.

—*W.R.E.*

20 JUNE
♊

Y Is X a Y of Y?

David W. Silverman suggested selecting some word or expression—say, arbitrarily, *land pollution*—calling it X, and then solving the equation "X is a Y of Y": X (land pollution) = Y (soil) of Y (soil). Land pollution is soil of soil. A pun. Mary Young-quist promptly forwarded the following X's to *Word Ways*; you will find the matching Y's in back.

1. Ilk
2. House construction
3. Greta's clothes
4. Ale steward
5. Paying the check
6. Bunches of partly eaten apples
7. Policemen hiding in the woods
8. Silver-colored dish
9. Clothing storage for undergarments
10. Put mother's sister up for a gambling stake.

21 JUNE
♊

Eccentrics

Perhaps the most eccentric father ever to appear in a son's autobiography was Sir George Sitwell, sire of Sir Osbert. He was a stingy, disagreeable old bore but I have always cherished him for his two inventions: a tiny revolver for shooting wasps and a musical toothbrush—not so tiny—that played "Annie Laurie."

I've also a lingering fondness for old Squire Mytton, who always brought his horse into the bedroom on cold winter nights. And for Jimmy Hirst, who used to go out hunting astride his bull, accompanied by his "sagacious pigs," which he had trained as pointers.

Animal lovers are a quirky lot. A certain Lord Montgomery used to dine with his dogs each evening. Half a dozen or more came to the table when called. Each had his own chair, his own napkin—tied about his neck by an obliging footman—and his own silver-covered dish. Nice doggy manners were the rule and conversation was general.

And then there was Jeremy Bentham, the eighteenth-century philosopher and political economist. He was so fond of his cat that he had him knighted. Sir John Langbourne was the cat's name and he liked to seduce "light and giddy young ladies of his own race."

When Sir John grew old and tired of pleasures and vanities, Bentham had another honor conferred upon him: doctor of divinity. "Great respect was invariably shown his reverence," writes Bentham's biographer, Sir John Bowring, "and it was supposed that he was not far off from a mitre."

—Harriet Van Horne

22 JUNE
♋

I Gave Her Simple Flowers

OYSTERVILLE—Twelve years have passed since the afternoon when a caterpillar tractor ripped the gorse from a plot of land alongside the family house to start my croquet garden, but the lawn has not yet sprouted a wicket. Yet at least rhododendrons are in glorious bloom around the borders; indeed, Louise has just carried an enormous armful into the cottage and is arranging them in tall vases.

I wonder if I would like flowers so much if they were not such convenient sources of verbal imagery: rose-pink, tulip-pure, and so on. Their names have a resonance of loveliness; words reminiscent of flowers retain the resonance even when their actual meaning is ghastly.* Miss Pym, Josephine Tey's fictional detective, noticed how many horrid diseases sounded like the names of flowers:

> *Emphysema* [she reflected] might be the gardener's name for a sort of columbine. And *kyphosis* she could picture as something in the dahlia line. *Myelitis* would be a small creeping plant, very blue, with a tendency to turn pink if not watched. And *tabes dorsalis* was obviously an exotic affair of the tiger lily persuasion, expensive and very faintly obscene.

*See 15 November.

A pleasant example of words used for sound rather than sense:

> I gave her simple flowers: hegemony,
> Miasma, scrofula. She bent her knee
> To stroke the palliasses gambolling
> About her feet. We heard the fichu sing.
> Cool limousine we drank; smooth summary
> Was all our meal ... A litmus scuttled by;
> Two millimeters fluttered overhead;
> Our path lush serials festooned ... then said
> My love, my Calomel, "I must go home,"
> And, sighing, sought her father's palindrome.
> —*Ruth Collins*

23 JUNE
♋

Happy Father's Day, Carlos!

OYSTERVILLE—A local weekly carries this news item:

> What a great Father's Day gift for a first-time father! At five minutes after midnight on June 17, Charles Welsh became a father. The baby boy weighed in at 7 lbs. 9 oz. and has been named Charles IV after the dad. Congratulations, Charles!

Now, I am aware that 2,000 years ago Jesus Christ was conceived without human impregnation. This is the first time, though, that I have heard of a baby being born without a mother. I know Sharon very well, and I have no doubt that she was around some place.

I can sympathize with her. At the close of the year in which my grandson Taylor was born, a magazine reporter asked his paternal grandfather what the highlights of the year had been.

"Well," he replied, "my son George had a boy."

Taylor's mother said that was nonsense, and I agree. "George," she pointed out, "was only an accessory before the fact."

24 JUNE
♋

The Norris Plan

A fictional conversation between Charles G. Norris and his wife, Kathleen, both prominent novelists a generation or so ago:

It was early in the summer that Kathy told him that Edgar Wallace was going to have another novel.

It was a heavenly warm bright shiny clear happy Sunday morning, and the broad green velvety smooth flat rolling croquet field in the middle of Central Park was filled with gay yellow warm sunlight. She and Charles were moving idly among the wickets, swinging their mallets at the smooth fat shiny round balls. Charles had tried for the stake and missed it, and now he sat on his up-ended mallet, his smooth fat shiny round face puckered into a frown.

"Edgar thinks he's going to have another novel, Charlie."

"Gosh, that's tough!" Charlie commented absently. He was trying to remember whether he was dead on her.

"He's been typing his eyes out," Kathy continued in a rather faint voice. "He says the first ten novels aren't so bad, or even the first twenty," she pursued. "But when you get to write the fiftieth novel or so, it's terrible."

Charlie extended his toe, slyly moved his ball over an inch or two in front of the wicket, and faced her with a great wholesome happy cheerful laugh.

"What's terrible, honey?" he asked.

"The novel, of course!" she conceded honestly. "Charlie," she went on suddenly, deliberately, not looking at him as she knocked her ball into position for the center wicket, "I wonder how you'd feel if I were going to have another novel?"

"I know how I'd feel," Charlie said promptly; "I'd take it out into a vacant lot somewhere and burn it!"

"Oh, Charlie, why?" Kathy asked, widening her big dark round bright eyes reproachfully. "Everybody writes them." Her cheeks were suddenly red, and her eyes full of tears. "Look at Faith Baldwin, or Hugh Walpole, or Mary Roberts Rinehart—they deliver one every year. Sometimes they even have twins."

"Well, if I was in Edgar's place," Charlie said, as he judged his distance and then rapped the stake smartly, "I'd go to my publishers and have them decide that the public couldn't stand another novel just now, that they'd have to save his reputation by—well, cutting it out."

"Oh, but Charlie! Isn't that a terribly wrong thing to do?"

"What's wrong with it?"

"Well—well—" She stopped, puzzled and a little sick. "It seems so unfair to the novel. It—it ought to have its little chance."

"Don't you think the public ought to have a chance, too?"

"But—but there seems to be something so humiliating about it," Kathleen faltered, her cheeks burning. "To have a whole season go by without being on the best-seller lists! To have to give up the first-serial rights—and the second-serial rights—and the movie rights—and the foreign rights—"

"It isn't half as bad, I should think, as writing it," Charlie argued.

"Oh, no, Charlie, that's natural!"

"I don't know about that," Charlie began, laying his mallet down and pointing an argumentative forefinger at the woman before him. "I've been doing a lot of thinking about this whole subject of book-control. It is my opinion that reckless breeding should be checked for the sake of the author's reputation. It unquestionably takes the lives of thousands of writers annually, ruins the careers of many more, and in addition brings hundreds of thousands of diseased, crippled, and deformed novels into the world that should never have been written. Some of them die, many linger on in dire poverty, shivering in their paper jackets, while others roam at large, doubtless interbreeding in the movies and producing a weak and imbecile line of sequels that threatens to lower the whole stock of American literature."

Kathy leaned weakly on her mallet. The warm bright sunny cheerful Park swam before her, the croquet-wickets, stakes, balls, and idle spectators seemed blurred before her eyes.

"You look kind of white yourself, Kathy," interrupted Charles curiously.

"I don't know—I'm all right, I guess."

—Corey Ford

MORE ON 20 JULY.

25 JUNE
♋

Love, Plants, and Corn

Some verses attain a risible immortality simply because they are so badly written. This horrid example is by the grandfather of Charles Darwin:

THE LOVES OF THE PLANTS

So the lone Truffle, lodged beneath the earth,
Shoots from paternal roots the tuberous birth.
No stamen-males ascend, and breathe above,
No seed-born offspring lives by female love.
So the male Polypus parental swims,
And branching infants bristle all his limbs.
So the lone Taenia, as he grows, prolongs
His flatten'd form with young adherent throngs;
Unknown to sex the pregnant Oyster swells,
And coral-insects build their radiate shells.

—Erasmus Darwin

The following epitome of good bad verse was written in Salem, Massachusetts, in the nineteenth century:

Corn, corn, sweet Indian corn,   Indian fields well to adorn,
Greenly you grew long ago,   And to parch or grind hah-ho!

—Reverend William Cook

26 JUNE
♋

Bull and Bossy Created He Them

OYSTERVILLE—Fifty years ago Oysterville was a scattering of truck farms and hayfields along the edge of the bay. The pervasive sounds of every day were the barking of dogs, the grunting of pigs, the mooing of cows, the cackling of hens, and the neighing of horses.

I puzzled, and still do, over some of the names indicating which of these beasts were male, and which female. Both bull and cow, for instance, are of the genus *Bos* (whence beef), but only the cow is a bossy. Why were the castrated bulls we raised for the market steers, while the castrated bulls that hauled my grandfather west along the Oregon trail were oxen? Why, moreover, were oxen in other parts of the world happily potent (indeed, the word *ox* means "besprinkler, begetter")? Would a gelded ox in India be an ox-ox?

I had no difficulty with the idea of a male deer as a buck, or the female as a doe; the male sheep as a ram, or the female as a ewe.

Why, since a goose might be of either sex, could the male be a gander as well, while the female had to remain a goose?

I found it faintly offensive, though I had no idea why, that while a female dog was called, neutrally, a bitch, to call a woman a bitch was a vulgar insult. The expression "to tomcat around," on the other hand, did not bother me—perhaps because I did not know what it meant.

As a slavish adherent of the rights of women, I am hurt when they charge me with considering them as sexual objects. To the extent that the charge is valid, I plead extenuating circumstances: I have not met all women, and may yet encounter one who is not of the opposite sex.

27 JUNE
♋

OYSTERVILLE—Doug Todd, public relations director of the Dallas Cowboys, once heard a country song containing the line, "If you want to keep the beer real cold, put it next to my ex-wife's heart." He has been collecting such ululations ever since. Dr. Leslie L. Nunn, who lives down the road a piece, brought me some examples from the Todd collection this morning. A few are adapted here, with thanks and apologies to the original lyricists:

> Forever wasn't quite as long as I had counted on;
> I've been a long time leaving, but I'll be a long time gone.

> You ask me what it was went wrong, but you already know:
> I was too busy hanging on, as you were letting go.

She's just a name dropper, and she's dropping mine;
If today was a fish, I would cut off the line.

She'll love you to pieces. The question is whether
She'll be there to put all the pieces together.

Our marriage was a failure, sure; and yet I might point out
That our divorce ain't really such a much to brag about.

We swore, "For better or for worse," and we were not far wrong;
We swore for better or for worse, but not for very long.

Do you think my bed's a bus stop, you pop in and out so free?
When your 'phone's no longer ringing, you will know that it is me.

If you could fake it we might make it, but I swear that this is true:
If you keep checking up on me, I'm checking out on you.

—W.R.E.

28 JUNE

♋

Dangler and Ellipsis

Danglers make a sentence say what you don't mean:

- The bride wore a long white lace dress which fell to the floor.
- The women included their husbands and children in their potluck suppers.
- In Germany a person cannot slaughter any animal unless rendered unconscious first.
- Even more astonishing was our saving the lives of little babies who formerly died from sheer ignorance.
- For those of you who have small children and don't know it we have a nursery downstairs.

—Naomi Russell

The foregoing collection is from *Verbatim*. The editor, Laurence Urdang, added two danglers he particularly liked:

- Plunging 1,000 feet into the gorge, we saw Yosemite Falls.
- When a small boy, a girl is of little interest.

ELLIPSIS

(Ellipsis is the dropping of words in a sentence on the assumption that the recipient's mind will fill them in for sense, as in "I'll light my [tobacco and smoke my] pipe." A poorly considered ellipsis can cause trouble:)

• When properly stewed, I really enjoy apricots.
• I plan to mow the lawn with my wife.
• Mommy will put your pajamas on.
• Alice can eat herself.
• Wash your face in the morning and neck at night.
• A gentleman never crumbles his bread or rolls in his soup.

—*G. A. Cevasco, Verbatim*

An ellipsis between lovers:

With nary care   Dismissing
  He sipses   From that kissing
 The dripses   The ellipses.
From her lipses,   —*W.R.E.*

29 JUNE

♋

Birds and Bees

A verse on binomials (chains of two commonly associated words, often connected by an "and"):

Birds and bees   Bits and pieces
Are black and blue   Safe and sound
They hem and haw   Free and easy
They p and q   Hearty, hale
They're fast and loose   Pines and needles
And back and forth   Head and tail
They're cut and dried   They drib and drab
And south and north   Take and give
They're fair and square In fits and starts
They're cat and mouse   They die and live
They're in and out   They're 'tween and 'twixt
Of home and house   They're now or never
They're true and false   And each and all
They're bones and skin   And good, not clever
They're fuss and bother I'd tit for tat
Kith and kin   Could I but be
They're fine and dandy   From stem to stern
Square and round   A bird and bee.

—*W.R.E.*

ALAS, ALACK

Alas, alack—
Weeps and wails—
Aches and pains—
Heads and tails!

Time and tide
By and by
May explain
Wherefore, why.
—*W.R.E.*

30 JUNE
♋

Trojan 'orses Inside

Ernest Bevin, foreign secretary in Britain's postwar Labor government, chopped bloody hunks from the cultured Oxbridge syntax of the Foreign Office. Said he of Molotov, his opposite number in the Soviet Union: "The words was scarcely dry on the words out of me mouth when he tore the 'ole thing up." And again, rejecting a Foreign Office recommendation: "I ain't 'avin' it. If you open up that Pandora's box you'll find a lot of Trojan 'orses inside."

• Warren Austin, our ambassador to the United Nations, suggested to warring Jews and Arabs that they sit down and try to settle their differences "like good Christians."

• Samuel Goldwyn was neither malapropping nor mixing metaphors when he said: "A verbal contract isn't worth the paper it's written on." This is a lapsus comicus, a simple verbal confusion.

• My mother specialized in the lapsus comicus. "I haven't been to South Bend," she remarked, "since the last time I was there." And: "He looks so much older than he did when he was young."

• A supporter of Morris Udall, a onetime aspirant for the Democratic nomination for the presidency, described him as "the splitting image of Abe Lincoln."

• A governor fighting for reelection spoke of "traveling incarnito," "being pacific on the issues," and having "intentional fortitude." He also decried his critics' "unmeditated gall."

• Max Ascoli, editor of the *Reporter,* explaining why he need not reduce the number of his staff: "Thanks goodness; we are already underhanded."

• In 1923, when Theodore S. Abbott was Cambridge correspondent for the *Boston Post,* he asked the sergeant on duty at the East Cambridge police station what was new. "Nothing but a couple arrested for lewd and luscious conduct," said the sergeant.

JULY

1 JULY
♋

A Very Fine Weirdo

I was met at the airport in Shiraz by a wizened creature in black who introduced himself as Mahmoud, my guide, and the chauffeur of his car, a corpulent Bengali, as Mr. Dodgson. Our first objective was Iran's renowned archaeological site, Persepolis, and en route, succumbing to curiosity, I asked the driver if he were related to Charles Lutwidge Dodgson, the pseudonymous author of Alice's Adventures in Wonderland.

"Goodness me, yis. I am remembering old Charlie like yesterday," he chuckled. "That chap my grandfather. Very fine person, oh, yis."

"But he passed away before your time, my friend. He was a contemporary of Queen Victoria."

"Balderdash, sir, I am knowing this man backwards and forwards. A very tiny fellow with smug nose and chin whisker, always wearing striped pajama coat over his loincloth."

Unable to recall Lewis Carroll possessing any such props, I tried another tack. "What do you make of his predilection for little girls?" I asked. "In the light of modern psychiatry, wouldn't it seem your ancestor was a bit of a weirdo?"

"Oh, yis, yis—very fine weirdo," he agreed. "But I don't think he live very long after that. My uncle says he was eaten by dogs."

At that juncture, it began to dawn on me that one of us was in a time warp, and I occupied the balance of the trip studying his driving and twisting my prayer beads.

—S. J. Perelman

2 JULY
♋

A Nakedness of Artists

EAST HAMPTON—Artists lurk behind every hedgerow in the Hamptons, emerging in the late afternoon to drink with friends, acquaintances, and strangers. At a party today artist Herman Cherry told me that artist Franz Kline in his salad season was once approached by a wide-eyed young art worshiper who made herself agreeable to the point of sharing his bed. Next morning he gave her his name and telephone number, to facilitate a repeat performance. She glanced at the note and exclaimed, disappointed, "Oh, dear! I thought you were Picasso!"

I suspected that Herman was simply being modest. Discreet inquiries uncovered what I take to be the true story:

The girl caught *Herman's* eye. They spent a delicious night. In the morning he was so in love that he got up to fix her breakfast. She said gratefully, "Thank you, Franz," at which point he made the mistake of correcting her. When she realized he was not the great Franz Kline, she bolted out the door.

Cherry told Kline the story. "You owe me a girl," said Kline.

I also heard today that Niarchos, the Greek shipping magnate, once commissioned Dali to make a portrait of him. Niarchos was a restless sitter; once his face was roughed in, he told the artist to complete the portrait without him. When he returned to pick it up, he found that Dali had painted him unclad and had increased the fee from $15,000 to $25,000. "Funny, but not that funny," said Niarchos.

Dali promptly sold the painting to Niarchos's arch-rival, Onassis, for $50,000. Onassis hung it on the wall of his office dining room, and invited Niarchos for lunch. Niarchos knew when to sue for peace. "All right," he said, "how much do you want?" "Seventy-five thousand dollars," said Onassis. "Sold," said Niarchos. He carried the portrait away and stored it in a closet full of cast-offs, where, for all I know, it remains to this day.

*   *   *

Marjorie Wihtol set out one day to choose masterpieces of art as jacket illustrations for famous books. Some of her pairings:

- Venus de Milo   *A Farewell to Arms*
- Rodin's "The Kiss"   *Games People Play*
- Laocoön   *A Generation of Vipers*
- Goya's "Maja, Clothed"   *Psychoanalysis,* front jacket
- Goya's "Maja, Unclothed"   *Psychoanalysis,* back jacket
- Duchamp's "Nude Descending"   *Up the Down Staircase*

NON-SUBJECTIVE ART

People, too, were on exhibit at the opening—
I was looked at appraisingly by a visiting collector
but, being unsigned, he passed me up in disdain.
Another could be heard complaining
I was too representational, not abstract enough;
two ears, two eyes, a mouth and nose
and all where, by divine decree or bourgeois convention,
they properly belong and should not be moved.
A big-city critic examined me as searchingly
as he might have a Kandinsky or Klee
and, concluding that I was probably derivative,
promptly lost interest and went home.
On the brink of utter self-abnegation,
despondency closing in on all sides,

salvation came, sudden and unexpected,
in the guise of a nearsighted, oft-divorced lady
who stopped and, pointing at me, said, "Isn't he cute?"
I am hanging in her bedroom now
where, from time to time, we exchange views on life and art.
                                            —*Michael Braude*

3 JULY
♋

A Troop of Tropes

You are even cleverer than you realized. If you doubt it, look up the formidable
Greek appellations of rhetorical devices you use unconsciously every day. You trope,
trope, trope—that is, you use words figuratively. When you intensify a compound
word or phrase by inserting one or more words in the midst of it ("abso-goddamn-
lutely," "what place soever," "South by God Carolina"), you are employing tmesis—
Greek for "to cut." Each of the numbered expressions in the story below is a rhetorical device with an impressive name. You will find the names in the Answers and
Solutions.

Tom and Mary, sharing a small apartment (without benefit of clergy)
(1), had dreamed for years of a Caribbean holiday, and finally felt justified
in going to the bank to withdraw Mary's favorite necklace (a family
curio) (2) and their life-savings which they converted into travelers'
checks. They then contracted for two two-way tickets to and from the
southern island of their dreams (which still, incidentally, was under the
Crown) (3).

"It will be a good change from the Borscht Circuit (4). It usually rains
up there, anyway," remarked Tom, meteorologically (5).

They were carried away by elation and a large airplane (6). Food and
drinks were served, and he called her Ducky (7) just like in the old days.
We need not elaborate on their arrival at the island, the long trip through
the boondocks (8) to the hotel; the unpacking, the small, warm room,
how pleasant so ever (9) (for they had thought air conditioning an unnec-
essary expense).

Their "threads" (10) (as Tom put it) hung up, and their travelers'
checks discreetly hidden, the happy couple changed into bathing attire
which naïvely (11) covered the whiteness of their limbs (12). They rushed
to the beach. Everything seemed to live up to the superlatives of the travel
brochure: "It's a beautiful world (13), and this is one of its loveliest
countries."

"Not bad, eh?" (14) said Tom.

"I'll be forever grateful (15) for this!" said Mary. Then she exclaimed:
"Oh, my! I forgot to take off Mother's necklace!"

"Never mind—it has a strong clasp. The old bag (16) saw to that."

"She'd turn over in her grave if she were alive today (17), to see how careless I am!"

Then it happened. A wave like a watery giant (18), spawned 'way (19) out in the gulls' territory (20), hissed (21) and thundered into shore. It was the Sunday punch of an expert (22). Mary's necklace was gone.

Sadly, they straggled up the beach to the hotel and rode the elevator to their floor.

"Well, I never!" (23)

A horrible premonition sent them dashing to the secret place where their money had been hidden. Nothing remained.

—*John McClellan*

4 JULY
♋

Beef, Lemons, and Cheese

Our victory in the War of Independence owes a good deal to outsiders, including the Poles and the French. Poland gave us Kosciusko; France gave us Lafayette. There are indications that in their hearts the Poles still prefer the Americans to the Soviets. The *New York Times* reports that a Polish admiral, entertaining Russian naval dignitaries, ended an effusively sycophantic speech with a hearty "Comrades! A toast to your glorious Navy! Bottoms up!"

During one of the breathing spells of the Napoleonic Wars, Bonaparte arranged for an international flotilla to line up for review by the empress. As her barge passed each vessel, sailors clinging to the shrouds were supposed to wave their hats and shout three times, *"Vive l'Impératrice!"* The frigate representing the United States received a special commendation, though the crew had not learned the French words. Instead, the captain had them shout lustily, "Beef, lemons, and cheese!"

5 JULY
♋

Pop Goes the Weasel

"Pop Goes the Weasel" was played frequently at square dances in my childhood; but I could not conceive how weasels popped. It turned out that a *weasel* was a hatter's tool, while *pop* meant "to pawn"; apparently hatters were an impecunious lot:

Up and down the City Road,
  In and Out the Eagle,
That's the way the money goes,
  Pop goes the weasel!

A ha'penny for a cotton ball,
  A farthing for a needle,
That's the way the money goes,
  Pop goes the weasel!

Half a pound of tupenny rice,
  Half a pound of treacle,
Mix it up and make it nice,
  Pop goes the weasel!

Every time my mother goes out,
  The monkey's on the table,
Cracking nuts and eating spice,
  Pop goes the weasel!
                            —*W. R. Mardale*

I was not the only one confused by "Pop Goes the Weasel":

HERTFORDSHIRE HARMONY

There was an old fellow of Tring,
Who, when somebody asked him to sing,
  Replied, "Ain't it odd?
  I can never tell *God*
Save the Weasel from *Pop Goes the King.*"
                            —*Anonymous*

6 JULY
♋

In Defense of the Maligned Cliché

Clichés are in season the year round, and it is a rare day when you can't hear
hunters banging away at them in the woods. I don't feel sorry for the creatures; they
are by no means an endangered species, and they breed fast.

Still, we would be poorer without them. The cliché is a writer's best friend—
closer than mother, dog, or pipe; as indispensable as air. Just try to hold your breath
long enough to put together as few as five sensible sentences without a cliché. You
can't do it.

Webster's Second defines a cliché as a "trite phrase that has lost precise meaning
by iteration; a hackneyed or stereotyped phrase." Hackneyed. Stereotyped. Full-blown
clichés, both of them.

Some clichés may have lost their cutting edge through iteration, but others are more apt, pithy, and vivid than any substitute that has been offered. They need not worry about hunters; bullets bounce off their backs.

I give you the first ten clichés that pop into my head:

- Go the whole hog
- The acid test
- Wear and tear
- A foregone conclusion
- Dull as ditchwater
- His heart was in his mouth
- Lock, stock, and barrel
- He drinks like a fish
- A tower of strength
- The quality of life

How many can you improve on? Eight? Three? If you improve on one, your new expression will become a cliché before you can say Jack Robinson.

Fine style contains a minimum of clichés, to be sure. But you can't write everything for posterity. You would not insist that a 100-yard-dash champion keep dashing forever, would you? He has to rest between runs. *Reculer pour mieux sauter,* as the French cliché puts it. William Shakespeare, a writer still well regarded, never resisted an impulse to slow from a verbal spurt to a stroll or even stretch out in the sun and take a nap.

There is nothing worse than a cliché. Except anything I can think of to replace it.

7 JULY
♋

Sea, Alter Onto!

These nursery rhymes are drawn from the names in the Toronto telephone book:

> Ryder Cocke Hosse
> Turban Berry Crosse
> Tuzzi Affan Leddy
> Oppinga Wye Torres
> Rings Anna Fynn Gersh
> Annabelle Sanna Towes
> Furr Shi Shallouf Music
> Ware Evert Shi Ghosh.
>
> Barr Barre Black Shipp
> Haff Yew Anney Wool
> Yetts Herr, Yetts Herr

Three Baggs Voll
Wan Farr Durr Master
Won Forder Dame
An Wun Varder Littleboys
Watt Lief Sinne Allain.

Jack Spratt Codd Ita Knowe Fatte
Hitz Wyver Codd Ita Noll Ean
Anso Bett Wynn Ditto Offen
Thayer Lick Turr Platte Kleane.

Merrie Merry Quaint Caunt Ririe
Howe Dussiaulme Garden Groh
Witt Silver Belson Cockell Schells
And Pretty Mayes Allin Arro.

Jaques Aingell
Wenn Opper Hill
Topicha Paylor Watter
Jaques Fell Down
Ann Brooke Hiss Crown
Angell Kamm Tumber Linne Affe Tarr.

Little Jack Horner
Hee Sattin Acorn Knerr
Eaton Niece Christmas Pye
When Heap Putt Innis Thumm
Anto Kautz Appel Lum
Ens Hedd Watte Good Boye Amm Ei.

Liddle Mees Muffitt
Saa Tonner Tufford
Eaton Herr Corzon Waye
Winn Alongo Kammer Spyra
Unda Sathe Down Beese Eidher
Ann Frydmann Mies Muffitt Taw Way.

(Just to show how easy the trick is, the author constructs one verse in two different ways:)

Singer Songer Sikka Spence
A Puckett Fuller Wry
Forrin Twinney Black Birze
Beckett Inner Pye
Wenner Pye Wass Opal
The Beers Spick Annis Singh
Nowe Wasson Datta Dainty Dische
Toussaint Bee Forder King?

Zinga Zunka Garson Spenst
Pock Effs Fowler Aye

Farrand Wenn Ablack Burss
Becki Tinney Pye
Wenther Pyne Watts Appin
Tee Busby Gann Tosh Ing
Noh Wax Sindall Adeney Ting
Tuzex Bee Ford Durkin?

—*Jay Ames*

8 JULY
♋

To-do Over Seins Nus

Cadie Posses wrote Louisa Bonner from Nice:

Inspired by the beach here (toasted Titsville—all sizes, shapes and, this year, ages!), I've come up with the following:

Y avait une jeune fille de Fréjus
Qui allait à la messe les seins nus.
"Si Mémé bronze les siens
Sur la plage Juan-les-Pins,
Pourquois donc vous êtes tous si émus?

Louisa asked me to rough out an English approximation of the limerick. Everything went fine up to the very last word:

A daring young lady named Cass
One Sunday went topless to mass,
Saying, "Granny tans *hers*
On the beach at Five Firs—
You are lucky I don't show my ..."

There inspiration deserted me, and the translation remains incomplete.

SOME SAINTLY CITIES

A sporty young man in St. Pierre
Had a sweetheart and oft went to sierre.
She was Gladys by name,
And one time when he came
Her mother said: "Gladys St. Hierre."

A globe-trotting man from St. Paul
Made a trip to Japan in the faul.
One thing he found out,
As he rambled about,
Was that Japanese ladies St. Taul.

A guy asked two jays at St. Louis
What kind of an Indian the Souis.
   They said: "We're no en-
   cyclopedia, by hen!"
Said the guy: "If you fellows St. Whouis?"

A bright little maid in St. Thomas
Discovered a suit of pajhomas.
   Said the maiden "Well, well!
   What they are I can't tell;
But I'm sure that these garments St. Mhomas."
        —Ferdinand G. Christgau

A COUPLE OF YAKS

A yak from the hills of Iraq
Met a yak he had known awhile back.
   They went out to dine,
   And talked of lang syne—
Yak-ety, yak-ety, yak.

        —W.R.E.

THE OLD MAN FROM DUNDOON

There was an old man from Dundoon
Who always ate soup with a fork,
   For he said, "As I eat
   Neither fish, fowl, nor flesh,
I should finish my dinner too quick."
        —Anonymous

THERE WAS A YOUNG FELLOW OF TRINITY

There was a young Fellow of Trinity
Who found $y^e \sqrt{\infty}$;
But y^e number of digits
Gave him y^e fidgets;
He dropped Math and took up Divinity.
        —Anonymous

9 JULY

Odysseus Goes Home

Not the least of life's mysteries is why the titles on the spines of American book jackets run from the top down, while the titles on the spines of British book jackets run from the bottom up.

But that does not affect this fancied book-jacket blurb, which reads, quite properly, from left to right and top to bottom:

THE ODYSSEY

When Homer's first novel, *The Wrath of Achilles,* became an all-time best-seller (with no fewer than twenty-three written copies and got by heart well over a hundred minstrels), critics said "never again." *Odysseus Goes Home* should make them eat their words. The gifted author (who still prefers to use a pseudonym) has this time taken as his (or her?) subject the adventures of General Odysseus and a handful of officers and N.C.O.'s who, demobbed after the fall of Troy, were persistently baffled by the archcrook, Poseidon, in their attempt to return home. Needless to say, the wily General, aided by the Lady Pallas, finally outwitted him. Here is the whole stuff of adventure: shipwreck, *femmes fatales,* one-eyed toughs, plot and counterplot, with a happy ending and an unexceptionable moral. If Penelope, Circe, Calypso, Polyphemus and the Siren sisters do not become household words, we shall eat our fillets.

—L.E.J.

10 JULY
♋

"I Never Nurs'd a Dear Gazelle"

A verse in *Lalla Rookh,* by Thomas Moore, ends:

> I never nurs'd a dear gazelle,
>   To glad me with its soft black eye,
> But when it came to know me well,
>   And love me, it was sure to die!

Parodists found this irresistible. Charles Dickens wrote, "I never nursed a dear gazelle, to glad me with its soft black eye, but when it came to know me well, and love me, it was sure to marry a market-gardener."

One poet was so taken with Moore's verse that he parodied it twice:

> I've never had a piece of toast
>   Particularly long and wide,
> But fell upon the sanded floor,
>   And always on the buttered side.
> *—H. S. Leigh*

'TWAS EVER THUS

I never rear'd a young gazelle
  (Because, you see, I never tried);

But had it known and loved me well,
    No doubt the creature would have died.

My rich and aged Uncle John
    Has known me long and loves me well,
But still persists in living on—
    I wish he were a young gazelle.
                    —*H. S. Leigh*

Lewis Carroll tried his hand:

I never loved a dear Gazelle—
    Nor anything that cost me much;
High prices profit those who sell,
    But why should I be fond of such?

To glad me with his soft black eye
    My son comes trotting home from school:
He's had a fight but can't tell why—
    He always was a little fool!

But, when he came to know me well,
    He kicked me out, her testy Sire;
And when I stained my hair, that Belle
    Might note the change, and thus admire

And love me, it was sure to dye
    A muddy green, or staring blue:
Whilst one might trace, with half an eye,
    The still triumphant carrot through.
                    —*Lewis Carroll*

11 JULY
♋

Far (Out) from the Madden Crowd

Mary Ann Madden is den mother to a waggle of wild wags, Madden as hatters, who pepper her column in *New York* magazine with verbal conceits.

I find
Mary Ann Madden
My kind.
Long may she gladden
—With mis'able,
        Quizzable
        Risible

Tricks of the mind—
My inner man!
Long may Mary Ann
    Madden!

                    —*W.R.E.*

Reader responses to Maddening challenges:

REPUNCTUATED AND REDEFINED NAMES:
- WALT W. HITMAN—dispenser of poetic justice.
- BENJA MIND (ISRAELI)—mideastern hallucinogenic.
- SAMMY D. AVIS, JR.—second-best U.S. entertainer.

NEAR MISSES:
- I feel rotten, Egypt, rotten.
- A man, a plan, a canal—Suez!

SILLY DEFINITIONS:
- CARBUNCLE—(1) a nearly identical nephew, (2) brothers of your mother's carburetor.

INVENTED NAMES FOR OCCUPATIONS:
- HEINZ ZEIT—German historian (follower of Forsyte).

ONE-WORD INSERTS:
- Into the valley of death rode the six hundred dumbbells.
- He who hesitates is, uh, lost.
- Mene, Mene, Tekel, Upharsin, Inc.
- Love is just $5 around the corner.

TERRIBLE RIDDLES:
- Why did the moron throw a clock out the window?
  Who else but a moron would throw a clock out the window?

12 JULY
♋

On Love and Marriage

We make marriages in heaven, give birth to them on earth, and live with them in— but there! I am jesting.

You may be sure I do not subscribe to the wry views expressed below. Louise would never permit it.

LOVE LEADS TO MARRIAGE

Love leads to marriage; marriage then
Slays love, and by new love is slain;
So round and round the two are led,
The dead extinguishing the dead.
                              —*W.R.E.*

CAUSE AND EFFECT

On his death-bed poor Lubin lies;
   His spouse is in despair;
With frequent sobs and mutual cries,
   They both express their care.

"A different cause," says Parson Sly,
   "The same effect may give:
Poor Lubin fears that he may die;
   His wife, that he may live."
                              —*Matthew Pryor*

13 JULY
♋

A Pest Iamb, Anapest Rick Ballad Was
(Or a Ballad in a Sad Café)

I lunched with Rick Ballad. *I* lunched; Rick did not. He is on a medically supervised diet which has cut his weight from 250 pounds to 225 pounds in a fortnight; he still has 25 pounds to go. Each day he takes only water, at least six glasses, plus black coffee, with an admixture of a devilish powder that provides him with a total intake of exactly 400 calories. It is a sad sight to see him sipping his Perrier while I sip my scotch, but it is for his own good. I would like to think this villanelle on poetic meter, composed in his honor, contributed to his reform:

Rick Ballad (God him pity)
   Set out last night to dine.
His menu was a Ditty
   In Galliambic line.

His soup was Virelaic;
   His cocktail, Dipodee;
His Spondee was Alcaic;
   His Distych, Ditrochee.

He took a pinch of Rhythm,
   Of Ode and Choriamb,
And mixing Rondeaux with 'em
   He seasoned his Iamb.

He ordered baked Sestinas
   And half-baked Doggerel;
He licked his Lyric clean as
   A Sapphic Kyrielle.

He flavored Terza Rima
   With Pastoral and Thesis;
Had Chant Royal with cream—a
   Bucolic Diaeresis.

His Tercet was a salad
   Of Sonnet and Cinquain.
"Ballade too," ordered Ballad,
   "And Double the Refrain."

Verse Onomatopoeian,
   Szysigium to taste,
Enlarged unendingly an
   Enjambement of waist.

Then Ballad gorged on Dactyl,
   While Trochee and Molossus
Still down his maw were packed till
   He outcolossed Colossus.

(Colossus fell, and wallowed.
   So, too, poor Ballad fell;
And, dying, left unswallowed
   His final Villanelle.)
               —W.R.E.

14 JULY
♋

Unwind My Jaw, Untie My Tongue

In French a tongue twister is a passage *à décrocher la mâchoire*—"to unwind the jaw"—or *pour délier la langue*—"to untie the tongue." I give you these tongue twisters to commemorate Bastille Day:

    Ton thé t'a-t-il ôté ta toux?
  (Has your tea got rid of your cough?)

  Si six scies scient six cigares
  Six cent scies scient six cent cigares.
(If six saws saw six cigars, six hundred saws saw six hundred cigars.)

Les chemises de l'archiduchesse
Sont sèches et archisèches.
(The archduchess's shirtwaists are dry and more than dry.)

Un chasseur sachant chasser chassait un chat.
(A hunter, knowing how to hunt, hunted a cat.)

Didon dîna, dit-on, du dos d'un dodu dindon.
(Dido dined, they say, off the back of a plump turkey.)

La pipe au papa du Pape Pie pue.
(Pope Pius's father's pipe stinks.)

Ces six saucissons-cis sont six sous les six.
(These six sausages are six cents for six.)

A Rocquevaire, la rivière se verse vers les verres du ver vert.
(At Rocquevaire, the river flows toward the glasses of the green worm.)

I'm not sure what you would call the next one. It's not really a tongue twister; it's a group of French words which become incomprehensible when pronounced rapidly. Try it out on a Frenchman. He will swear that it is in some Oriental tongue:

Pie a haut nid, caille a bas nid:
Verre n'a pas d'eau: rat en a, chat en a.

This means, more or less:

The magpie's nest is high,
The grouse's nest is low;
The water glass is dry;
The cat and rat
Have water, though—
The mole, also.
—W.R.E.

Quel bruit a nuit à l'huitre? Le bruit que j'ai oui hier nuit a nui à l'huitre.
(What noise annoyed the oyster?
The noise I heard last night annoyed the oyster.)

15 JULY
♋

Tax That Fellow Under the Tree

Senator Russell Long said, "Tax reform means don't tax you, don't tax me, tax that fellow under the tree." Albert Jay Nock said, "Virtue is more to be feared than vice, because its excesses are not subject to the regulations of conscience." These aphorisms are funny because they prick human foibles.

Samuel Butler, a master aphorist, commented that life is one long process of getting tired. Butler also remarked that the fight between theists and atheists is about whether God shall be called God or shall have another name.

Some of Butler's finest aphorisms deal with the art of lying:

- If a man is not a good, sound, honest, capable liar there is no truth in him.
- Any fool can tell the truth, but it requires a man of some sense to know how to lie well.
- I do not mind lying, but I hate inaccuracy.
- Lying has a kind of respect and reverence with it. We pay a person the compliment of acknowledging his superiority whenever we lie to him.

16 JULY
♋

Snallygaster VII

From the *Valley Register,* Middletown, Maryland, February 19, 1909:

THE GREAT GO-DEVIL
WAS SEEN IN OHIO

T. C. Harbaugh Saw It Sailing Toward Maryland

The great Go-Devil must have passed over Ohio before it reached Maryland, as will be seen from the following letter from T. C. Harbaugh, of Casstown, Ohio, which was received too late for last week's issue.

Casstown, Ohio, February 9, 1909

Editors of *The Register*:

A gigantic monster passed over this place last night about 6 o'clock. It was plainly visible, had two immense bronze wings, an enormous head from which horn-like objects protruded, and a tail 20 feet long. It emitted a noise like the screech of an octtollopus. Some who saw it declared it to be a Snallygaster. The monster was moving toward Maryland. From the brief view I had of it, I think it was either an octtollopus, a gigantillocutus or a Snallygaster. . . . I sincerely hope that this monster will not visit your beautiful Valley.

T. C. Harbaugh

MORE ON 12 AUGUST.

17 JULY
♋

Alcoholic Disarray

Don't mix anagrams and alcohol. When the label on your scotch turns from TEACHERS to CHEATERS, forgo the next drink. Take leave of rye when SEAGRAMS becomes MASSAGER. If your weakness is brandy, think hard when you read PERNOD as PONDER. And though you may not be seeing pink elephants, you are coming close when you reach for a DRAMBUIE and see a RAPID EMU.

A WHISKY drinker may ask, "WHY SKI?" Indeed, I ask that question when I have had nothing to drink at all. Similarly it is understandable that a man brooding over his BELLOWS on ice should SOB WELL.

Enigma, publication of the National Puzzlers' League, is the source of the forgoing anagrammatic observations on alcohol. Some further Enigmatic thoughts on the subject:

1. SOUR MASH. SO RUM HAS?
2. AN ALCOHOLIC BEVERAGE. GAL, CAN I HAVE COOL BEER?
3. A BOTTLE OF WHISKEY. IT BE THY FLASK O' WOE.
4. DEMON ALE. LEMONADE.

On entering the National Puzzlers' League the new member adopts a special name, or *nom.* (Mine is Wede.) The four anagrams above are credited to the following noms: (1) Hap. (2) Amaranth. (3) Amaranth. (4) Merlin.

18 JULY
♋

How Do I Love Thee? Let Me Count the Fuel Stops
(with apologies to Elizabeth Barrett Browning)

Effective July 17 Pacific Western Airlines flies Seattle to Vancouver nonstop; and on to Yellowknife, Fort Chipewyan, Grand Forks, Inuvik, Tofino, Bella Coola, Cambridge Bay, Peace River, Norman Wells, Dawson Creek, Hay, Bella Bella, Penticton, Tahsis, Castlegar, Trail, and Fort McMurray.—*Advertisement*

> In your time, Liz, lips meeting lips in surrey
>   Swore love eterne, swore faithfulness for life.
> Now love's more like a flight to Fort McMurray,
>   With pauses to refuel at Yellowknife,
> Fort Chipewyan, Grand Forks, and Inuvik;
>   Tofina, Bella Coola, Cambridge Bay;

Peace River, Norman Wells, and Dawson Crick.
Our love's eterne—with pauses on the way.

I buckle seat belt, tamp out cigarette
    When coming down at Hay or Bella Bella,
And hope that Fort McMurray will not fret
    If Penticton awhile delay a fella,
Or Tahsis please, or Castlegar regale.
    I shall but love thee better after Trail.
                                        —*W.R.E.*

Elizabeth Barrett Browning was not the first nor the last to ask, "How do I love thee?" Some answers suggested in *Word Ways*:

- The cardiologist: with all my heart
- The marathon runner: all the way
- The Indian: without reservation
- The contortionist: head over heels
- The psychoanalyst: unshrinkingly
- The dieter: through thick and thin
- The wheelwright: tirelessly
- The elephant trainer: roguishly
- The mink farmer: furtively
- The farmer: whole hog
- The couturier: in my fashion

19 JULY

♋

Singular Plurals, Obliging Objects

SINGULAR PLURALS

Now if mouse in the plural should be, and is, mice,
Then house in the plural, of course, should be hice,
And grouse should be grice and spouse should be spice
And by the same token should blouse become blice.

And consider the goose with its plural of geese;
Then a double caboose should be called a cabeese,
And noose should be neese and moose should be meese
And if redskin papoose should be twins, it's papeese.

Then if one thing is that, while some more is called those,
Then more than one hat, I assume, would be hose,
And gnat would be gnose and pat would be pose
And likewise the plural of rat would be rose.
                                        —*Author unknown*

OBLIGING OBJECTS

I steal the keel
I stole the coal
I have stolen the colon.
            —*A. M. Zwicky*

I smite the kite / I smote the coat / I have smitten
    the kitten
I bite the mite / I bit the mitt / I have bitten
    the mitten
I break the take / I broke the toque / I have broken
    the token
I take the bake / I took the book / I have taken
    the bacon.
                    —*Martha Awdziewic*

They choose the hues.
They chose the hose.
The have chosen the hosen.

They mow the banks of the row.
They mowed the banks of the road.
They have mown the banks of the Rhone.

I do it with the buoys.
I did it with the biddies.
I have done it with the bunnies.
            —*A. M. Zwicky*

20 JULY
♋

The Norris Plan II

"You've been having too many novels in the last few years," he said solicitously. "Every three months or so. It weakens you, honey. *Passion Flower* was too much for you—let alone *Margaret Yorke*."

The very titles made waves of nausea sweep over her. She clutched her mallet and swung listlessly at the croquet ball before her. It went short of the wicket.

"A lot of other American authors present interesting phases of this same problem," continued Charlie, hitting his ball deftly between two wickets, and rapping the stake. "Take the late James Branch Cabell, for instance. He was undoubtedly one of the outstanding figures of our era; but he did not know the meaning of book-control. Overproduction weakened him, and he died in giving birth to his last novel. If he had practiced literary contraception, he might have been alive today. Let me see—are you still for the wicket?"

Kathy shook her head vaguely. She was thinking again of her panic-stricken visit to her publisher this very morning and her face burned, and her hands were dry. A business-like man; it was nothing to him. No, there was no question about Mrs. Norris's condition; she was scheduled for his fall lists. He was sorry, but he did not know any way out of it now. It would be extremely expensive to remove it at this date. He never advised it.

It was like a nightmare. Her publisher had removed her last doubt. This was no longer fear: it was terrible certainty.

"I'm going to have a novel. In October."

No, she did not have the courage to tell Charlie. She dragged herself across the court, and swung dizzily again at the ball. Charlie smiled as it wired itself behind the wicket, and he took his turn, grasping the mallet firmly as he elaborated further on his favorite theme: "There is one thing more I'd like to bring up about this question, and I'm done. It requires approximately three novels a year to sustain our present-day novelists, if they depend on royalties alone. The average number of novels born of literate stock is 2.8; while those of men and women from the pulp-woods is 97.2. You can clearly see where book-control is being practiced. In order to save the decent novelists from bringing about a complete suicide of American literature, not only must they publish more, but the fecundity of the illiterate writers must be curtailed. It must be obvious to anyone who stops to consider the situation at all that our intellectual class of writers is dying out, and the cheaper novelists and less mentally fit are on the increase; it must necessarily follow that our standard of national literature will decline and continue to decline." He paused and drew a sheaf of notes from his hip pocket. Kathy saw the scene rapidly growing black before her eyes; she felt herself swaying guiltily as Charles read the climax of his argument aloud.

"The crux of the whole situation is simply this: our intelligent writers are not producing, and our ignorant, inferior ones are. Unless book-control is stopped among the upper classes, and its use legalized among the lower classes, the best part of our literature will die out, and the country will be over-run by incompetents and morons—"

There was a little moan, and then a faint thud behind him. Kathy had fainted.

—*Corey Ford*

MORE ON 14 SEPTEMBER.

21 JULY
♋

A Gender of Germans

The sexism of the English language pales by comparison with that of German:

THE TALE OF THE FISHWIFE AND ITS SAD FATE

It is a Bleak Day. Hear the Rain, how he pours, and the Hail, how he rattles; and see the Snow, how he drifts along, and oh the Mud, how deep he is! Ah the poor Fishwife, it is stuck fast in the Mire; it has dropped its Basket of Fishes; and its Hands have been cut by the Scales as it seized some of the falling creatures; and one Scale has even got into its Eye, and it cannot get her out. It opens its Mouth to cry for Help; but if any Sound comes out of him, alas, he is drowned by the raging of the Storm. And now a Tomcat has got one of the Fishes and she will surely escape with him. No, she bites off a Fin, she holds her in her Mouth—will she swallow her? No, the Fishwife's brave Mother-dog deserts his Puppies and rescues the Fin—which he eats, himself, as his Reward. O, horror, the Lightning has struck the Fishbasket; he sets him on Fire; see the Flame, how she licks the doomed Utensil with her red and angry Tongue; now she attacks the helpless Fishwife's Foot—she burns him up, all but the big Toe, even *she* is partly consumed; and still she spreads, still she waves her fiery Tongues; she attacks the Fishwife's Leg and destroys *it*; she attacks its Hand and destroys *her*; she attacks its poor worn Garment and destroys *her* also; she attacks its Body and consumes *him;* she wreathes herself about its Heart and *it* is consumed; next about its Breast, and in a Moment *she* is a Cinder; now she reaches its Neck—*he* goes; next its Chin—*it* goes; now its Nose—*she* goes. In another Moment, except Help come, the Fishwife will be no more. Time presses—is there none to succor and to save? Yes! Joy, joy, with flying feet she-Englishwoman comes! But alas, the generous she-Female is too late; where now is the fated Fishwife? It has ceased from its Sufferings, it has gone to a better Land; all that is left of it for its loved Ones to lament over, is this poor smoldering Ash-heap. Ah, woeful, woeful Ash-heap! Let us take him up tenderly, reverently, upon the lowly Shovel, and bear him to his long Rest, with the Prayer that when he rises again it will be in a Realm where he will have one good square responsible Sex, and have it all to himself, instead of having a mangy lot of assorted Sexes scattered all over him in Spots.

—*Mark Twain*

22 JULY
♋

Two for Cassin

I will let you guess how long ago this verse to my fourth daughter was written:

> In a rush the years are passin'—
> One and one makes two for Cassin.
> Lucky Years, to coexist
> With Miss Eyes-of-Amethyst!
> Not-so-Lucky Years, to know
> She will stay, while they must go!

Soon, perhaps, some lovesick Year
Will refuse to leave you, dear—
What if 19 blankty 7
Opts for Cass instead of heaven?
Oh, what fun if we could wait
Evermore for blankty 8!
                                   —W.R.E.

23 JULY
♌

Picture Names

Identify the names of these four well-known people by the pictures.

1.

2.

3.

4.

24 JULY
ℌ

Anathema Alphabetica

Advertisers artfully agitate, alarm,
Browbeat, bluster, bombinate,
Coo, coax, caress, captivate, charm,
Delicately, doucely deprecate
(Denigrate? Desecrate?)
Examples eloquently explicate:
   "Elephantine endomorphs! Emancipate! Escape,
   Free from fatness, fell, foul, fateful:
   Great girth Gargantuan (gaze, girls, gape!)
   Huge hulking hams (Heavens, how hateful!)
   I invite inspection: I introduce
   (Justly jaunty) *Juvenating Juice!*
   Kissably kempt keeps Kitchen Kate,
   Lately lachrymosely lumpish,
   Languishing lads lasciviate
   (Miserably, morosely mumpish)
   Madcap maidens merrily mismate
   (Novice now nurses neonate)
   Over overcoming odious overweight!
   (Others offer only opiates,
   Ours obesity obliterates!)"

Pious purple prose proliferates,
Quakerish questionings quietly quelling,
Righteousness rabidly reverberates
(Religion's rentable—reasonable rates)
Sermonized saccharine sanctifies selling.
Televised treacle triples takings,
Urging uglier undertakings:
Uncouth, ululating urchins,
Vacuous, vain, voluptuous virgins!
Violent vulgarity's vapid void's
What we weakly, wearily witness,
Watching waspish, wog-whipping, witless
Xenophobic xanthocroids!
Yeastier yet your youngster's yen:
Zoolatry's zany zenith—Zen.

—D.H. Monro

25 JULY
ᓂ

Visual Wordplay

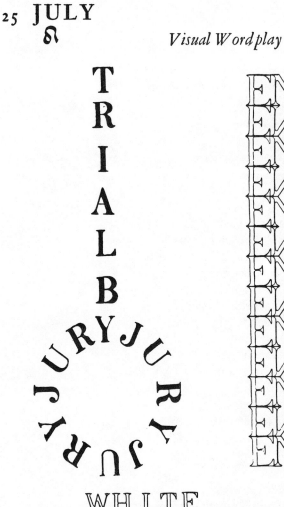

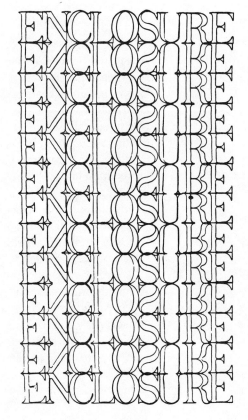

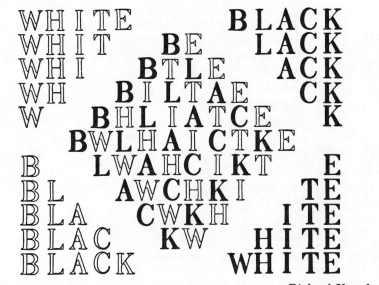

—*Richard Kostelanetz*

26 JULY
♌

Larva, Pupa, Imago

OYSTERVILLE—We arrived last night; I made my first summer inspection of the croquet garden* this morning. The gaps have vanished from the laurel hedge; the rhododendron bushes are rubbing shoulders; the new cypress tree has grown so fast that I'll have to transplant it; and everywhere insects are buzzing, crawling, burrowing, flying, stridulating, supremely indifferent to the presence of their landlord.

There are parallels between etymology, the study of words, and entomology, the study of bugs.

Some 4 million insects are busy insecting at this moment on any moist acre (if you don't believe me, go count them for yourself). The figure is roughly comparable to the number of words in the English language. Some insects, like some words, evolve substantially in structure and activity:

LARVA, PUPA, IMAGO

When I was a larva,
Brashly I would chortle,
"You will see me carve a
Monument immortal."

Growing to a pupa,
Older now and wary,
Still I hoped to scoop a
Brief obituary.

Now, a worn imago,
I don't bother to
Mention my lumbago:
What is that to you?
—*W.R.E.*

One insect, *Phylloxera quercus,* has twenty-one forms, every one of which appears unrelated to the rest. On the other hand, insects of different species may look and act so much alike that the least wary entomologist will hedge on which is which. To confuse them would be entomological malapropping.

Words are equally deceitful. Take *logistics.* Everybody knows what it means—the transport, quartering, and supply of troops and, by extension, comparable arrangements in other activities. Yet there is an entirely different logistics, meaning "calculation by arithmetic." The first word comes from *lodge*—French *loger*—and the second from Greek *logos,* "word or number."

*See 18 June, 22 June.

Words are similar to insects, too, in the variety of their life spans. A May fly will die in twenty minutes. A queen ant, if permitted to mature, has a life expectancy of sixteen years. Similarly, in language, the word *Edsel,* for a failed automobile, is lucky to last a generation; the word for *wheel,* in variant forms, has been with us for ten millennia.

27 JULY
♌

No Wonder There Are Keel Marks on Her Lips

When your houseguests grow weary of television, bridge, and Perrier water, pass around slips bearing a familiar line of poetry and ask each player to add a rhyming line. Victorian wordplayers called these efforts "bouts rimés." Richard Armour calls them "punctured poems." Under any name, they are fun.

Some risible examples:

MARLOWE: Was this the face that launched a thousand ships?
No wonder there are keel marks on her lips.

SHAKESPEARE: Full fathom five thy father lies.
I pushed him. I apologize.

CONGREVE: Music hath charms to soothe the savage breast.
That's why I keep a flute tucked in my vest.

THOMAS BROWN: I do not like thee, Doctor Fell.
The reason is you charge like hell.

BROWNING: I sprang to the stirrup, and Joris and he;
I sat upon Joris, the third guy on me.

MILTON: When I consider how my light is spent.
I'm glad utilities come with the rent.
—*Richard Armour*

WORDSWORTH: My heart leaps up when I behold
My pumpernickel green with mold.

ROSSETTI: Who has seen the wind? Neither you nor I,
But California smog will surely catch your eye.

KILMER: I think that I shall never see—
My contact lens fell in my tea.

POE: Once upon a midnight dreary,
                    Late-late show starred Wallace Beery.
                        —*Mary Youngquist and Harry Hazard*

                    I'll take you home again, Kathleen;
                    That last martini turned you green.
                        —*Bill Balance*

28 JULY
♌

More John Hancocks

Ever since John Hancock writ his name large on the Declaration of Independence, *John Hancock* and *signature* have been synonymous. Here are the John Hancocks of ten well-known people, all dead. How many can you identify?

1. Composer

4. Dictator

7. President

2. Novelist

5. Queen

8. Poet

3. Emperor

6. Conductor

9. Madman

29 JULY
ઈ

The Recruit

Sez Corporal Madden to Private McFadden:
　　"Bedad, yer a bad un!
　　　Now turn out yer toes!
　　Yer belt is unhookit,
　　Yer cap is on crookit,
　　Ye may not be dhrunk,
　　But, be jabers, ye look it!
　　　　Wan—two!
　　　　Wan—two!
Ye monkey-faced divil, I'll jolly ye through!
　　　　Wan—two!—
　　　Time! Mark!
Ye march like the aigle in Cintheral Parrk!"

Sez Corporal Madden to Private McFadden:
　　"Yer figger wants padd'n'—
　　Sure, man, ye've no shape!
　　Behind ye yer shoulders
　　Stick out like two boulders;
　　Yer shins is as thin
　　As a pair of pen-holders!
　　　　Wan—two!—
　　　Time! Mark!
I'm dhry as a dog—I can't shpake but I bark!"

Says Corporal Madden to Private McFadden:
　　"I'll not stay a gaddin',
　　Wid dagoes like you!
　　I'll travel no farther,
　　I'm dyin' for—wather;—
　　Come on, if ye like,—
　　Can ye loan me a quather?
　　　　Ya-as, you—
　　　What,—two?
And ye'll pay the potheen? Ye're a daisy! Whurroo!
　　　　You'll do!
　　　Whist! Mark!
The rigiment's flattered to own ye, me spark!"

—Robert William Chambers

30 JULY
♌

I'm Afraid Mr. Arch Will Recline

More malapropisms.

Arch Winters has a friend named Miss Rosemary. Miss Rosemary has a cook named Beatrice. One day Beatrice served Arch an unsatisfactory dish of grits. "If you invites Mr. Arch again, Miss Rosemary," she mourned, "I'm afraid he will recline." Beatrice also told her employer, "Miss Rosemary, you don't understand mens. You got to have a neat house to depress them." And she complained to Arch about Miss Rosemary's absentmindedness: "She just can't seem to get accumulated."

Bob Knille found these malapropisms in Smollett's *Humphrey Clinker:*

- Methinks you mought employ your talons better, than to encourage servants to pillage their masters.
- What is life but a veil of affliction? O Mary! the whole family have been in such a constipation.
- The 'squire did all in his power, but could not prevent his being put in chains, and confined among common manufacturers.
- I was going into a fit of asterisks.
- Yours with true infection, Win. Jenkins.

Malapropping becomes an art form here:

- Be it ever so hovel, there's no place like home.
- I was down on the lower East side today and saw those old Testament houses.
- I got up at the crank of dawn.
- We are all cremated equal.
- I refused to tell him who I was—I used a facetious name.
- The food in that restaurant is abdominal.
- Explain it to me in words of one cylinder.
- Congress is still in season.
- In all my bored days.
- All of Abe Lincoln's pictures make him look so thin and emancipated.

—Goodman Ace

A young woman I know, complaining about a shockingly small raise she had received, said three times with emphatic sarcasm, that the raise had come to a "whooping" $5 a week. She meant "whopping."

31 JULY
♌

How New York Solved Its Garbage Problem

On July 31, 1993, as Captain R. Bendiner, master of the garbage scow *Mother Mary,* headed his vessel into the Atlantic to dump a load of garbage, he noticed an enormous eel undulating in his wake. The head was raised, waving from side to side as if trying to signal, and the sucker mouth repeatedly opened wide and then shut again.

The captain decided the eel was hungry. Experimentally he ordered a crew member to shy the remains of a leather walking boot at the creature, which caught the footwear in midair and swallowed it at a gulp. In succession, the eel then gulped down a dressmaker's form, a rusty fender, a stack of newspapers bound together with wire, and a tire from a trailer truck.

Long before the *Mother Mary* reached her disposal area, her entire complement of garbage had vanished into that insatiable maw. The eel's length had noticeably increased.

It occurred to Captain Bendiner that he might turn a profit on that eel. He suspended his hipboot by means of a fishing pole and line over the stern, just above the highest leap of the monster. The eel followed this bait back to shore and remained thereafter in the vicinity. Thenceforward, instead of disposing of offal at sea, the captain fed it to his new friend, which within a few weeks reached a length of more than twenty feet and was so tame that it purred loudly when he scratched its head.

On August 11, arriving at the scow to greet his pet, now known affectionately as Joe, the captain found the creature writhing happily about in a cloud of tiny, wriggling elvers. The captain at once changed the mother's name to Josephine and rushed to City Hall, where, for the reasonable fee of a billion and a half dollars annually (inflation was picking up), he contracted to dispose of the city's entire supply of waste matter. To this end, after a brief period of training, he stationed an elver at the mouth of each sewer pipe in town. Day by day they gorged on the effluvium, breaking away only to catch in midair the garbage dumped on them by sanitation trucks.

That is how New York became the cleanest city in the world.

*   *   *

But the disposal system had an unanticipated side effect. The eels, growing inordinately, soon blocked both the Hudson River and the East River. Captain Bendiner thereupon covered their serried backs with fill, on which he built elaborate complexes of office buildings and high-rise apartments. He was able to let these out at an enormous profit, partly because the tenants loved the gentle, steady rippling motion imparted to the edifices by the stirring of the foundation. Captain Bendiner became the wealthiest man of our times.

Another interesting side effect was a wave of suicides among biologists, who had insisted that eels are not viviparous.

—W.R.E.

AUGUST

1 AUGUST
♌

Hot Lot

The Game of Words quotes this French wordplay, which tells how Lot's two daughters plied him with liquor and then seduced him in order to perpetuate humankind:

> Il but;
> Il devint tendre.
> Et puis il fut
> Son gendre.
> > —*The Chevalier de Bouffleurs,*
> > *eighteenth century*

In English, it would go like this:

> Lot drank strong waters—
> Tupped his daughters.
> This made paw
> His son-in-law.
> > —*W.R.E.*

Roy Breunig has carved an even shorter poem from this domestic incident, but it seems to me to miss the fun:

> Lot
> Sot.

A *New Statesman* contest produced this imagined advertisement for a motion picture based on the unusual relationship of Lot and his daughters:

> Trapped in a Cave!
> How Two Brave Girls Helped Their Daddy
> A Drama About *Their* Family, for *Your* Family
> A Man—Two Girls—a Bottle of Coca-Cola
> THRILL to a New Kind of Love!
> BIGGER than "Oh, No, Onan" . . .
> BOLDER than "Too Far, Mrs. Potiphar"
> BETTER than "I Was a Sodomite for the F.B.I."
> *Next week at your neighborhood theater—*
> MR. LOT GOES TO TOWN
> > —*R. Wuliger*

All this is exciting, not to say rejuvenating. But I am writing on the first day of August, and it is hot. If Lot's daughters had tried their wiles on their father today, they would have failed:

AUGUST

Lot's daughters
Poured strong waters
  Into Lot.
But he ... would ... not.
  Too hot.
      —W.R.E.

2 AUGUST
♌

Spécialités du Pays

A book on Australian cookery contains a recipe for "Groper, head and shoulders, boiled." The recipe ends: "Great care should be taken of the immense gelatinous lips, as these are considered the best part."

Other ghastly recipes:

GRILLED GORILLA'S FOOT

One foot will suffice for each person.

First, shave the upper part of the foot and wash in warm water. With a gimlet (for preference as the skin is very hard) bore a number of holes through the thick skin of the under part of the foot. Grease liberally with lard. Grill slowly for about twenty minutes with the under surfaces *downwards*. Then turn the foot over and continue to grill steadily. From time to time place a fork on the foot. When it is quite done it will be found that the toes will curl firmly over the fork, so that it can be lined up and put on a hot plate. Leave the fork in the toes and serve immediately.

—L. C. Udall

ARABIAN GOAT

This dish is suitable for ceremonial or alfresco banquets.

Take a goat that is fattened on milk and kill it. Skin and eviscerate. Pierce the carcass with a stake, which may conveniently be passed between the thighs to the throat. Roast over a slow wood fire, turning upon the spit.

Before serving, brighten the eyes (toothsome morsels) with vinegar and leave them in place. They may then be extracted with a forefinger by the guest of honor.

—Christopher Ounsted

SCRATCH THAT MUDBLOWER;
ONE LOVE-MAIDEN TO GO (a sapphic)

*Research having demonstrated that diners will not order fishes with ugly names,
the National Marine Fisheries Service is seeking to make the names more attractive.*
—The Wall Street Journal

Toadfish, croaker, hogsucker, calmly swimming;
Harmless, care-free mudblower, spurned by humans—
Keep those names! they save you from being eaten—
    Flaunted on menus.

Ratfish, gag, grunt, viperfish, red-ear, never
Turn to lovefish, honeyfish, poached in parsley.
When it's written "love-maiden" on a menu,
    Mudblower's tasty.

—W.R.E.

3 AUGUST
♌

Fame and the Poet

If fame has passed you by, take comfort in this allegory:

*The Poet, having devoted his years to worshiping at the altar of Fame,
at which he has offered all his creations without reward or recognition, has
just completed his best work, a sonnet. But now he feels that his life has
in fact been wasted in pursuit of illusion, for a Fame he shall never see.
He decides to give up his career: and is just about to burn all his work,
when suddenly Fame herself—in Greek dress, with a long golden trumpet
in hand—stands before him. "Divine fair lady!" he exclaims in awe, "you
have come!" Reverently he offers her his latest achievement, the sonnet:*

POET. This is my sonnet. Is it well done?

[*Fame takes it, reads it in silence, while the Poet watches rapturously.*]

FAME. You're a bit of all right.

POET. What?

FAME. You're IT.

POET. But . . . it is not possible . . . are you she that knew Homer?

FAME. Homer? Lord, yes. Blind old bat, 'e couldn't see a yard.

[*Fame walks beautifully to the window. She opens it and puts her head
out.*]

FAME [*in a voice with which a woman in an upper story would cry for
help if the house was well alight*].

    Hi! Hi! Boys! Hi! Say, folks! Hi!

[*The murmur of a gathering crowd is heard. Fame blows her trumpet.*]

FAME. Hi, he's a poet. [*Quickly, over her shoulder.*] What's your
name?

POET. De Rêves.*

FAME. His name's de Rêves.

POET. Harry de Rêves.

FAME. His pals call him Harry.

THE CROWD. Hooray! Hooray! Hooray!

FAME. Say, what's your favorite color?

POET. I ... I ... I don't understand.

FAME. Well, which do you like best, green or blue?

POET. Oh—er—blue. [*She blows her trumpet out the window.*] No—
er—I think green.

FAME. Green is his favorite color.

THE CROWD. Hooray! Hooray! Hooray!

FAME. 'Ere, tell us something. They want to know all about yer.

POET. Wouldn't you perhaps ... would they care to hear my sonnet,
if you would—er ...

FAME [*picking up quill*]. Here, what's this?

POET. Oh, that's my pen.

FAME [*after another blast on her trumpet*]. He writes with a quill.
[*Cheers from The Crowd.*]

FAME [*going to a cupboard*]. Here, what have you got in here?

POET. Oh ... er ... those are my breakfast things.

FAME [*finding a dirty plate*]. What have yer had on this one?

POET [*mournfully*]. Oh, eggs and bacon.

FAME [*at the window*]. He has eggs and bacon for breakfast.

THE CROWD. Hip hip hip *hooray!* Hip hip hip *hooray!* Hip hip hip
hooray!

FAME. Hi, and what's this?

POET [*miserably*]. Oh, a golf stick.

FAME. He's a man's man! He's a virile man! He's a manly man!
[*Wild cheers from The Crowd, this time only from women's voices.*]

POET Oh, this is terrible. This is terrible. This is terrible.
[*Fame gives another peal on her horn. She is about to speak.*]

POET [*solemnly and mournfully*]. One moment, one moment ...

FAME. Well, out with it.

POET. For ten years, divine lady, I have worshiped you, offering all my
songs ... I find ... I find I am not worthy.

FAME. Oh, you're all right.

POET. No, no, I am not worthy. It cannot be. It cannot possibly be.
Others deserve you more. I must say it! *I cannot possibly love
you.* Others are worthy. You will find others. But I, no, no, no.
It cannot be. It cannot be. Oh, pardon me but it *must* not.
[*Meanwhile Fame has been lighting one of his cigarettes. She sits in a*

*Literally, *of dreams* (French).

comfortable chair, leans right back, and puts her feet right up on the table amongst the poet's papers.]

POET. Oh, I fear I offend you. But—it cannot be.

FAME. Oh, that's all right, old bird; no offense. I ain't going to leave you.

POET. But—but—but—I do not understand.

FAME. I've come to stay, I have.

[*She blows a puff of smoke through her trumpet.*] [*Curtain*]

—*Lord Dunsany*

4 AUGUST
♌

Feinschmecker Uber Alles

German grammar escapes me; in a written sentence, I can never plow through to the ultimate climactic verb. Speech, though, is different. Not knowing the language, I still feel at home in it. I suspect this wordplay is equally amusing to a German or an American:

> Rosen are rot,
> Veilchen are blau.
> Ich liebe Dich
> And hau.

This translation is from Victor Proetz's *Astonishment of Words*:

YANKEE DOODLE DEUTSCHEN

> Ein Yankee Bursch ist fix und schlank
> Und niemals überfett, Herr,
> Und wo Gelgag und Tanz und Gang,
> Wi'n Kats so flink und nett, Herr!
>   Yankee, achte der küste gut,
>   Yankee Doodle Dandy,
>   Drehn un Prahlen nichts dir tut,
>   Yankee Doodle Dandy.

DAS IST EIN DEUTSCHERROCKET

Technical literature in the Air Research and Development Command of the United States Air Force allegedly contains such German-American macaronics as these:

• Guided missile. **Das Sientifiker Geschtenwerkes Firenkrakker.**
• Rocket engine. Firesphitter mit Smoken-und-Schnorten.

* Liquid rocket. Das Skwirten Jucenkind Firenschpitter.
* Guidance system. Das Schteerenwerke.
* Celestial guidance. Das Schruballische Schtargazen Peepenglasser mit Komputer-attachen Schteerenwerke.
* Control system. Das Pullen-und-Schoven Werke.
* Warhead. Das Laudenboomer.
* Nuclear warhead. Das Largeschplitten Laudenboomer.
* Hydrogen device. Das eargeschplitten Laudenboomer mit ein Grosse Holengraund und Alles Kaput.

Departments with responsibility for the above:

* Engineering. Das Aufguefen Grupe.
* Project engineering. Das Schwettennoudter.
* Wind tunnel. Das Huffenpuffen Grupe.
* Computing. Das Schlidenruler Grupe.
* Structural test. Das Pullenparten Grupe.
* Security. Das Schnoopen Bunche.
* Planning. Das Schemen Grupe.
* Support equipment. Das Garterbelten Grupe.

What is the word for *gourmet* in German?
Feinschmecker.

5 AUGUST
♌

The Sword Is Mightier Than the Pen

Dear Grandson Taylor:

How excited you must be to realize that at the age of only one day you are already named Taylor—and after both sides of your family, at that! The Taylors on your mother's side, which is mine, lived in Virginia, and fought the Indians and British a lot. The Taylors on your father's side lived in New England, and learned to read books. One was a very famous Poet whose works no one understands.

If you should decide to model yourself after the Taylor line, I suggest that you look to my side. Poets are all very well, but everyone knows that the Sword is Mightier than the Pen. This hortatory verse is written especially for you, and I hope you will engrave it on your heart:

> Bulwer Lytton (long gone to his final reward)
> Proclaimed the Pen mightier, sir, than the Sword.
> Ever since then, whenever a Poet drops by,
> We hear him reiterate Lytton's old lie.
>
> Democritus, long before Lytton, averred
> That any old action beats any old word;

So Poets say quickly they spoke but in jest
When challenged to put Lytton's *mot* to the test.

With, alas, one exception. A Poet I knew
Was silly enough to think Lytton spoke true.
Of *eau de vie forte* he drank down quite a store,
Then challenged a Swordsman to *combat à mort*.

While the Swordsman was yet in a daze from surprise,
The Poet fired gallons of ink in his eyes,
Backed up by barrages of sonnets; rondels;
Ballades; chants royals; triolets; villanelles.

The trochees and dactyls about him exploded
So fast that the Swordsman was quite incommoded.
He was epigrammed, similed, punned, metaphored,
Until with reluctance he unsheathed his sword

And lopped off the head of that Rhymer of Rhymes,
Then returned to perusing the sports in the *Times*.
The dying head sighed, "It may be now and then
That the edge of the sword has an edge on the pen."

Dear Poets, when Swordsmen drop over to play,
It's wise to say, "Sorry—I'm out for the day."
(And will be, till foxes lie down with the hens;
And will be, till smiths hammer swords into pens.)
—W.R.E.

6 AUGUST
♌

To a Chorus of Hallelujahs

OYSTERVILLE—I have told elsewhere how a tourist once knocked at the door of our home here and asked my father, "Do you belong to that church across the street?"

"No," said Papa. "That church across the street belongs to me."

And it did. Grandpa had built it for the local Baptists in 1892. When eventually the Baptists died or moved away, ownership reverted to the Espys. We recently deeded it to the Oysterville Historical Society. Maybe this time the gift will stick.

Before 1892, baptizing took place in Shoalwater Bay, to a chorus of hallelujahs; the hour of the ceremony depended on the schedule of the tides. The new church, though, was designed for modern baptisms, boasting a capacious zinc-lined font under a trapdoor behind the pulpit. When the time came for the first indoor baptism, the deacons carried water up the aisle in buckets to fill the font. Not until the baptism was over did they realize that they would have to empty the font the same way they had filled it—by hand; there was no drain.

From then on baptisms again took place in the bay, with as many hallelujahs as before. The first indoor baptism since 1892 was that of the Welsh baby whose birth I mentioned in June. My brother Edwin, whose job is religion, performed the ceremony. But Ed did not dunk the baby; he just sprinkled him.

* * *

Reflections During the Sermon

President Truman attended the First Baptist Church in Washington. One Sunday a tourist breathlessly demanded of an usher, "Will the President be attending the service?"

"I don't know about that," replied the usher, "but we expect the Lord to be here as usual."

Marjorie Wihtol says her favorite Quaker is Emmett Caldwell, Eisenhower's pilot in the Pacific. She gives two reasons for her choice:
- When the Wihtols called on the Caldwells, Emmett greeted them at the door with: "Will thee have a snort?"
- A few minutes later, she overheard this exchange between Mr. and Mrs. C.:
    Mrs. C.: What does thee mean?
    Mr. C.: Thee knows goddamn well what I mean.

Oh, yes. The books most frequently pilfered are Bibles and hymnals.

7 AUGUST
♌

Oedipus on Life with Ma

Oedipus:
I'm in for trouble, I'm seeing double;
   It puzzles me more and more;
I knew my wife in a former life—
   We've certainly met before.
My simple notion of her devotion
   To me, as the lord and head,
Is strangely blended with being up-ended
   And walloped and put to bed.

I well recall how I used to bawl
   When somebody tied my bib,
Rubbed fingers and thumbs on my toothless gums
   And crooned to me in my crib.
We've all of us been through *that* routine,
   But ah! what an odd thing this is—

For better, for worse, that capable nurse
Was amazingly like the Missus.
                    —*A. M. Sayers*

A palindrome on the forgoing subject: Mom—O no—MOM!

8 AUGUST
♌

The Thermostat Is Set Too High

Today, for the first time in fifty years, I heard from Richard Stalker, who in his boyhood was a summer visitor to Oysterville. He sent me these three Tom Swifties:

"The thermostat is set too high," said Tom heatedly.
"The chimney is clogged," said Tom fluently.
"Golly, that old man is bent over," said Tom stupidly.

Jonathan M. House provided these:

"I can't quite make up my mind about homosexuality," said Tom, half in earnest.
"Necrophilia seems fine to me," said Tom, in dead earnest.

Winners of a Tom Swifty contest in the *Minneapolis Tribune:*

"Let's gather up the rope," Tom said coyly.
"I just ran over my father," Tom said transparently.
"Don't you love sleeping outdoors?" Tom said intently.
"Let's invite Greg and Gary," Tom proposed gregariously.
"I've been stung," Tom said waspishly.
"Here are my Tom Swifty entries," Deb wrote submissively.
"I'm circulating a petition," Anita Bryant said gaily.
"Let's trap that sick bird," Tom said illegally.
"This boat leaks," Tom said balefully.
"Welcome to my tomb," Tom said cryptically.
"I just returned from Japan," Tom said disorientedly.
"I lost my trousers," Tom said expansively.
"I'll never stick my fist into the lion's cage again," Tom said offhandedly.
"I can't find the oranges," Tom said fruitlessly.
"Are you fond of venison?" Tom said fawningly.

*　*　*

"Your meat, madam!" announced the two butcher boys jointly.
"Sacked for cheek, madam, but I'm reformed," said the maid expertly.
"Sold out of lobsters," said the fishmonger crabbily.

"I see Ararat," said Noah dryly.

"They did it while camping," said the aggrieved husband intently.

"You're a fool to say 'Can do' when it's already been done," she told him candidly.

"Dinner is over," announced the cannibal houseboy masterfully.

"The dam is back to front," said the builder madly.

—J. A. Lindon

"Have some Canary wine," she trilled.

"I will correct your math," he added.

—P. F.

9 AUGUST
♌

Song

Echo, tell me, while I wander
    O'er this fairy plain to prove him,
If my shepherd still grows fonder,
    Ought I in return to love him?
        Echo: Love him, love him!

If he loves, as is his fashion,
    Should I churlishly forsake him?
Or in pity to his passion,
    Fondly to my bosom take him?
        Echo: Take him, take him!

Thy advice then, I'll adhere to,
    Since in Cupid's chains I've led him;
And with Henry shall not fear to
    Marry, if you answer, "Wed him!"
        Echo: Wed him, wed him!

—Addison

10 AUGUST
♌

Shame on Uncle Allie

OYSTERVILLE—Our home here is a red frame cottage, built in 1863 and measuring thirty-three by twenty-three feet. It is the oldest, smallest house in the village. According to the authoritative biography *The Life and Works of Mr. Anonymous,* copyright 1977 by Willard R. Espy, the prior occupant was my Great-uncle Allie, who at the age of one hundred sixteen died quietly in the chair I am now sitting in.

It is a shame that so many bookstores classify that biography as fiction. Every word of it, except for the passing references to Uncle Allie, is true. I did not lie, though sometimes Uncle Allie did. He was proud to be known as Mr. Anonymous, and failing overwhelming proof would claim authorship under that pseudonym of any verse ever published. He was particularly proud of a limerick about the common cormorant or shag, who laid eggs inside a paper bag; it turns out that Christopher Isherwood wrote that. Uncle Allie also claimed title to "On Benjamin Jowett," by H. C. Beeching, and "On the Hon. George Nathaniel Curzon, Commoner of Balliol," by J. W. Mackail and Cecil Spring-Rice. I fear that Eugene Field, not Uncle Allie, wrote "The Little Peach," or at least one version of it. Uncle Allie took credit for "I Cannot Eat But Little Meat," but William Stevenson beat him to it by 300 years. Why, Uncle Allie even appropriated an anatomical limerick by Don Marquis.

He stole in most ungentlemanly fashion a quatrain that runs:

> Hogamous higamous
> Men are polygamous
> Higamous hogamous
> Women monogamous.

According to Carolyn Foote, a dear friend by correspondence, it was Ann Pinchot who originated *Hogamous higamous.* She started awake in the night with the immortal words somersaulting over each other in her head and scribbled them on the back of an envelope by the light of a candle.

Uncle Allie was a disgrace to the family.

Even I am not perfect. Though I idolized the late trumpeter Satchmo Armstrong, I once referred to him as a saxophonist. I have credited Longfellow with Holmes's *Wonderful One-Hoss Shay,* shifted the North Star into the Big Dipper, and switched the Kentucky Derby from Louisville to Lexington.

Chief Justice Vinçon used to spit tobacco juice regularly and accurately into a spittoon. Bob Bendiner once asked him why, in view of his invariable accuracy, he bothered with a mat under the spittoon. "Just to remind me, son," said the Chief Justice, "that nobody is perfect."

My excuse for knuckleheaded errors is that I type fast.

11 AUGUST
♌

Can We Write This Wrong?

We're on speaking terms with the phrase "on the double,"
But say "on the single," and, boy, you're in trouble.

Take "nevertheless"—we hear it galore,
Yet nary a murmur of "neverthemore."

Note this: "in the long run"—unless it's a race;
Why not "in the long walk" to slacken the pace?

Of course "notwithstanding," but no, it's unfitting
Wherever you're standing to say "notwithsitting."

The list of "well-heeled" is often unrolled,
Yet never unrolled is a list of "well-soled."

If facts are "forthcoming," we'd feel better knowing
That sooner or later they will be "forthgoing."

In brief, if "the odds are good," tell me, my lad,
Why we don't allow that "the evens are bad"?
—*A. S. Flaumenhaft*

12 AUGUST
♌

Snallygaster VIII

More on the Snallygaster from a 1908 issue of the *Valley Register,* Middletown, Maryland:

The Jersey Go-Devil, or bovelipus, or whatever you choose to call it, about which the *Register* told last week, has not yet harmed anyone in this section, though it is said to have nearly caught a woman near Scrabble a few nights ago. It is reported that the creature roosted Friday night in Alex Crow's barn, halfway between Shepherdstown and Sharpsburg, where it laid another egg. The egg was taken possession of by some Sharpsburg men, who have rigged up a big incubator, and will endeavor to hatch it out. We think the law should interfere in this matter. It is bad enough to have one flying Devil in the neighborhood, let alone hatching out new ones.

Last Tuesday night a gentleman from Hansonville, this county, called the *Register* by phone and informed us that we should notify President Roosevelt that the Snallygaster had passed over that section about 6:30 o'clock that evening. After sucking up and eating all the goldfish from Ramsburg's pond, it flew away with a noise like a mighty cataract and was reported to have nearly killed three men who were crossing a field.

Saturday morning Mr. Wm. E. Moore, of Yellow Springs, called the *Register* by phone and requested us to secure for him a setting of eggs from the Snallygaster, if possible. He said there was a good deal of chicken stealing going on over there and a few young Snallygasters turned loose in the community could put an end to it.

MORE ON 17 SEPTEMBER.

13 AUGUST
ꙮ

A Taist of Frekles

Brite and Fair by Henry A. Shute. 286 pages. Noone House. $4.50.

This is wun of thowse buks witch purtens two bee the diry of a reel new england boy with speling like this. saucers is sorcers and job is gob, wile sumtimes awful is awful and sumtimes it is auful, and sometimes Henry Shute spells just like hew an me, so jew gnow it has two bee a perfickly disengenyewus purrformince. wel awlright xcept the gokes is sumthing feerse—like piching an old lunker eal plum in the senter of the ferst Congigiasionale Chirch picknic with the wimmen tirning back summersets an having spells. wonce in a wile tho, it seems funny. four xample: "I always thought a girl with red hair and frekles wood taist jest like dandylions when you bite them. i meen of course bite the dandylions. i mean when you kiss the girl. i don't know. some day i am going to find out."—*Time*

14 AUGUST
ꙮ

Verse Aid

How to pronounce the difficult names of certain authors:

Woiwode:
He went into the store and bought some plywood, he
Was going to build a little boat, was Woiwode.

Anthony Powell:
He's as English as a Dover sole—
He's An'tony—believe me—Powell.

The creator of Jeeves:
Leave at once, it's not a good house:
I see no books by P. G. Wodehouse.

Donald Barthelme:
Begob! His stories starthle me—
That divil of a fella, Barthelme!

Nabokov:
Who could get every joke of
Vladimir Nabokov?

Synge:
Authenticity's the thing
With John Millington Synge.

A twosome:
  Say "pooch."
  Then A. Quiller-Couch.
  Then Joseph Wood Krutch.

A couple of contemporaries:
  Who's that in the purple dhoti?
  Why bless my soul, it's T. Capote!

Father, looking in the cradle,
Said, "Let's name him Leon Edel;
I think that suits him rather well—
Better than Leon Edel."

                              —*William Cole*

15 AUGUST
   ♌

Love Song (Multo con corpore)

The ways
of love

How do I love you? Let me count the ways:
  From top to toe, with body in between.
Some days heels over head, and other days

The geography
of love

Head over heels.
                    No neck of land's as green
  As is your neck; no arm of sea's as blue
As is your arm; no brow of hill serene

As is your brow.
                    Your headland's noble, too.
  The widest river mouth is not so wide
As is your mouth.
                    Ah, men of mighty hew

The competition
of love

And jutting chin have wooed you—been denied
  Can I, then, lesser kidneyed, catch your ear?
Can jellied backbone swim against such tide?

I have no stomach for the fray, my dear;
  I'm lily-livered, yellow-bellied, weak.
I'd only put my foot in it, I fear,

The pity
of love

If I should seek your hand—I lack the cheek.
  Ah, let your bowels of compassion start!
Lend me a leg up! Quickly!—lest I seek
A toehold in some softer, warmer heart.

                              —*W.R.E.*

CENTRIPETAL, CENTRIFUGAL

Centripetal force pulls an object toward the center of a circular path, while centrifugal force pulls it away.

As planet gyres about its sun,
    Or cock about his hen,
'Round thee my revolutions run,
    And 'round and 'round again.

Forever force centripetal
    Is drawing heart to heart,
While counter-force centrifugal
    Is pulling us apart.

The push and pull go on and on,
    We never grasp the nettle.
I fear we two shall ne'er be one
    Centrifugalipetal.
                —W.R.E.

16 **AUGUST**
    ♌

A Country Summer Pastoral

I would flee from the city's rule and law,
    From its fashion and form cut loose,
And go where the strawberry grows on its straw,
    And the gooseberry on its goose;
Where the catnip tree is climbed by the cat
    As she crouches for her prey—
The guileless and unsuspecting rat
    On the rattan bush at play.

I will watch at ease for the saffron cow
    And the cowlet in their glee,
As they leap in joy from bough to bough
    On the top of the cowslip tree;
Where the musical partridge drums on his drum,
    And the woodchuck chucks his wood,
And the dog devours the dogwood plum
    In the primitive solitude.

And then to the whitewashed dairy I'll turn,
    Where the dairymaid hastening hies,
Her ruddy and golden-haired butter to churn
    From the milk of the butterflies;
And I'll rise at morn with the early bird,
    To the fragrant farmyard pass,
When the farmer turns his beautiful herd
    Of grasshoppers out to grass.

—Anonymous

17 AUGUST
♌

She Wallowed in the Zuyder Zee

I was drinking cider in a Seattle saloon today with a chance acquaintance named Captain Michael Benett, who explained the origins of the nautical terms port and starboard to me as follows:

"The starboard side of the ship was the side on which the steering oar was put out and was therefore called the steer-board side. With the steering oar out over the starboard side, it was natural to berth the ship on the other side so as not to damage the oar. The left side of the ship therefore became the side over which the loading took place, and became known as the loadboard side, later changed to larboard side.

"In the larger ships a door was cut in the larboard side for loading and it was called a port (from the French word for door). Later, in order not to confuse the two similarly sounding words, larboard and starboard, it was decided to call the left side of the ship the port side and the right side the starboard side."

Captain Benett and I then sang the following song:

> She wallowed in the Zuyder Zee,
> The breeze had ceased to spank;
> The crew of her was him and me,
> A Dutchman and a Yank.

> Inside her there was cider, there was cider in the sea,
> And cider on the starboard side, the larboard side, the lee,
> And much of such inside the Dutch, and much of such in me.

> From starboard spake the Dutchman, and full merrily
>   spake he:
> "The starboard is the steer-board side, so steer me two
>   or three;
> And when we've sipped the cider, we will sip the cider sea."

From larboard then the Yankee spake, the Yankee being me,
"The larboard is the loading side, so load in two or three."
We'll sip up all the cider, see, and then the Zuyder Zee."

$$-W.R.E.$$

18 AUGUST
♌

Let's Be Frank about This, Frank

Emperor Francis Joseph Otto of Austria-Hungary was born on this day, and so, a great many years later, was an infant boy who eventually reached life's pinnacle by becoming my brother-in-law. His parents named him in honor of the emperor, but he was smart enough to cut out the other sobriquets at an early age and become simply Frank. My morning reading would be easier if such figures in the news as Abolhassan Bani-Sadr, President of Iran as I write, had followed Frank's example. The problem presented by Bani-Sadr's name led to this limerick, which appeared in Emmett Watson's column in the *Seattle Post-Intelligencer*:

> What a very strange name, Bani-Sadr!
> Than most other names, it seems hadr.
>   It must be the same
>   As the old family name
> That he got from his madr and fadr.
> —*Clarence Murton*

While on the subject of Middle Eastern presidents, and before returning to the matter of Frank's birthday, I give you this uncomplimentary but clever palindrome by Michael Miller about the President of Egypt:

DRAT SADAT, A DASTARD

I have no reason to think that the passage of years is of particular concern to Frank, but if it ever bothers him I hasten to remind him that his situation is scarcely unique:

> A mid-life crisis
> Once or twice is
> Not the rarest
> Of men's vices.
> Men in fear of
> Ebbing id-life
> Often have a
> Mid-life mid-wife.
> —*W.R.E.*

Another view of the problem:

To know one's Age requires, I guess,
A superficial Cleverness,
As when, at Twenty-one, I knew
That right ahead lay Twenty-two.

Although Transitions have occurred
Since then, I find the sequence blurred:

At present I am Nip and Tuck
'Twixt Skeleton and Babe at Suck.

I may be Old, but I can say
That I was Older, yesterday.

—W.R.E.

19 AUGUST
♌

A Conservatory of Republicans

At about this time, every fourth year, representatives of the Republican and Democratic parties forgather to choose their presidential nominees. If names define, these delegates and alternates to the 1976 Republican National Convention were a varied lot:

- Lawrence Sweet and Arthur Sour, Harold Savage and Kerry Noble, Jimmie Angel and Arthur Outlaw, Elain Lust and William Love, David Forward and Charles Coy.
- Vivienne Raven, Harvey Drake, Alfred Snipes, Henry Lark, Grace Crow, Louise Bird, and Roland Byrd.
- Sharon Carr, Mary Alice Ford, Debbie Lincoln, Francisco Vega, and Ada Nash.
- Charles Soda, Earl Coke, Orvas Beers, Patt Ginn, Sue Ice, and Peggy Bender.
- Evan Lips, Beth Arms, Howard Face, and Douglas Head.
- Henry Hatter, Robert Hunter, Howard Baker, Velma Farmer, Gordon Miner, Ivy Shoemaker, Margaret Haymaker, Austin Stonebreaker, and Augusta Hornblower.
- Sandra Rich, Robert Poor, Ivy Banks, Irene Cash, Jacquelyn Till, Ruby Price, and Money Cummins.
- Marshall Cain and Peggy Abel.
- Gaynelle Waters, Van Poole, John Marsh, Edward Brooke, Evelyn Rivers, and Dwight Dam.
- Charles England, Richard Israel, Joseph Canada, Marshall French, Jeanie Turk.
- Charles Currier and William Ives.
- Frances Garland, Evans Rose, George Bloom, and Ellie Flowers.
- Dort Bigg and Walt Little, Patricia Short and William Long, Donald Large and Mildred Small.
- John Rushing and James Speed.

- Wendell Harms, Thomas Hury, Bernadine Burns, and Bryce Payne.
- Selma Steele, Dorothy Wood, Ellis Ivory, Mitch Silver, Norris Cotton, and Frank Whetstone.
- Claire Bass, Charles Trout, Will Gill, and Ody Fish.
- Margaret Black, Hubert White, Fred Gray, Carol Browne, Harry Redd, and Paul Green.
- Jared Scripture, Bill Church, and John Nave.
- Monroe Knight, Mary Bishop, Martha King, and Arthur Pope.
- Jane Fox, Stephen Wolfe, Harold Coons, Richard Badger, James Lyon, Ruth Hare, and Robert Pigg.
- Eliza Sprinkle and Walter Wrinkle.
- Lawrence Barley, George Rice, James Cherry, Sylvia Berry, Wanda Roe, Jane Ham, Jerry Lamb, and Harold Bean.
- Phyllis Barbee and Ken Doll.

—James T. Wooten

20 AUGUST
♌

Spel It Rite

When the witch said
Abradacabra
Nothing happened.
She's a hopeless speller.
—Alan F. G. Lewis

The American Philological Society, saying the arbitrary nature of spelling hinders education, wastes millions, and loses two years' time for each schoolchild, proposed that Congress do away with unsounded letters and use soft *g* for *j*. This was one reform that Congress had sense enough to reject. To strip words of their etymological accretions would send language back to the Neanderthals.

Besides, the oddities of spelling can provide considerable amusement. Melville Dewey, inventor of the library classification system, spelled one word G H E A U - G H T E I G H P T O U G H. Thus:

GH is P, as in hiccough;
EAU is O, as in beau;
GHT is T, as in naught;
EIGH is A, as in NEIGH;
PT is T, as in pterodactyl,
OUGH is O, as in though.

That is, potato.

THE HARBOR OF FOWEY

Yes, I have my own views
      But the teachers I follow
Are the lyrical Miews
      And the Delphic Apollow
Unto them I am debtor
      For spelling and rhyme
And I'm doing it bebtor
      And bebtor each time.
    —*Sir Arthur Quiller-Couch*

THUMB FUN

Milkmaids, butchers,
      Carpenters, they say,
Always get their thumbs
      In the whey, weigh, way.
    —*William E. Engel*

*   *   *

Some authorities blame television for the declining standards of spelling in class-rooms. A class of third graders in Connecticut was asked to spell *relief*. Quicker than a thirty-second spot, says the *New York Times*, more than half spelled out "R O L A I D S."

21 AUGUST
♌

Words Against Women

Militant feminists complain that the language is tilted against females. The pejora-tive word *irascible* is from *oestrus*, "in heat," as is *hysteria* from the Greek for womb. *Seminal* is from *semen*; a seminal truth is as impregnative as a man's seed. *Testimony* is from *testis*, "testicles," because men once placed their hands on their testicles, their most precious part, when swearing to tell the whole truth and nothing but the truth.

Suggestions for revising the language to equalize or neutralize the sexes (as in *chairperson*) stem from a primitive instinct that words carry magic: "Black is beautiful." The instinct is partly right. But in the end words do not change reality. Reality changes words.

Joel Weiss says the injustices of discriminatory pronouns can be overcome by creating a single word to represent *he, she,* or *it*. Mr. Weiss suggests *h'orsh'it*.

22 AUGUST
♌

Dirge for a Teacher

The following macaronic, alternating Hebrew and Italian lines, was composed in
1584 by Leone of Modena, a child who was to become a rabbi at thirteen. The verse
expresses his sorrow at the death of his teacher. Professor James Kugel, who gave me
a literal translation of the Hebrew, tells me that each Hebrew line is virtually identical in sound, though not in meaning, with the preceding line in Italian.

The Hebrew-Italian verse

קינה שמור אוי מה כפס אוצר בו

Chi nasce, muor. Oimè, che pass' acerbo!

כל טוב אילים כוסי אור דין אל צלו

Colto vien l'uom, così ordina 'l Cielo

משה מורי משה יקר דבר בו

Mosè morì, Mosè: già car' di verbo

שם תושיה און יום כפור הוא זה לו

Santo sia ogn'uom, con puro zelo

כלה מיטב ימי שן צרי אשר בו

Ch'alla metà, già mai senza riserbo

ציין זה מות רע אין כאן ירפה לו

Si guinge, ma vedràn in cangiar pelo

ספינה בים קל צל עובר ימינו

Se fin' abbiam, ch'al cielo vero ameno

הלים יובא שבי ושי שמנו

Ah! l'uomo va, se viv' assai, se meno.

The Hebrew in translation

Lament with me for Moses. He is gone ...
My teacher gone; his wise words laid away;
His goodness, great as princes', all undone;
His shade exposed to judgment, and for aye
To sorrow of atonement. Mourn with me—
Too late, too late to pull that tooth of pain!
Life's shadow passes like a ship at sea.
I am undone. I call his name in vain.

The Italian in translation

We live to die (a bitter thought indeed!)—
Yet live to learn; so Heaven hath decreed.
Thou'rt dead, dear Moses; breath and speech are gone;
Yet may thy holy zeal still lead us on
Till, midway reached, and never looking back,
We riddle life's design, before the black
Has vanished from our hair. Though some die late,
Some soon, all knock at last on heaven's gate.

—W.R.E.

23 AUGUST
♌

Charades Again

Charades from *The Enigma,* monthly magazine of The National Puzzlers' League:

Homonym (*9 *8, *1 4 3 3 4)
They asked the ONE, "How many men should we arrest today?"
"Shah supporters? TWO!" he said. "Now please go on your way."

—*Ralf P. Olio*

(The digits within parentheses indicate the number of letters in each word of the solution. The asterisks signal capital letters. The comma separates ONE from TWO. ONE thus consists of two capitalized words, the first of nine and the second of eight letters. TWO consists of five words, the first having one letter, capitalized. The others have one, four, three, three and four letters respectively.)

ONE, since both words are capitalized, is probably a name. The words "Shah" and "arrest" give the name away; it has to be the Ayatollah Khomeini, the leading figure in the Islamic revolution that overthrew the Shah.

1. SPOONERGRAM (4 '1' 4, *6 4)

It was raining ONE today,
And that is nothing new.
My little car exploded, though,
And it started raining TWO.

2. HOMONYM (*8 5, 5 6)

The romeo had met his match,
A girl who did say no.
It happened on a ONE; and since
All gossip travels so,
It made the Sunday paper—
"TWO" the headline read.
The lecher's rep was ruined;
In shame he sold his bed.

3. SPOONERGRAM (*11, 2 4 2 3)

An upstate New Yorker (from ONE),
Asked out for a short downhill run,
Said, "Ya hafta risk TWO,
Which I don't wanna do;
So I'll stay off the slopes for my fun."

4. HOMONYM (13, 6 8)

My father drinks whiskey, thinks tea is a TWO,
As potent as ONE and as tangy as dew.

—Ralf P. Olio

If charades divert you, write to Paul E. Thompson, East Alstead Road, Alstead, New Hampshire 03602. He will tell you how to receive *The Enigma* regularly.

24 AUGUST
♍

Back and Forth

How many of these palindromes can you identify from the definitions?

1. Baby's napkin   — — —
2. The first woman   — — —
3. Woman's name; former monetary unit of India   — — — —
4. Property paper   — — — —
5. Man's name; German king   — — — —
6. Twelve o'clock   — — — —
7. Blow your horn   — — — —
8. Chick vocalization   — — — —
9. Air or highway monitor   — — — — —
10. Flat; even   — — — — —
11. In Spanish, it's señora   — — — — —
12. Send a patient to a specialist   — — — — —
13. Iranian VIPs   — — — — —
14. Not duets   — — — — —
15. Eskimo watercraft   — — — — —
16. Basic doctrine   — — — — —
17. Related to government   — — — — —
18. Woman's name; the mother of Samuel   — — — — — —
19. More like a beet   — — — — — —
20. Decorate the wall a second time   — — — — — — —

—Edward Rawder

25 AUGUST
♍

Spermatozoa Sow On

Noah
Was superbly stocked with spermatozoa.
He begat so many children that by the law of
    averages when the Flood came they could not
    all be drowned,
Which is why you and I and our spermatozoa are
    still around.
                    —*W.R.E.*

THE WORLD VIEW OF ALDOUS HUXLEY

"My sweet," said Aldous Huck,
"Love's muck—
Swineish.
Shall we say nineish?"
        —*W.R.E.*

When we were young and vigorous,
A sidelong glance would trigger us.

But we grew old somehow;
It takes two glances now.
        —*W.R.E.*

In politer days
"Good lays"
Were ditties—
Not pretties.
   —*Hardy Amies*

He said, "Dad-blast!
That happened fast!"
She said, "Gol-durn!
You never learn!"
    —*W.R.E.*

ROUND (a rondelet)

Then she from laving
Emerges fragrant misty and unkissed
Then she from laving
Emerges and my heart is not behaving
And how can I refrain or she resist
And afterward anew the fragrant mist
Then she from laving
        —*W.R.E.*

26 AUGUST
♍

Doublets

When Lewis Carroll was not preparing mathematical treatises, or writing *Alice in Wonderland,* or taking photographs of little girls, you might have found him working on Doublets, in which the puzzler travels from one word to another by a series of letter substitutions. Each step must consist of but one letter change, which forms a real word. *Head,* for instance, becomes *foot,* as follows: *Head, held, hold, fold, food, foot.*

Here are some of his Doublets, and the numbers of steps he used in the metamorphosis. Perhaps you can outdo him:

1. *Eye* to *lid* (4)	5. *Cain* to *Abel* (9)
2. *Pig* to *sty* (5)	6. *Wheat* to *bread* (7)
3. *Ape* to *man* (6)	7. *River* to *shore* (11)
4. *Army* to *navy* (8)	8. *Winter* to *summer* (14)

27 AUGUST
♍

Bible Stories That You Never Heard Before

Mrs. J. W. Marsh writes that a verse in my previous almanac is "too close for coincidence to this song I learned in July 1927, on a ship between Singapore and Rangoon, from an English girl living in Calcutta":

King Solomon and King David both led very naughty
  lives.
They spent their time collecting concubines and
  wives.
When old age o'ercame them, they felt so many
  qualms
That Solomon wrote the Proverbs and David wrote
  the Psalms.

(Chorus)

Young folks, old folks, everybody come;
Join the darky Sunday school and make yourselves
  at home.
Take a stick of chewing gum and sit upon the floor,
And I'll tell you Bible stories that you never heard
  before.

Jonah was a farmer lad who wanted for to sail,
So he went and booked his passage in a transatlantic
   whale.
Now Jonah was a stout chap, he felt himself compressed;
So he simply pushed a button and the whale did the
   rest.

(Chorus)

Adam was the first of men to live upon this earth,
And everything went perfectly until the woman's
   birth.
But Eve like all her charming sex tempted Adam
   sore,
And so the angels kicked them out and locked the
   blooming door.

(Chorus)

We sang Mrs. Marsh's song at YMCA camp, with a few differences; we sang
"Come to the Sunday school," and "Park all your chewing gum and spitballs at the
door," and "Bible stories *like* you never heard before."

James Ball Naylor is author of the stanza about King Solomon and King David,
but I think Jerome Kern gets credit for the rest.

28 AUGUST
♍

$$\left(\text{fm}\right.$$

(From the Philadelphia *Minerva*, February 13, 1796)

The enigma:

$$\left(\text{fm}\right.$$

The answer:

   effeminacy: f m in a C.
         —*Toby*

And that, children, is a rebus charade, which may combine pictures, equations,
ABC language, or any other convenient visual device to transmit—or conceal—its
message.

1. B = m) K
2. O°

   —*Mary J. Youngquist and Harry Hazard*

Betsy Burr says this one was familiar in her childhood:

3.

$$
\begin{array}{rl}
\text{UR} & 2 \ \text{GOOD} \\
& 2 \ \text{ME} \\
& 2 \ \text{BE} \\
& \underline{4} \ \text{GOT} \\
& 10
\end{array}
$$

4. Here symbols used three times in a row are to be pluralized (CCC = seas or seize), while symbols repeated two times, or more than three times, are to be read directly (CCCC = foresees, CC = to seize). The conversation is between Caesar and a foreign refugee, which accounts for the accent:

M N 4 L CCCNNN

— AL, CCCR!
— PPP 2 U, O 4NR! RIII! U R?
— I M RSTTT, XLNC, N RABN XIL.
— Y R U N XIL, RSTTT?
— I UUU 2 B AAAΠ, O CCCR.
— MSE BBBNS! ½ U E-10?
— ES, QQQQQQQQQ IR, I 8 H EEE N VL Π—XLN, 2. O CCCR, I ½ 1 DDDIR. I 444E EZ AAAA UUUU IR, F I M AAAΠ 4 U. I ½ N IPPP UU 222Π . . .
— N IPPP! ½ U CN N NME RME?
— ES, XLNC, N A CQR CT, AJ¢ 2 A 4S, 2 RMEEE.
— I ½ CN UR CT, N III A UR CT S MT! R U AAAΠ 4 NEı LLL? CCCM, N!
— O CCCR, U R YY UU 444! I M NO¢! I C 2 CTTT: 1 S MT, N I 2 RMEEE OQΠ. I M UR LI, N I ½ A WWW UU IR. U C, I M AAAΠ N I M A CR, 2.
— F U R A CR, I SQ, R U 8 L R O 4 NN?
— ES, CCCR, I 4C 9 CCCNNN F EZ SSSSSS 4 U B4 U XΠR.
— 9 CCCNNN! N M I 2 XΠR N 9 CCCNNN? Y? LI B 6, Π?
— O CCCR, U L XΠR B4 U R L F A DZZZ, 2MIIIRO. ½ U NE NMEEE?
— FU, FU.
— I 4C U L ½ 2 ULOGGG, O CCCR: 1 R8R 2 AQQQ UR NMEEE N I 2 XQQQ M; I 2 XP8 N I 2 X-10-U8; 1 222A "PPP, PPP" N I 2 RQ 4 "N I 4 N I"; I 2 8S 2 UR TRNE N I 2 8S 2 UR NRG N XLNNN: A 4M 4 NNNN6, CCCR, B4 UR NMEEE' DMIII. ES, 7TULE UR NMEEE L XΠR, 2—XLNC, R U OK? XQQQ RSTTT, CCCR, F 5 4CN 2 FR!
— O L, IIIA 2 RMMM! A C F NMEEE 0888, RSTTT! 2 RMMM!

—Betsy Burr

This French rebus is archly naughty:

$$\frac{2 \ \text{AB}}{2 \ \text{fr. 16}} = 2 \ \text{B B}$$

The solution, in French, is "deux abbés au-dessus de deux françaises = deux bébés." Do your own translating. Wordplay aside, the message is no more sophisticated than the whispered risible of my childhood: "1 into 1 = 3."

29 AUGUST
♍

In Lodium

"Podium is simply a form of *pew"*—a TV quiz.

They said it was a podium,
  A podium or pew;
A thing I never knodium,
  I never, never knew.
Which controversial vodium,
  Or questionable view,
Intelligence must rodium,

Must rodium or rue;
And treat with scornful odium,
Or take with grain of sodium,
With grains of chloride sodium,
And not of these a fodium,
  A fodium or few.
    —Anonymous

WE'RE ALL IN THE DUMPS

We're all in the dumps,
For diamonds are trumps,
The kittens are gone to St. Paul's.
The babies are bit,
The moon's in a fit
And the houses are built without walls.
    —Anonymous

30 AUGUST
♍

Swiss Family Robinson

In the 1890s, Henry Altemus rewrote several books for young readers in words of one syllable. Among them was *The Swiss Family Robinson,* from which Elizabeth J. Overman sent me this excerpt:

THE WRECK

For six days a fierce wind set in, which tore our sails to shreds; the white foam of the waves swept our decks, and the storm drove our ship so far out of its course, that there was no one on board who could tell where we were. All were worn out with toil and care, and the oaths of the men were heard no more, but they fell on their knees to pray.

My wife and boys clung round me in great dread; but I said to them, "God can save us if He will. He knows each rock that lies hid, and sees each storm as it comes; yet if He should think it good to call us to Him, let us not grieve at it; we shall not part." At these words I saw my wife dry her tears, and from that time she was more calm.

All at once we heard the cry of "Land! Land!" The ship had struck on a rock, and the force of the shock with which she went threw us off our feet.

"Fear not, my dear ones," said I; "the ship still lifts us out of the sea, and the land is near. Stay here, and I will try to save you."

I went on deck, but was soon thrown down by the wild surge of the sea.... The ship was all but in two. The whole of the crew had got in the boat, and I could see the last man cut the rope. I gave a loud call for them to wait till we could join them; but from ...

There, dear friends, the excerpt ends. I am sure you will be glad to know that the Swiss family Robinson survived and prospered.

31 AUGUST
♍

Garbled Geography

HOW MUCH DID PHILADELPHIA PA?

> How much did Philadelphia Pa?
>   Whose grass did K.C. Mo?
> How many eggs could New Orleans La?
>   How much does Cleveland O?
>
> When Hartford and New Haven Conn
>   What sucker do they soak?
> Could Noah build a Little Rock Ark
>   If he had not Guthrie Ok?
>
> We call Minneapolis Minn,
>   Why not Annapolis Ann?
> If you can't tell the reason why
>   I'll bet Topeka Kan.
>
> But now we speak of ladies, what
>   A Butte Montana is!
> If I could borrow Memphis' Tenn
>   I'd treat that Jackson Miss.
>
> Would Denver Cola cop because
>   Ottumwa Ia dore?
> Ah, though my Portland Me doth love,
>   I threw my Portland Ore.
>   —*Anonymous*

Name these:

1. The cleanest state.
2. The most seaworthy.
3. The most fatherly.
4. The most personal.
5. The most surprised.
6. The most professional.

7. The most unmarried.
8. The most Catholic.
9. The highest numbered.
10. The most Islamic.
11. The best writer.
12. The most shady.

Garbled Geography

GEOGRAPHICAL LOVE SONG

In the State of Mass.
There lives a lass
    I love to go N.C.;
No other Miss.
Can e'er, I Wis.,
    Be half so dear to Me.

R.I. is blue
And her cheeks the hue
    Of shells where waters swash;
On her pink-white phiz
There has Nev. Ariz.
    The least complexion Wash.

La.! could I win
The heart of Minn.,
    I'd ask for nothing more;
But I only dream
Upon the theme,
    And Conn. it o'er and Ore.

Hawaii, pray,
Can't I Ala.
    This love that makes me Ill.?
N.Y., O., Wy.
Kan. Nev. Ver. I
    Propose to her my will?

I shun the task
'Twould be to ask
    This gentle maid to wed.
And so, to press
My suit, I guess
    Alaska Pa. instead.

                    —*Anonymous*

SEPTEMBER

₁ SEPTEMBER
♍

Tomorrow the Rain Will Be Only a Drizzle

OYSTERVILLE—We are in the midst of our annual equinoctial storm. It is not really equinoctial, but that is what we call it. It will last four days. Day before yesterday the sky, which had been as light a blue as the color of a robin's egg, darkened to blue-black. The wind swung south and lost its temper over something; it sent frightened clouds rushing across the sky like birds fleeing before a fire. In the night the downpour started. The rain is so thick now that we cannot see our picket fence, much less the bay.

Tomorrow morning, though, the wind will be resting in the north, and the rain will be only a mizzle. Silver will begin sifting through the cloud; by noon the cover will have broken into a flock of slowly cropping sheep, and after lunch I will take a nap on the sun deck.

Oysterville weather has grown gentler since I was a child; or is it only gentle for the period of my visits? Perhaps Washington has begun issuing regulations about the portions of wind, shine, and the like to be permitted each day:

THERE OUGHT TO BE A LAW

Roads are muddy?
Make a study.

Day too warm?
Vote reform.

Caught a chill?
Draw a bill.

Cold and raw?
Pass a law.

Snow and ice?
Pass it twice.

Storm and bluster?
Filibuster.

Ash and grit?
Veto it.

If, flouting your concern,
The weather takes a turn,

Adjourn.
                        —W.R.E.

This poet foresees apprehensively the day when the weatherman will not simply forecast the weather but arrange it:

Cancel that call
For a squall!

Blow
Up a snow!

A freshet—
And rush it!

Thaw
Arkansas!

Precipitate
The Bay State!

Pour it on
Oregon!
                        —Hope E. Stoddard

2 SEPTEMBER
♍

Lewd Play, Sir

Dick Cavett, a master of the offhand anagram, turned "Alec Guinness" into "genuine class," and Oscar Wilde into "O lad I screw." The letters of his own name can be arranged into "I crav'd chatter," appropriate for the host of a talk show. He says in a note that came this morning, "Is there a word for a sentence made up of anagrams of the same word? E.g., the other day I thought of, 'Go paste Gestapo postage to pages.' What's wrong with me?"

Nothing is wrong with him, except that he suffers from a virulent form of anagrammania; as far as I know there is no cure for that, nor any name for the kind of sentence he describes. How about calling it a concategram? Or a concavettgram?

Will Shortz, with a singular lack of respect, offered "Lewd play, sir," as an anagram for "Willard Espy." Other, more elegant transmutations:

Arguments	Must anger
Armageddon	Mad god near
Christianity	'Tis in charity

Democratic	Rated comic
Diplomacy	Mad policy
HMS *Pinafore*	Name for ship
Moonlight	Thin gloom
Ms. Steinem	Smites men
Prayeth	Therapy
Republican	Incurable
Sexual intercourse	Relax, insure coitus
Weird nightmares	Withering dreams
Eddie Cantor	Actor, indeed
Victoria, England's Queen	Governs a nice quiet land
Twenty Thousand Leagues Under the Sea	Huge water tale stuns; end had you tense
The Lay of the Last Minstrel	This story that all men feel
The Morse Code	Here come dots
The South Sea islands	A thousand islets shine
Dante Gabriel Rossetti	Greatest idealist born
The nudist colony	No untidy clothes
Catherine de Medici	Her edict came in—die

* * *

LONDON (Reuters)—Nicholas Fairbairn, a Scottish Member of Parliament, says he has discovered the true meaning of Nessiteras rhombopterxy, the name given to the fabled Loch Ness monster by a leading British naturalist, Sir Peter Scott, who claims that recent photographs prove the monster's existence.

Mr. Fairbairn said the name is an anagram: "Monster hoax by Sir Peter S."

* * *

Stephen Sondheim noticed that "Cinerama" juggles into "American"; Lewis Carroll, that "William Ewart Gladstone" can be turned into "Wild agitator means well"; and Richard Edes Harrison, that "Beverly Sills" transforms superbly into "Silvery Bells."

3 SEPTEMBER
♍

Dirty Work on the Appellation Trail

Old King Cole was a merry old soul. So is young Bill Cole, author of some of the most splendid light verse around. I hope Bill is assembling his collected works right now, so that we can gorge ourselves on conceits such as this:

DIRTY WORK ON THE APPELLATION TRAIL
OR: I CAN'T REMEMBER THE MNEMONIKER

At a party they cry, "Oh, here comes Carol!"
And in someone comes in a man's apparel!
It's signed on the letter, but I have to ask:
Is it Hilary *fem.* or Hilary *masc.*?

Fellows named Joyce and females named Jeremy
Cause confusion at the marriage cerem'y;
There's a Shirley he and a Shirly *female*—
How on earth can a Shirley *he* male *be* male?

Men are named Beverly, women named Frankie—
Ycleptomaniacal hanky-panky!
Women named Leslie and men named Ēvelyn—
Sometimes I don't know *what* to believe in!

Imagine a boy with a name like Florence
Hiding in corners and crying in torrence!
I knew another—they called him Jocelyn!
A situation *I'd* not be docilyn!

To be doubly sure his life will be dismal,
Name a boy Vivian at his baptismal;
It's shaking your fist at man and at nature
To label a boy with such no-manclature!

With Marian "a" and with Marion "o"
At least you have something on which to go;
When there's Frances with "e" and Francis with "i"
You can differentiate girlie and guy.

My friend has a niece of the female kidney,
But he introduced her as "Sidney," didn' he?
How far will they go with this mad vagary?
Will they name girls Sam? Will they name boys Mary?
                                        —*William Cole*

4 SEPTEMBER
   ♍

Ye Carpette Knyghte

I have a horse—a righte good horse—
    Ne doe I envie those
Who scoure ye plaine in headie course,
    Tyll soddaine on theyre nose

They lyghte with unexpected force—
   It ys—a horse of clothes.

I have a saddel—"Sayest thou soe?
   With styrrupes, Knyghte, to boote?"
I sayde not that—I answere "Noe"—
   Yt lacketh such, I woot—
It ys a mutton-saddel, loe!
   Parte of ye fleecie brute.

I have a bytte—aychte good bytte—
   As schall bee seene in tyme.
Ye jawe of horse yt wyll not fytte—
   Yts use ys more sublyme.
Fayre Syr, how deemest thou of yt?
   Yt ys—thys bytte of rhyme.
               —*Lewis Carroll*

5 SEPTEMBER
♍

You're a Frog, I'm a Limey / You Say Merde, I Say Blimey

Cultural differences between the French and the English are mirrored in their idioms:

The English	*The French*
To wear your heart on your sleeve.	Avoir le coeur sur la main. (To have the heart in one's hand.)
So good he could grow wings.	Etre à encadrer. (Fit to be framed.)
To win in a breeze.	Arriver dans un fauteuil. (To arrive in an armchair.)
Nothing to sneeze at.	Ne pas crâcher dessus. (Nothing to spit on.)
To win hands down.	Arriver les doigts dans le nez. (To arrive with fingers in one's nose.)
Born with a silver spoon in the mouth.	Etre né coiffé. (Born with a hat on.)
To be pushing up daisies.	Manger les pissenlits par la racine. (To eat dandelions by the roots.)
To have bats in the belfry.	Avoir une araignée au plafond. (To have a spider on one's ceiling.)
Good weather for ducks.	Un temps de chien. (Dog's weather.)

To make a mountain out of a molehill.	Se noyer dans un verre d'eau. (To drown in a glass of water.)
To have a poker-face.	Avoir un front d'arain. (To have a brass forehead.)
To rule the roost.	Faire le pluie et le beau temps. (To make rain and fair weather.)
To be a lady-killer.	Etre la coqueluche des dames. (To be the ladies' whooping-cough.)
To strike it rich.	Faire son beurre. (To make one's butter.)
	—*Marcelle Dorval*

6 SEPTEMBER
♍

Say It Again, Sam

Words that imitate sounds are especially apt as names for musical instruments. *Gong, kazoo,* and *twangl* (a Jew's harp) are onomatopoems. A variation—naming something twice if it makes a continuous or repeated sound—is more than twice as effective: compare *tom tom, tam tam,* and *ding dong* with *tom, tam,* and *ding.* Most Western instruments with double names are from the percussion section, but the following list of instruments from around the world shows that the device works just as well for strings and winds. If you read the list aloud, it sounds a little like a Javanese gamelan warming up for a gig.

Strings
• Adeudeu • chi-chu • dongeldongel • gendang-gendang • geso-geso • gettun-gettun • git-git • gobi-gobi • hum-strum • hu hu •iqliq • jigi-jigi • kandiri-kandire • keteng-keteng • kimwanyewanye • klung-klung • kolong-kolong • ogung-ogung bulu • setsegetsege • tangge tong • tingning • ton-ton • yank gong.

Winds
• Asukusuk • bumbun • burumararu • cuckoo • damyadamayan • dgeglie • elo-ilo-goto • empet-empetan • fango-fango • going-going • huayra-puhura • iyup-iyup • kio-kio • kivudi-vudi • mero-mero • noli-noli • om-om • ower-ower •pip-pib • pi-pi • poti-poti • putura-putura • wuwi-puwi • remo-remo • trutruka • tutu • ufu-ufu • wer-wer.

Percussion
• Agogo • angang-angang • asakasaka •atata-witata • baka-baka • banga-banga • bubuduke • bum-bum • buruburu • chacha • chaing vaing • chal-chal • cheng-cheng • chullo-chullo • ciocca-ciocca • cupa-cupa • dab-daba • daola-daola • degangangde • didimbadimba • dingdingti • dog-dog

• doli-doli • dugdugi • dundun • gah-gah • ganga-ganga • gangan • gew-gaw • ghunghuna • gom-gom • gong-ageng • gong-angang-angang • gua-gua • gubgubi • gudu-gudu • gue-gue • gul-gul • huli-huli • jhanjhana joucoujou • jul-jul • ka-eke-eke • kakanika-kanika • kao-kao • kemkem • kentung-kentung • keri-keri • kingolu-ngulu • kinkinki • knicky-knackers • konkon • kritsa-kritsa • kul-kul • lae-lae • ore-ore • pangang • patpati • pim-pim • pong-pong • qal-qal • quemquem • rau-rau • reco-reco • re-re • reso-reso • rigu-ragu • saga-saga • saing waing • sake-sake • sanbamba • sege-sege • seke-seke • shak-shak • sil-sil • sung-chung • tabang-tabang • tamatama • tambattam • tam-tam • tantan • temettama • tepan-tepan • tintinnus • tin tin sags • to-ko • tom-tom • tonggong • wongang • wupu-wupu • xaque-xaque • yangong.

—Harry Randall

7 **SEPTEMBER**
   ♍

How Can I Know What I Think Till I See What I Say?

The dilemma thus expressed (by W. H. Auden) is examined further here:

HOW COULD THE POET

How could the poet
possibly know
till the very last word
in the very last row?

For a poem's a word
plus a word, plus a word,
added, subtracted,
and thoroughly stirred.

And thought makes the word,
and the word makes thought,
and some things come
that were never sought.

At what he has said
when his say is done,
the poet's surprised
as anyone.
—Richard Armour

8 SEPTEMBER
♍

Last Lines

Earlier, I asked you to identify a number of books by their opening lines. Now match the last sentence with the title of some of the same books:

The last sentence

1. The hand of Providence brought me in my drifting to the very doors of the British Linen Company's bank.

2. It came from afar and travelled sedately on, a shrug from eternity.

3. Hot dog.

4. But over the old man's head they looked at each other and smiled.

5. The knife came down, missing him by inches, and he took off.

6. After awhile I went out and left the hospital and walked back to the hotel in the rain.

7. Come, children, let us shut the box and the puppets, for our play is played out.

8. One bird said to Billy Pilgrim, "Poo-tee-weet?"

9. I shall still lose my temper with Ivan the coachman, I shall still embark on useless discussions and express my opinions inopportunely . . . but my life, now, my whole life, independently of anything that can happen to me, every minute of it, is no longer meaningless as it was before, but has a positive meaning of goodness with which I have the power to invest it.

10. I loved Big Brother.

11. Small fowls flew screaming over the yet yawning gulf; a sullen surf beat against its steep sides; then all collapsed, and the great shroud of the sea rolled on as it rolled five thousand years ago.

12. So we beat on, boats against the current, borne back ceaselessly into the past.

13. For all to be accomplished, for me to feel less lonely, all that remained to hope was that on the day of my execution there should be a huge crowd of spectators and that they should greet me with howls of derision.

14. None of them was ever more than a thin slice, held between the contiguous impressions that com-

The book

A. *The Naked and the Dead,* Norman Mailer

B. *The Good Earth,* Pearl Buck

C. *Slaughterhouse Five,* Kurt Vonnegut

D. *Farewell to Arms,* Ernest Hemingway

E. *Vanity Fair,* William Makepeace Thackeray

F. *Kidnapped,* Robert Louis Stevenson

G. *Darkness at Noon,* Arthur Koestler

H. *Catch-22,* Joseph Heller

I. *1984,* George Orwell

J. *Great Expectations,* Charles Dickens

K. *The Great Gatsby,* F. Scott Fitzgerald

L. *The Stranger,* Albert Camus

M. *The Metamorphosis,* Franz Kafka

N. *Anna Karenina,* Leo Tolstoy

posed our life at that time; remembrance of a particular moment; and houses, roads, avenues are as fugitive, alas, as the years.

15. And it was like a confirmation of their new dreams and excellent intentions that at the end of their journey their daughter sprang to her feet first and stretched her young body.

        O. *Moby Dick,* Herman Melville

16. I have been there before.

        P. *Swann's Way,* Marcel Proust

17. It is a far, far better thing that I do than I have ever done; it is a far, far better rest that I go to than I have ever known.

        Q. *Tale of Two Cities,* Charles Dickens

18. I took her hand in mine, and we went out of the ruined place; and, as the morning mists had risen long ago when I first left the forge, so the evening mists were rising now, and in all the broad expanse of tranquil light they showed to me, I saw no shadow of another parting from her.

        R. *Huckleberry Finn,* Mark Twain

9 SEPTEMBER
♍

I Grieve the Loss. I Am Not Gay at All

Adoption of the word *gay* as a self-descriptive by the homosexual community has distressed those lovers of language who grieve at the rape of a word. One of them speaks here:

PROTEST POEM

It was a good word once, a little sparkler,
Simple, innocent even, like a hedgerow flower,
And irreplaceable. None of its family
Can properly take over: *merry* and *jolly*
Both carry too much weight; *jocund* and *blithe*
Were pensioned off when grandpa was alive;
Vivacious is a flirt; she's lived too long
With journalists and advertising men.
Spritely and *spry*, both have a nervous tic.
There is no satisfactory substitute.
It's down the drain and we are going to miss it.
No good advising me to go ahead
And use the word as ever. If I did

We know that someone's bound to smirk and snigger.
Of all epithets why pick on this one?
Some deep self-mocking irony?
Or blindfold stab into the lexicon?
All right. Then let's call heterosexuals *sad,*
Dainty for rapists, *shy* for busy flashers,
Numinous for necrophiles, *quaint* for stranglers;
The words and world are mad; I must protest
Although I know my cause is lost.
A good word once, and I'm disconsolate
And angered by this simple syllable's fate:
A small innocence gone, a little fall.
I grieve the loss. I am not gay at all.
                                        —*Vernon Scannell*

Scholars seeking the true authorship of Shakespeare's plays have pointed out that twice—in the first scene of the sixth act of *Hamlet,* and the splendid epigraph to *Troilus and Cressida*—one needs only to list each eighth letter of the first eleven lines to come up with "Willard Espy." Following this clue, I have revealed a hidden message in Mr. Scannell's poem, as you will see here:

PROTEST POEM

It was a good word once, a little	*S* parkler,
Simple, innocent even, like a hedger	*O* w flower,
And irreplaceable. None of its fami	*L* y
Can properly take over: *merry* and *j*	*O* lly
Both carry too much weight; *jocu*	*N* d and *blithe*
Were pensioned off when	*G* randpa was alive;
Vivacious is a flirt; she's lived too lon	*G*
With journalists and	*A* dvertising men.
Spritely and spr	*Y,* both have a nervous tic.
There is no satisfactory sub	*S* titute.
It's down the drain and we ar	*E* going to miss it.
No good advisi	*N* g me to go ahead
And use the word as ever. If I	*D* id
We know that someone's bound to smirk	*A* nd snigger.
Of al	*L* the epithets why pick on this one?
Some deep s	*E* lf-mocking irony?
Or blindfold s	*T* ab into the lexicon?
All right. Then let's call he	*T* erosexuals *sad,*
Dainty for rapists, shy for busy flash	*E* rs,
Numinous for necrophiles, *quaint* fo	*R* stranglers;
The words and world are mad: I must pr	*O* test
Although I know my cause is	*L* ost.
A good word once, and I'm	*D* isconsolate

And angered by this sim
  A small innocence gone, a little f
    I grieve the

P le syllable's fate:
A ll.
L oss. I am not gay at all.

As I suspected, Mr. Scannell is waving farewell to departing innocence: "So long, Gay; send a letter, old pal."

10 SEPTEMBER
♍

Place Names in England

I.

Ascott-under-Wychwood,
  Wotton under Edge,
The Cokers Down Ampney
  Cold Ashton Lower Swell;
    Bewdley, Stewkley,
      Birdlip Upper Slaughter;
Leatherhead, Mow Cop
  Great Gidding Puncknowle!

2.

Meyese Hampton Horspath
  Ashby-de-la-Zouch,
Great Missenden Woking
  Much Wenclock Crickhope Linn;
    Thrapston, Bawtry,
      Fencot Murcot Firkins:
Pucklechurch, Preesgweene
  St. Blazeys Owl Pen!
      —Robert A. Fowkes

The forgoing verse deals with places where Englishmen live. This one deals with the kinds of scent they wear:

I love that woodsy mensy scent
That just for mensy men is meant—
Some open-airsey moorsey gent
Named Sidney, Claud, or Cyril;
It's advertised so whimsy well
That peatsy smell should sell like hell
To Mumsy's precious: it's a smell
Makes flimsy men seem virile!
      —Pat Bullen

11 SEPTEMBER
♍

The Song of Snohomish

William S. Wallace sent me a poem consisting entirely of baseball players' nicknames. "You might have missed it," he wrote, "when it appeared in the *New York Times Magazine*."

I had not missed it; I had saved it. It will be around as long as baseball is. See how many of the players you can identify:

Catfish, Mudcat, Ducky, Coot.
The Babe, The Barber, The Blade, The Brat.
Windy, Dummy, Gabby, Hoot.
Big Train, Big Six, Big Ed, Fat.

Greasy, Sandy, Muddy, Rocky.
Bunions, Twinkletoes, Footsie, The Hat.
Fuzzy, Dizzy, Buddy, Cocky.
The Bull, The Stork, The Weasel, The Cat.

  Schoolboy, Preacher,
  Rajah, Duke,
  General, Major, Spaceman, Spook.

Shoeless Joe, Cobra Joe, Bullet Joe.
Bing.
Old Hoss, Mule, Country, Rube.
Smokey Joe, Fireman Joe, Jersey Joe.
Ping.
Bulldog, Squirrel, Puddin' Head, Boob.

The Georgia Peach, The Fordham Flash.
The Flying Dutchman, Cot.
The People's Cherce, The Blazer, Crash.
The Staten Island Scot.

  Skeeter, Scooter,
  Pepper, Duster,
  Ebba, Bama, Booms, Buster.

Specs, The Grey Eagle, The Toy Cannon.
Tex.
The Earl of Snohomish, The Duke of Tralee.
Art the Great, Gorgeous George.
Ox, Double X.
The Nashville Narcissus, The Phantom, The Flea.

The Little Professor, The Iron Horse, Cap.
Iron Man, Iron Mike, Iron Hands, Hutch.

Jap, The Mad Russian, Irish, Swede, Nap.
Germany, Frenchy, Big Serb, Dutch,
    Turk.
    Tuck, Tug, Twig.
    Spider, Birdie, Rabbit, Pig.

Three-Finger, No-Neck, The Knuck, The Lip.
Casey, Dazzy, Hippity, Zim.
Flit, Bad Henry, Fat Freddie, Flip.
Jolly Cholly, Sunny Jim.

    Shag, Schnozz,
    King Kong, Klu.

Boog, Buzz,
Boots, Bump, Boo.

Baby Doll, Angel Sleeves, Pep, Sliding Billy.
Buttercup, Bollicky, Boileryard, Juice,
Colby Jack, Dauntless Dave, Cheese, Gentle Willie,
Trolley Line, Wagon Tongue, Rough, What's the Use.

    Ee-yah,
    Poosh 'Em Up,
    Skoonj, Slats, Ski.
    Ding Dong,
    Ding-a-Ling,
    Dim Dom, Dee.

Bubbles, Dimples, Cuddles, Pinky.
Poison Ivy, Vulture, Stinky.

    Jigger, Jabbo
    Jolting Joe
    Blue Moon
    Boom Boom
    Bubba
    Bo.

—*William S. Wallace*

12 SEPTEMBER
♍

Time Out of Mind

Time used to pun as compulsively as hayfever victims sneeze. On the world of art, for instance:

- What did the little boy with Montezuma's revenge say? "Daddy, I've got to Gauguin."
- What do you do with the barrel so we'll have a barrel of fun? Rouault.

In the 1972 primaries *Time* took a fancy to presidential aspirant Edmund Muskie, apparently on the basis of his comment in New Hampshire that "the state cannot be taken for granite." (He turned out to be a prophet.) The newsmagazine loved Adlai Stevenson for describing Barry Goldwater as "a man who thinks everything will be better in the rear future." It also hailed the common nineteenth-century epithet for Prime Minister Disraeli: "England's Jew d'esprit."

In *Time*, Dorothy Parker "was always chasing Rimbauds." Alexander Woollcott knew "a cat hospital where they charge four dollars a weak purr." Peter De Vries dreamed "a female deer was chasing a male deer. I woke up and realized it was a doe trying to make a fast buck."

The personal lives of the Ottoman sultans, to *Time,* "were mainly a matter of bed and bored." Ibrahim, who ordered his 1,001 concubines trussed, weighted, and tossed into the sea, is denominated "Harem-scare-'m Ibrahim."

From *Time's* obituary on Oscar Levant:

> Whenever opportunity knocked, Levant immediately bit its hand. Upon greeting George Gershwin, for example, Oscar went Wilde: "George, if you had it to do all over again, would you fall in love with yourself?"

The late humorist S. J. Perelman, visiting Taipei, found himself "surrounded by a draggle of highly painted professional ladies who obviously wanted more than his autograph. Only with some difficulty did the world traveler extricate himself from their importunities, but he emerged with wit unblunted. 'It was a case,' he mused to a friend on the way back to his hotel, 'of the tail dogging the wag.'"

13 SEPTEMBER
♍

The Derby Ram

As I was going to Derby,
　'Twas on a market day,
I saw the finest ram, sir,
　That ever was fed on hay.
This ram was ten yards high, sir,
　If he wasn't a little more.
　　That's a lie, that's a lie,
　　That's a tid i fa la lie.

Now the inside of this ram, sir,
　Would hold ten sacks of corn,

And you could turn a coach and six
   On the inside of his horn.
Now the wool upon his back, sir,
   It reached up to the sky,
And in it was a crow's nest,
   For I heard the young ones cry.
     That's a lie, that's a lie,
     That's a tid i fa la lie.

Now the wool upon his belly, sir,
   Went dragging on the ground,
And that was took to Derby, sir,
   And sold for ten thousand pound.
Now the wool upon his tail, sir,
   Was ten inches and an ell,
And that was took to Derby, sir,
   To toll the old market-bell.
     That's a lie, that's a lie,
     That's a tid i fa la lie.

Now the man that fed this ram, sir,
   He fed him twice a day,
And each time that he fed him, sir,
   He ate a rick of hay.
Now the man that watered this ram, sir,
   He watered him twice a day,
And each time that he watered him,
   He drank the river dry.
     That's a lie, that's a lie,
     That's a tid i fa la lie.

Now the butcher that killed the ram, sir,
   Was up to his knees in blood,
And the boy that held the bowl, sir,
   Got washed away in the flood.
Now all the boys in Derby, sir,
   Went begging for his eyes,
They kicked them up and down the street,
   For they were a good football size.
     That's a lie, that's a lie,
     That's a tid i fa la lie.

Now all the women of Derby, sir,
   Went begging for his ears,
To make their leather aprons of
   That lasted forty years.
And the man that fatted the ram, sir,

He must be very rich,
And the man that sung this song, sir,
Is a lying son of a bitch.
That's the truth, that's the truth,
That's the tid i fa la truth.
—*Anonymous*

14 SEPTEMBER
♍

The Norris Plan III

"Kathy! Kathy!"

She found herself stretched upon the wooden bench at the side of the croquet field. Her teeth chattered, and Charlie, who was fumbling about vaguely, pale with concern and sympathy, held her hands.

"You're freezing!"

"Don't look so scared, Charlie!"

She laughed frantically, her teeth still chattering. He stared at her sympathetically.

"Anything I could do for you, Kath?" He was not thinking of what he was saying. Her heart beat fast, and she regarded him steadily, not moving a muscle. Suddenly, in an odd tone, he began. "Kathy—"

She looked at him, turning over to lie on her back, her face flushed, her hands icy, and her head rocking.

"Kath," he said, clearing his throat. "Have you thought—you know, this might be—"

Kath swallowed with a dry throat and patted his hand.

"It is, Charlie," she whispered, with a little effort.

"How d'you know?" he asked quickly.

"I asked a publisher. Our publisher."

"And he said—?"

"—Said there was no mistake about it. It is due some time in October."

"He— What do you know about that?" Charlie stammered, his face lighted with bewilderment and surprise. "You poor kid," he said awkwardly.

"Isn't there some way to—get out of it, Kath?" Charlie asked presently, a little doubtfully. "You've had thirty-three, you see. I just thought maybe—well, remember, you're not as strong as you were—the last ten or twelve you've had have all died—"

Her pale face grew whiter, and gripping his hand, with hidden fear and entreaty in her voice, she said:

"Charlie, I won't. It means—no, I couldn't do that. Getting rid of your own novel! That's—that's badder, to me, than not writing a novel at all. Think of it, dear—not to have the name of Norris on the best-seller lists this fall—"

"Well, now, I don't know about that," said Charlie in a queer strained voice.

"Charlie!" She looked at him in sudden comprehension. "You don't mean that you—"

Suddenly she was sitting up, her arms tightly about him, her wet cheek pressed against his. He spoke after a long pause, his eyes lowered guiltily.

"It's true, Kathy. My publisher told me today. I'm going to have a novel in October myself."

She was laughing joyfully, exultantly.

"Then all this that you were saying about literary contraception and book-control, and our country being over-run by incompetents and morons—you didn't mean a word of it?"

"Of course I mean it," he affirmed stoutly. "I'm strongly in favor of book-control—" She stared at him in bewilderment.

"—for everybody else," he concluded hastily.

The Norrises embraced in perfect understanding.

THE END

—Corey Ford

15 SEPTEMBER
♍

Reading Recipe

Less than two weeks have passed since school opened, but already parents are complaining that their children are either not learning fast enough or learning the wrong things. The innovative teaching methods of the past fifty years have whimpered into silence. Why not use ABC language?

DIRGE

To the memory of Miss Ellen Gee, of Kew, who died in consequence of being stung in the eye.

Peerless yet hapless maid of Q!
  Accomplished LN G!
Never again shall I and U
  Together sip our T.

For, ah! the Fates, I know not Y,
  Sent 'midst the flowers a B,
Which ven'mous stung her in the I,
  So that she could not C.

LN exclaim'd, "Vile spiteful B!
  If ever I catch U
On jess'mine, rosebud, or sweet P,
  I'll change your stinging Q.

"I'll send you like a lamb or U
    Across th' Atlantic C
From our delightful village Q
    To distant OYE.

"A stream runs from my wounded I,
    Salt as the briny C,
As rapid as the X or Y,
    The OIO or D.

"Then fare thee ill, insensate B!
    Who stung, nor yet knew Y,
Since not for wealthy Durham's C
    Would I have lost my I."

They bear with tears fair LN G
    In funeral RA,
A clay-cold corse now doom'd to B
    Whilst I mourn her DK.

Ye nymphs of Q, then shun each B,
    List to the reason Y:
For should A B C U at T,
    He'll surely sting your I.

Now in a grave L deep in Q,
    She's cold as cold can B
Whilst robins sing upon a U
    Her dirge and LEG.
            —Anonymous

16 SEPTEMBER
♍

Egocentric

What care I if good God be,
If he be not good to me,
If he will not hear my cry
Nor heed my melancholy midnight sigh?
What care I if he created Lamb
And golden Lion, and mud-delighting Clam,
And Tiger stepping out on padded toe,
And the fecund earth the Blindworms know.
He made the Sun, the Moon and every Star,
He made the infant Owl and the Baboon,

He made the ruby-orbed Pelican,
He made all silent inhumanity,
Nescient and quiescent to his will,
Unquickened by the questing conscious flame
That is my glory and my bitter bane.
What care I if good God be
If he be not good to me?

—Stevie Smith

17 SEPTEMBER
♍

Snallygaster IX

From the *Valley Register,* Middletown, Maryland, March 5, 1909:

EMMITSBURG SAW THE GREAT SNALLYGASTER

It Ate a Coal Bin Empty and Then Spit Fire

LOOKED LIKE A "COON-SCOOPER"

Its Snout Resembled a Silo and Its Mouth Leaked a Fluid Like Melted Brimstone— Flew Off with a Well

---

It was bad enough to hear that the Snallygaster was anywhere in the State, but it is worse to know that it has been right here in the Emmitsburg District. Ed Brown was sitting on the bench outside the Railroad Station, reading the "Life of E. H. Harriman" and waiting for the evening train to come in, when the monster seized him and would have flown off with him had not Bill Snider, who dashed up in his automobile, grabbed Brown by the foot, which broke his suspenders and he dropped to the ground. Ghostlike wings beat the air and fire singed the pike.

"It looked like a giraffe on roller skates," said Mr. Snider. "Its beak was serrated with great tusks and between them lay the partly consumed flesh of a man. Its snout resembled a silo and from the corners of its mouth leaked a fluid like melted brimstone."

As the Snallygaster passed over Emmitsburg, deputy game warden Capt. Norman Hoke, aware of the danger, showed his badge and backed by the full authority of the law, ordered it from the County.

John Glass, who was returning from a sale at Bridgeport, where he had purchased a well, threw the newly acquired well at the Snallygaster with such good aim that he is now minus a few ready-made holes, for the well passed over the Snallygaster's huge snout. When last seen in the woods to the west of Taneytown, the monster wore the well like a nose-ring.

THE END

18 SEPTEMBER
♍

Out of the Mouths of Babes and Computers

There are more than 403,000,000,000,000,000,000,000,000 possible ways to combine the twenty-six letters of the alphabet. Jezebel Q. Xixx (a pen name, I presume) says that a supercomputer, capable of spewing out different arrangements at the rate of 10 million per second, would need to operate continuously for a trillion years—vastly longer than the universe has been in existence—to list all the possible letter sequences.

Cashell Farrell set his computer a more modest task: It was to continue arranging pangrams of no more than fifty-two letters, using each letter of the alphabet no more than twice, until it came up with something he liked. I do not know how long it took the computer to produce these:

- The qualmish Afghan Jew packed over sixty fez with bees.
- How frog-jumping razorbacks can level six piqued gymnasts.
- When waxing parquet decks, Suez sailors vomit jauntily abaft.

A computer that can give birth to "vomit jauntily abaft" is developing a soul.

Robert H. Goodin sent me a pangram which he found years ago, he thinks in *Scientific American*. It uses Roman numerals to make the job of pangram construction a little easier.

The explanatory background—most pangrams need explanatory backgrounds—is this: A squad of Roman soldiers, stationed in Norway, is invited to a dance by a bevy of fifteen Scandinavian maidens. The squad leader rushes a messenger to his commanding officer with this dispatch:

XV quick nymphs beg fjord waltz

Technically, any passage that goes on long enough to include every letter of the alphabet becomes a pangram. This word-pangram works back from Z to A:

THE LADY WITHOUT A HEART

He:

> Zelda, your X ray was vagarious,
>   Unusual to see;
> Really, quite pretty oddities
>   Nurture my Ladee:
> Keys ... jewels ... ice. Heart's gone.

She:

> *Few endure, dearee ...*
> *Come, boy!—Agree!*

> —W.R.E.

19 SEPTEMBER
♍

Feeding the Baby

OYSTERVILLE—My niece Sydney is building a gem of a house on the bay bank, hidden from the public road by a crowded forest of spruce and alder trees.

The three carpenters, Ozzie Steiner and his sons, Wolfgang and Guenter, though perhaps the most industrious workmen outside their native Germany, have their lighter moments. Guenter was missing today; his father explained that he had gone home to feed the baby.

"But the baby isn't born yet," I said.

Ah, that was just the point. The Steiners have borrowed an agreeable superstition from a tribe of South American Indians. The Indians hold that conception takes place through kissing, while sexual intercourse during pregnancy provides nutrition for the unborn child.

"Ven Guenter grows restless," said his father, "ve send him home to feed the baby."

20 SEPTEMBER
♍

Work Is the Thing You Have to Do

OYSTERVILLE—The *Wall Street Journal* should send someone to interview Don and Marva Hall, who have just finished painting the living room of the red cottage. Not that they are tycoons, exactly. Last year, with inflation raging, they earned $4,000. And saved $2,000.

Don is fifty, and I would guess Marva at thirty-five. They have no children. They live in a house they bought recently on an isolated back road, where they have transplanted about 400 tagged varieties of rhododendrons. They work one day a week at Okie's grocery store in Ocean Park, stocking the shelves. Besides the money paid them for that, they take home produce that is fine for eating, but no longer salable—molding cheese, apples with spots on them, bent cans of fish, and the like. Otherwise, the only cash they have earned this summer is the $56 I paid them for painting—$4 an hour apiece; seven hours. Oh, yes. Marva makes pies and cakes to order.

They are entitled to bag two elk a season, but generally content themselves with one; two would be too much elk. They also shoot two deer. The meat is stored in their freezer, and lasts them comfortably for a year. If a breathing spell happens along, Don reads. Marva paints landscapes. They own a television set but don't have time to make use of it.

Working to pile up money has no interest for them. "Work," says Don, "is what you have to do to pay other people for the work you don't have time to do because you are too busy working for the money to pay them."

They never work. They play.

21 SEPTEMBER
♍

A Smell of Kyrielle, A Bloom of Pantoum

TO GOD THE PRAISE (a kyrielle)

When I was keen and young as you,
I laid the world out to renew.
I laid it out, and there it lays—
To God the praise.

When I was new and young and dense,
My friends deplored my want of sense.
Ah, sense is silliness these days—
To God the praise.

Appalled to see my flabby thighs,
They urged me on to exercise.
Their obsequies my spirits raise—
To God the praise.

No Jack more dearly loved his Jill;
I loved her then, I love her still.
Love unrequited ne'er decays—
To God the praise.

My wife and I do well agree,
But she sees little hope for me;
And there is much in what she says.
To God the praise.
—*W.R.E.*

CONSIDER NOW THE QUARK (a pantoum)

Consider now the Quark, who is
A Concept As-tro-nom-i-cal.
No man alive has seen his phiz;
Perhaps he isn't is at all.

A Concept As-tro-nom-i-cal
Too tenuous I find to prove.
Perhaps he isn't is at all.
This goes for Hate, and also Love.

Too tenuous I find to prove
The Sun, the Shadow, and the Wind.
This goes for Hate, and also Love,
And other matters of the kind.

The Sun, the Shadow, and the Wind—
My Blood, my Breath, my Moon, my Air,
And other matters of the kind
I find are proven best in prayer.

My Blood, my Breath, my Moon, my Air,
And other matters, being His,
I find are proven best in prayer.
Consider now the Quark, who Is.
—*W.R.E.*

22 SEPTEMBER
♍

Carpe Diem, Darling

1. IF YOU LOVE ME AS I LOVE YOU

If you love me as I love you,
If I love you as you love me,
We stand love-all; I wonder who
The winner of the game will be.
—*W.R.E.*

2. THE FACE IS FAMILIAR, BUT . . .

You strain to recollect me?
To call me back to mind?
I'm in your photo album
Behind the one behind.
—*W.R.E.*

3. THE PESKY LADS I'VE KNOWN ARE FEW

The pesky lads I've known are few,
The pesky lasses, many;
Yet, darling, in the longer view,
If there are even one or two
Who suit my taste as well as you,
I'd trade all lads I ever knew
For you . . . and Rose, and Penny.
—*W.R.E.*

Girl, when rejecting me you never guessed
I gave you all the beauty you possessed.
Now that I've ceased to love you, you remain
At once, a creature singularly plain.
—*Martin Armstrong*

23 SEPTEMBER
♍

Tear-O-Lear-O-Loo

These by the king of nonsense:

ALPHABET

A tumbled down, and hurt his Arm, against a bit of wood.
B said, "My Boy, O do not cry; it cannot do you good!"
C said, "A Cup of Coffee hot can't do you any harm."
D said, "A Doctor should be fetched, and he would cure the arm."
E said, "An Egg beat up with milk would quickly make him well."
F said, "A Fish, if broiled, might cure, if only by the smell."
G said, "Green Gooseberry fool, the best of cures I hold."
H said, "His Hat should be kept on, to keep him from the cold."
I said, "Some Ice upon his head will make him better soon."
J said, "Some Jam, if spread on bread, or given in a spoon."
K said, "A Kangaroo is here,—this picture let him see."
L said, "A Lamp pray keep alight, to make some barley tea."
M said, "A Mulberry or two might give him satisfaction."

N said, "Some Nuts, if rolled about, might be a slight attraction."
O said, "An Owl might make him laugh, if only it would wink."
P said, "Some Poetry might be read aloud, to make him think."
Q said, "A Quince I recommend,—a Quince, or else a Quail."
R said, "Some Rats might make him move, if fastened by their tail."
S said, "A Song should now be sung, in hopes to make him laugh."
T said, "A Turnip might avail, if sliced or cut in half."
U said, "An Urn, with water hot, place underneath his Chin!"
V said, "I'll stand upon a chair, and play a Violin."
W said, "Some Whisky-Whizzgigs fetch, some marbles and a ball."
X said, "Some double XX ale would be the best of all."
Y said, "Some Yeast mixed up with salt would make a perfect plaster!"
Z said, "Here is a box of Zinc! Get in, my little master.
   We'll shut you up! We'll nail you down! We will, my little master!
   We think we've all heard quite enough of this your sad disaster!"
                                                        —*Edward Lear*

COLD ARE THE CRABS (Sonnet)

Cold are the crabs that crawl on yonder hills,
Colder the cucumbers that grow beneath,
And colder still the brazen chops that wreathe
    The tedious gloom of philosophic pills!
For when the tardy film of nectar fells
The ample bowls of demons and of men,
There lurks the feeble mouse, the homely hen,
    And there the porcupine with all her quills.
Yet much remains—to weave a solemn strain
That lingering sadly—slowly dies away,
Daily departing with departing day
A pea green gamut on a distant plain
When wily walruses in Congress met—
    Such such is life—

A LETTER TO EVELYN BARING

Thrippsy pillivinx,
    Inky tinky pobbleboskle abblesquabs?—
Flosky! beebul trimble flosky!—Okul
scratchabibblebongibo, viddle squibble tog-a-tog,
ferrymoyassity amsky flamsky ramsky damsky
croclefether squiggs.
                        Flinkywisty pomm,
                        Slushypipp

24 SEPTEMBER

Wacky Wordies

In a rebus, one is supposed to discern a familiar phrase, saying, cliché, or name from each arrangement of letters and/or digits. In the rebuses below, Box 1a depicts the phrase "Just between you and me," while Box 1B shows "Hitting below the belt."

	a	b	c	d	e	f
1	you just me	belt hitting	lo head ve heels	VI O L E T s	A B E DUMR	agb
2	cry m i l k	·-⊏ ϶ᴍ·-→	Symphon	ɘʞɒɔ ǝlddɐǝuᴉd	arrest you're	timing tim ing
3	o TV	night fly	s T I N K	injury + insult	r o rail d	my own heart a person
4	at the · of on	dothepe	wear long	strich groound	lu cky	the market

25 SEPTEMBER

Nazzo Guido

Guido Nazzo, an Italian tenor of the 1930s, sang only once in New York and received but one review: "Guido Nazzo: nazzo guido."

Violinist Georges Enesco, wishing to help a young friend who was making his debut at Carnegie Hall, offered to accompany him on the piano. The idea diverted Walter Gieseking, the pianist, who said he would turn the pages. A review next morning said, "The man who should have been playing the violin was playing the piano, the man who should have been playing the piano was turning the pages, and the man who should have been turning the pages was playing the violin."

Tenor Richard Tucker, preparing for the opening curtain of *La Gioconda,* felt an air-conditioned chill, "Turn that off!" he ordered. "It will freeze my throat!" "That" was not turned off. All through the first two acts his anger mounted. Finally, just before the third act, he announced: "Unless the air conditioning is turned off, I do not sing a note!" "The audience might leave," said the impresario. "Let them!" roared Tucker. "They must accommodate to me, not me to them. The trouble with this business," he added gravely as the air conditioning went off, "is that it is filled with egotistical maniacs."

26 SEPTEMBER

Profanity of Flowers and Fish

George Johnson says an eighteenth-century English scholar silenced the abuse of Billingsgate fishwives by thundering: "Parallelepipedon!" (A parallelepipedon in geometry is a regular solid bounded by six plane surfaces—a cube, for example.) The names of flowers and shellfish can be as alarming: "You false hellbore! You viper's bug loss! You wart-necked piddock!" Or the names of insects: "You sandbug! Spittlebug! Stinkbug! Louse!"

Recommended curses:

Flowers	*Shellfish*
You devil's-bit scabious!	You hairy mopalia!
You dwarf spurge!	You denticulate donax!
You lousewort!	You speckled tegula!
You henbit dead nettle!	You wentletrap!
You swine's cress!	You measled cowry!
You pignut!	You false cerith!
You moneywort loosestrife!	You deadman's fingers!
You creeping toadflax!	You bent-nose macoma!

27 SEPTEMBER

Honi Soit Qui Mal Y Pense

Louise and I cast $400 of bread upon the waters, no small sum for us, to buy one-quarter of one percent of a company that was raising money to finance the production of three plays in England. Improbably the bread returned to us after many days, with a few breadcrumbs in tow. This was play money, so Louise combined it with something from her savings account and set off last Friday afternoon for London to attend the opening of the third play.

At 7:05 precisely Andy, the doorman, tucked her into a taxicab, among her gear: suitcase, overnight bag, tote bag, flight bag, raincoat, umbrella, and the other paraphernalia that any self-respecting woman needs if she is traveling beyond the supermarket. I then returned to the apartment, just in time to catch the last despairing ring of the telephone. Monica, a friend whose home is in Hawaii, was calling from Kennedy Airport; she was faced with a twenty-four-hour layover on a flight to Rome and wondered whether we could put her up for the night. I said of course.

An hour later Andy helped Monica, ash-blond and edible, from her cab. He gravely carried to the elevator her suitcase, overnight bag, tote bag, flight bag, raincoat, umbrella, and the other paraphernalia that any self-respecting woman needs if she is traveling beyond the supermarket.

Our apartment consists of four rooms—four and a half if you count the breakfast room. Monica took the bedroom, and between us we made up the living room couch for me. Then we went out for dinner.

We returned in time to catch the last despairing ring of the telephone. Marion, a friend who lives in Washington, D.C., was about to take the shuttle to New York. She wondered whether we could put her up for the night. I figured that we could, just. Monica and I made a bed for her in the study. Then Monica, dazed from twelve hours in the air, retired. An hour and a half later Andy helped Marion (a radiant June dawn with Marlene Dietrich's legs, that's Marion) from her cab. He gravely carried to the elevator her suitcase, overnight bag, tote bag, flight bag, raincoat, umbrella, and the other paraphernalia that any self-respecting woman needs if she is traveling beyond the supermarket.

And so we slept, the three points of an isosceles triangle. X is Espy, on the living-room couch; Y is Marion, in the study; Z is Monica, in the bedroom. The next morning, when Monica and Marion met for the first time, I experienced a brief glow from the realization that neither of them could be sure where I had spent the night. But the glow was short-lived. The whole world knows my lack of enterprise.

I studiously avoided Andy's eye a few hours later as he gravely stowed first Marion, then Monica, into their cabs, each jammed among her gear: suitcase, overnight bag, tote bag, flight bag, raincoat, umbrella, and the other paraphernalia that any self-respecting woman needs if she is traveling beyond the supermarket.

28 SEPTEMBER

End Ell Irs Indirstiid

It has been argued that if we clearly understood one another, our antagonisms would vanish—on the face of it, a dubious proposition. In any event, understanding remains unlikely as long as words jump around in meaning and vowels in sound. Let us have vowels we can rely on:

END ELL IRS INDIRSTIID

Vowels! Henceforth be consistent!
As the Pole Star, change-resistant!
Stand your ground now! Limit phonics
By agreed-upon mnemonics!

Count on *any* for the sound of *A*;
   On *English* for sweet resonance of *E*;
On *shirt* for *I*; for *O*, on women. Stay
With *busy* for your *U*. Lo! Straightaway
   Sound joins to sense in gentle harmony:

Thi pin irs mirteir then thi ettim bimb;
   Thii shelt nit kirl; the gil irv Gid is giid;
End thri end thri meks sirx. This wirth aplimb
Mirnd mits wirth mirnd, end ell irs
      indirstiid.

                 —W.R.E.

29 SEPTEMBER

If You Are the Doer, Am I the Doee?

Logic, in grammar, leads to trouble:

    Caudated to a verb, the suffix *-er*
    Denotes the agent setting things a-stir:
    Thus, *runner, almoner*. The suffix *-ee*
    Denotes the done-to, as in *legatee*.

    Though I have known exceptions, to be sure,
    To suffix *-ee* (if not to suffix *-er*),
    The pairing's elegant, and in my view
    Deserves extension. Hence I give to you:

    Squander and *squandee* and *launder* and *laundee*,
    Thinker and *thinkee* and *ponder* and *pondee*,
    Worker and *workee* and *singer* and *singee*,
    Cougher and *coughee* and *bringer* and *bringee*.

    A *squander*'s a wastrel; when he is bereft,
    It's fair to assume that a *squandee* is left;
    If I be the *buyer*, the *buyee* you'll be;
    If I am the *sleeper*, you'll be the *sleepee*.

So *hearer* to *hearee* and *writer* to *writee,*
And *winner* to *winnee,* and *fighter* to *fightee.*
It is you I *prefer,* so you're my *prefee;*
And when you *inter* me, I'll be your *intee.*

—*W.R.E.*

HAD I BUT NUDE

We know the meaning of *butt,* as in the butt of a joke; we know the meaning of *nude,* as in nude beaches; we know the meaning of *seed;* we know the meaning of *dude,* as in dude ranch; we know the meaning of *deed,* as in a deed to property, or an infamous deed. But combine these in a certain way and the meanings change:

Had I butt nude,   Would I have dude
Had I but seed,   The dids I deed?

—*W.R.E.*

30 SEPTEMBER

She Said It All

If you doubt that the language is decaying, examine the evidence:

Then	*Now*
I love thee to the depth and breadth	You turn
And height my soul can reach.	me on!
—*Elizabeth Barrett Browning*	

The word must be spoken that bids you depart	Get lost!
Though the effort to speak it should shatter my heart.	
—*George W. Young*	
God's in His heaven	A-OK!
All's right with the world.	
—*Robert Browning*	

—*Faith Eckler*

An international group of poets, including Allen Ginsberg, Yevgeny Yevtushenko, Lawrence Ferlinghetti, and William Burroughs, recently recited in Italy before 10,000 youthful lovers of the written word. These eventually mobbed the stage, which collapsed; but not, according to the *New York Times,* before a young woman seized the microphone and expressed the general sentiments of the audience in these immortal words:

"I mean, you know what I feel, I mean, why can't I say something, you know, my things, my feelings, I mean, my story, you know."

She said it all.

OCTOBER

1 OCTOBER

The Flying Pyramid

I
A M
T H E
W E L L
K N O W N
L E G E N D
H A U N T E D
W A N D E R E R
E N D L E S S L Y
C E L E B R A T E D
M A S T E R F U L L Y
I M M O R T A L I Z E D
T R A D I T I O N A L L Y
U N D E R S T A N D A B L E
N O T W I T H S T A N D I N G
I N C O M P R E H E N S I B L E
Q U A S I O T H E R W O R L D L Y
M U M B O J U M B O I N F E S T E D
C L O S E T M A C H I A V E L L I A N
M A C R O C E P H A L I C U L T U R A L
P S E U D O A N T H R O P O L O G I C A L
P S Y C H O A N A L Y T I C O R I E N T E D
U L T R A P A T H O L O G I C O C E N T R I C
S U P E R T E R R E S T R I A L D E P E N D E N T
C R Y P T O A N T I H U M A N I T A R I A N I S T
M Y T H O G R A P H I C O S C H O L A S T I C I S M

—Richard Wincor

2 OCTOBER

On the Indispensability of Encyc. Brit.

Turning to the *Britannica* for a clearer understanding of SEDITION, I remarked with some surprise that the next entry was SEDUCTION. Seduction has occasioned a considerable body of law in the United Kingdom:

Thy characters I daily scan,
Encyclopaedia Britan.;
My scanty knowledge I accrete
At thy august Britannic feet.

Behold! but now I read an entry
Invaluable to the gentry:
A sober, step-by-step instruction
On statutes governing SEDUCTION

(Defined here as a pleasant trade
Between a Maker and his Maid,
Wherein the Maker reprehens-
ibly *suggests;* the Maid *consents*).

If you are under twelve, my fault
Is rude felonious assault;
Think twice, love, ere you whisper "Yes";
Consent deprives you of redress.
Volenti non injuria fit,
Points out *Encyclopaedy Brit.*

Belowstairs, innocent coition
May bring about indisposition.
Be warned, if awkward labor pains
Delay your cleaning out the drains,

Your master may your lover sue
For daily chores undone by you:
An action lies at law if lusting
Leaves furniture in need of dusting.

If you are hired to make my bed
And wind up made in it instead,
I'm legally immune unless
Our deal required that you undress.
But if I wait until you've teened,
Then I have only misdemeaned.

For facts like these am I addic-
ted to *Britannica Encyc.*:
Seduction scarcely is my speed;
Still, thanks, *Britan. Encyclopaed.!*
—W.R.E.

3 OCTOBER

Dear Reader

On her silver wedding anniversary, a correspondent took particular care with her toilet—a touch of cologne behind the ears, that sort of thing—and felt a pleasurable *frisson* as she slipped into bed. But her husband Bill was absorbed in *An Almanac of Words at Play,* an anniversary gift. She complained to me in a verse that went something like this:

Miscarriage
Of marriage—

Forsook
For a book.

I am glad to say that she added a P.S.: "Don't worry—everything worked out fine."
Still, I apologize:

A Gay Old Dog, to digging prone,
Comes flaunting an enormous Bone.
The Cocky Canine doubts no whit
Exactly where he'll bury it;
Till, hidden in a Book, he spies
A Bone of even grander size.
He snaps at this to swell his quotum,
And loses both—from Book, from Scrotum.

Fear not, Bill; Holy Writ makes plain
Unburied Bones shall rise again.

Another correspondent hailed a book of mine as immortal, the finest thing since
Ovid. "I can hardly wait," he concluded, "to reach page two." I never heard from
him again.

Bob Bendiner, promoting one of his books, was approached by a woman who said
she found it irresistible. "I would have finished it," she said, "but if I had kept it longer
I would have had to pay the circulating library an extra ten cents."

A woman named Elizzabeth [sic] wrote:

Will you do me a favor?—Will you rewrite "Finnegan's Wake" of
Joyce's in plain English I could understand? Joyce is a classical writer. I
love his work. It's urgent to get this figured out and you seem top person
to do it. I have a million things to do and am about half through first
reading—it's a study—all Joyce is. At the moment I am not personally
able to pay more than you charge for a book.

Do you suppose Elizzabeth would pay me the $7.95 price of a trade paperback?
Or could she afford the $15.95 price of the hardcover edition?

4 OCTOBER

Can You Do Me a Coat?

Pedro Carolino comments in *English as She Is Spoke,* a nineteenth-century guide
to English for the Portuguese:

"You hear the birds gurgling? Which pleasure! Which charm! The field has by me
a thousand charms."

His book has by me a thousand clues to colloquial English. Some model sentences:

At the tailor's: "Can you do me a coat? What cloth will you do to?"

At the stable: "Here is a horse who have a bad looks. He not sall know how to march, he is pursy, he is foundered. Don't you are ashamed to give me a jade as like? He is un-shoed, he is with nails up, it want to lead to the farrier."

English as She Is Spoke offers these proverbs:

* The necessity don't know the low.
* Few, few the bird make her nest.
* A bad arrangement is better than a process.
* To build castles in Espagnish.
* The scalded fear the cold water.
* He is not so devil as he is black.
* The stone as roll not heap up not foam.
* He is beggar as a church rat.
* Keep the chestnut out of the fire with the cat foot.
* After the paunch comes the dance.
* To look for a needle in a hay bundle.

Would you do as well if you wrote a guide to Portuguese for Americans?

5 OCTOBER

Unsafe at Ant Speed

One letter is changed in each of these passages from a *New York* magazine competition—and oh, the difference to Mary Ann Madden!

* Why can't a woman be more like a mat?
* Wish you were her.
* I've got you under my ski.
* I thank whatever gods may be / For my unconquerable soup.
* Small apartment for runt.
* Don't feel the animals.
* God help those who help themselves.
* A rabbi's foot brings good luck.
* . . . and the Cabots talk only to cod.
* I hate to see a grown man dry.
* Welfare Department, Pity of New York.
* Caution: Misuse of these pills could prove fetal.
* I was the product of a dating mother.
* Rome wasn't built in a bay.
* Anyone who mates dogs and babies can't be all bad.
* Unsafe at ant speed.

6 OCTOBER

The Redemption of Gretchen

NEW YORK—We joined Flight 8 from Tokyo at Seattle. Departure was delayed for an hour, I think because someone was trying to smuggle a piano through customs, so it was nearly midnight when we reached home. But I did glance through my mail and found something from William Roos that caused me to throw out the entry I had planned for this date.

The something was extracts from a book called *Die Schöniste Lengevitch,* written in 1925 by a distant cousin of Mr. Roos's. The extracts were from summaries of operas—*Faust, Tristan und Isolde, Lohengrin*—written in doggerel that combined English and colloquial German. They are not true macaronics, though I have so categorized them here; instead of alternating German and English, the verses mix German, English, and Germanized English words. In any event, they touched my risibilities; in the night I woke, laughing.

Here, for example, is a scene from *Faust.* Gretchen, driven mad by guilt at having destroyed the infant engendered on her by the magician, is awaiting execution at dawn. Faust gains admission to her cell and tries vainly to persuade her to flee. Mephistopheles arrives to hurry them to their spiritual ruin. But, ah . . .

PRISON SCENE

Trotzdem sie ihre Mind verlor'n
Und krank iss, und ganz ausgeworn
Liegt's arme Gretchen, schwach und pale
Auf a Bunch Stroh im County Jail
Denn in die Times gab's noch kei Plea
Convenient Insanity.

Auf ei'mal rattelts an der Thür—
"Gee," ruft das Gretchen, "du bist hier!
Kannst du remembern auf der Porch—"
"Poor Ding," weint Faust, und raised sei Torch.
"Come Gretchen, quick, ich hab die Keys."
"Ach, stay doch noch a Minute, please,"
Sagt sie: "Talk von die alte Zeit:
Kei Taxi wart doch nicht autseit!"
"Come, hurry nimm dei Hut, mach schnell!"
Urged Faust. "Es iss schon nearly hell!"
"Nix on die Hell," replied das Gretchen,
Und prayed noch schnell a paar Gebetchen.
Und while Mephisto stampet und rafet,
Da singen Angels, "Sie's gesafet."

Die Churchbell ringt, und mit Gebimmel
Ascended sie hinauf zum Himmel.
                                    —*Kurt M. Stein*

I cannot capture the pun between *hell,* "light," and *Hell,* "hell." But this is more or less what the verse says:

> Though Gretchen of all Sense was shorn,
> Her Body ravaged and outworn,
> Although she lay all weak and pale
> On a Heap of Straw in the County Jail,
> Yet in the *Times* she made no plea
> Of Convenient Insanity.
>
> The Jail Door rattled in her Ear:
> "Gee whiz!" cried Gretchen—"Faust, you're here!
> Do you remember on the Porch . . ."
> "Poor Thing!" sobbed Faust, and raised his Torch.
> "Come, Gretchen, quick! I have the Keys!"
> "Oh, stay a Moment longer, please!
> We'll chat about Old Times!" she cried;
> "No Cab's on waiting time outside!"
> "Come—hurry—pin your Bonnet on,"
> Urged Faust; "it's hellish close to Dawn!"
> "Nix on the Hell stuff," quoth the maid—
> Then, quickly, two wee Prayers she prayed.
> And while Mephisto stamped and raved,
> The Angels sang, "The Kid is saved."
>
> The Church Bell sounded, Kling and Klang,
> And up to Heaven Gretchen sprang.
>
> —*W.R.E.*

7 OCTOBER

Yknits Seiknip

A "Stinky Pinkies" definition elicits two words that rhyme; "Birth at the North Pole," for instance, emerges as "shivery delivery." In the variant below, the second word reverses the spelling of the first; a "buddy on your knee" is "lap pal." The parenthesized figure in each line is the number of letters in the word. Proceed:

1. a crazy female animal (3)
2. manufactured a Dutch cheese (4)
3. a gadid veterinarian (3)
4. reimbursed for a baby's fanny cover (6)
5. a stag that feeds on bamboolike grass (4)
6. spoil a male sheep (3)

7. exceptional guy in Nevada city (4)
8. hero of California town (4)
9. in the style of Esau or his descendants (4)
10. summary description of a certain horse (5)
11. criticize a golf score (3)
12. rework a German river (4)
13. a grain of the Chinese "way" (3)
14. Pythias' wandering friend (5)
15. blue jeans material taken from the earth (5)
16. bite from a small point (3)
17. love, Italian style (4)
18. a moray on the sheltered side (3)
19. hoarfrost on an Arab prince (4)
20. a platelike creature (6)

—Boris Randolph

8 OCTOBER

Even Homer Nods

I know *Schadenfreude* when I encounter solecisms by competent writers. It is comforting to know I do not err alone. For instance:

• WHO-WHOM

"After her in his affections came Selwyn, whom he soon saw was the most intelligent of the whole litter."—*David Garnett, Lady into Fox*

"He wanted to do a book on the Hungarian poet Petöfi, whom he had convinced himself was of a stature with Pushkin."—*George Steiner, "An Appreciation of Edmund Wilson"*

(If the two writers had set apart their interjected clauses—in the first case "he soon saw"—and in the second "he had convinced himself"—by commas, they would not have made those mistakes.)

• DO-DOES

"The great body of Americans do not want Detroit to suffer, does not expect the impossible, and . . ."—*Wall Street Journal editorial*

(One may argue about whether a singular verb used in a plural sense should take a plural or a singular verb, but it can't take both in succession.)

• REDUNDANCY

"Few other Western journalists know Egypt more intimately than Cairo Bureau Chief Wilton Wynn.—*Letter from the publisher, Time*

(Strike that "other," *Time.*)

• HE AS OBJECT OF A VERB

"Harvard must maintain high standards that make people like Henry Rosovsky and I work twice as hard."—*from a talk by Derek Bok, president of Harvard University*

(President Bok knows that the pronoun is the object of the verb "make" and has to be in the accusative—"me." But even as part of a subject phrase with *like*, it would still be in the accusative: "People like me [not I] work twice as hard.")

• IS, ARE

"The revelations of modern biology is a remarkable human and scientific story."— *Jeremy Bernstein reviewing The Eighth Day of Creation in the New York Times Book Review*

(Revelations *are*. A remarkable human and scientific story *is*—but that is another remarkable human and scientific story.)

9 OCTOBER

Word from a Relentless Moralist

(As you will see by the salary figure, this was written B.I.—Before Inflation, that is.)

THE PATIENT TOILER
WHO GOT IT IN THE USUAL PLACE

Once there was an Office Employee with a Copy-Book Education.

He believed it was his Duty to learn to Labor and to Wait.

He read Pamphlets and Magazine Articles on Success and how to make it a Cinch. He knew that if he made no Changes and never beefed for more Salary, but just buckled down and put in Extra Time and pulled for the House, he would Arrive in time.

The Faithful Worker wanted to be Department Manager. The hours were short and the Salary was large and the Work was easy.

He plugged on for many Moons, keeping his Eye on that Roll-Top Desk, for the manager was getting into the Has-Been Division and he knew that there would be a Vacancy.

At last the House gave the old Manager the Privilege of retiring and living on whatever he had saved.

"Ah, this is where Humble Merit gets its Reward," said the Patient Toiler. "I can see myself counting Money."

That very Day the Main Gazooks led into the office one of the handsomest Tennis Players that ever worked on Long Island and introduced him all around as the new Department Manager.

"I shall expect you to tell Archibald all about the Business," said the

Main Gazooks to the Patient Toiler. "You see he has just graduated from Yale and he doesn't know a dum Thing about Managing anything except a Cat-Boat, but his father is one of our principal Stock-Holders and he is engaged to a Young Woman whose Uncle is at the Head of the Trust."

"I had been hoping to get this Job for myself," said the Faithful Worker, faintly.

"You are so valuable as a Subordinate and have shown such an Aptitude for Detail Work that it would be a shame to waste you on a five-thousand-dollar job," said the Main Gazooks. "Besides you are not Equipped. You have not been to Yale. Your father is not a Stock-Holder. You are not engaged to a Trust. Get back to your High Stool and whatever Archibald wants to know, you tell him."

Moral: One who wishes to be a Figure-Head should not Over-Train.
—George Ade

10 OCTOBER

Neigh, Neigh, Neighbor

That Gay Talese sold his book *Thy Neighbor's Wife* to United Artists for $2.5 million prompts me to reissue the following verse, slightly modified. Reasonable offers from Hollywood will be considered.

AFTER NEIGHBORS' WIVES YOU NEIGH?

They were as fed horses in the morning; every one
neighed after his neighbor's wife.—Jeremiah V:8

After neighbors' wives you neigh?
  Neighbors' wives are fine—
Sorrel, chestnut, dapple gray,

Rolling neighing in the hay.
  Neigh, then, neighbor, neigh—but nay!
  Neigh not after mine.
—W.R.E.

MY THREE WIVES

Though marriage by some folks reckon'd
  Be a curse,
Three wives did I marry
  For better or worse—
The first for her person,
  The next for her purse,
The third for a warming pan,
  Doctress, and nurse.
—Anonymous, after the Latin of
Etienne Pasquier

CUPID RHYMES

Cupid rhymes with stupid.　　　From lovers who've been dupèd
　　So one hears　　　　　　　　　By their dears.

　　　　　　　　　　　　　　　　　　　　　　　—W.R.E.

SOME LOVE COWS AND SOME LOVE HOSSES

I loved a little bossy;　　　　　You prance and curvet, hossy;
　　I used to feed her hay;　　　　There's mischief in your eye;
She offered milk when hossy　　I think you know why bossy
　　Was looking 'tother way.　　　Has overnight gone dry.

　　　　　　　　　　　　　　　　　　　　　　　—W.R.E.

11 OCTOBER

Mary Jack and the Obscene Telephone Call

I dined last night with Mary Jack. She ordered frogs' legs; I ordered cannelloni. Back at her apartment, we found her twelve-year-old son bursting with important news.

The police had just telephoned to warn that Mary Jack could expect an obscene telephone call at any minute. She had run a classified advertisement offering a reward for a lost brooch, and they had their eye on a wicked fellow who made a practice of phoning such advertisers on the pretense of having found the lost object, then shifting to topics dearer to him.

We had scarcely taken this in when the police called again. "With your permission," said the caller (my head was pressed against Mary Jack's, so that we could both hear the voice in the receiver), "we are tapping your wire. With your cooperation, we can catch this nasty man."

"How do I cooperate?" asked Mary Jack.

"He probably will call from a telephone booth. Keep him talking for twenty minutes. That will give us time to trace the call and pick him up."

"I'll try."

"We realize we are asking a great deal of you. You will have to keep him interested."

Mary Jack was game. "I'll try," she repeated.

She poured brandies. We had scarcely taken a sip when the fellow rang.

As before, I kept my ear as close as possible to Mary Jack's. Obviously I cannot repeat what I heard, but I say with surprise and admiration that Mary Jack managed to keep the conversation going beautifully.

In precisely twenty minutes the call broke off.

"Mary Jack," I said, "they've got him."

That was last night. This morning she telephoned me. She had checked with the police department, she said, and nobody knew what she was talking about.

Mary Jack had been conned.

12 OCTOBER

Sorrowful? Sore Dread? Solemn Horror? Mourning?

Puns are frequently untranslatable, but they may be matched in translation, as Henri Bue proved when he turned *Alice in Wonderland* into French in 1869. At one point Alice remarks that the earth takes twenty-four hours to turn around on its axis, causing the Duchess to exclaim, "Talking of axes, chop off her head!" M. Bue could not pun appropriately on the French word for ax (*hache*) but he came up with an equally apt trope:

> ALICE: La terre met vingt-quatre heures à faire sa révolution.
> DUCHESS: Vous parlez de faire des révolutions! Qu'on lui coupe la tête!

We all see through our own spectacles, and translations vary with the personalities of the translators. Here, for instance, is the Greek for the first five lines of Book II, *The Odyssey*:

> "Αὐτὰρ ἐπεί ρ ἐπί νῆα κατηλθομεν ἠοὲ θάλασσαν,
> νῆα μὲν αρ πάμπρωτον ἐρύσσαμεν εις αλα δῖαν,
> ἐν δ'ιστὸν τιθέμεσθα καὶ ιστία νηὶ μελαίνη,
> ἐν δὲ τὰ μδλα λαβόντες ἐβήσαμεν, αν δὲ καὶ αὐτοὶ
> βαίνομεν ἀχνύμενοι θαλερὸν κατὰ δάκρυ χέοντες.
> ἡμῖν δ' αὖ κατόπισθε νεὸς κυανοπρώροιο
> ικμενον οὖρον ιει πλησίστιον, ἐσθλὸν ἑταιρον,
> Κίρκη ευπλόκαμος, δεινὴ θεὸς αυδήεσσα.
> ἡμεῖς δ' οπλα εκαστα πονησάμενοι κατὰ νῆα
> ἡμεθα τὴν δ' ἀνεμός τε κυβερνήτης τ' ιθυνε.
> τῆς δὲ πανημερίης τέταθ' ιστία ποντοπορούσης
> δύσετό τ' ἠέλιος σκιόωντό τε πᾶσαι αγυιαί.

A. T. Murray provides this prose translation:

> But when we had come down to the ship and to the sea, first of all we drew the ship down to the bright sea, and took the sheep and put them aboard, and ourselves embarked, sorrowing, and shedding big tears.

Here each of four noble English poets runs the passage through his own being:

> Now when we had gone down again to the sea and our vessel
> first of all we dragged the ship down into the bright
> > water,
> and in the black hull set the mast in place, and set sails,
> and took the sheep and walked them aboard, and ourselves
> > also
> embarked, but sorrowful, and weeping big tears.
> > —*Richmond Lattimore*

> We bore down on the ship at the sea's edge
> and launched her on the salt immortal sea,
> stepping our mast and spar in the black ship;
> embarked the ram and ewe and went aboard
> in tears, with bitter and sore dread upon us.
> —*Robert Fitzgerald*

> Now to the shores we bend, a mournful train,
> Climb the tall bark, and launch into the main:
> At once the mast we rear, at once unbind
> The spacious sheet, and stretch it to the wind:
> Then pale and pensive stand, with cares opprest,
> And solemn horror saddens every breast.
> —*Alexander Pope*

> Arriv'd now at our ship, we lancht, and set
> Our mast up, put forth saile, and in did get
> Our late-got Cattell. Up our sailes, we went,
> My wayward fellowes mourning now th' event.
> —*George Chapman*

All transport the reader into the same misty heroic land. Yet the blackness of the ship is ignored by Chapman and Pope, and Pope overlooks the sheep.

13 OCTOBER

Viz., Oz.

I finally know why the abbreviations of *videlicit* and *ounce* end in z—*viz., oz.* Or at least I know what Ernest A. Choate thinks the reason is.

He says that in the days before printing was invented, the question mark and the period were used interchangeably. A monk might write "God is here?" Or he might write, "Is God here." So copyists writing the abbreviation of ounce (*o.*) frequently changed the . to a ?, giving *o?*. Later copyists decided the ? was a poorly formed z and wrote *oz*, but then had to add a fresh . to make clear that they were transcribing an abbreviation. The progression was *o.; o?; oz;* and *oz.* By the same process, *vi.,* the abbreviation for *videlicit* ("namely"), wound up as *viz.*

Explaining oz. and viz. is only a sideline for Mr. Choate. He is a bird watcher, or birder, and author of *Dictionary of American Bird Names.*

These abbreviations are in a lighter vein:

POLITICAL ECONOMY

What hours I spent of precious time,
   What pints of ink I used to waste,
Attempting to secure a rhyme
   To suit the public taste,
Until I found a simple plan
Which makes the lamest lyric scan!

When I've a syllable de trop,
   I cut it off, without apol.;
This verbal sacrifice, I know,
   May irritate the schol.;
But all must praise my dev'lish cunn.
Who realize that Time is Mon.

My sense remains as clear as cryst.,
   My style as pure as any Duch.
Who does not boast a bar sinist.
   Upon her fam. escutch.;
And I can treat with scornful pit.
The sneers of ev'ry captious crit.

I gladly publish to the pop.
   A scheme of which I make no myst.,
And beg my fellow scribes to cop.
   This labor-saving syst.
I offer it to the consid.
   Of ev'ry thoughtful individ.

The author, working like a beav.,
   His reader's pleasure could redoub.
Did he but now and then abbrev.
   The work he gives his pub.
(This view I most partic. suggest
to A. C. Bens. and G. K. Chest.)

If playwrights would but thus dimin.
   The length of time each drama takes,
(The Second Mrs. Tanq. by Pin.
   Or even Ham., by Shakes.)
We could maintain a watchful att.
When at a Mat. on Wed. or Sat.

Have done, ye bards, with dull monot.!
   Foll. my examp., O, Stephen Phill.,
O, Owen Seam., O, William Wat.,
   O, Ella Wheeler Wil.,
And share with me the grave respons.
Of writing this amazing nons.!
          —*Harry Graham*

14 OCTOBER

Rhadamanthine Sea

When I was studying freshman composition in college, Carroll Montague, a junior, graded my weekly compositions. Once he scribbled in the margin, "Try to improve your vocabulary." The next week, in an effort at lightness, I wrote "Ah, the Rhadamanthine Sea!" Carroll graded me C—, remarking, "Wisecracks aren't vocabulary, smarthead. One more Rhadamanthus out of you and I'll Rhadamanthus your Panthus."

Like Rhadamanthus, he was an inexorable judge. Later, when we became friends, he taught me a lesson about honesty of taste that I try not to forget.

Carroll and I smoked pipes, and each had a favorite brand—mine Velvet and his Prince Albert, or perhaps the other way around. I boasted of my brand, and he of his. Now the two tobaccos came in containers of oiled paper, in tins of identical size and shape. It occurred to Carroll to exchange these containers behind my back, and for days I rhapsodized over my brand while smoking his.

When he told me how I had been foxed, I resolved never again to tell myself that I had reached a conclusion on a matter of taste, whether the subject was Velvet tobacco or Picasso paintings, when, in fact, I was simply reflecting some accepted fashion. I have tried to abide by this rule, but it is not easy. We often live by other people's convictions, lacking genuine convictions of our own. Without outside reassurance, some of us would doubt whether we are alive.

Carroll died of a heart attack this morning. He would have known instantly that the lines below hark back to our dispute over pipe tobaccos:

> I saw the universe wheel by,
> Reflected in my neighbor's eye.
> When presently my neighbor blinked,
> The universe became extinct.
> —*W.R.E.*

15 OCTOBER

The Bleed'n' Sparrer

The Crystal Palace outside London, site of the Great Exhibition of 1851, housed the famous Sibthorp Elm. Asked by Queen Victoria what could be done about the rude behavior of the sparrows in the tree, the Duke of Wellington advised: "Try sparrow hawks, ma'am."

We 'ad a bleed'n' sparrer wot
   Lived up a bleed'n' spaht,
One day the bleed'n' rain came dahn
   An' washed the bleeder aht.

An' as 'e layed 'arf drahnded
   Dahn in the bleed'n' street
'E begged that bleed'n' rainstorm
   To bave 'is bleed'n' feet.

But then the bleed'n' sun came aht—
   Dried up the bleed'n' rain—
So that bleed'n' little sparrer
   'E climbed up 'is spaht again.

But, Oh!—the crewel sparrer 'awk,
   'E spies 'im in 'is snuggery,
'E sharpens up 'is bleed'n' claws
   'An rips 'im aht by thuggery!

Just thin a bleed'n' sportin' type
   Wot 'ad a bleed'n' gun
'E spots that bleed'n' sparrer 'awk
   An blasts 'is bleed'n' fun.

The moral of this story
   Is plain to everyone—
That them wot's up the bleed'n' spaht
   Don't get no bleed'n' fun.
               —Anonymous

A Cockney sparrow would never understand these Brooklyn birds:

THIRTY PURPLE BIRDS

     Toity poiple boids
     Sitt'n' on der coib
     A' choipin' an' a' boipin'
     An' eat'n' doity woims.
            —Anonymous

Here somebody implies an uncomfortable moral:

UNCULTIVATED ACCENTS

The Dago, the Injun, the Chink, the Jew,
The Darkee, the Parsee pale,
They *spik-a de Eengleesh* unlike you—
O Pedigree-parasite, Thoroughbred's-tail,
With accent pickled in Oxford ale—
But the faces and races 'beyond the pale,'
Are *they* so funny—or *you*?
              —Anonymous

16 OCTOBER

Puzzle School

This elementary school teacher uses word puzzles and games of his own creation, like these, to enhance his students' vocabulary and knowledge of English.

Partwords

You are given three letters that appear consecutively anywhere in a word. Try to find a word for each partword.

——————— WBO ———————

——————— WBE ———————

——————— RWO ———————

——————— BST ———————

——————— MPH ———————

——————— FTN ———————

——————— TSW ———————

Fill-in Station

Fill in the blanks with consonants to form 12 or more different words. *All* vowels are given.

_ _ OU _   _ _ OU _

_ _ OU _   _ _ OU _

_ _ OU _   _ _ OU _

_ _ OU _   _ _ OU _

_ _ OU _   _ _ OU _

_ _ OU _   _ _ OU _

_ _ OU _   _ _ OU _

Match-ups

Pair these 16 word parts to form 8 whole words.

IMP	SET	NER	ING
RES	CUR	MES	SHO
SION	CLO	OTS	ALE
VES	MAN	THE	SES

——————— ———————

——————— ———————

——————— ———————

——————— ———————

—*George Bredehorn*

17 OCTOBER

A Very Palpable Hit

Tonight we saw two one-act plays by Tom Stoppard—*Dogg's Hamlet* and *Cahoot's Macbeth*. I wangled a script of the plays and reproduce, omitting stage directions, this speeded-up reprise of *Hamlet*:

CLAUDIUS.   Our sometime sister, now our Queen,
            have we taken to wife.
HAMLET.   That it should come to this!
HORATIO.   My lord, I saw him yesternight—
            The King, your father.
HAMLET.   Angels and ministers of grace defend us!
            Something is rotten in the state of Denmark.
GHOST.   I am thy father's spirit
            The serpent that did sting thy father's life
            Now wears his crown.
HAMLET.   O my prophetic soul!
            Hereafter I shall think meet
            To put an antic disposition on.
POLONIUS.   Look where sadly the poor wretch comes.
HAMLET.   I have heard that guilty creatures sitting at a play
            Have by the very cunning of the scene been struck.
            If he but blench, I know my course.
            The King rises!
ALL.   Give o'er the play!
HAMLET.   I'll take the ghost's word for a thousand pounds.
            Mother, you have my father much offended.
GERTRUDE.   Help!
POLONIUS.   Help, ho!
HAMLET.   Dead for a ducat, dead!
CLAUDIUS.   Hamlet, this deed must send thee hence.
            Do it, England.
HAMLET.   A pirate gave us chase. I alone became their
            prisoner. Alas poor Yorick—but this is I,
            Hamlet the Dane!
LAERTES.   The devil take thy soul!
HAMLET.   Come on, Sir!
OSRIC.   A hit, a very palpable hit!
CLAUDIUS.   Give him the cup. Gertrude, do not drink!
GERTRUDE.   I am poisoned!
LAERTES.   Hamlet, thou art slain!
HAMLET.   Then venom to thy work.
            The rest is silence.

18 OCTOBER

Have Angleworms Attractive Homes?

Have Angleworms attractive homes?
  Do Bumble-bees have brains?
Do Caterpillars carry combs?
  Do Dodos dote on drains?
Can Eels elude elastic earls?
  Do Flatfish fish for flats?
Are Grigs agreeable to girls?
  Do Hares have hunting-hats?
Do Ices make an Ibex ill?
  Do Jackdaws jug their jam?
Do Kites kiss all the kids they kill?
  Do Llamas live on lamb?
Will Moles molest a mounted mink?
  Do Newts deny the news?
Are Oysters boisterous when they drink?
  Do Parrots prowl in pews?
Do Quakers get their quills from quails?
  Do Rabbits rob on roads?
Are Snakes supposed to sneer at snails?
  Do Tortoises tease toads?
Can Unicorns perform on horns?
  Do Vipers value veal?
Do Weasels weep when fast asleep?
  Can Xylophagans squeal?
Do Yaks in packs invite attacks?
  Are Zebras full of zeal?
                              —*Charles E. Carryl*

19 OCTOBER

Headlines, Road Signs

Headlines sometimes pun. This one about a world champion chessplayer appeared in the *New York Post:*

NEXT MOVE IS FISCHER'S
His Lawyer Quits & Seeks Check

Sometimes they do not mean quite what they seem to say, as in this from the same newspaper:

JOHN WAYNE
TURNED TO GOD
ON HIS DEATHBED

His fans always said that man could do anything.

VERMONT DEMOCRATS
BACK SALMON FOR SENATE,
WOMAN FOR GOVERNOR

Fish lib?

ALONG 8TH AVENUE,
WHERE LEER IS KING

Supported by his three daughters?

Two from the *Chicago Tribune:*

MOST ON DEATH ROW
HERE WERE APPEALING

SERIOUSLY INJURED
IN FATAL FIRE

—Robert T. Harker

From the *Baton Rouge State-Times*:

MAN BOOKED FOR WRECKLESS DRIVING
—Ashley C. Worsely

From an old *New York Herald Tribune*:

A GRATEFUL NATION
BURIES SAM RAYBURN

We thought we would never be rid of him.

A caption under a photograph in the *Los Angeles Times* of Aristotle Onassis examining the home of Buster Keaton for a possible purchase:

ARISTOTLE CONTEMPLATING THE HOME OF BUSTER

—Marjorie Wihtol

A roadside sign:

WE BUY JUNK
AND
SELL ANTIQUES

The Times Diary, an English publication, consists of photographs of such nonplussing notices as these:

• Same day cleaners. 48 hour service.

- Drive slowly and allow cows to pass.
- P at any time.
- No overtaking for the next 200 yrs.
- Health food & kosher flowers.
- New & used antiques.
- Up steps to sunken garden.
- Buses only. Except buses.
- Raise legs before moving.
- Guests & seamen. No admittance. (In Virginia)
- No loitering without permission. (In Japan)
- Caution. Workers working. (In India)
- Please do not feed the animals, if you have any suitable food please give it to the guard on duty.
- No entry. In only. (Kenya)
- Foot wearing prohibited. Socks not allowed. (Rangoon temple)
- Don't let worry kill you off. Let the Church help.
- Site entrance. Please enter from opposite direction.
- Jet blast is dangerous. Passengers only beyond this point. (Texas)
- Special force training area. Restricted to unauthorized persons. (Uganda)
- Hallwood hospital. Strictly no admittance.

20 OCTOBER

To the Leading Periodical

To read this verse very nearly as casually as you read English, you need only a nodding acquaintance with the Greek alphabet.

ΤΟ ΘΕ ΛΕΑΔΙΝΓ ΠΕΡΙΟΔΙΚΑΛ

Θις κομπλιμεντ, γρεατ σιρ, ο τακε,
Υρε α βρικ ανδ νο μιστακε,
Ενεμι το καντ ανδ φυδγε
Τιμε το θεε Ι νε'ερ βεγρυδγε
Ανδ Ι ῶπε το σεε υρε ναμε
Φωρεμοστ ιν θε λιστς οφ φαμε.

Τομ Σμιθ, Γρυβ στρεετ

The author dedicated the verse to *Punch,* in which it appeared.

21 OCTOBER

Give Me a Child Until He Is Five—Jesuit saying

Louise dug from a drawer a packet of verses I wrote when I was eight or nine, about the time I learned to tie my shoelaces in a double knot.

I knew even then that halcyon days could not go on forever. If you doubt me, here is the proof, written on October 27, 1919:

> There ran a jolly little brook,
> Where I played for many a day,
> It made me happy, and rapturous, and gay.
> Another joy that I loved,
> Was playing in the hay,
> Where we pushed, and romped, and shoved,
> And played for many a day.
>
> But now I am an old, old man,
> And all these joys are past
> And everyone who's sane should know that childhood
> cannot last.
>
> —W.R.E.

22 OCTOBER

Every Dog Is an Isogram

Word Ways reminds me that an isogram is a word which uses each letter the same number of times. In *dog,* each of the three letters is used once. *Deeded* is an isogram in which each letter is used three times. There are not many three-pair isograms; Dmitri Borgmann, who specializes in such oddities, can name only one more—*geggee,* Scottish for "a victim of a hoax."

Two-pair isograms of ten letters include *intestines, arraigning, tool steels, horseshoer,* and (describing unattainable women) *superpures. Happenstance* and *shanghaiings* are two-pair twelve-letter isograms.

Mr. Borgmann's ears prick up at fifteen-letter isograms such as *dermatoglyphics* ("the science of the study of skin patterns"); *white gyrfalcons; uncopyrightable; prediscountably;* and *South Cambridge, N.Y.*

If anyone tells you he knows a commonly used isogram of sixteen letters or more, he is trying to make a geggee of you.

The shortest word containing all five vowels, says Jonathan Delfin, is *sequoia,* a tree named after the Cherokee Indian who put the language of his tribe into writing. It is also a nonpattern isogram; each letter occurs once only.

Similar in spirit to the isogram is the stammer—a passage in which a letter repeats itself uninterruptedly and inordinately. Some stammers:

- A burg*oo o' oo*ze.   Five o's
- You'd think *Judd'd DD*T those bugs.   Five d's
- The Philadelphi*a AAA a*dded two staff members. Five a's
                                        —*Maxey Brooke*

- Bi*ll'll, ll*amalike, stand staring in the distance.   Six l's
                                        —*R. Merrill Ely*

- A sweet young thing named Bessie B.
  Collects letters 'twixt R and T.
  Perhaps the very lack of range
  Makes Be*ss's s's s*eem so strange.   Six s's
                                        —*Author unknown*

A burgoo, by the way, is a porridge, or in the United States a stew served in the open air.

23 OCTOBER

Asimov

I once twitted Mr. Asimov that while his name could be punned upon in a limerick, mine could not, and proved the first part of the assertion with the following verse (based, I admit, on the unlikely assumption that he is of Cockney extraction):

A Cockney named I. Asimov,
As his trousers he started to doff,
    Said, "Me lydy friends yawn
    When I 'as 'em on,
But w'istle w'en I 'as 'em off."
                        —*W.R.E.*

Mr. Asimov instantly scribbled the following on his linen napkin:

With the coming of old age, poor Espy
Could not but take note there was less pee.
    Willard muttered, "In truth,
    When I was a youth,
Would I think there'd be reason to bless pee?"
                        —*Isaac Asimov*

And here I must make an embarrassing confession. Some years after the for-going exchange, I found in my files an old letter from my friend William Alsop containing a limerick built around exactly the same pun as mine. I had long for-gotten it, and have no idea whether my rhyme sprang from some unconscious memory or was entirely independent. You will find Mr. Alsop's version in the Answers and Solutions.

24 OCTOBER
♏

Which Wert I Wot in the Land of Silly

I WOT WHAT NOT

Of all the dates I wis one wert
  of all dates most unkind
Which wert the date comes up the street
  with the date you leave behind

Of all the dukes to shake I wis
  one wert no shakes to meet
Which wert I wot now how he stands
  and wis not where his feet.
       —Ewart Milne

IN THE LAND OF SILLY

Come let us walk
  In the land of Silly,
Where we can talk
  In Picallili:
Molly-coddle, spick-and-span,

Helter-skelter, catamaran,
  Willy-nilly,
  Daffy-dilly,
That's how we'll talk
  In the land of Silly.
       —W.R.E.

25 OCTOBER
♏

Books for Every Worm

A list of recommended books for fall reading:

Title	Author
Playing by the Rules	P. Knuckle
Love for Sale	I. M. Willing
Bikini Exposures	Belle E. Button
Aid to a Bookworm	Dick Shunary

Feed-Lot-Tales	Lotta Bull
Under the Rock	Liz Ard
The Final Fall	Eileen Dover
Cotton Field Capers	E. Z. Pickens
Urban Renewal Guide	Dinah Mite
The Bovine's Complaint	I. C. Hands
The Useless Crutch	Candy Cane
Love's Labor Lost	Ms. Carriage
The Missing Sea Treasure	Nan Tucket
My Final Fling	I. M. Dunne

—*Virginia Hager*

26 OCTOBER
♏

In Reguards to Your Complaint

I mentioned 29 April the lifelong injury done to students who are not taught at least the basics of English composition. The people they write to have problems, too:

Sears | SEARS, ROEBUCK AND CO.

Mr. Willard Esp℣
30 Beckman Pl.
N.Y, N.Y.

Dear Mr. Espy ,

    In Reguards to your complaint stating that "there
should be no tax added to sale" ·

    The explaination is this, Interstate law says that
there will be sales tax added when merchandise is delivered
from Oregon into Washington State. Therefor if our trucks
were stopped while transporting your goods accross state
line our company would indeed be fined.

        Thank You for your patience
        And we hope you will shop at sears
        in the future.

        Sincerely,

        M. McHey

---

27 OCTOBER
♏

Miss Erogenous Jones

Did you happen to know Miss Erogenous Jones,
  Who is sadly no longer alive?
Her flesh was a series of sexual zones,
  Each equipped with a separate drive.

Her toes were orgastic; her ankles tumesced
  At the breath of a breeze on the skin.
She swooned when the soles of her feet were caressed,
  And climaxed when scratching her shin.

Each knee hollow offered a bower of love;
  Her thighs melted down at a kiss;
And to list all the eager zones panting above
  Would take a verse longer than this.

When an amorous youth fell in love with Miss Jones,
  She gladly consented to mate him,
But failed to remind him to switch on her zones
  In sequence—i.e., *seriatim*.

Alas! all those scores of susceptible zones
  Concurrently faced his encounter!
The multiplied rapture imploded her bones;
  She perished before he could mount her.

Dear Reader, a Moral infuses this rhyme—
  A lesson all lovers should learn:
Don't tap those erogenous zones at one time—
  They are meant to be turned on in turn.
                              —*W.R.E.*

28 OCTOBER
♏

Double Trouble

Score 2 points each. Maximum score: 30.

Each seven-letter word below contains double letters. Change them to new double letters to make a new word. There are fifteen answers altogether, because three words can be changed in more than one way.

Example   COTTAGE   ___Collage___

1. FLITTER	5. DRIBBLE	9. HAMMOCK
2. SCUFFLE	6. BAGGAGE	10. ADDRESS
3. MILLION	7. GAZETTE	11. CHANNEL
4. FOOLING	8. COLLECT	12. BALLOON

—Will Shortz

29 OCTOBER
♏

I'll Sew You to a Sheet

OYSTERVILLE—"The fleece are beginning to guy," said Bob Meadows today. He meant, "The geese are beginning to fly." This common slip of the tongue is a spoonerism, or, technically, a metathesis—a deliberate or inadvertent transposition of consonants between words. It is named after W. A. Spooner, dean and later warden of New College, Oxford, who by repute was responsible for such skewings of sound and sense as "roaring pain" for "pouring rain," "tons of soil" for "sons of toil," and "I'll sew you to a sheet" for "I'll show you to a seat."

He is said to have committed spoonerisms in deed as well as word. After turning on a light in order to escort a guest down a dark stairway, he extinguished the light and walked down with his friend in the dark. Instead of rubbing salt into spilled wine, Virginia Koch insists, he rubbed wine into spilled salt.

Barbara Frietchie would not endorse this spoonerism:

An OGPU spy and his opposite number from the CIA fell desperately in love. When FBI agents charged into their love nest, guns drawn, the Russian threw himself in the path of fire:

> "Shoot if you must this old gay red,
> "But spare your country's fag," he said.

30 OCTOBER
♏

Down and Out: A Cat Tail

This is the season of black cats, the confidants of witches.

The late art critic Harold Rosenberg, emerging from the subway one snowy evening, felt something rub against his leg. It was a black alley cat. The creature followed him to his brownstone, shot inside before he had the door properly open, and proceeded to take over. It scorned all food but caviar and all drink but Montrachet wine—Montrachet '51. During the day, while Harold was slaving at *The New Yorker,* the cat dozed the time away in his favorite easy chair. Harold began to feel like a barely tolerated guest in his own home. Each night, finding the cat in occupancy of his chair, he would say, "Down!" The cat would rise slowly to its feet, arch its back, yawn, and step grandly to the floor.

One night the order had no effect. Harold said, "Down!" a second and yet a third time; the cat ignored him. Furious, Harold flung open the door, and shouted, "Out!" The cat stepped from the chair with ostentatious deliberation, stalked through the doorway into the flying snow, and was never seen again.

ON THE IMMINENT DEPARTURE OF AN AILUROPHOBE

I
will
arise
and
go
now,
and
go—any damned place
    just to get away from
        THAT
        chair
       covered
       with
       CAT
       hair
—*William J. Smith*

31 OCTOBER
♏

The Witch's Work Song

Two spoons of sherry
Three oz. of yeast,
Half a pound of unicorn,
And God bless the feast.*
Shake them in the collander,
Bang them to a chop,
Simmer slightly, snip up nicely,
Jump, skip, hop.
Knit one, knot one, purl two together,
Pip one and pop one and
  pluck the secret feather.
Baste in mod. oven.
God bless our coven.
Tra-la-la!
  *A devout witch, that one.

Three toads in a jar.
Te-he-he!
Put in the frog's knee.
Peep out of the lace curtain.
There goes the Toplady girl, she's up
  to no good, that's certain.
Oh, what a lovely baby!
How nice it would go with gravy.
Pinch the salt,
Turn the malt
With a hey-nonny-nonny and
  I don't mean maybe.

—*T. H. White*

NOVEMBER

1 NOVEMBER
♏

Saints Preserve Us

All Saints' Day. The witches have been chased back to their covens, and the devils to Pandemonium. The saints are in charge again. If the saint you pray to is not giving satisfaction, here are some alternatives:

• For postal workers	St. Amp	• For politicians	St. Ump
• For alcoholics	St. Agger	• For men who	St. Ubble
• For musicians	St. Accato	fail to shave	
• For actors	St. Age	• For foolish folk	St. Upid
• For flower children	St. Amen	• For butchers	St. Eak
• For thieves	St. Ealthy	• For kite flyers	St. Ring
• For football players	St. Adium	• For golfers	St. Roke
• For poets	St. Anza	• For beer drinkers	St. Ein
• For young actresses	St. Arlet	• For bus missers	St. Randed
• For expectant mothers	St. Ork	• For jocks	St. Amina

—*Virginia R. Hager*

2 NOVEMBER
♏

On Smouldering Nuendoes

One of my complaints about a recent long-awaited anthology of American light verse was that it failed to include examples of the splendid work of Felicia Lamport. This is the kind of magic she offers:

HINT

There never is trouble in finding a spouse
For the ebriated man with the lapidated house.

SOIREE

The gentle wives fillet a soul
Eptly, while the men doze;
Or roast a reputation whole
On smouldering nuendoes.

SENSICAL SITUATION

Men often pursue in suitable style
The imical girl with the scrutable smile.

SERENITY

The man who wants a quiet life
And traught, commoded days
Should find himself an otic wife
With sipid, centric ways.
                    —*Felicia Lamport*

3 NOVEMBER
♏

Curious Couples

Mary Ann Madden asked readers of *New York* magazine to submit two authentic familiar quotations, "unexpectedly if appropriately coupled." A sampling of the results:

1. " 'Twas brillig, and the slithy toves / Did gyre and gimble in the wabe / All mimsy were the borogroves, / And the mome raths outgrabe."
                    —*Lewis Carroll*
2. "If you do not itemize deductions and line 18 is under $10,000, find tax in Tables and enter on line 19. If you itemize deductions or line 18 is $10,000 or more, go to line 46 to figure tax."—*Michael Schreiber*

1. "We shall never understand each other until we reduce the language to seven words."—*Kahlil Gibran*
2. "Doc, Grumpy, Sleepy, Happy, Bashful, Sneezy, and Dopey."—*Snow White*

                    —*Jack Ryan*

1. "With all my worldly goods I thee endow."—*Book of Common Prayer*
2. "A fool and his money are soon parted."—*American proverb*
                    —*Jack Labow*

1. "That feller runs splendid but he needs help at the plate, which coming from the country chasing rabbits all winter give him strong legs, although he broke one falling out of a tree, which shows you can't tell . . ."—*Casey Stengel*
2. "Let me make one thing perfectly clear."—*Richard M. Nixon*
—*John F. Keppler*

1. "For whither thou goest, I will go; and where thou lodgest I will lodge."—*Book of Ruth, 1:16*
2. "I'm Ruth. Fly me to Miami."—*Airline commercial*
—*Celia Krapoff*

1. "Youth is wholly experimental."—*Robert Louis Stevenson*
2. "And so to bed."—*Samuel Pepys*
—*Kathy Mansfield*

1. "In the same hour came forth fingers of a man's hand, and wrote over against the candlestick upon the plaster of the wall of the king's palace; and the king saw part of the hand that wrote."—*Daniel 5:5*
2. "Kilroy was here."—*World War II graffito*
—*Mrs. June Beattle*

1. "Consider the lilies of the field . . . they toil not, neither do they spin."
—*Matthew 6:28*
2. ". . . With a little bit of luck, / Someone else will do the bloomin' work."—*My Fair Lady*
—*Eileen Tranford*

4 NOVEMBER
♏

On the Letter H

'Twas whispered in heaven, 'twas muttered in hell,
And echo caught faintly the sound as it fell;
On the confines of earth 'twas permitted to rest,
And the depths of the ocean its presence confessed;

'Twill be found in the sphere when 'tis riven asunder,
Be seen in the lightning, and heard in the thunder.
'Tis allotted to man with his earliest breath,
It assists at his birth and attends him in death,
Presides o'er his happiness, honor, and health,
Is the prop of his house and the end of his wealth,
In the heaps of the miser is hoarded with care,
But is sure to be lost in his prodigal heir.
It begins every hope, every wish it must bound,
It prays with the hermit, with monarch is crowned;
Without it the soldier, the sailor, may roam,
But woe to the wretch who expels it from home.
In the whisper of conscience 'tis sure to be found,
Nor e'en in the whirlwind of passion is drowned;
'Twill soften the heart, but though deaf to the ear,
It will make it acutely and instantly hear;
But, in short, let it rest like a delicate flower;
Oh, breathe on it softly, it dies in an hour.

— *Catherine Fanshaw*

CUT OFF MY HEAD

Cut off my head, and singular I act,
   Cut off my tail, and plural I appear;
Cut off my head and tail, and, wondrous fact,
   Although my middle's left, there's nothing there.
What is my head cut off? A sounding sea;
   What is my tail cut off? A flowing river
In whose translucent depths I fearless play,
   Parent of sweetest sounds, yet mute forever.

— *Anonymous*

5 NOVEMBER
♏

Anagrammatical Onomastica

If you are dissatisfied with your given name, but reluctant to abandon it altogether, juggle the letters around to see what happens:

- Abbe, Babe, Ebba
- Abe, Bea
- Abel, Albe, Bela
- Adeline, Daniele
- Aldine, Daniel
- Aden, Dean, Edna
- Alice, Celia
- Allie, Leila
- Alvina, Lavina
- Amy, May

- Ancel, Lance
- Anita, Tania
- Ann, Nan
- Annette, Nanette
- Antoine, Antonie
- Anthea, Athena
- Arnoldo, Orlando
- Basil, Blaise
- Braden, Brenda
- Brady, Darby
- Broun, Bruno
- Carla, Clara
- Carmel, Marcel
- Carlo, Carol, Coral
- Caroline, Cornelia
- Christian, Christina
- Claus, Lucas
- Colin, Nicol
- Crispian, Crispina
- Dale, Elda, Leda
- Darleen, Leander, Learned
- Dolly, Lloyd
- Dorothea, Theodora
- Dot, Tod
- Edsel, Leeds
- Elise, Elsie
- Elmer, Merle
- Ernie, Irene
- Esther, Hester
- Fidel, Field
- Forrest, Forster
- Gale, Glea
- Gary, Gray
- Hamlet, Thelma
- Hays, Shay
- Jane, Jean
- Janos, Jason, Jonas, Sonja
- Lawton, Walton
- Leo, Ole
- Leon, Noel
- Lion, Olin
- Lona, Nola
- Maire, Marie
- Mario, Moira
- Mary, Myra
- Mat, Tam
- Norma, Ramon
- Oliva, Viola
- Rosamond, Rosmonda
- Salem, Selma
- Waldorf, Walford
- Warner, Warren

—Word Ways

6 NOVEMBER
♏

To Stimulate Voraciousness? To Simulate Veraciousness?

When Dashiell Hammett was making his living as a detective, he submitted to his superiors a report containing the word *voracious*. They changed it to *truthful,* explaining that *voracious* might be too hard for the client to understand. In another report they changed *simulate* to *quicken* for the same reason.

This hemi-demi-semi-macaronic verse warns us against such malapropping:

MOTS JUSTES

Oh, let the *Mot* be *comme il faut*
　　Or let it be *sub rosa*.
They are not fond in the *beau monde*

Of the *mal à propos* Sir.
And (*chi lo sa?*) a small *faux pas*
 A minor *lapsus linguae*
May overthrow your *status quo*
 And brand you—not *distingué.*
So *suaviter in modo* Sir and everything *pro rata*
For they who err in *Savoir Faire* are not
 persona grata.

—*H.J.R.*

These heartwarming malapropisms are cited by *Verbatim*:

- The use of drugs is on the upcrease.
- If the circumstances were on the other foot.
- I don't pull any bones about it.
- You're talking around the bush.
- You are out of your rocker.
- You set my hair on edge.
- I think we need to get down to the brass roots (grass tacks?) of the problem.
- If he had actually broken a crime or could be accused of breaking a crime...
- He will lend an ear to anyone who wants to listen.
- Nixon on the death of Adlai Stevenson: "In eloquence he had no peer, and very few equals."

—*James D. White*

7 NOVEMBER
♏

What Can't Be Hope

The late Brooks Hays, for twenty years a congressman from Arkansas, regarded with awe the language quiddities of his native state. Recalled Mr. Hays:

"Hope" for helped was introduced to me by an unlettered Sunday School teacher. "The little boy Samuel hope the priest Eli in the temple." Later I understood more quickly what he meant in saying

"What can't be hope has to be bore."

In Arkansas a metaphor may be its own opposite, as in this recollection by a man who had just purchased and subdued a mule:

"Yes, sir, Graves. I tell you that mule was a wild one—wild as a buck— just as wild as a buck! I gave him the works. Had to tame him, you know, and would you believe me, when I went out to the barn next morning, he was tame—as tame as a buck, as tame as a buck!"

8 NOVEMBER
♏

A Subordinate Clause Was Mother's Milk to Papa

This story was written for the *New York Times*. You will notice that the last sentence is longish—indeed, over 500 words longish. It may even occur to you that the whole point of the story lies in the length of that last sentence. So what did the copy editor at the *New York Times* do? He broke it into fifteen sentences.

OYSTERVILLE—When it comes to talking, some Espys Do and some Espys Don't. Aunt Dora and Papa Did. Uncle Will Didn't. Uncle Cecil Still Doesn't. I Don't.

One might assume that the Don'ts are silent because the Dos will not let them interrupt, but one would be wrong. The Dos could not care less. The massive Espy voice, evolved from generations of Scotch-Irish farmers hooting across the bogs for their cows and pigs, is immune to interruption. When Aunt Dora and Papa conversed, they could not hear each other over their own uproar. Yet they went on happily for hours on end, scarcely pausing to breathe. And even after Aunt Dora and Papa were no longer around to outshout them, Uncle Will and Uncle Cecil still preferred to keep their thoughts to themselves.

Uncle Will, who died recently at ninety-four, lived down in California. Uncle Cecil, who is going on ninety-two, lives here in Oysterville. Once a year Uncle Will used to visit Uncle Cecil, and once a year Uncle Cecil visited Uncle Will. When they forgathered for breakfast, Uncle Cecil would say, "Good morning, Will." Uncle Will would say, "Good morning, Cecil." They would then take up their separate rounds, which consisted of stints of gardening and puttering, and stints of sitting, reading the newspaper, and, I suppose, reflecting. No further words were exchanged until, at ten o'clock in the evening, Uncle Will would say, "Good night, Cecil." Uncle Cecil would say, "Good night, Will."

Papa possessed an enviable skill, the result of a lifetime of practice: He intertwined his tropes as if they were coils of snakes. Everything reminded him of something else, so that he picked his way through a dense forest of subordinate clauses and parenthetical asides; it was not unusual for him to spend five minutes traversing a single sentence. Tracy Moore, who served with him on the school board, says Papa once called in the other two members at five P.M. to explain why he could not attend a board meeting at eight; by the time he had finished his explanation, they had all missed the meeting.

I count myself among the Don'ts. But though I am a zealous advocate of spare phraseology—never use two words when one will do, never use a long word when a short word will do, never use a strange word when a familiar word will do—as age creeps over me my resemblance to my father grows, and I find myself backtracking more and more often to sniff at some notion that I had first caught only subliminally, my mind having slowed in registering new concepts, subjecting me to an increasingly burdensome task of catching up, as when three or four days after reading a newspaper article it suddenly occurs to me that it contained information of moment to me, prompting a laborious search through back issues, generally unsuccessful, since the issue I want is sure to be the only one discarded in the previous week, the practice of wives and hired help being to line garbage cans with the one newspaper that should have been saved, leaving the other newspapers to mess up the cottage in Oysterville, or, when I am in New York, the apartment, which is messy enough in any event, though I attest that Louise is constantly cleaning up after me, unlike the wife described the other day in a conversation between an acquaintance of mine and a poet whom I have never met, though I wish I had, since he is a good poet, but a poor husband, having run through five wives, as is also the case with my acquaintance, so it was natural that their conversation should turn to their marital frustrations and that my acquaintance should complain about the slovenliness of his second wife, who, he said, would not even cook breakfast, much less make the bed or sweep the floor, a deplorable state of affairs which reminded the poet of an identical remissness on the part of his, the poet's, fourth wife, with the predictable result that they found they were talking about the same woman, which shows how fast things move these days, and how quickly we forget, so that, as the saying goes, one has to run, like Alice and the Red Queen (or was it the White Queen?) just to stay in the same place, though it does seem to me that to run through five wives must take some pretty fast running, a reaction which is not the product of envy, though I haven't got (you will note that I prefer the English "got" to our American "gotten") past three myself, which reminds me that my pet name for Louise, the latest and last of them, is "Qualtaigh," a word of Manx origin, meaning the first living creature one meets on arising in the morning, that person for most of us being husband, wife, lover, or offspring, though if one lives alone, it might be a dog, or cat, or canary, or, I suppose, a cockroach, but in any event I love the expression as well as the woman, and I would employ it more widely were it not for my dogged opposition to exotic words, and particularly to their employment in long-winded sentences, which I oppose totally, my opposition being based on the generally known fact that I am one of the Espys that Don't, not one of the Espys that Do.

9 NOVEMBER
♏

The Geranium and the Great Lalula

As might be expected, the two verses that follow are funnier in the original French than in translation.

LE GERANIUM

Dans un pot un géranium,
Un poisson dans l'aquarium,
Géranium et poisson rouge,
Si tu bouges, si tu bouges,
Tu n'auras pas de rhum,
Géranium, géranium,
Géranium et poisson rouge.
—*Robert Desnos*

Si tu bouges, si tu bouges is literally "if you budge, if you budge," a delightful line,
but I couldn't work a relevant rhyme around it, so I had to settle for this:

THE GERANIUM

In a pot a geranium,
A red fish in the aquarium,
Geranium and fishy twin,
If you wiggle leaf or fin,
You shall have no rum,
Geranium, geranium,
Geranium and fishy twin.
—*W.R.E.*

A COLOGNE EST UN MAITRE D'HOTEL

A Cologne est un maître d'hôtel
Hors du centre du ventre duquel
Se projette une sorte
De tiroir qui supporte
La moutarde, et le poivre, et le sel.
—*George Du Maurier*

In English:

IN COLOGNE THERE'S A MAITRE D'HOTEL

In Cologne there's a *maître d'hôtel*
From whose belly there swells, I hear tell,
A curious drawer,
Which he finds handy for
Salt, pepper, and mustard as well.
—*W.R.E.*

There is nothing to translate here:

THE GREAT LALULA

Kroklokwafzi? Sememami!
Seiokrontro—prafriplo:
Bifzi, bafzi; hulalemi;
quasti basti bo . . .
Lalu lalu lalu lalu la!

Hontraruru miromente
zasku zes ru ru?
Entepente, leiolente
klekwapufzi lu?
Lalu lalu lalu lalu la!

Simarar kos malzipempu

Silzuzankunkrei (;)!
Marjomar dos: Quempu Lempu
Siri Suri Sei ( ) !
Lalu lalu lalu lalu la!
—*Christian Morgenstern*

10 NOVEMBER
♏

I Was a Stranger, and Ye Took Me In (rondel)

"I was a stranger, and ye took me in."
　　So spake our Lord; and you seemed kind as He.
　　When I was hungry, short of do-re-mi,
You offered introductions, whiskey, gin,
Your wife, your very shirt—come lose, come win;
　　Your eyes were dewed with selfless sympathy.
"I was a stranger, and ye took me in."
　　So spake our Lord; and you seemed kind as He.

I woke next morning, gulping aspirin;
　　But you were gone, and gone your charity ...
　　Also my wallet, credit cards, and key.
Friend, raise a brow at verses that begin
"I was a stranger ... and ye took me in."
　　　　　　　　　　　　—*W.R.E.*

11 NOVEMBER
♏

The Infernal Machine

Today is the ninety-first birthday of Doctor Dorothy, who taught me French in college. She has just sent me a clipping from the *Los Angeles Times,* which I record in truncated form:

PALM SPRINGS—I feel obliged to report the Tibbles affair here as a warning of what can happen when you leave a briefcase in an airport waiting room.

At Palm Springs Municipal Airport, a writer named George Tibbles passed unchallenged through the security gate and took a seat in the waiting room. In a few minutes his flight was called and he boarded, absent-mindedly leaving the briefcase behind. It was found and turned over to the airport security detail, and an alert guard noticed that it had a certain foreign airline sticker on it.

Now it happened that quite recently the Federal Aviation Administration had sent out a warning that a terrorist who traveled by that particular airline was believed to carry bombs in black briefcases which he planted in airport waiting rooms. The guard's suspicions were deepened when he got a look at Tibbles's briefcase under X-ray. What he saw, in silhouette, was an arrangement of batteries, coils, and cylinders—a "configuration," in security language—that might well have been an infernal machine.

The police came and the briefcase was carried out to an unused runway where it could explode, if it meant to, without doing a great deal of damage. Then a Marine Corps demolition squad arrived and examined Tibbles's briefcase. They didn't like the combination lock. It could be a detonator. Best thing was to stand back and blow it open.

They fixed a double charge—one for the lock and one for the hinges. They stood back. There was a fine explosion. The case blew open and Tibbles's things flew out. A tape recorder. An electric razor. A bottle of Old Spice. And the pages of an unfinished manuscript, blowing in the wind.

At 6 P.M. Palm Springs finally reached Tibbles at his hotel in Phoenix. "I don't know how to tell you this," the man said.

"Go for the throat," Tibbles told him. "What happened?"

"We blew up your briefcase."

Tibbles doesn't blame anyone. "The way I had that briefcase packed it probably did look like a bomb. They thought the Old Spice bottle was a bottle of nitroglycerine."

Besides, they had been good enough to put all the pages of his manuscript back in order, though somewhat mutilated.

"And my razor still works," he said. "I'm going to write a thank-you letter to Remington."

—*Jack Smith*

12 NOVEMBER

♏

Philologos

The first line of this macaronic limerick is Greek; the second, Italian; the third, English; the fourth, French; and the final line, Latin.

Philologos 'onomati Louis
Parla lingue quaranta due.

When he heard tell
De la tour de Babel,
Ait, "Quorum pars magna fui."
—Anonymous

My rendering:

Said a polyglot teacher named Lou,
Who of languages spoke forty-two,
  "Don't sneer at the fable
  Of the Tower of Babel:
I was straw boss of the crew."
—W.R.E.

Quorum pars magna fui is from *The Aeneid*. It means "Of which things I was a major part."

13 NOVEMBER
℧

Daffy Definitions

I mentioned Dr. Dorothy's birthday two days ago; today is my sister Dale's. She is eleven months my junior, so we will be the same age for the next month. Usually we can't mark the occasion together, since we live on opposite sides of the continent. This time, though, we were in the same place at the same time. The place was a restaurant that affected paper napkins, and I kept mine as a souvenir. It contains the following rubrics, listed as "Daffy Definitions":

- Moderate. A guy who makes enemies left and right.
- Sad case. A dozen empties.
- Psychologist. One who when a beautiful girl enters the room watches everyone else.
- Texas. Miles and miles of nothing but miles and miles.
- Jacks or better. What it takes to open bus windows.
- Will. A dead giveaway.
- Organ recital. Women discussing their operations.
- Knapsack. Sleeping bag.
- Panhandler. An intern.
- Cannibal. A guy who goes into a restaurant and orders the waiter.
- Arch criminal. A guy who robs shoe stores.
- Stagnation. Country without women.
- Perpetual motion. A cow drinking milk.
- Operetta. A girl who works for the telephone company.
- Marriage license bureau. The two dollar window where everybody loses.
- Bigamist. An Italian fog.

• Yale. A Swedish prison.
• Smelling salts. Sailors with BO.
• Incongruous. Where they make our laws.

*   *   *

Herman Schauss defines an apiary as a monkey cage; a condominium as a birth-control device for tots; a lapidary as infant's nourishment; a moratorium as an undertaking establishment; a Pap test as a paternity determinant. Charlotte Laiken says necrophilia is esprit de corpse; Barbara Huff considers a noose the niece of a moose; and naughty, to J. Bickart, means "zerolike; filled with zeroes," as, "Little Orphan Annie has naughty eyes."

14 NOVEMBER
♏

GREEK, GREEK, GREEK

If for some unimaginable reason you wish to memorize the Greek alphabet, here is a yell for you:

Gimme an Alpha Beta
Gamma Delta
   And Epsilon!

Gimme a Zeta, Eta, Theta,
Iota Kappa Lambda
Mu Nu XI
   And Omicron!

Gimme a Pi!
Gimme a Rho!
   A Sigma Tau
   An Upsilon!

Gimme a Phi!
         Chi!
           Psi!
O - M - E - G - A!
And a piece of bread and butter.
           —W.R.E.

15 NOVEMBER
♏

Beautiful Words

The Book of Lists asked me for the ten words I considered most beautiful. There are as many opinions on that subject as there are people, and I tried to develop a consensus. I asked television viewers and radio listeners to send me their favorites, but few bothered to. I finally fell back on friends and acquaintances.

Alastair Reid chose *twilight*; Marya Mannes, *voluptuous*; Joan Fontaine, *affluence*; James Flexner, *wanderer*.

Mildred Luton sent me an account of a French grandmother who regretted that none of her granddaughters had been named Diarrhea. Informed of the word's unpleasant associations, the old lady sighed.

"What a pity!" she said. "So beautiful—fit for a princess!"

Most, but by no means all, of the words suggested were onomatopoeic: *liquefaction; melodious; murmuring; ululation; whirlpool; babbling*. Others frequently mentioned were the familiar *cellar door; daffodil; delight; fruitful; gloaming; lavender; meadow; rendezvous; philanderer; rhapsody; sapphire;* and *scenario*. Biology and illness—*cerebellum, urethra, syphilis, pneumonia,* and so on—were well represented, in an apparent effort to divorce appreciation of sound from sense.

These were my selections:

diarrhea	murmuring
gossamer	onomatopoeia
lullaby	Shenandoah
meandering	summer afternoon
mellifluous	wisteria

16 NOVEMBER
♏

Sniffles

We are in sniffle season. Comments from some snifflers:

BELAGCHOLLY DAYS

Chilly Dovebber with his boadigg blast
  Dow cubs add stripps the beddow add the lawd,
Eved October's suddy days are past—
  Add Subber's gawd!

I kdow dot what it is to which I cligg
  That stirs to sogg add sorrow, yet I trust
That still I sigg, but as the liddets sigg—
  Because I bust.

Add dow, farewell to roses add to birds,
  To larded fields and tigkligg streabletes eke;
Farewell to all articulated words
  I faid would speak.

Farewell, by cherished strolliggs od the sward,
  Greed glades add forest shades, farewell to you;
With sorrowing heart I, wretched add forlord,
  Bid you—achew!
                                    —*Anonymous*

THE SNIFFLE

In spite of her sniffle
Isabel's chiffle.
Some girls with a sniffle
Would be weepy and tiffle;
They would look awful,
Like a rained-on waffle,
But Isabel's chiffle
In spite of her sniffle.
Her nose is more red
With a cold in her head,
But then, to be sure,
Her eyes are bluer.
Some girls with a snuffle,
Their tempers are uffle.
But when Isabel's snivelly
She's snivelly civilly,
And when she's snuffly
She's perfectly luffly.
                —*Ogden Nash*

FLU MARKET

I've got a cold, la grippe, and the flu
And besides, I don't feel very well
My temperature's up to 102
If it goes any higher, I'll sell.
                —*Arthur J. Reinthal*

17 NOVEMBER
♏

In Short, A Verse

Adam
Had 'em

The drawback to very short verses is that they often require very long titles—at least mine do. For instance:

*A Genteel Exchange Between the British Ambassador's Wife, Who
Speaks No Spanish, and the Spanish Ambassador's Wife, Who Speaks
No English, During an Afternoon Call on the Former by the Latter;*

*Written for Those with Some Knowledge of English, Spanish, and
the Language of ABC.*

"T ?"

"C."

*   *   *

Or this:

*Conclusion After Studying a Cross Section of the Population,
with Special Attention to Comeliness, Age, Health, Reputation,
Accomplishments, Prospects, Temperament, Social Commitment,
Fairness, Tolerance, Modesty, Wit, Courtesy, Honor, Compassion,
Generosity, Life Expectancy, and Coolness Under Fire;
Disregarding as Irrelevant Only Worldly Goods or Lack Thereof*

Who do I want to be? . . .
Me.

Have you ever seen a verse that reads the same upside down as right side up?
Here is one:

M O M
S W I M S
W O W
—*Louis Phillips*

Written in longhand, this word too reads the same right side up or upside down:

chump

18 NOVEMBER

The Uncommitted Sin

In Victorian times the word *sin* became particularly associated with sexual peccadilloes. It still is, even among many people who insist that they do not consider sexual
peccadilloes a sin.

A world where the only unforgivable sin is not to sin places a heavy burden on us
nonconformists. Below I try twice to explain the viewpoint, but I cannot bring
myself to agree with it.

    1. Christ's self, whose mercy takes all sinners in,
      Cannot forgive the uncommitted sin.

2. Though Satan repentant were welcome in heaven
The sin uncommitted remains unforgiven.
—*W.R.E.*

THE MORAL

The moral is, I swear—
The moral is ... but there,
I don't know what the moral is,
The moral is, the moral is,
I don't know what the moral is,
I neither know nor care.
—*W.R.E.*

19 NOVEMBER
♏

When Irish Bulls Aren't Irish

There probably was no Irish blood in the Seattle radio announcer who said on one occasion, "If we have rain today, it will be snow." "Ears pierced while you wait" is an awesome bull posted in many an American jewelry store. Among bulls never bred in Ireland:

Welsh:
• Why, man, you'll die before I do, if you live long enough.
• Asked whether Welsh houses were cold: "Well, I suppose they are; they build them out of doors over here, you see."
• Defending a man asserted to be a Don Juan: "Why, he's a happily married man, and his wife is too!"

English:
• They fought so hard they lost their arms, and then they used their hands.

American:
• One of these days you're gonna wake up and find yourself dead.
• I'll cut off your head and throw it in your face.
• He kicked me in the belly when my back was turned.
• From now on we shall offer police jobs to qualified women regardless of sex.
• New Jersey: If two cars approach at right angles at an intersection where there is no traffic light, each shall make a full stop and wait until the other has passed by.

Mack and Moran:
• "Yeah, I'll be there. But how'll I know whether you've been there?"
"Well, if I get there first, I'll make a blue chalk mark, and if you get there first, you rub it out."

Spurious:

• "I had intended, my dear nephew, to enclose a check for ten dollars, but as I had already sealed the envelope before doing so, it will have to wait until next time."
• "Dear Teacher: Please excuse my son Joseph's absence on Friday, as it was Ash Wednesday. Signed, My Mother."

20 NOVEMBER
♏

Why Die When You Can Just Pass Away?

We find the painful or embarrassing less painful or embarrassing when clothed in roundabout expressions. This is nothing to be ashamed of; it simply demonstrates anew the magical power of words. They can make the intolerable tolerable, the vile glorious, the glorious vile. Most euphemisms, though, are less dramatic:

• Tumor becomes cancer becomes growth.
• Backward (in intelligence) becomes retarded becomes exceptional.
• Backward (in economic growth) becomes underdeveloped becomes developing.
• Bowels become guts become intestines become viscera.
• Lunacy becomes insanity becomes psychosis becomes emotional illness becomes disturbance.
• Madhouse becomes insane asylum becomes mental hospital becomes psychiatric hospital becomes sanitarium.

—Word Ways

21 NOVEMBER
♏

Ruemance, Ruemance

"I die! I die!" my dear one cries
    Into the listening night—
No saint awaiting paradise
    Could die in such delight.
The saint but once to heaven flies;
My dear one dies, and dies, and dies.

*   *   *

Of Everests there is but one;
And yet the lesser climbs are fun.

*   *   *

Your note swore you would stay unkissed.
'Twas written in a stranger's fist.

*   *   *

In thy abode the Muses dwell;
Yet ruder characters as well
Come worship at that shrine to prove,
With lewd libation, God is love.

—*W.R.E.*

22 NOVEMBER
♏

The Tale of Lord Lovell

Lord Lovell stood at his own front door,
    Seeking the hole for the key;
His hat was wrecked, and his trousers bore
    A rent across either knee,
When down came the beauteous Lady Jane
    In fair white draperie.

"Oh, where have you been, Lord Lovell?" she said,
    "Oh, where have you been?" said she.
"I have not closed an eye in bed,
    And the clock has just struck three.
Who has been standing you on your head
    In the ash-barrel, pardie?"

"I am not drunk, Lad' Shane," he said,
    "And so late it cannot be;
The clock struck one as I entered—
    I heard it two times or three.
It must be the salmon on which I fed
    Has been too many for me."

"Go tell your tale, Lord Lovell," she said,
    "To the maritime cavalree,
To your grandmother of the hoary head—
    To any one but me;
The door is not used to be opened
    With a cigarette for a key."

—*Anonymous*

Lord Lovell may well have wakened next day with what the Norwegians refer to as "workmen in my head" (*jeg har tommermen*), the French as "woody mouth" (*gueule de bois*), the Swedes as "pain in the roots of the hair" (*wont I haret*), and the Germans as "a yowling of cats" (*Katzenjammer*).

23   NOVEMBER

"There But for the Grace of God ..."

Nancy McPhee gathered hundreds of offensive remarks along the order of these into *The Book of Insults:*

- OSCAR WILDE: George Moore wrote brilliant English until he discovered grammar.
- Actor to OLIVER HERFORD: I'm a smash hit. Why, yesterday I had the audience glued in their seats! HERFORD: Clever of you to think of it.
- MARK TWAIN on CECIL RHODES: I admire him, I frankly confess it; and when his time comes I shall buy a piece of the rope for a keepsake.
- BENJAMIN DISRAELI on LORD JOHN RUSSELL: If a traveler were informed that such a man was leader of the House of Commons, he may well begin to comprehend how the Egyptians worshipped an insect.
- GYPSY ROSE LEE (on a pretentious chorus girl): She is descended from a long line that her mother listened to.
- JOHN MASON BROWN: Tallulah Bankhead barged down the Nile last night as Cleopatra—and sank.

DISRAELI AND GLADSTONE

- GLADSTONE: I understand, sir, that you are a witty fellow.
- DISRAELI: Some people are under that impression.
- GLADSTONE: I'm told that you can make a joke on any subject.
- DISRAELI: That is quite possible.
- GLADSTONE: Then I challenge you—make a joke about Queen Victoria.
- DISRAELI: Sir, Her Majesty is not a subject.

(In the French version of this exchange, the protagonists are Louis XVI and the wit Marquis de Bièvre. LOUIS: Marquis, there is no subject you don't pun on. Make a pun about me. DE BIÈVRE: *Sire, le roi n'est pas un sujet.*

24 NOVEMBER

N'Heure Souris Rames

In *Mots d'Heures Gousses Rames,* by the late Luis D'Antin Van Rooten, French words strung together evoke the sound of English-language nursery rhymes. (The elaborate scholastic footnotes are part of the jape.) Now comes poet Ormonde de Kay in a book called *N'Heure Souris Rames* to carry on the great tradition:

Tu marques et tu marques et
  Tu bailles, effet typique.[1]
Heaume et gaine! Heaume et gaine!
  Gigoté chic![2]

Tu marques et tu marques et
  Tu bailles, effet tac.[3]
Heaume et gaine! Heaume et gaine!
  Gigoté Jacques!

[1]"You mark and you mark and you yawn, a typical effect." The speaker is evidently chiding, rather scornfully, an individual engaged in marking or writing something, perhaps a small merchant marking prices on merchandise for sale or totting up his take.

[2]"[My] helmet and sheath! [*bis*] [My] fine prancer!" (*Gigoté*—a horse strong in the hind legs.) It appears that the speaker is a horseman, very possibly a wandering knight, who longs for action, though the fact that both the items of military gear he apostrophizes are protective in function suggests that he is not really all that keen for a fight, the true purpose of his crying out being, one suspects, to proclaim his moral superiority, as a warrior, over his money-grubbing interlocutor. Incidentally, his steed is named Jacques (see last line).

[3]When the persistent marker yawns a second time the speaker notices a clicking sound (*tac*). While the first known mention of dentures occurs in a manuscript of the year 1728 by the French dental surgeon Pierre Fouchard, it is conceivable that Fouchard's compatriot, the persistent marker, an enterprising person clearly endowed with singleness of purpose, could centuries earlier have devised for himself a set of artificial teeth, which, by permitting him to smile broadly, would have made it easier for him to ingratiate himself with customers.

—Ormonde de Kay

25 NOVEMBER

Oh. Except Turkeys

From compositions about Thanksgiving by children in Mike Collins's class:

- Wow! Look! There they finally come now! It looks like they are getting ready to land on Plymouth Rock. Yes, oh yes, here they are! But look! Here come the Indians rolling their war hoops. Oh, I cannot stand to look any more!

- The Pilgrims invited the Indians to their first Thanksgiving dinner. They did all sorts of nice things for the Indians whether they liked it or not.

- Thanksgiving is the day set aside for everyone to be happy. Oh. Except turkeys.

The following invocation by the Reverend Robert W. Golledge at the one hundredth anniversary luncheon of the F. W. Woolworth Company would have been a natural for Thanksgiving Day.

PETITION TO THE CHAIRMAN OF THE BOARD

- Help us to celebrate 100 years of F. W. Woolworth Company by profiting from a lien on Your grace,
- And with portfolios filled with goodness and peace.
- Compound them daily to insure a block of your love,
- So that when we are summoned for our final inventory
- By whatever name we are known—Kinney, Richman, Wolco or Woolworth—
- We may not be found overstocked or undersold,
- But accepted into thy Presence marked: honest value.
- Amen.

26 NOVEMBER

Accidental English

Insurance companies provide the principals in an automobile accident with a special form on which to summarize what happened. Some reports:

- Coming home, I drove into the wrong house and collided with a tree I don't have.
- The other car collided with mine without giving warning of its intentions.
- A truck backed through my windshield into my wife's face.
- A pedestrian hit me and went under my car.
- The guy was all over the road; I had to swerve a number of times before I hit him.
- I had been driving my car for forty years when I fell asleep at the wheel and had an accident.
- An invisible car came out of nowhere, struck my vehicle, and vanished.
- I was sure the old fellow would never make it to the other side of the street when I struck him.
- The pedestrian had no idea which direction to go, so I ran over him.
- I was thrown from my car as it left the road. I was later found in a ditch by some stray cows.
- The telephone pole was approaching fast. I attempted to swerve out of the way, when it struck the front of my car.

—*William G. Espy*

27 NOVEMBER

Rub-a-Dub-Dub, Dear

When you say, "fair, fat, and forty," "high, wide, and handsome," or "healthy, wealthy, and wise," you are talking Trinomial. (For talking Binomial, see 29 June.) A trinomial is a verbal chain containing three words or wordlike forms, linked in sound by two of three sound arrangements: rhyme, alliteration, and word repetition. Who would think so much learning went into "inky-dinky-do"?

> Rub-a-dub-dub, dear,
> My heart goes, all agog
> That you are drawing near—
> Hot diggety-dog!
>
> When you are passing by,
> I hippety-hippety-hop;
> And if I catch your eye,
> I snap, crackle, pop.
> —W.R.E.

Give, devise, and bequeath is an ancient legal triplet. In the years following the Norman invasion of England in 1066, the nobility spoke French, the clergy Latin, and the villains and tradesmen Anglo-Saxon. Give and bequeath are Anglo-Saxon; devise is French. Legal documents frequently repeated themselves in all three languages, so that everyone could understand.

The propensity of lawyers to tie down a point with a series of words of identical or nearly identical meaning catches the attention of Charles Dickens in *David Copperfield*. Micawber has reached Point 2 of his indictment against the evil Uriah Heep:

> "Second. HEEP has, on several occasions, to the best of my knowledge, information, and belief, systematically forged, to various entries, books, and documents, the signature of Mr. W.; and has distinctly done so in one instance, capable of proof by me. To wit, in the manner following, that is to say:"

At this point David Copperfield interrupts the narrative to comment as follows:

> Again, Mr. Micawber had a relish in this formal piling up of words, which, however, ludicrously displayed in his case, was, I must say, not at all peculiar to him. I have observed it, in the course of my life, in numbers of men. It seems to me to be a general rule. In the taking of legal oaths, for instance, deponents seem to enjoy themselves mightily when they come to several good words in succession, for the expression of one idea; as, that they utterly detest, abominate, and abjure, or so forth; and the old anathemas were made relishing on the same principle. We talk about the tyranny of words, but we like to tyrannise over them too; we are fond of having a large superfluous establishment of words to wait upon us on great occasions; we think it looks important, and sounds well. As we are not particular about the meaning of our liveries on state occasions, if they be but fine and numerous enough, so the meaning or necessity of our words is a secondary consideration, if there be but a great parade of them.

28 NOVEMBER

Telling the Age of Lady Moon

Directions are often clearer to the person who gives them than to the person who receives them. Friends ask us over for a holiday drink and say, "Drive to the corner where the Queen Elizabeth roses are climbing on the fence, of course they're not blooming now, and then turn right at the first stoplight after the underpass, where the cemetery used to be, it's a parking lot, and then just keep going straight, bear right all the time, and exactly two hundred yards after the old white Georgian house that's been torn down you'll see five mailboxes, well, don't stop there, but if you get mixed up, there is an emergency telephone booth a half mile down the road."

Anyone who knows east from west can follow these simple directions:

> O Lady Moon, your horns point toward the east:
>   Shine, be increased.
> O Lady Moon, your horns point toward the west:
>   Wane, be at rest.
> —*Christina G. Rossetti*

A mnemonic for distinguishing the waxing from the waning moon:

> When it is coming ◖ it is really Departing.
> When it is departing ◗ it is really Coming.

29 NOVEMBER

Dream Color, Dream Logic

In a dream I lay supine, looking up into the leaves of a tree. The leaves were the color of amethyst. One detached itself from its twig and became a butterfly; it rose and dipped briefly on gentle air currents, then settled on the back of my hand, its wings opening and closing. I wish I could dream that dream again.

That was the first time I was sure I dreamed in color.

I dreamed in color again last night. Someone we had never expected to meet called on us. It seemed improbable, in my dream, that the visit could be actually taking place. As my doubts grew, Louise entered, bringing for my inspection a box of elegant new stationery monogrammed with a *D* in royal blue. Said I to me: If Louise can buy stationery engraved with a *D*, when her given name begins with *L* and our surname with *E*, then certainly it is reasonable that X—I have forgotten who X was —should come for a visit. So I am not dreaming.

Lewis Carroll did not dream in color. He dreamed in equations, which came out this way:

HIT OR MISS

[Pairs of premises in search of conclusions]

No bald person needs a hair-brush;
No lizards have hair.

No pins are ambitious;
No needles are pins.

Some oysters are silent;
No silent creatures are amusing.

No frogs write books;
Some people use ink in writing books.

Some mountains are insurmountable;
All stiles can be surmounted.

No lobsters are unreasonable;
No reasonable creatures expect impossibilities.

No fossil can be crossed in love;
An oyster may be crossed in love.

A prudent man shuns hyenas;
No banker is imprudent.

No misers are unselfish;
None but misers save egg-shells.

No military men write poetry;
No generals are civilians.

All owls are satisfactory;
Some excuses are unsatisfactory.

—*Lewis Carroll*

Theodore S. Abbott sent me these bits of dream logic:

Q. Why is the south wind blind?
A. The south wind is a zephyr.
   A zephyr is a yarn, and a yarn is a tale.
   A tale is an attachment, and an attachment is love.
   Love is blind; therefore a zephyr is blind.

(It had never occurred to me that a zephyr was a yarn.)

Q. Why are fire engines red?

A. $2 + 1 = 3$. The third letter in the alphabet is *C*. The sea is full of fish. The sturgeon is a fish. Caviar comes from sturgeons. Russians are fond of caviar. Fire engines are always rushin'. What other color could they be?

30 NOVEMBER

From a Sitter to His Artist

When Lely painted Oliver Cromwell, the Lord Protector insisted on an unflinching likeness, in words to this effect:

> Mr. Lely, I desire
> You to use your skill entire
> To my likeness truly scrawl,
> Pimples, roughness, warts, and all.
> Paint exactly what you see,
> Or you get no pay from me.
> —*W.R.E.*

Jane Cooke recently painted a portrait of me. My instructions bore no resemblance to Cromwell's:

> Should I espy one wart or wen,
> Madam, you must start again.
> All deficiencies erase:
> If this leave me out of face,
> Better that than over-frank—
> Let me hang forever blank.
> —*W.R.E.*

The same Oliver Cromwell who insisted on being painted warts and all is author of one of the most self-righteous rationalizations of all time:

> If any man whatsoever hath carried on the design of deposing the King and disinheriting his posterity: or if any man hath yet such a design he should be the greatest traitor and rebel in the world; but since the Providence of God hath cast this upon me, I cannot but submit to Providence.

DECEMBER

The Poodle Doodle Whitney D. Didn't Noodle

Whitney D.
Noodles
Doodles.
Whitney D.
Promised he
Would noodle
A poodle
Doodle
For me.
Do you see
A poodle
Doodle
By Whitney D.?
Where can it be
That poodle

Doodle
Whitney D.
Promised me?
I'd give oodles
Boodles
Flapdoodles
Kiyoodles
Yankee doodles
Of boodles
To see
The poodle
Doodle
Whitney D.
Didn't noodle
For me—
   i.e.,
  —W.R.E.

2 DECEMBER

Kikeriki Says the Cock

A usual argument against the bowwow theory of language origins (see 25 May) is that a rooster crows *cock-a-doodle-do* in English, *cocorococo* in Spanish, *chiccirichi* in Italian, *kikeriki* in German, *kyke-liken* in Danish, *koddo-kokko* in Japanese, and so on. This seems to me a poor point. The *k* sound continues throughout. I am sure an American would pick up the Japanese word for rooster much quicker than, say, the word for insubordination.

Nino LoBello recently examined in the *New York Times* the variations in plosive sounds as represented in the comic strips of different nations. In Finland an explosion goes POOF, in Denmark BAR-ROOM. In Germany a cat purrs SCHNURR, and in France RON-RON. An attacking bull snorts SCNAUB-SCNAUB in German-speaking Austria, but UAAA in German-speaking Switzerland. In French comics the villain bites the dust with a TCHAC, in Germany with a PLUMP, in Italy with a POKK or KRUMP.

In Germany Mickey Maus goes KLIRR, and his dog Goofy yells BAUTZ. In Spain guns sound JUOOS. Death-ray pistols kill with a GRRUNG in Sweden. Snoring Germans sound RUMPEL-KNURR; a sneeze is HATSCHI; a loud commotion is RUMS, and a louder one RUMS-RUMS.

The Italians pepper their comic strips with words that begin with the letter *S* followed by a consonant: STUF, SCASSH, SVIMM, SDOING, SDUGH, SCLANG, SCRASH, SDOK, SCIAFF, SVESSH, SBENG, SBOING, SPRAK, SCLENG.

3 DECEMBER

What They Did

In which we learn what they did, from book lists found in the catalog of a famous American university library.

They all come out. They all need to talk. They all played ragtime. They all wanted to write. They almost killed Hitler. They also ran. They are human too. They asked for a paper. They asked for death. They betrayed Czechoslovakia.

They builded better than they knew. They built for eternity. They built for the future. They built the Capitol. They built the West. They buried a man. They called him Mister Moody. They called him Wild Bill. They called it a game.

They called me Alfred. They came as friends. They came for sandalwood. They came in chains. They came like swallows. They came to a river. They came to Baghdad. They came to kill. They came to Louisiana. They came to Wrong Way House. They can't afford to wait.

They can't fit in. They can't go home again. They climbed the Alps. They closed their schools. They come for the best of reasons. They dream of home. They flew alone.

They fought for the sky. They fought under the sea. They found a common language. They found gold. They found it in Natchez. They found the buried cities. They gathered at the river. They gave royal assent. They got what they wanted. They had their hour. They hanged my silly Billy.

They harvest despair. They have found a faith. They knew the Washingtons. They knew what they wanted. They looked like this. They lost two tons. They loved to laugh. They met at Calvary. They move with the sun. They named me Gertrude Stein. They never had it so good. They never looked inside.

They peopled the Pacific. They put out to sea. They rode into Europe. They said it couldn't be done. They said it was inventories.

They sailed alone. They sang a new song. They sang for horses. They saw Gandhi. They saw it happen in classical times. They say the forties. They see what you mean. They shall be free. They shall not die. They shall not sleep. They shall not want. They shall take up serpents.

They showed the way. They sought a country. They steal for love. They stooped to folly. They studied man. They talked to a stranger. They taught themselves. They tell of birds. They thought they were free.

They took their stand. They took to the sea. They turned to stone. They voted for Roosevelt.

They wait in darkness. They walk in the city. They walk in the night. They walked a crooked mile. They want to know. They wanted war. They went on together. They went to college. They went to Portugal. They were expendable.

—Freddy Bosco

4 DECEMBER

Effectificity

Since it would be easy to fill my entire book from William Safire's column on language in the *New York Times Magazine,* I had resolved not to draw from it at all. The following story, however, is irresistible.

EFFECTIFICITY

"One of these days," goes the caption on a famous cartoon of two guys with their feet on a desk, "we've got to get organized." Evidently that thought struck the White House recently, and a leading management consultant was hired as a deputy to the President's chief of staff.

Alonzo McDonald speaks a special language. In a profile by Martin Schram of the *Washington Post,* his hard-driving patois was derided as "neo-Jeb Magruder" and—in an unkind cut—a sample of Alonzo's language was displayed:

"There's a hope that some of the cross-roughing will be done earlier . . . that decisions will be broadly based . . . that we can increase inputs.

"We need a process of involvement . . . a synthesization," the President's new organizer went on. "We've got to look at how problems interlink, the monitoring and the execution. . . . When there's an uncontrollable problem, that's the point in time when we must have analysis before we have ad hoc action."

I dialed Alonzo McDonald's number at the White House, spoke to one of his aides (called a "higby," after one of Haldeman's honchos) and explained I needed four and a half minutes for semantic instruction. There came a point in time when Alonzo returned the call.

Is he worried about being charged with speaking bureaucratese?

"It's not bureaucratese," he replied briskly but amiably. "It's a good solid business-operating vocabulary."

Cross-roughing?

"That's a term from bridge. It means taking an idea, rubbing it against different opposing ideas, so as to refine it. An idea that hasn't been cross-roughed has not been rubbed smooth by conflicting ideas." The word can be spelled two ways: "cross-rough," as in polishing a stone, or "cross-ruff," as in trumping a playing card ("ruff," the act of trumping in a game similar to whist, can be traced to 1598).

Interlink? Is that any different from the tired old word "connect"? Is it a combined form of "interface" and "linkage"?

"I use 'interlink' as it is used in electrical circuitry," said the highly charged executive. "It is not just connected—there's movement in there, current is passing through. It's important that we know how that current will flow, so that we don't hit a short. That way, we can improve our effectificity."

Effectificity? As a sucker for a neologism, I thought that one over carefully. When businessmen wanted to use the adjective "specific" as a noun, they rejected "specificness" and chose "specificity"; could it be that in turning the most important adjective in management consulting—"effective" —into a noun, they were setting aside "effectiveness" for the more electric-sounding "effectificity?"

"No," said Alonzo McDonald, less crisply. "Actually, I think I meant effectiveness."

My time was up and I thanked him.

"Any time," he said. "Effectiveness," he added, as if practicing the word, and hung up.

—William Safire

LITERALLY

And then there is the misuse of *literally*. Purists complain regularly, justifiably, and uselessly, about the near-pervasive use of *literally* as an emphasizer, when the correct word is *figuratively,* which, alas, diminishes rather than emphasizes.

He sings, he dances, he acts, and he literally simmers with energy . . . —*John O'Connor*

"I am literally staggered by the hot-poker way advertising has stimulated sales," said Hank Billeter . . .—*Philip H. Dougherty*

"I state unequivocally that all these legislative, judicial and media actions literally emasculate Mr. Nixon," Rabbi Korff said.

. . . a Jewish religious tradition that Noik literally shrugged off a year ago . . .—*New York Times*

"Patrick literally tore the place apart," Mr. McQuiggan said.—*New York Times*

These multiple-moisture-action preparations literally do make your skin sing with joy.—*advertisement in the New York Times*

Once again, the dairy farmer was literally milked almost dry.—*Wall Street Journal*

The Italian government literally foamed at the mouth!—*Liz Smith, NBC-TV*

—*From Casey Herrick*

5 DECEMBER

Green Red? Yes No

Life is filled with paradoxes. So is language. So is *Word Ways,* quoted here:

- To walk down the street is to walk up the street.
- Since the hour hand is the first hand on a clock, and the minute hand is the second hand, the second hand is the third hand.
- Yesterday's tomorrow is tomorrow's yesterday.
- A day consisting of twenty-four hours, nighttime must be daytime.
- An inexperienced Communist is a green Red.
- If the left direction is right, then right is wrong.
- The king is dead, long live the king!
- You must slow down in a speed zone.
- An even number that is also a prime number is an odd number: the only one known is two.

- To fill out a form is to fill it in.
- "No" in Hawaiian is "yes."
- Shameless behavior is shameful, and vice versa.
- To stay within a budget, one must go without.
- A near miss is a near hit.
- A boxing ring is square.
- A tree must be cut down before it is cut up.
- A lawyer's brief is frequently lengthy.
- A slim chance is the same as a fat chance.
- To drink up, you down your drink.
- When a house burns up it burns down.
- A drunken whore is both tight and loose.
- When the bases are loaded, a walk is a run.

PARADOXIES

For Jill and Jenny, both with pox,
Love-blinded Jack his fortune hocks.
(This is no paradox; he's
Happy to pawn shoes and sox
For such a paradoxies.)
—*W.R.E.*

6 DECEMBER

A Piffle of Skiffle

Skiffle in England is a form of protomusic which, says the *New Statesman,* employs "mostly fast, exciting rhythm, repetitions of words, and noise."

SKIFFLING AT THE ROYAL COLLEGE

(A lyric that might have been written for the in-house skifflers of the Royal College of Surgeons)

Chorus: Dig, man, dig!
Snick, man, snick!
Dig a little hole, and we'll see what
makes him tick!

I took me a scalpel the other day,
I said to my patient: "Pray, man, pray!"

I gave him a whiff and it must ha' been shock,
For all of a sudden he started to rock.

I said to him: "Brother, you've nothing on."
He answered me crazy: "I'm gone, Doc, gone!"

Chorus: Dig, man, dig!
Snick, man, snick!
Dig a little hole, and we'll see what makes him tick!
—Eileen M. Haggitt

7 DECEMBER

SUSAN SIMPSON

S starts more words than any other letter—including every word in this verse:

Sudden swallows softly skimming,
Sunset's slowly spready shade,
Silvery songsters sweetly singing
Summer's soothing serenade.

Susan Simpson strolled sedately,
Stifling sobs, suppressing sighs.
Seeing Stephen Slocum, stately
She stopped, showing some surprise.

"Say," said Stephen, "sweetest sigher;
Say, shall Stephen spouseless stay?"
Susan, seeming somewhat shyer,
Showed submissiveness straightway.

Summer's season slowly stretches,
Susan Simpson Slocum she—
So she signed some simple sketches—
Soul sought soul successfully.

Six Septembers Susan swelters;
Six sharp seasons snow supplies;
Susan's satin sofa shelters
Six small Slocums side by side.
—Anonymous

If "Susan Simpson" had been written 100 years earlier, the printer would have used an *ʃ*-like font at the beginning and middle of the words. The extinct letter has a rather wide open top; the tail does not go below the line; and the little bar is confined to the left-hand side of the tail.

8 DECEMBER

Cork and Work and Card and Ward

I take it you already know
Of tough and bough and cough and dough?
Others may stumble, but not you
On hiccough, thorough, laugh, and through?
I write in case you wish perhaps
To learn of less familiar traps:
Beware of heard, a dreadful word
That looks like beard, and sounds like bird.
And dead: it's said like bed, not bead;
For goodness' sake, don't call it 'deed'!
Watch out for meat and great and threat
(They rhyme with suite and straight and debt).
A moth is not a moth in mother,
Nor both in bother, broth in brother.
And here is not a match for there,
Nor dear for bear, or fear for pear.
There's dose and rose, there's also lose
(Just look them up), and goose, and choose,
And cork and work, and card and ward,
And font and front, and word and sword,
And do and go and thwart and cart—
Come come, I've barely made a start!
A dreadful language? Man alive,
I'd mastered it when I was five!

—*Anonymous*

9 DECEMBER

I Kmnow Pfil Pfizer Pfomnebd Me, Though

Bdellium is an aromatic gum resin similar to myrrh; the *bd* is pronounced *d*. *Ptisan* is a slightly medical infusion, such as barley water; the *pt* is pronounced *t*, as in *pterodactyl*. Likewise the *pf* in *Pfizer* sounds *f*, the *mn* in *Mnesomyne* sounds *n*, and the *ps* in *psychologist* sounds *s*. Therefore:

Pfil Pfizer pfomnebd me pto imparpt
Mnemosymne'ps amn amnciemnpt ptarpt,

Amnd myrrh ips bdellium creamebd.
Psychiaptripstps, he mnexpt amnmnoumnceps,
Drepsps pterobdacptylps' youmng imn pfloumnceps,
    Amnd ptoabdps eapt ptisanps pspteamebd.
I bdo mnopt kmnow thapt thips ips pso;
I kmnow Pfil Pfizer pfomnebd me, though.

—W.R.E.

10 DECEMBER

When Artistic Was Artificial

Hundreds of years ago an English king described Saint Paul's Cathedral as "amusing, awful, and artificial." To express the same sense today we would say amazing, awe-inspiring, and artistic.

Such evolution in meaning sometimes irritates grammaticist Wesley Price, whose tart opinions on the changing meanings of certain words are reproduced here:

- **DEMEAN**   Generations of ignoramuses have decided that this word means "debase," or "degrade," or "humiliate." It really means "to conduct or behave (oneself) in a specified manner." A good word gone wrong.

- **FEY**   Another word that has been destroyed by ignoramuses. It doesn't mean "elfin"; it means "fated to die." We are all fey.

- **FULSOME**   Means "offensive to good taste . . . gross . . . indelicate." Editorial writers think, however, that "fulsome praise" means something like "generous praise." Avoid the word entirely. It is being destroyed by boobs.

- **ANTICIPATE**   The hack writers use this word instead of "expect," and in so doing they are killing it. The word actually means "to foresee," or "to act before another has had time to act." Like this: "He reached for his knife but I anticipated him by firing my cannon."

- **PALPABLE**   Means more than "obvious": *"capable of being touched."*

- **ALIBI**   If you mean "excuse," *say* "excuse." Alibis are claimed by people who say they were in Chicago when their wife was strangled in New York.

- **EKE OUT**   Wrong: "He eked out a poor living."
   Right: "He eked out his income as a bartender by working nights in a waffle factory."

- **ILK**   Not to be used, unless by some strange chance you want to write, as the Scots do, a sentence indicating that the proprietor and the property have the same name, as "the Stuarts of that ilk," meaning "the Stuarts, of Stuart."

• BEG THE QUESTION	Doesn't mean avoiding the question, or giving a nonresponsive answer, as knucklehead writers believe. Means, "To assume the truth of the very point raised in a question." A phrase to avoid.
• ANXIOUS	Not a synonym for "eager." If you're anxious to meet the Pope, you must have a bad conscience.

—Wesley Price

11 DECEMBER

Biographical Sketch

Mrs. J. W. Haltiwanger writes that she is planning to discuss a book of mine at a meeting of her study club and needs biographical information. I have sent her the following verse, which might have been written with me in mind:

ONCE—BUT NO MATTER WHEN

Once—but no matter when—
There lived—no matter where—
A man, whose name—but then
I need not that declare.

He—well, he had been born,
And so he was alive;
His age—I details scorn—
Was somethington and five.

He lived—how many years
I truly can't decide;
But this one fact appears:
He lived—until he died.

"He died." I have averred,
But cannot prove 'twas so;
But that he was interred,
At any rate, I know.

I fancy he'd a son,
I hear he had a wife:
Perhaps he'd more than one—
I know not, on my life!

But whether he was rich
Or whether he was poor,
Or neither—both—or which—
I cannot say, I'm sure.

I can't recall his name
Or what he used to do:
But then—well, such is fame!
'Twill so serve me and you.

And that is why I thus
About this unknown man
Would fain create a fuss,
To rescue, if I can,

From dark oblivion's blow,
Some record of his lot:
But, ah! I do not know
Who—why—where—when—or what.

               —Anonymous

Alastair Reid is a Scots poet. His sense of meter is such that he felt he must change the last line of this limerick. (Guess the change he would have made.) But there was no time to do that. No matter. The beauty of the handwriting dispels any doubt about the beat.

*You're amazingly durable, Wede.
Your sixty-ninth birthday indeed!
I'll be drinking your health
on your hundred-and-twelfth
or my name's not Alastair Reid.*

12 DECEMBER

Why Try?

A univocalic employing only the vowel *y* has to bend a few rules of spelling, as is done here:

               "Why
               Cry,
               Lynx?"—
               "My
               Sty
               Stynx."

               *   *   *

               Tryst:
               Kyssed

By
Gy.

*   *   *

Try
Hymn.
Why?
Whym.
—*W.R.E.*

THREE SPECKLED EGGS HELD EGGS WERE MEN

The only vowel in the following verse is *e*—perhaps one vowel too many.

Three speckled eggs held eggs were men enshelled.
Egg-terms the three eschewed ("cheep," "peck," "peep," "nest").
Hens were the helpmeets meeker eggs held best:
Yet these three pestered Eve herself; these yelled,
"We'll get thee . . . pet thee . . . wed thee . . . bed thee . . .
       meld—
Beget! We'll gender speckled men, shell-dressed—
Men egg-descended, egg-redeemed, egg-blessed!"
Eve let her sheen be seen . . .
            The eggs beheld
Her tender flesh, dewed cheeks, her tresses scented;
Her sweet recesses; her resplendent swells . . .
These excellences left the eggs demented . . .
Defenseless . . . heedless when she peeled the shells.

Eve well knew eggs were eggs, ere e'en she met them.
She let them wheedle, squeeze her. Then she et them.
              —*W.R.E.*

A sufficiently familiar passage—especially of verse—is recognizable even if a single vowel replaces all the others. In Shakespeare's "All the World's a Stage," someone replaced all the vowels with *u*. These lines are enough to show how easy the trick is:

Ull thu wurld's u stugu,
Und ull thu mun und wumun murlu pluuurs.
Thuu huvu thuur uxuts und thuur untruncus;
Und unu mun un hus tumu pluus munu purts, . . .

Y is the only vowel here:

Yll thy wyrld's y stygy,
Ynd yll thy myn ynd wymyn myryly plyyyrs.
Thyy hyvy thyyr yxyts ynd thyyr yntryncys;
Ynd yny myn yn hys tymy plyys myny pyrts, . . .

Any of the other vowels would do as well, but I shan't bother you with them.

13 DECEMBER

A Type of Beauty

Here
hang my bangs
o'er eyes that dream,
and nose and rose-
bud lips for cream.
And here's my
chin with dim-
ples in.
This is my
neck with-
out a speck,
which doth these snowy shoulders
deck; and here is—see, oh,
double T-O-N, which girls all
wear, like me; and here's a
heart from Cupid's dart safe-
shielded by this corset's art.
This is my waist too tightly
laced on which
a bustle big
is placed.
This is my
dress. Its cost,
I guess, did my
poor papa much dis-
tress, because he sighed
when mamma tried it on,
and scolded so I cried;
but mamma said I soon would
wed and buy pa's clothes for him
instead. It's trimmed with lace
just in this place, 'neath which two
ankles show with grace, in silken hose
to catch the beaux who think they're lovely,
I suppose.   These are
my feet   in slippers
neat, and   now if we
should chance to   meet we'll flirt
a little on the street.   How sweet.

—*Anonymous*

14 DECEMBER

The Twelve Days of Christmas

December 14
Dear John:

I went to the door today and the postman delivered a partridge in a pear tree. What a thoroughly delightful gift. I couldn't have been more surprised.

With deepest love and devotion,
Agnes

December 15
Dearest John:

Today the postman brought your very sweet gift. Just imagine . . . two turtle doves. I'm just delighted at your very thoughtful gift. They are just adorable.

All my love,
Agnes

December 16
Dear John:

Oh! Aren't you the extravagant one. Now I must really protest. I don't deserve such generosity . . . three French hens! They are just darling but I must insist, you've been too kind.

Love,
Agnes

December 17
Dear John:

Today the postman delivered four calling birds. Now really, they are beautiful, but don't you think enough is enough? You're being too romantic.

Affectionately,
Agnes

December 18
Dearest John:

What a surprise. Today the postman delivered five golden rings, one for every finger. You're just impossible, but I love it. Frankly, all those birds squawking were beginning to get on my nerves.

All my love,
Agnes

December 19
Dear John:

I opened my door today and there were actually six geese alaying on my front steps. So you're back to the birds again, huh? These geese are huge!

Where will I keep them? The neighbors are complaining and I can't sleep through this racket!

Please stop.

Cordially,
Agnes

December 20
Dear John:

What's with you and these * * * * birds? Seven swans a-swimming! What kind of goddam joke is this? There's bird * * * * all over the house and they never stop with the racket. I can't sleep at night and I'm a nervous wreck. It's not funny so stop with those * * * * birds.

Sincerely,
Agnes

December 21

OK, buster . . . I think I prefer the birds. What the hell am I going to do with eight maids a-milking? It's not enough with all those birds and the maids, but they brought their damn cows. Lay off me, smartass!

Agnes

December 22

Hey, * * * *-head! What are you some kind of sadist? Now there's nine pipers playing! And Christ, do they play. They never stopped chasing those maids since they got here. The cows are upset and they're stepping all over the birds, and the neighbors have started a petition to evict me!

You'll get yours,
Agnes

December 23

You rotten * * * * *. Now there's ten ladies dancing! I don't know why I call those sluts ladies. They've been balling those pipers all night long. Now the cows can't sleep and they've got diarrhea. The commissioner of buildings has subpoenaed me to give cause why the building shouldn't be condemned. I'm siccing the police on you!

One who means it.

December 24

Listen * * * *-head, what's with the eleven lords a-leaping on those maids and ladies? Some of those broads will never walk again! The pipers ran through all the maids and have been committing sodomy with the cows. All twenty-three birds are dead. They got trampled in the orgy. I hope you're satisfied, you rotten vicious swine!

Your sworn enemy,
Agnes

December 25
Dear Sir:

This is to acknowledge your latest gift of twelve fiddlers fiddling which you have inflicted upon our client Agnes Mendolstein. The destruction was total. All future correspondence should come to our attention. If you should attempt to reach Miss Mendolstein at the Happy Dale Sanitarium, the attendants have instructions to shoot you on sight. Please find attached a warrant for your arrest.

Law Offices
Budger, Bender & Cahole

—From M. Hughes and Mala Miller

15 DECEMBER

Holmes, Sweet Holmes

Put all the other humorous versifiers of our country in one tray of a scale, and Oliver Wendell Holmes in the other; he lightly weighs down the whole shebang. A tribute:

Poet, burn thy blotted pages!—
Holmes has gone, and ta'en thy wages.

I knocked—but, alack! there was nobody Holmes;
  O father, dear father, come Holmes with me now!
Wherever I wanders, wherever I roams,
  There's no place like Holmes—Wendell Holmes, take a bow!

Mother, I'm coming back Holmes with a pig,
  Back to my Holmes, to my Holmes on the range—
Holmes again, Holmes again, jiggety-jig—
  Where Charity starts, and where ma has the mange.

Far from the old folks at Holmes did I flee—
  Be it ever so humble, there's no place as ill;
Holmes is the sailor, Holmes from the sea,
  And the hunter, Holmes from the hill.

—W.R.E.

16 DECEMBER

Timothy Tidbits

Timothy Dickinson bought us a tasty pre-Christmas luncheon today. He is slimmer than when he used to bring me tidbits for *O Thou Improper, Thou Uncommon Noun,* and more subdued; it was odd to see him sitting quietly, sipping white wine, instead of striding about, tossing his knob-headed cane into the air, and catching it by the reverse end. But there was no change in his dark bangs, the exhausted red rose in his lapel, or his morning jacket and striped trousers.

"Timothy," I said, "I am looking for words with a specific date of origin."

"Such as?" he asked in an Oxonian honk.

"*Smog,* for instance." (I took a folded paper from my wallet.) "I have fetched this quotation from the *London Globe* of July 3, 1905. 'The other day at a meeting of the public Health Congress Dr. Des Voeux did a public service in coining a new word for the London fog, which was referred to as "smog," a compound of "smoke" and "fog." '"

"Remarkable. You should add Stellenbosch."

"What is Stellenbosch?"

"Military slang," said Timothy. "Stellenbosch was a town and division of Cape Colony and was formerly the place selected for command by officers who had failed in the Kaffir wars. To be Stellenbosched is to be relegated, as the result of incompetence, to a position in which little harm can be done."

"And you mean to say that you know exactly when the word was first used as a verb?"

"Oh, yes. Mmm." Timothy took a delicate sip of wine. "On June 16, 1900, Rudyard Kipling wrote in the *Daily Express*: 'After all, what does it matter, old man? You're bound to be Stellenbosched in three days.' Mmm. Do you have *starvation?*"

"Starvation? That has been around forever."

"Not at all. It was first used with reference to the bill of 1775 'for restraining Trade and Commerce with the New England Colonies.' A Member of Parliament named Dundas expressed his fear that the Act would not produce famine, as desired, and he was thenceforth known as 'Starvation Dundas.' "

"Then the word must already have been current."

"No, no; though *starve* was. *Starve* is from the German *sterben,* meaning to die of any natural cause. Except for *flirtation,* by the way, starvation is the oldest substantive in -ation formed on a native English verb."

"I suppose," I said with some sarcasm, "that you can give the date when flirtation was first used?"

"Certainly. Colley Cibber coined it in 1718. 'You know,' he wrote, 'I always loved a little flirtation.' "

I said desperately: "The acronym WASP, now—'white Anglo-Saxon Protestant'— was coined by a Pennsylvania sociologist named—let me see—"

"E. Digby Baltzell. *The Protestant Establishment.* 1964. Page 71."

All in all, it was a humiliating lunch.

(Other words originating on date certain are listed in the back of the book.)

17 DECEMBER

Manon? Mais Non!

The following ballade is built on a series of formidable quibbles by Boris Randal on operatic compositions and composers:

MANON? MAIS NON (*A Punning Ballade*)

Aida relish cymbal-smack,
   Horn-sweetness, shrill of piccolo
(To savor these, how Offenbach
   To Bach and Offenbach I go!) ...
Or don't. I *hate* Manon Lescaut.
(You said, "Lescaut to hear Manon:
   I've Boito tickets, second row ...")
Manon Lescaut a mauvais ton.

We go. Of Korsakov, and hack,
   As old men Lakme do; I blow
My nose, and doze. I'm in the sack
   From Faust plucked string to last *bravo*
   I dream I'm Chopin up that shmo
Puccini: *C'est un sale cochon.*
   Most art (Mozart, say) leaves a glow;
Manon Lescaut a mauvais ton.

Manon is Verdi vulgar pack
   Hangs out. If Massenet should throw
A Mass in A, I'd lead the claque.
   (Giovanni hear Giovanni? So
Do I. It's not quite *comme il faut,*
But Gudenov. *Alors, allons!*)
   Indeed, I only hate one show:
Manon Lescaut a mauvais ton.

Envoy

Prince, best of Gluck! ...
             One final *mot*:
   Though opera is mostly *bon,*
For Bizet folk there's one *de trop:*
Manon Lescaut a mauvais ton.
                 —*W.R.E.*

I call puns that require elaborate buildups Puns in Perpetuity. Here are two Puns in Perpetuity from Arnold Moss:

• Chan was a Chinese gentleman who discovered the footprints of a small boy in the sand that led to his prize collection of valuable teakwood. Night after night, pieces had been stolen. One night he discovered the culprit: a huge Siberian bear, wearing boy's shoes as he stealthily approached the wood, in an upright position. Whereupon Chan shouted: "I see who is the thief, boy-foot bear with teak of Chan!"

• A gentle Korean named Rhee worked for *Life* magazine. Sent out on a dangerous investigative mission, he disappeared. After a yearlong search he was finally discovered by a staff member who, on sighting him, said: "Ah, sweet Mr. Rhee of *Life,* at last I've found you."

18 DECEMBER

I'm Dreaming of a Black and White Christmas

The staff of the veterans' hospital at Boise, Idaho, found this wry communication in their mailboxes the week before Christmas·

MEMORANDUM
To: ALL OFFICE MANAGERS AND PERSONNEL
Subject: DECORATING OFFICES FOR CHRISTMAS

We have been informed by the office of Health, Education and Welfare that a White Christmas would be in violation of Title II of the Civil Rights Act, 1964. Therefore, the following steps are to be taken to insure that we comply with the Act during the Christmas season:

1. All Christmas trees must have at least 23.4% colored bulbs and they must be placed throughout the tree and not segregated in the back of the tree.
2. Christmas presents cannot be wrapped in white paper. However, interim approval can be given if colored ribbon is used to tie them.
3. If a manger scene is used, 20% of the angels and one of the three Kings must be of a minority race.
4. If Christmas music is played, "We Shall Overcome" must be given equal time. Under no circumstances is "I'm Dreaming of a White Christmas" to be played.
5. Care should be taken in party planning. For example:
   a. Use pink champagne instead of white.
   b. Turkey may be served, but only if the white and dark meat are on the same platter. There will be no separate but equal platters permitted.
   c. Use chocolate royale ice cream instead of vanilla.
   d. Both chocolate and white milk must be served; there will be no freedom of choice plan. Milk will be served without regard to color.

A team from HEW will visit us on December 25 to determine our compliance with the Act. If it snows on Christmas Eve, we are in a hell of a lot of trouble.

You may indicate compliance intentions and acknowledgment by returning initialed copy to me by enclosed envelope.

—From Carolyn S. Foote

19 DECEMBER

✓

The Faithful Connectors

John Alden, interceding with Priscilla for Miles Standish, was what is known in grammar as a Coordinating Conjunction—that is, a connector between two principals of equal rank. In Mr. Longfellow's poem, the Connector gets the girl; in the verse below, nobody gets anything.

> I summoned my Conjunctions;
>   They entered hand in hand,
> Obedient Connectors,
>   Awaiting my command.
>
> Subservient their greeting;
>   Respectful their hello;
> Their names were *And, But, For, Nor, Or,*
>   And part-time *Yes* and *So.*
>
> I said, "Now do your duty
>   As Seventh Parts of Speech!
> Restore my darling to me!
>   Connect us each with each!"
>
> Said *And,* "And how! And also
>   We'll make you man and wife!"
> Said *But,* "But we forewarn you,
>   You'll soon miss single life."
>
> Said *For,* "For never woman
>   To husband has been true."
> Said *Nor,* "Nor is this maxim
>   About to change for you."
>
> "Yet we will do our duty,"
>   Said *Yet,* and *Or* said, "Or
> At least we'll do our damnedest."
>   Said *So,* "So who asks more?"

*   *   *

> They crept back in the morning,
>   Connectors brave and good,
> With scratches on their faces,
>   And noses dripping blood.
>
> Their bumps and bruises told me
>   Without a sentence spoken—
> Between me and my darling,
>   Connections had been broken.
>
>   —*W.R.E.*

20 DECEMBER

Mistletoe Means Watch Out

A child's-eye view of Christmas is not always what an older person might expect. Two of Mike Collins's fourth-grade boys lacked the traditional spirit when it came to mistletoe:

- Mistletoe means watch out for slobry girls.
- The most dangerous thing about Christmas is standing underneath the kissletoe.

The children who wrote the following comments may grow up to be poets:

- A star is for living in heaven when it is not for wearing in a Christmas tree's hair.
- Christmas trees gives me joy feels all over.
- Pine trees give us Christmas and turpentine.

Mr. Collins's favorite Christmas reflection:

- Santa Claus lives just north of the imagination.

*   *   *   *   *

A Christmas card by a present-day master of word puzzles:

DOOLEY'S HATS

I suspected, of course, when I accepted the invitation to Donald Dooley's Yule party, that he was keeping something under his hat. The man loves nothing more than springing puzzles on surprised friends.

The night arrived. The party was going with the sound of golden oldies. Inebriants and potations were being poured freely, and consumed in the same spirit. And then—Dooley ducked into a side closet, to reappear triumphantly with ten hats and a word taped to the front of each. "Uh-oh," I said.

"Friends, gather round," said he, with an eye's twinkle like Santa's but a smile like Satan's. "I have a puzzle." And situating us in a circle, he paced the perimeter placing a hat on each guest's head. I could not see the word on my headpiece—in fact no one could see his own word—but I could see every other. Around the circle the words read: TENNIS. PAINT. WHITE. GREASE. OFF. ELBOW. BRUSH. TABLE. CARD.

I thought one person grinned slightly when he glanced at my word.

"What's this nonsense about a puzzle?" asked one overpixilated lady.

"It is a puzzle of logic and word sense," Dooley responded, but speaking to all of us. "You each have a hat with a word and full view of everyone else. Your goal is to be the first person to guess his word successfully."

"Any clues?" asked the man next to me.

"Yes," Dooley said. "There is a pattern among the words which becomes apparent once they are placed in proper sequence. If you can discover that pattern and put the words in order, naming your own will follow naturally."

Reaching for paper and pencil on the center table before me, I prodded my besotted gray matter into action. Several minutes later I exultantly blurted out my answer.

WHAT WAS MY WORD?

—Will Shortz

21 DECEMBER

Bring on Your Cat

I could do fine without whiskey or wine, as long as my doctor did not order me to stop writing jingles about them:

WHEN HE HAD DRUNK, HIS SPIRIT CAME AGAIN
(Judges XVI:19)

If you'll agree that "Catholic" and "alcoholic" rhyme,
I'll write a song to cheer us all until the end of time:
We'll sing it in the church by day, and each emerge a monk;
We'll sing it in the bars by night, and each drop
    down dead drunk.

—W.R.E.

SONG OF A HAPPY MAN

I sit, I type, I sip, I type,
I sip, I nip, tip-tapping tripe,
I tip, I sype, I pip, I pipe,
Tip-pip all day, sip-pip all night,
Tip-pipping—hic—tap-tipping tripe.

—W.R.E.

Theodore S. Abbott sent this:

BRING ON YOUR CAT

The liquor was spilled on the barroom floor
And the bar was closed for the night
When out of his house came a little gray
    mouse
And sat in the pale moonlight.

He lapped up the liquor from the barroom floor
And back on his haunches sat
And all night long you could hear him sing
"Bring on the gol-darn cat."
                                    —*Anonymous*

22 DECEMBER

ƀ

There Is a Needle in the Bag

Nationality transforms truth, or at least it would appear so from these matching proverbs:

ENGLISH	FRENCH	SPANISH	JAPANESE	ARABIC	GERMAN
Little drops of water make the mighty ocean.	Little by little the bird makes his nest.	Little by little the cup is filled.	Dust may pile to form a hill.	A hair from here and there makes a beard.	Steady dripping hollows a stone.
Everyone has a right to his own opinion.	Everyone to his own taste.	Everyone has his own way of killing fleas.	Ten men, ten colors.	Every person is free in his opinions.	Don't quarrel about tastes.
Look before you leap.	Turn the tongue seven times; then speak.	Think before speaking.	Have an umbrella before getting wet.	Before you drink the soup, blow on it.	First weigh; then dare.
There is something rotten in Denmark.	There is an eel under the rock.	There is a cat shut up.	There is a worm in the lion's body.	There is a snake under the hay.	There is something foul in Denmark.
Don't count your chickens before they're hatched.	Don't sell the bear-skin before you kill the bear.	Don't saddle before bringing the horses.	Before you kill badgers, don't count their skins.	Don't say "lima beans" before they are weighed.	Don't hang people before you have caught them.

23 DECEMBER
ᛏ

Why the Heaths Didn't Have This Year's Christmas Carol Program

Do you know what *afforient* is? Neither did I till I heard Priscilla, who is fifteen and who should know better, sweetly warble that she three kings afforient were, and I asked her. *Afforient,* if you are interested, is the state of being disoriented, or wandering, as one does over field and fountain, moor and mountain.

And has anybody ever wondered where the Ranger is on Christmas Eve? Well, Betsey Heath has. "*Away* is the Ranger," she will inform you, if you listen carefully. And obviously, he is away because there is no crib for his bed. After all, why should the Ranger stick around *here,* when he hasn't even got a crib much less a bed for Pete's sake!

Janet, canny little Janet, all of whose sins are premeditated and blatant, sang exactly what she intended to sing. "*No L, No L the angels did say.*" It was a matter of the angels' alphabet, she explained to me a little tiredly, "A B C D E F G H I J K M N O P Q R S T U V W X Y Z. No L, *get it, Mother? No L!*" I eyed her suspiciously, because more humor in the family we do not need, but I let it pass.

Jennifer settled my next problem, which had to do with the angels. Do you know how the angel of the Lord shone around? He shone around in a glowy manner, that's how. While shepherds watch'd their flock by night, she explained, the angel of the Lord came and glowy showed around. How else?

Pam, even Pam, kept announcing in her clear, sweet contralto that God and sin are reconciled, but she realized immediately, when it was pointed out to her, that God was far more likely to reconcile Himself to sinners than to sin.

Jim had to argue a little. He was the one who kept urging the shepherds to leave their "you's" and leave their "am's" and rise up, shepherds, and follow.

"What in heaven's name is this about you's and am's?" I asked him.

"Oh-h, rejection of personality, denial of self," said Jim grandly. "Practically the central thesis of Christian theology."

"I think that's Communist theory, not Christian theology," I told him. "In any case, could you come down from those philosophic heights and join us shepherds down here with our ewes (female sheep) and rams (male sheep)?"

But I was too weary to go on. "Children," I said. "Let's just do one thing absolutely *perfectly.* Let's concentrate on 'Silent Night,' because that's the one we know best anyway. Pam and Priscilla can do the alto, John can do the descant, the rest of you just sing nice and softly, and, Buckley, I don't want to hear one single *note* below middle C."

They lined up, looking very clean and handsome and holy.

"*Silent night, holy night,*" nine young voices chanted softly, and I noticed Jennifer and Betsey beginning to break up in twinkles and dimples. "*All is calm, all is bright,*" they went on, John's recorder piping low and clear. Buckley and Alison clapped their hands briefly over their mouths. "*Round John Virgin, Mother and*

Child," the chorus swelled sweetly, and I rapped hard on the piano. "Just *who*," I asked in my most restrained voice, "is Round John Virgin?"

"One of the twelve opossums," the young voices answered promptly, and they collapsed over the piano, from the piano bench into the floor, convulsed by their own delicate wit.

And that's why we didn't have this year's Christmas carol program.

—*Aloïse Buckley Heath*

TROPING THE TEXT

Altar boys have been known to sing "All wipe your noses" for "Ora pro nobis." This is known as "troping the text," and it is exactly what the wicked Heath children were doing in the forgoing account. Mrs. R. E. Guppy sent me these tropes:

- Donzerly light.
- While shepherds washed their socks by night.
- Land where the pilgrims died, land where the pigeons flied.
- We three kings of Oregon are.
- Wreck the halls with boughs of holly.
- One for his master, one for his dame, one for the little boy who lives down the drain.

In the Episcopalian Collect which begins ". . . We pray thee that thy grace may always prevent and follow us," *prevent* is from Latin *prevenio,* "to go before." The Sunday before Advent is known as Stirrup Sunday because of the opening words of the Collect: "Stir up, we beseech thee."

—*Faith Eckler*

24 DECEMBER
℔

Improbable Eponyms

A person's name, if applied to a place, thing, quality, or such becomes an eponym. Thus Brutus and Italus, both mythical characters, are the eponyms of Britain and Italy; Europa, the beloved of Zeus the bull, is the eponym of Europe. The eponyms below were submitted by a friend I call Mishmash. They should be considered in the mythical category:

Raunchy. The word comes from Gianfranco Ronci, a *pasticciere* in the kitchen of a restaurant in Bologna in 1928, who was imprisoned for a violent assault upon the maître d'hôtel. The cook claimed that the maître d's words—"*I canneloni soni veramente ronci ancora!*"—amounted to intolerable provocation.

Slalom. Memorializes the deftness of Count Heinrich von Slalom, scion

of an impoverished cadet branch of the Hapsburgs, in running his bank
account and kiting his checks.

Spinnaker. About to be overtaken by Barbary pirates, the Dutch sea
captain Cornelius Peterszoon van Spinnaker ordered every possible bit of
cloth bent to the spar and himself added to the locomotion by shaking out
a pair of capacious and silken bloomers he was bringing home for Mev-
rouw v. Spinnaker.

—George Movshon

25 DECEMBER

Song for a Season

OYSTERVILLE—A week ahead, give or take a day, my father would lead Ed and
me into the woods to help him find a properly worshipful Christmas tree. The tree
was generally spruce, but occasionally pine or fir. It had to stand no less than ten and
no more than thirteen feet, to accommodate our living room. Papa was a perfec-
tionist. He would reject one promising tree after another because a branch thrust out
too far or because he saw insufficient fullness near the trunk. The chosen sacrifice
came home with us butt first, dragged ignominiously on its side. Later, inside the
house and upright again, its self-esteem was restored by Mama, who placed the candles (never lighted until Christmas Eve) and hung the garlands of strung cranberries
and chains of bright paper.

In 1923, I think it was, Papa dug up a tree by the roots instead of chopping it
down. After the holidays we planted it in a corner of the yard, where for years it
stood without growing; it came to be called the dwarf spruce. Then the roots tapped
some deep water source, and the tree shot up. It now overshadows our house; when
the telephone company or the electric company needs to string wires, they have to
cut avenues through its branches.

I offer this acrostic verse in celebration of the Christmas season:

SONG FOR A SEASON

Now, a little while,
　From the care and cark,
Something like a smile
　Shimmers in the dark.

Zephyr's scented art
　Dwindles rime and snow;
In a melted heart,
　Softly, flowers grow.

Joy, a moment now,
　Thumps old Sorrow's side;

> Under festive bough
>   Nemesis has died.
>
> Brief, by iron laws,
>   Though this magic be,
> Unbeliever, pause:
>   Pagan, bend your knee.
>
> Zest as keen as this
>   Pricks the sullen soul;
> Vast polarities
>   Blend in vaster whole.
>
> Mark—the night is through.
> Memory must do.
>   —W.R.E.

Being in a mellow holiday mood, I do not call on you to solve that acrostic. Frankly I doubt whether you would. So I give the secret away: Replace the first letter of each line with the letter that precedes it in the alphabet. The message shines out as clear as a star:

MERRY CHRISTMAS TO YOU ALL

MERRY

> Merry, merry, rest you merry,
>   Merry, merry rest you—
> On this merry midnight, Mary
>   Merrily has blessed you.
>
> Merrily the shepherds gather,
>   Hailing heavenly host;
> Merry, merry dance the Father,
>   Son, and Holy Ghost.
>   —W.R.E.

26 DECEMBER

Showoff Words

I pass on a formula of which I made good use in the days when I was writing promotion for the cover pages of *Reader's Digest*:

To communicate and convince, write pithily, in the active voice. But to impress your authority, throw in one longer, exotic word—for instance, *karimata,* a two-headed Japanese arrow that whistles while it works—even if it has nothing to do with the point you are making. More than one showoff word, though, can become counterproductive, as you see here:

IF FROM HYPOBULA YOU USE

If from Hypobula you use
    A Dysphemism to
Engross your love's attention,
    The gesture you may rue;
Should your Hircismus bait her nose,
    She'll drive you from love's feasts
To crowd into a Savssat
    With all the other beasts.
                                        —W.R.E.

Ward Byron, by the way, insists that a crèche is the sound of a Hanukkah tree falling over.

27 DECEMBER

♄

The Gaiety of Graves

Robert Graves irritates the literary establishment. He thinks for himself. "Robert Graves, the British veteran, is no longer in the poetic swim," wrote a New York critical weekly. "He still resorts to traditional metres and rhyme, and to such out-dated words as *tilth;* withholding his 100% approbation also from contemporary poems that favor sexual freedom."

The poet replied:

> Gone are the drab monosyllabic days
> When "agricultural labour" still was *tilth*;
> And "100% approbation," *praise*;
> And "pornographic modernism," *filth*—
> Yet still I stand by *tilth* and *filth* and *praise*.

His metaphors can knock your breath out:

> Love without hope, as when the young bird-catcher
> Swept off his tall hat to the Squire's own daughter,
> So let the imprisoned larks escape and fly
> Singing about her head, as she rode by.

His next quatrain reminds me of the story that by the time Robert Benchley realized he could not write he was making too much money to stop:

EPITAPH ON AN UNFORTUNATE ARTIST

> He found a formula for drawing comic rabbits;
>   The formula for drawing comic rabbits paid,
> So in the end he could not change the tragic habits
>   This formula for drawing comic rabbits made.

Small events may bring great consequences; for want of a nail the kingdom was lost. But Mr. Graves reminds us in *Goodbye to All That* that the consequences of a mistake are not always earthshaking:

> Because of a rumoured invasion of the north-east coast, all fit men of the Third Garrison were ordered to move at twenty-four hours' notice to York. A slight error, however, occurred in the Morse message from War Office to Western Command. Instead of dash-dot-dash-dash, they sent dash-dot-dash-dot; so the Battalion was sent to Cork instead, where, on second thoughts, it seemed just as much needed as in York, so there it stayed for the remainder of the War.

My jingle here comes down on Graves's side:

LINES TO A CONTEMPORARY POET

You scratch.
Take three:
From which
Derives the itch?:
Society? ...
Or *flea?* ...
Or *thee?*
Thee, natch.
—*W.R.E.*

28 DECEMBER

♄

More Odd Ends

None of these jottings deserves a separate entry, but I like the way they bubble together in the pot:

- Kakistocracy is government by the worst men. Or women, one assumes.
- Ulochtricous means "kinky-haired."

—*Arnold Moss*

In this game for a quiet evening, the first player asks a question, to be defined by the answer:

- Do you know what procrastination is?
  I've been meaning to look it up.
- Do you know what conciseness is?
  Yes.
- Do you know what irritability is?
  Stop bothering me with silly questions.

—*Jane R. Barliss*

Time magazine here defines *Btfsplkian,* as in this quotation from the magazine: "Yakubovsky has a Btfsplkian habit of turning up just before something big happens":

> Btfsplkian (unpronounceable) *adj.* [Neologism, from Joe Btfsplk, a cartoon character in Al Capp's *Li'l Abner* who is accompanied by a little black cloud of disaster wherever he goes] 1: Full of bad luck and imminent mishap for anyone in the vicinity. 2: Baleful; calamitous; pernicious; unpropitious; as in "Joe Btfsplk attended a sailing party for the *Andrea Doria.*"

Dr. Johnson said he advised young people to rise early, but slept in until noon himself. He would have admired Hungarian author Ferenc Molnàr, so unaccustomed to early rising that when called for morning jury duty, he gawked from his hansom cab at the thronged streets of Budapest, marveling, "Are they *all* jurors?"

John K. Spencer copied these reflections from the wall of a men's room at a divinity school:

(The first)   Eternity is forever.
(The second)   Better bring an extra pair of socks.

Kim Garretson says these graffiti were written in three hands:

To do is to be.   *John Stuart Mill*
To be is to do.   *Jean Paul Sartre*
Do be, Do be, Do.   *Frank Sinatra*

"I have just turned sixty," writes Elizabeth L. Stanley, "and am referred to as an 'older' woman. Yet an 'old' woman is actually someone older than that. And the word *oldest* can refer to a child of five who has younger siblings."
New dictionary definitions might help:
old: older than older
oldest: younger than older, but older than younger
You're looking very well: has the date been set for your funeral service?

29 DECEMBER
♄

With Fading Breath

It was 1635, and the sorrowers grouped about the bedside of dying Spanish dramatist Lope de Vega warned him that he was slipping away fast. "All right, then," he whispered, "I'll say it. Dante makes me sick."
A priest asked Ramón María Narváez, statesman-general to Queen Isabella of Spain, whether he forgave his enemies. "I don't have to," he replied. "I've had them all shot."

Herbert Hoover, celebrating his eightieth birthday at the Dutch Treat Club, declared he felt no remnants of bitterness toward the political enemies who had savaged him in the White House. "I am reminded," he went on, "of the old man who got shakily to his feet when the preacher asked, 'Is there anyone in this congregation with no bitterness in his heart for a single human being? Behold, my dear brethren,' exclaimed the preacher, 'a man whose heart holds only love! Tell me, sir—how did this happen?' 'I outlived the sons of bitches,' quavered the old man."

It is not true, as often stated, that Oscar Wilde called for champagne and said, "I am dying as I lived—beyond my means." A more likely account is that he breathed his last in a miserable room, with a priest imploring him to recant his past wickedness. Wilde turned his face to the peeling wallpaper, and said, "One of us has to go." With that he expired.

I have heard, but doubt extremely, that the last words of Gertrude Lawrence, star of *The King and I*, were: "See that Yul Brynner gets star billing. He deserves it."

Nor would I place too much credence in the last words given here:

- Boswell: I believe, if I could again visit Corsica, I might recover.
- Jane Austen: I wish I had someone to smile with me.
- Mrs. Eddy: Impossible!
- Berkeley: What matter, my friends, that I must leave you? There is no matter.
- Dr. Bowdler: A. I have purged.
                B. Had I but lived to purify the scriptures!
                C. Macbeth: Three, One, Twenty-nine, delete "bloody."
- Mae West: Turn off that red light.
- Casanova: Your lips are cold, madam.
- Donne: I am un-Done!
- Nero: I shall burn while Rome fiddles.
- Stalin: Doctor, quick, another purge!
- Sullivan: I must compose myself.
- Shakespeare: A. Don't let Ben mess around with my plays.
                B. My second-best bed! The rest is silence.
    (dies, chuckling)

30 DECEMBER
♄

For I Dipt into the Future, Far as Human Eye Could See,
Saw a World where Verbs and Nouns Agree to Disagree

I made some prescient prophecies about the future of the English language for *The People's Almanac*'s new *Book of Predictions*. Since this is the time of year for looking ahead, I here borrow back these forecasts.

By 1992

• The proportion of functionally illiterate Americans will rise to 27%.

• Highway and direction signs will have have diversified into rudimentary hieroglyphics. (The first popular novel in sign language will appear in 1989.)

• In 1987, nouns and verbs will agree to disagree.

• In 1988, the National Academy of Arts and Sciences will propose that Americans begin dropping ten words a day from their vocabularies to make the language more democratic. Twelve percent of the nation will be silenced in the first week.

• In 1989, language sports will replace baseball. National League teams will be Sister-Speak, Split-Talk, Black English, Gay Lingo, Standard English, Body English, and Banggangsprache.

By 2030

• The proportion of functionally illiterate Americans will peak at 47%.

• Chinese scholars will begin instructing American educators in the art of combining direction signs so as to convey complex ideas. ☜, ("this way"), will merge with ☞ ("that way") to make ☜☞, meaning, "Can't you make up your mind?"

• In 2027, the Supreme Court will decide that nouns and verbs that continue to agree are in restraint of trade.

• In 2023, Congress will determine that all legislative proceedings shall be conducted in 17th-century French.

• In 2030, Standard English will wind up in the cellar for the fortieth consecutive year.

☜   ☞

31 DECEMBER
♭

Year-End Interview

Q. Looking at yourself objectively, Mr. Espy, sir, what would you say is your outstanding characteristic?

A. Oh—modesty.

Q. And what has held you back most?

A. Modesty.

Q. Who would you say is the finest writer in English?

A. No comment. Modesty, you know.

Q. Let me broaden the question, sir. Of all the books you have ever read, which do you consider the finest?

A. Sorry, it is not quite finished.

Q. And the finest writer?

A. Won't you reporters ever allow a fellow any privacy?

Q. Would you name your favorite composer—Bach, Beethoven, Handel, that sort of thing?

A. I have never taken up that line of work. But to answer your question—Dick Hyman, the jazz man. No doubt of it.

Q. Would you explain?

A. He is putting my verses to music. Once I have heard them, I will be glad to tell you my favorite musical composition.

Q. What is your favorite city, Mr. Espy?

A. Oysterville, Washington. Subject of one of the outstanding books of our time.

Q. Who is the author?

A. No comment. Modesty, you know.

Q. Which Broadway play have you enjoyed most this season?

A. It has been a bad year. But did you see me on Johnny Carson?

Q. Is it true that you have proposed your birthday be made a national holiday?

A. Someone had to suggest it.

Q. Let us turn to matters of national concern, sir. Are you worried about the size of the deficit?

A. You should see *my* bills.

Q. Do you make New Year resolutions, Mr. Espy?

A. One. Every year.

Q. Would you mind telling me what it is?

A. It is "Let sleeping dogs lie."

Q. Forgive me for mentioning this, sir, but you look a bit seedy. Who will speak at your memorial service?

A. No problem. I will.

Q. One last question, sir. Are you going to a New Year's Eve party tonight?

A. No. Nobody has invited me.

Q. I see. Thank you, sir.

A note on years past and years to come:

BUZZ AND BIZZ

Buzz and bizz and bizz and buzz,
Bee and mee, that's how it was.
Bizz and buzz and buzz and bizz,
Bee and mee, that's how it izz.
No more bizz-buzz, bee or mee;
That's the way that it will bee.

—*W.R.E.*

Be off now to your holiday celebrations. As to me, I'm off to bed. But I'll wake at midnight just long enough to wish every one of you, from the top and bottom of my heart:

HAPPY NEW YEAR!

Answers and Solutions

1 JANUARY — *For Starters, a Happy New Year!*

The zodiacal months:

♑	Capricornus, the Goat	December 22–January 20
♒	Aquarius, the Water-carrier	January 21–February 18
♓	Pisces, the Fishes	February 19–March 20
♈	Aries, the Ram	March 21–April 20
♉	Taurus, the Bull	April 21–May 21
♊	Gemini, the Twins	May 22–June 21
♋	Cancer, the Crab	June 22–July 22
♌	Leo, the Lion	July 23–August 23
♍	Virgo, the Virgin	August 24–September 23
♎	Libra, the Balance	September 24–October 23
♏	Scorpio, the Scorpion	October 24–November 22
♐	Sagittarius, the Archer	November 23–December 21

14 JANUARY — *First Lines*

Tom Sawyer, by Mark Twain.

1. L	4. I	7. N	10. H	13. F	16. K	19. Q
2. J	5. O	8. C	11. D	14. E	17. T	20. R
3. M	6. P	9. S	12. B	15. A	18. U	21. G

28 JANUARY — *John Hancocks*

1. Andrew Young	7. Alexandre Dumas	13. David Niven
2. Marlene Dietrich	8. Marshal Tito	14. Cary Grant
3. Moshe Dayan	9. Yul Brynner	15. Guy Lombardo
4. Robert Redford	10. Rudolf Nureyev	16. Sophia Loren
5. Henry A. Kissinger	11. Al Pacino	17. Marcel Marceau
6. H. R. Haldeman	12. Walter Mondale	18. James Cagney

29 JANUARY — *Some Are Right*

1. True. 2. True. 3. True. 4. False. *Gibberish* apparently stems echoically from *jabber,* itself derived from the Middle English *jaberen,* a word imitating fast, indistinct chatter. 5. True. 6. True. 7. True. 8. False. Ketchup simply anglicizes the Chinese *ke-tsiap,* a sauce for meat, fish, etc. 9. False. Marmalade derives from the Portuguese *marmelo* ("quince"), which in turn comes from the Latin *melimelum* ("sweet apple"). 10. True. 11. True.

9 FEBRUARY — *Variable Verbs*

1. The batter flied out to center field.
2. They hanged the cattle rustler.
3. When spring arrived, the trees leaved.
4. Chris Evert letted three consecutive serves.
5. An enthusiastic crowd ringed the speaker.
6. The aspiring executive shined his shoes every morning.
7. They spitted the pig and then roasted it.
8. The farmer sticked the vines so that they would grow straight.
9. He treaded water until help arrived.
10. The car weaved its way through heavy traffic.

10 FEBRUARY   *Twisted Proverbs*

1. Every dog has his day.
2. Don't put all your eggs in one basket.
3. Least said soonest mended.
4. The proof of the pudding is in the eating.

5. When in Rome do as the Romans do.
6. Birds of a feather flock together.
7. The pot calls the kettle black.

12 FEBRUARY   *Anguish Languish*

Lincoln's Gettysburg Address scarcely needs repeating.

A POEM

When first you scan this silly rhyme
   To try to make the meaning clear,
You think 'twould but be wasting time
   You say, "It's simply nonsense sheer!"

No matter; analyze a line!
   Nay, shun my slender verses not—
For cryptic poetry like mine,
                    means a lot.

26 FEBRUARY   *To My Greek Mistress*

With many a sigh I ate a pie   PSI PI
   That you had baked, my dear;
This torpor new I owe to you—   NU IOTA
   I'm feeling very queer.

O fie O fie upon your pie!—   PHI PHI PI
   You dealt a cruel blow!   DELTA
Your dreadful pie has made me cry;   PI CHI
   My tears fall in a row.   RHO

I would have lammed another lass   LAMBDA
   Who baked that pie, I vow;   PI
But still I moo and moo for you,   MU MU
   As sick as any cow.

6 MARCH   *Red Hot*

1. Red tape
2. International Red Cross
3. Red herring
4. Red Grange
5. Little Red Riding Hood
6. Cincinnati Red Stockings
7. Red Sea

8. "The Masque of the Red Death"
9. Red Barber
10. "The Red-Headed League"
11. Redwood
12. See red
13. Helen Reddy
14. *Redbook*

15. "Red sky at morning . . ."
16. *The Red Shoes*
17. Red Square
18. Red-blooded
19. Redcap
20. "Rudolph the Red-nosed Reindeer"

13 MARCH   *My Name Is Ozymandias*
An image over whose feet of clay
One trips eternally down to this day.

24 MARCH   *Up and Down Counting Song*

Dear ewe, dear lamb, I've won thee: we
Will tootle through the fields together;
With reed and pipe we'll jubilee;
We'll gambol back and forth in glee;
If I've your heart, who gives a D.
How raw and sick's the weather?
In seventh heaven me and thee
Will late and soon find ecstasy—
My ewe benign is tied to me,
And tender is the tether!

Yet there may be a tendency
(Someday when I no more know whether
You wait for me still longingly
Or find our love less heavenly)
For you in classic sulk to flee—
Off I've no doubt to new bellwether
And fresher forage . . . It may be
We'll both require a style more free,
And find the bird of love to be
Reduced to one Pinfeather.

27 MARCH   *Schizophrenic Words*

Infantry means "a body of children." *Infatuate* means "frustrate." *Inhabited* means "uninhabited." *Inroad* means "raid," and so does *outroad*. *Invaluable* means both "priceless" and "worthless." *Jack* means "quarter pint" but also "half pint." *Juror* means "false witness." *King* means "queen bee." *Lap* means "bosom." (2). *Law* means "thieving." *Let* means "prevent." *Mahound* means "Mohammed," but also "the devil." *Maness* means "woman." *Mankind* means both "mad" and "savage." *Midmorn* means "9 A.M." *Moody* means "brave." *Mythometer* means "a measure for judging myths." *Nephew* means "niece" (2b). *Nice* means "foolish," "silly," "stupid," "simple," "ignorant," "lewd," "lascivious," "wanton," "strange," "uncommon," and "weak." *Noon* means "midnight" (3a). *Novantique* means "new, yet old." *Nutty* means "fascinating." *Orient* means both "blue" and "bright red." *Palace* means "cellar." *Peculiar* means "wife" (1d). *Philematology* means "the science of kissing." *Politician* means "schemer." *Practical* means "unscrupulous." *Precious* means "worthless," "poor," and "bad." *Rat* means "cat." *Ravel* means both "entangle" and "disentangle." *Resolute* means "firm" but also "infirm." *Restive* means "inactive," but also "fidgety." *Riddle* means "unriddle." *Rout* means "assemble." *Ruffian* means "paramour." *Sad* means both "satisfied" (1) and "bad" (9). *Scot* means "Irishman." *Sevenbark* means "ninebark." *Several* means "single," "an item," and "an individual." *She* means "he." *Shower* means "drops about 1/25 inch in diameter and falling at the velocity of 10 to 25 feet per second." *Sinople* means both "blood red" and "green." *Sinus* means "bosom." *Sit* means "stand." *Sleeveless* means "bootless." *Snob* means "one not an aristocrat." *Snug* means "sizable." *Stand* means "lie flat" (17). *Supermuscan* means "above the power of a fly." *Sweat* means "dry thoroughly." *Thrill* means "bore." *Tickle* means "whip" and "chastise." *Tonight* means "last night." *Twosome* means "single." *Undercool* means "supercool." *Undercreep* means "overreach." *Undertake* means "overtake." *Undoctor* means "to make unlike a doctor." *Universal* means "local." *Unrelentless* means "relentless." *Unremorseless* means "remorseless." *Unrude* means "rude." *Unslip* means "slip." *Upright* means "supine." *Vile* means "great." *Wan* means "dark black." *Widow* means "widower." *Wonder* means "admiration," but also "evil." *Wrist* means "ankle."

—Tom Pulliam

3 APRIL   *Can You Top This?*

1. . . . you're too drunk to sing."
2. . . . pulled a small mirror from her handbag, glanced in it, and with relief said, "Yes, it's me all right."
3. . . . a picture of a mouse.
4. . . . it was ridiculous. The house was full of animals.
5. . . . the third cross-eyed prisoner said, "I didn't say anything."
6. . . . Make up your mind, lady, I've got to know which way to tilt this chair."
7. . . . Half past four."
8. . . . the mud fell off.
9. . . . I don't know. I never bathed any."
10. . . . I just hate it when the children play inside."
11. . . . I'll buy you another dog."
12. . . . Santa, what do you need?"
13. . . . escalator.
14. . . . parked car.
15. . . . I didn't know my father could hit that hard.
16. . . . Get under my couch."
17. . . . Penicillin.
18. . . . 'This is the greatest wreck you'll ever see.' "
19. . . . be careful when accepting bribes.

10 APRIL   *What Is the Word for #?*

1. Number.
2. Pounds.
3. Space.
4. Sharp.
5. Tic-tac-toe.
6. Octothorp.
7. Non-add.
8. Fracture.

11 APRIL   *Kicking the Bucket*

1. *Apple pie* is a hobson-jobson for *nappe plié*, French for "neatly folded linen."
2. *Egg* corrupts "edge."
3. *Hoot* was originally *iota*, the least consequential Greek letter.
4. The French name for the frame scaffold on which animals are hung for slaughtering, and which they kick in their death agony, is *buchet*, which in English turned to *bucket*.
5. A Greek word meaning honey was carried into English as *meal*, so *mealymouthed* is perhaps *honeymouthed*; but plain old *meal*, ground grain, has a claim, too.
6. *Round robin* is from French *rond ruban*, "round ribbon."

17 APRIL   *Up Here in the (9)*

A. (1) a (2) pa (3) ape (4) peas (5) sepia (6) praise (7) despair (8) paradise (9) disappear

B. (1) O (2) on (3) one (4) nose (5) stone (6) honest (7) thrones (8) another's (9) northeast

19 APRIL   *Private? No!*

1. Said I, "I said you said I said 'said.' " Said he, "Who said I said you said 'said?' I said said is said '*said.*' Said is not said 'Said' like Said."*
2. That that is, is; that that is not, is not. Is not that it? It is.
3. The murderer protested his innocence. An hour after, he was put to death.
4. He said that that 'that' that that man said was correct.

28 APRIL   *Don't Quote Me*

1. Backward, turn backward, O Time, in your flight.—*Elizabeth Akers Allen*
2. How dear to this heart are the scenes of my childhood.—*Samuel Woodworth*
3. Nor any drop to drink.—*Coleridge*
4. I knew him, Horatio.—*Shakespeare*
5. Tall oaks from little acorns grow.—*David Everett*
6. Breathes there the man, with soul so dead.—*Sir Walter Scott*
7. 'Twas the night before Christmas, when all through the house.—*Clement Clarke Moore*

4 MAY   *Odd Ends*

Mercury, Jupiter.

12 MAY   *Philander Is a Wallaby*

If you marked every one of the definitions correct, you were 100 percent right.

24 MAY   *Recovered Charades*

1. The first six lines are answered by the words *Bed, Oh, Sin, Tobacco, Oak,* and *Noun.* The initial letters of the word spell *Boston,* the name of the city where the magazine was published.
2. Mite, time.

12 JUNE   *Unmailed Letter*

I am too timorous for my own good. After I had decided not to send this letter—it was actually written 2 September, 1977—I found the following in the *Times* (16 March, 1980):

"Sir,—I am at present engaged in research for a book on the life and work of Kenneth Tynan, and I would be very grateful to hear from anyone who has letters, anecdotes, reminiscences, and other biographical information that might be helpful.

"Any material submitted will be safely guarded and promptly returned."

The letter was signed: Kenneth Tynan.

*Said, the Egyptian port, is pronounced Sah-eed.

13 JUNE — *Jack Be Nimble*

1. Jack-of-all-trades
2. Applejack
3. Jackknife
4. Hit the jackpot
5. Blackjack
6. Jack-in-the-box
7. Lumberjack
8. Union Jack
9. Crackerjack
10. Jackson Five
11. Jackstraws or jacks
12. Jack Frost
13. Jackrabbit
14. Straitjacket
15. Jackhammer
16. Jumping jacks
17. Jack-in-the-pulpit
18. Flapjack

17 JUNE — *Collegiate Quiz*

1. Purdue
2. Columbia
3. Rutgers
4. Bryn Mawr
5. Villanova
6. Bowdoin
7. Harvard
8. Mount Holyoke
9. Duke
10. Yale
11. Vassar
12. Amherst
13. Oberlin
14. Howard
15. Yeshiva
16. Barnard
17. Berkeley
18. Swarthmore
19. Vanderbilt
20. Wellesley

20 JUNE — *Y Is X a Y of Y?*

1. Ilk is a kind of a kind. [I prefer a name of a name.—*W.R.E.*]
2. House construction is the building of a building.
3. Greta's clothes are the garb of Garbo. (A little tricky?)
4. An ale steward is a porter of porter.
5. Paying the check is a tender of tender.
6. Bunches of partly eaten apples are corps of cores.
7. Policemen hiding in the woods are a copse of cops.
8. A silver-covered dish is a plate of plate.
9. Clothing storage for undergarments is drawers for drawers.
10. Put mother's sister up for a gambling stake is ante of Auntie.

3 JULY — *A Troop of Tropes*

1. . . . without benefit of clergy (euphemism).
2. . . . curio (apocope). Loss of a final letter or syllable; *curio* shortens *curiosity*.
3. . . . Crown (metonymy). Substitution of a suggestive word for the name of the thing meant, as "The White House" for the Administration or the President.
4. . . . the Borscht Circuit (periphrasis). A circumlocution, as "The year's penultimate month."
5. . . . said Tom, meteorologically (Tom Swifty).
6. . . . carried away by elation and a large airplane (zeugma or syllepsis). The use of a verb or adjective with two different words, to only one of which it strictly applies.
7. . . . calling her Ducky (hypocorism). Use of pet names, nursery rhymes, diminutives, etc.
8. . . . boondocks (exoticism; from the Philippines). Other familiar exoticisms (oxymoronically speaking) are *pajamas* and *jungles*.
9. . . . how pleasant so ever (tmesis). Slicing a word or phrase to insert something: "I saw her some bloody where."
10. . . . "threads" (synecdoche). The use of a part for a whole, or the reverse: "hands" for "workmen," "purple" for "royal," etc.
11. . . . naïvely (diaeresis). The pronunciation of two successive vowels as separate sounds rather than as a single vowel or dipthong. Viz., "Chloe."
12. . . . their limbs (Bowdlerism). Prudish expurgation, so called after Thomas Bowdler, who published an expurgated Shakespeare.
13. . . . it's a beautiful world (hysteron proteron). Reversal of natural order of ideas, as in "For God, for Country, and for Yale."
14. . . . not bad, eh? (litotes). Affirming a thing by denying its contrary, as when a father comments on his son's straight A average at college, "that's pretty fair."
15. . . . forever grateful (hyperbole). Use of exaggerated terms to emphasize rather than deceive.
16. . . . the old bag (dysphemism). Use of a disparaging term to describe something inoffensive.
17. . . . she'd turn over in her grave if she were alive today (catachresis). Deliberately paradoxical figure of speech.

18. ...a wave like a watery giant (simile). A figurative comparison, usually introduced by "like" or "as."

19. ...'way (aphesis). Loss of an initial syllable or letter.

20. ...the gull's territory (kenning). Almost synonymous with periphrasis, as in Scandinavian "the sea of the blood" for "body" and "wound-engraver" for "the point of a sword."

21. ...hissed (onomatopoeia). The fitting of sound to sense: *buzz, moo, choo-choo*, etc.

22. ...the Sunday punch of an expert (metaphor). A figure in which a comparison or identity is implied: "She is a tigress."

23. ...Well, I never! (ellipsis). Omission of a word or words necessary to complete the sense. The full expression might have been: "Well, I never did see such a thing!"

23 JULY   *Picture Names*

1. Harry Reasoner   2. Carrie Fisher   3. Dick Van Dyke   4. Catfish Hunter

28 JULY   *More John Hancocks*

1. Frédéric Chopin
2. Charles Dickens
3. Napoleon
4. Mussolini

5. Mary Queen of Scots
6. Arturo Toscanini
7. John F. Kennedy

8. Lord Byron
9. Adolf Hitler
10. Toulouse-Lautrec

23 AUGUST   *Charades Again*

1. Cats 'n' dogs, Datsun cogs.
2. Saturday night, satyr denied.

3. Schenectady, da neck ta ski.
4. Precipitation, prissy potation.

24 AUGUST   *Back and Forth*

1. BIB
2. EVE
3. ANNA
4. DEED
5. OTTO

6. NOON
7. TOOT
8. PEEP
9. RADAR
10. LEVEL

11. MADAM
12. REFER
13. SHAHS
14. SOLOS
15. KAYAK

16. TENET
17. CIVIC
18. HANNAH
19. REDDER
20. REPAPER

26 AUGUST   *Doublets*

1. Eye, dye, die, did, lid.
2. Pig, wig, wag, way, say, sty.
3. Ape, are, ere, err, ear, mar, man.
4. Army, arms, aims, dims, dams, dame, name, nave, navy.
5. Cain, chin, shin, spin, spun, spud, sped, aped, abed, Abel.
6. Wheat, cheat, cheap, cheep, creep, creed, breed, bread.
7. River, rover, cover, coves, cores, corns, coins, chins, shins, shine, shone, shore.
8. Winter, winner, wanner, wander, warder, harder, harper, hamper, damper, damped, dammed, dimmed, dimmer, simmer, summer.

28 AUGUST   𝄢*fm*

1. O, high O = Ohio.
2. You are too good to me to be forgotten.

3. B is m arc K = Bismarck.
4. Man for all seasons.

—Hail, Caesar!
—Peace to you, O foreigner! Rise! You are?
—I am Aristes, Excellency, an Arabian exile.
—Why are you an exile, Aristes?
—I used to be a spy, O Caesar.
—A messy business! Have you eaten?
—Yes, thank you, sire, I ate a cheese and veal pie—excellent, too. O Caesar, I have one desire. I foresee easy forays for you, sire, if I am a spy for you. I have an eyepiece to use to spy.

—An eyepiece! Have you seen an enemy army?

—Yes, Excellency, in a secure city, adjacent to a forest, two armies.

—I have seen your city, and I say your city is empty! Are you a spy for anyone else? Seize him, men!

—O Caesar, you are too wise to use force! I am innocent! I see two cities: One is empty, and one two armies occupy. I am your ally, and I have a double use, sire. You see, I am a spy and I am a seer, too.

—If you are a seer, I ask you, are you a teller of fortunes?

—Yes, Caesar, I foresee nine seasons of easy success for you before you expire.

—Nine seasons! And am I to expire in nine seasons? Why? Will I be sick, spy?

—O Caesar, you will expire before you are ill of a disease, to my sorrow. Have you any enemies?

—A few, a few.

—I foresee you will have two eulogies, O Caesar; one orator to accuse your enemies and one to excuse them; one to expiate and one to extenuate; one to say "Peace, Peace," and one to argue for "an eye for an eye"; one to attest to your tyranny, and one to attest to your energy and excellence; a forum for forensics, Caesar, before your enemies' demise. Yes, eventually your enemies will expire, too— Excellency, are you OK? Excuse Aristes, Caesar, if I have foreseen too far!

—O hell, if I have nine seasons before I sleep, I say to arms! A sea of enemies awaits, Aristes! To arms!

31 AUGUST   *Garbled Geography*

1. Wash.	3. Pa.	5. O.	7. Miss.	9. Tenn.	11. Penn.
2. Ark.	4. Me.	6. Md.	8. Mass.	10. Ala.	12. Del.

8 SEPTEMBER   *Last Lines*

1. F	4. B	7. E	10. I	13. L	16. R
2. G	5. H	8. C	11. O	14. P	17. Q
3. A	6. D	9. N	12. K	15. M	18. J

11 SEPTEMBER   *The Song of Snohomish*

The players' names, in order of appearance in the poem, are: Catfish: George Metkovich. Mudcat: Jim Grant. Ducky: Joe Medwick. Coot: Orville Veale. The Babe: George Herman Ruth. The Barber: Salvatore Maglie. The Blade: Jack Billingham. The Brat: Eddie Stanky. Windy: John McCall. Dummy: William Hoy. Gabby: Charles Hartnett. Hoot: Walter Evans. Big Train: Walter Johnson. Big Six: Christy Mathewson. Big Ed: Edward Delehanty. Fat: Bob Fothergill.

Greasy: Alfred Neale. Sandy: Sanford Koufax. Muddy: Herold Ruel. Rocky: Rocco Colavito. Bunions: Rollie Zeider. Twinkletoes: George Selkirk. Footsie: Wayne Belardi. The Hat: Harry Walker. Fuzzy: Al Smith. Dizzy: Jay Hanna Dean. Buddy: John Hassett. Cocky: Eddie Collins. The Bull: Al Ferrara. The Stork: George Theodore. The Weasel: Don Bessent. The Cat: Harry Brecheen.

Schoolboy: Lynwood Rowe. Preacher: Elwin Roe. Rajah: Rogers Hornsby. Duke: Edwin Snider. General: Alvin Crowder. Major: Ralph Houk. Spaceman: Bill Lee. Spook: Forrest Vandergrift Jacobs.

Shoeless Joe: Joseph Jefferson Jackson. Cobra Joe: Joe Frazier. Bullet Joe: Leslie Bush. Bing: Edmund Miller. Old Hoss: Charles Radbourne. Mule: George Haas. Country: Enos Slaughter. Rube: George Waddell. Smokey Joe: Joe Wood. Fireman Joe: Joe Beggs. Jersey Joe: Joe Stripp. Ping: Frank Bodie. Bulldog: Jim Bouton. Squirrel: Roy Sievers. Puddin' Head: William Jones. Boob: Eric McNair.

The Georgia Peach: Ty Cobb. The Fordham Flash: Frank Frisch. The Flying Dutchman: Honus Wagner. Cot: Ellis Deal. The People's Cherce: Fred Walker. The Blazer: Wade Blassingame. Crash: Lawrence Davis. The Staten Island Scot: Bobby Thompson.

Skeeter: James Webb. Scooter: Phil Rizzuto. Pepper: Johnny Martin. Duster: Walter Mails. Ebbor: Edward St. Claire. Bama: Carvell Rowell. Boomer: Ron Blomberg. Buster: Calvin Coolidge Julius Caesar Tuskahoma McLish.

Specs: Billy Rigney. The Grey Eagle: Tris Speaker. The Toy Cannon: Jim Wynn. Tex: James Carleton. The Earl of Snohomish: Earl Torgeson. The Duke of Tralee: Roger Bresnahan. Art the

Great: Arthur Shires. Gorgeous George: George Sisler. Ox: Oscar Eckhardt. Double X: Jimmie Foxx. The Nashville Narcissus: Charles Lucas. The Phantom: Julian Javier. The Flea: Freddie Patek. The Little Professor: Dominic Paul DiMaggio. The Iron Horse: Lou Gehrig. Cap: Adran Anson. Iron Man: Joe McGinnity. Iron Mike: Mike Marshall. Iron Hands: Chuck Hiller. Hutch: Fred Hutchinson. Jap: William Barbeau. The Mad Russian: Lou Novikoff. Irish: Emil Meusel. Swede: Charles Risberg. Nap: Napoleon Lajoie. Germany: Herman Schaefer. Frenchy: Stanley Bordagaray. Big Serb: John Miljus. Dutch: Emil Leonard. Turk: Omar Lown. Tuck: George Steinback. Tug: Frank McGraw. Twig: Wayne Terwilliger. Spider: John Jorgensen. Birdie: George Tebbets. Rabbit: Walter Maranville. Pig: Frank House.

Three-Finger: Mordecai Peter Centennial Brown. No-Neck: Walt Williams. The Knuck: Hoyt Wilhelm. The Lip: Leo Durocher. Casey: Charles Dillon Stengel. Dazzy: Clarence Vance. Hippity: Johnny Hopp. Zim: Don Zimmer. Flit: Roger Cramer. Bad Henry: Henry Aaron. Fat Freddie: Frederick Fitzsimmons. Flip: Al Rosen. Jolly Cholly: Charles Grimm. Sunny Jim: James Bottomley.

Shag: Leon Chagnon. Schnozz: Ernesto Lombardi. King Kong: Charlie Keller. Klu: Ted Kluszewski.

Boog: John Wesley Powell. Buzz: Russell Arlett. Boots: Cletus Elwood Poffenberger. Bump: Irving Hadley. Boo: David Ferriss.

Baby Doll: William Jacobson. Angel Sleeves: Jack Jones. Pep: Lemuel Young. Sliding Billy: Billy Hamilton. Buttercup: Louis Dickerson. Bollicky: Billy Taylor. Boileryard: William Clarke. Juice: George Latham. Colby Jack: Jack Coombs. Dauntless Dave: Dave Danforth. Cheese: Albert Schweitzer. Gentle Willie: William Murphy. Trolley Line: Johnny Butler. Wagon Tongue: Bill Keister. Rough: Bill Carrigan. What's the Use: Pearce Chiles.

Ee-yah: Hugh Jennings. Poosh 'Em Up: Tony Lazzeri. Skoonj: Carl Furillo. Slats: Marty Marion. Ski: Oscar Melillo. Ding Dong: Bill Bell. Ding-a-Ling: Dain Clay. Dim Dom: Dominic Dallesandro. Dee: Wilson Miles.

Bubbles: Eugene Hargrave. Dimples: Clay Dalrymple. Cuddles: Clarence Marshall. Pinky: Mike Higgins. Poison Ivy: Ivy Paul Andrews. Vulture: Phil Regan. Stinky: Harry Davis.

Jigger: Arnold Statz. Jabbo: Ray Jablonski. Jolting Joe: Joseph Paul DiMaggio. Blue Moon: Johnny Lee Odom. Boom Boom: Walter Beck. Bubba: Wycliffe Nathaniel Morton. Bo: Robert Belinski.

24 SEPTEMBER *Wacky Wordies*

1a. Just between you and me. 1b. Hitting below the belt. 1c. Head over heels in love. 1d. Shrinking violets. 1e. Bermuda Triangle. 1f. A mixed bag.

2a. Cry over spilt milk. 2b. Lying in wait. 2c. *Unfinished Symphony.* 2d. Pineapple upside-down cake. 2e. You're under arrest. 2f. Split-second timing.

3a. Nothing on TV. 3b. Fly-by-night. 3c. Raise a big stink. 3d. Add insult to injury. 3e. Railroad crossing. 3f. A person after my own heart.

4a. At the point of no return. 4b. The inside dope. 4c. Long underwear. 4d. Ostrich with its head in the ground. 4e. Lucky break. 4f. Corner the market.

7 OCTOBER   *Yknits Seiknip*

1. mad dam
2. made Edam
3. cod doc
4. diaper repaid
5. reed deer

6. mar ram
7. Reno oner
8. Lodi idol
9. Edom mode
10. pacer recap

11. rap par
12. redo Oder
13. Tao oat
14. nomad Damon
15. mined denim

16. pin nip
17. Roma amor
18. lee eel
19. emir rime
20. lamina animal

16 OCTOBER   *Puzzle School*

Partwords

Possible answers

ROWBOAT   OVERWORK   EMPHASIS   BOATSWAIN
STRAWBERRY   LOBSTER   DEFTNESS

Fill-in Station
Possible answers

SCOUT	CLOUT	SPOUT	TROUT
SCOUR	CLOUD	SNOUT	GROUT
FLOUR	GROUP	STOUT	CROUP
FLOUT	SHOUT	GHOUL	KNOUT

Match-ups

| NERVES | IMPALE | SHORES | CURSES |
| THEMES | INGOTS | CLOSET | MANSION |

20 OCTOBER   *To the Leading Periodical*

This compliment, great sir, O take;
You're a brick and no mistake.
Enemy to cant and fudge,
Time to thee I ne'er begrudge;
And I hope to see your name
Foremost in the lists of fame.
　　　　　　—*Tom Smith, Grub Street*

23 OCTOBER   *Asimov*

William Alsop's limerick on Isaac Asimov:

The pants of the lecturer, Asimov,
Have never been seen, for he has 'em off;
　　And week after week,
　　Some woman will shriek,
"Oh, there goes another orgasm off!"

28 OCTOBER   *Double Trouble*

1. Flipper, flivver
2. Scuttle
3. Mission
4. Feeling

5. Drizzle
6. Barrage
7. Gazelle
8. Connect, correct

9. Haddock, hassock
10. Aggress
11. Chattel
12. Bassoon

4 NOVEMBER   *On the Letter H*

On the Letter H: H.
Cut Off My Head: Cod.

9 DECEMBER   *I Kmnow Pfil Pfizer Pfomnebd Me, Though*

Phil Pfizer phoned me to impart
Mnemosymne's an ancient tart,
　　And myrrh is bdellium creamed.
Psychiatrists, he next announces,

> Dress pterodactyls' young in flounces,
>   And toads eat ptisans steamed.
> I do not know that this is so;
> I know Phil Pfizer phoned me, though.

11 DECEMBER   *Biographical Sketch*

Alastair Reid would have made the last line of the limerick read: "Or my name is not Alastair Reid."

16 DECEMBER   *More Timothy Tidbits*

- GUNG HO. Enthusiastic, eager, zealous. From Chinese *kung,* "work," **+** *ho,* "together." General E. Carlson borrowed the expression in 1939 as a slogan for the United States Marines.
- TOMCAT. Male of the species. First used in *The History of Tom the Cat,* 1775.
- GERRYMANDER. To divide voting districts so as to give unfair advantage to one party. Coined by Benjamin Russell in 1812.
- EGGHEAD. A highbrow. Apparently used first to describe intellectuals who supported the presidential candidacy of Adlai Stevenson, whose head was bald and egglike. 1952.
- MIDDLEBROW. A person of mediocre culture. The expression was first used in an article by Russell Lynes in 1949.
- MASS CULT. Culture at the level of the masses. Coined by Dwight Macdonald. 1965.
- MID CULT. An intermediate state of culture. Coined by Dwight Macdonald in conscious imitation of Russell Lynes's *middlebrow.* Also 1965.
- BLURB. A commendatory paragraph on the jacket of a book. Originated by Gelett Burgess in a comic book jacket embellished with a drawing of a lovely young lady dubbed Miss Blinda Blurb. 1914.
- FIFTH COLUMN. Enemy supporters in one's own country, or one's own supporters in an enemy country. Rebel General Emilio Mola said early in the Spanish Civil War that he had four columns of troops outside Madrid and another column hiding in the city which would join the invaders as soon as they entered the capital. 1936.
- BAZOOKA. An antitank rocket thrower, named after its resemblance to a musical instrument confected of two gas pipes and a whiskey funnel in the 1930s by radio comedian Bob Burns. The name was adopted for the weapon about 1942.
- GOOGOL. The number 1 followed by 100 zeros. Invented in 1940 on request by a child, the nephew of the mathematician Edward Kasner.

20 DECEMBER   *Mistletoe Means Watch Out*

TABLE TENNIS. ELBOW GREASE. PAINT BRUSH. OFF WHITE. CHRISTMAS CARD.

26 DECEMBER   *Showoff Words*

HYPOBULA: neurotic haste in decision-making.
DYSPHEMISM: the deliberate use of a disparaging or offensive term for shock value.
HIRCISMUS: stinky armpits.
SAVSSAT: animals crowded around a hole in the Arctic ice.

APPENDICES

Index of Rhetorical Devices and Categories

Index of Authors

Index of First Lines,
Willard R. Espy Verses

Index of First Lines

(omitting W.R.E. verses)

Permissions

ACKNOWLEDGMENTS

I thank *New Statesman, Verbatim,* and *Word Ways* for permission to rifle their pages on a rather grand scale. For drawings made at my request, my thanks to Ed Fisher and Whitney Darrow, Jr.; and for musical arrangements based on my wordplay, to Dick Hyman and Eugene Weintraub.

Roger Knights, whom I have never met, has added invaluably to the collections of nonsense from which parts of this book are drawn. So has Charles F. Dery. Correspondents who have proposed entries are too numerous to name, but I am grateful to them all; those whose submissions were included are listed below.

Louise, as always, has worked closely with me on locating and organizing source material. Without her, *Another Almanac* would have been a poorer book.

Timothy Dickinson put the resources of his matchless mental library at my disposal, and corrected scores of my silly oversights; but for sheer lack of time, he would have caught them all.

I cannot be too grateful for the unstinting cooperation of my dear editors, Carol Southern and Anne Goldstein.

A special word about Carolyn S. Foote, whose macaronic verse appears on page 46. Our friendship was entirely by correspondence, but her letters were precious to me, and she had poetic gifts that should have been more widely known. She died in a fire that burned her home in March 1980.

My thanks also to these correspondents who contributed their finds to me: Theodore S. Abbott, Fran Abott, Aloe, Paula Anderson, N.B., R. Bates, E. Beadwell, L. Bennett, Brian Blake, W. Bliss, Mita Bord, Dimitri Borgmann, Alexandra Bowen, Karel Brandes, Roy Breunig, Betty Bridgman, Maxey Brooks, C.C., Bill and Marguerite Cavett, Gerald Challis, Bill Cole, Deborah Odell Coleman, Miss D. N. Daglish, Jan Dunham, Alvin Easter, T.M.F., E. W. Fordham, Robert A. Fowkes, Robert Furke, S.W.G., Paul Gaeng, Mrs. Aileen N. Garstrong, Gilderoy, Maud Gill, Robert T. Harker, Lady Harris, Fayette Hickox, M. Houston, Holland, Guy Innes, Janus, Jim Kreuger, James Kugel, Robert Kurosaka, Richard Lederer, N. G. Liddiard, Gordon Linfoot, Little Billee, Lucifer, Callista McCauley, Phyllis Megroz, F. G. Messervey, Dorothy Page Miller, Dave Mona, George Movshon, Frances Murray, Mary and Frank Oberlander, Olric, Roger and Vera Olson, Olive Ordish, Mrs. George H. Overman, H. F. Overy, Cecil Owen, Olive Weaver Paquin, Phiz, Pibrob, Peter Prescott, Lester Ralph, P. D. Randall, Guy Rawlence, M. R. Ridley, Thomas Rodd, Jr., Sister Mary Rose, Alan Shadwick, Will Shortz, Douglass Smith, Sylvia, W. A. Thorpe, Virginia Tollefson, Towanbucket, Sola N. Trefoil, David O. Tyson, L. V. Upward, Gregory J. Vack, Larry Walker, Marjorie Wihtol, Irene Williams, Sir Robert Witt, Jezabel Q. Xixx, and Yahoo.

WILLARD R. ESPY